THE CAMBRIDGE
COMPANION TO

RALPH WALDO EMERSON

The Cambridge Companion to Ralph Waldo Emerson is intended to provide a critical introduction to Emerson's work. The tradition of American literature and philosophy as we know it at the end of the twentieth century was largely shaped by Emerson's example and practice. This volume offers students, scholars, and the general reader a collection of fresh interpretations of Emerson's writing, milieu, influence, and cultural significance. All essays are newly commissioned for this volume, written at an accessible yet challenging level, and augmented by a comprehensive chronology and bibliography.

Cambridge Companions to Literature

Continued on page following Index

THE CAMBRIDGE
COMPANION TO
RALPH WALDO EMERSON

EDITED BY

JOEL PORTE
Cornell University

AND

SAUNDRA MORRIS
Bucknell University

CAMBRIDGE
UNIVERSITY PRESS

PUBLISHED BY THE PRESS SYNDICATE OF THE UNIVERSITY OF CAMBRIDGE
The Pitt Building, Trumpington Street, Cambridge, United Kingdom

CAMBRIDGE UNIVERSITY PRESS
The Edinburgh Building, Cambridge CB2 2RU, UK   http://www.cup.cam.ac.uk
40 West 20th Street, New York, NY 10011-4211, USA   http://www.cup.org
10 Stamford Road, Oakleigh, Melbourne 3166, Australia

©Cambridge University Press 1999

First published 1999

Printed in the United States of America

Typeface Sabon 10/13 pt.   *System* DeskTopPro$_{/UX}$® [BVC]

A catalog record for this book is available from the British Library

Library of Congress Cataloging-in-Publication Data
The Cambridge companion to Ralph Waldo Emerson / edited by Joel Porte,
Saundra Morris.
p.   cm. – (Cambridge companions to literature)
Includes bibliographical references and index.
ISBN 0-521-49611-X (hardbound)
1. Emerson, Ralph Waldo, 1803–1882 – Criticism and interpretation.
I. Porte, Joel. II. Morris, Saundra, 1956– . III. Series.
PS1638.C32   1999
814.3 – dc21   98-36892
CIP

ISBN 0 521 49611 X hardback
ISBN 0 521 49946 1 paperback

CONTENTS

CONTENTS

CONTRIBUTORS

PHYLLIS COLE is Associate Professor of English and Women's Studies at Pennsylvania State, Delaware County. She has written numerous articles on American Transcendentalism and women writers and recently published *Mary Moody Emerson and the Origins of Transcendentalism* (Oxford, 1998).

JULIE ELLISON is Professor of English and Associate Vice President for Research at the University of Michigan, Ann Arbor. She is the author of *Emerson's Romantic Style* (Princeton, 1984) and *Delicate Subjects: Romanticism, Gender, and the Ethics of Understanding* (Cornell, 1990).

MICHAEL LOPEZ, currently an independent scholar, was Associate Professor of English at Michigan State University. His writing has appeared in *Prospects, Harvard English Studies, ESQ, Prose Studies,* and *Philosophy and Literature.* He is the author of *Emerson and Power: Creative Antagonism in the Nineteenth Century* (Northern Illinois University, 1996) and is the editor of an *ESQ* symposium on Emerson and Nietzsche (1997).

ROBERT MILDER is Professor of English at Washington University in St. Louis. He is editor of *Critical Essays on Melville's Billy Budd, Sailor* (G. K. Hall, 1989) and, with John Bryant, of *Melville's Evermoving Dawn: Centennial Essays* (Kent State, 1997). He is the author of *Reimagining Thoreau* (Cambridge, 1995).

SAUNDRA MORRIS is Assistant Professor of English at Bucknell University. She published, in 1997, an essay on Emerson's poetry in *American Literature* and is coeditor, with Joel Porte, of the forthcoming *Prose and Poetry of Ralph Waldo Emerson, A Norton Critical Edition.* She is currently completing a book on Emerson's poetry.

JOEL PORTE is Ernest I. White Professor of American Studies and Humane Letters at Cornell University. Among his books are *The Romance in Amer-*

ica: Studies in Cooper, Poe, Hawthorne, Melville, and James (Wesleyan, 1969), *Representative Man: Ralph Waldo Emerson in His Time* (Oxford, 1979), and *In Respect to Egotism: Studies in American Romantic Writing* (Cambridge, 1991). He has edited *Emerson: Prospect and Retrospect* (Harvard, 1982), *Emerson in His Journals* (Harvard, 1982), *Emerson: Essays and Lectures* (Library of America, 1983), and *New Essays on* The Portrait of a Lady (Cambridge, 1990).

ROBERT D. RICHARDSON, JR., is an independent scholar living in Middletown, Connecticut. He has taught at Harvard, The University of Denver, the University of Colorado, Queens College and the Graduate Center of CUNY, Sichuan University, Yale, and Wesleyan. He is the author of *Literature and Film* (University of Indiana, 1968), *Myth and Literature in the American Renaissance* (University of Indiana, 1978), *Henry Thoreau: A Life of the Mind* (Berkeley, 1986), and *Emerson: The Mind on Fire* (Berkeley, 1995). He has edited, with Burton Feldman, *The Rise of Modern Mythology* (Indiana, 1972).

DAVID M. ROBINSON is Distinguished Professor of American Literature at Oregon State University and president of the Ralph Waldo Emerson Society. He is the author of *Apostle of Culture: Emerson as Preacher and Lecturer* (University of Pennsylvania, 1982) and *Emerson and the Conduct of Life* (Cambridge, 1993).

JEFFREY STEELE is Professor of English at the University of Wisconsin–Madison. He is the author of *The Representation of the Self in the American Renaissance* (University of North Carolina, 1987) and editor of *The Essential Margaret Fuller* (Rutgers, 1993).

CATHERINE TUFARIELLO received her PhD from Cornell University in 1994. She is currently an independent scholar living in Brooklyn, New York.

ALBERT J. VON FRANK is Professor of English and American Studies at Washington State University and the author of *The Sacred Game: Provincialism and Frontier Consciousness in American Literature, 1630–1860* (Cambridge, 1985), *An Emerson Chronology* (G. K. Hall, 1994), and *The Trials of Anthony Burns: Freedom and Slavery in Emerson's Boston* (Harvard, 1998). He is also coeditor of *The Poetry Notebooks of Ralph Waldo Emerson* (University of Missouri, 1986) and general editor of *The Sermons of Ralph Waldo Emerson* (University of Missouri, 1989–92).

ROBERT WEISBUCH is president of the Woodrow Wilson National Fellowship Foundation and Professor of English at the University of Michigan,

Ann Arbor. He is the author of *Emily Dickinson's Poetry* (University of Chicago, 1975) and *Atlantic Double-Cross* (University of Chicago, 1986). He is also coeditor of *Dickinson and Audience* (University of Michigan, 1996).

R. JACKSON WILSON is Professor of History at Smith College. He is the author of *In Quest of Community: Social Philosophy in the United States, 1860–1920* (Wiley, 1968) and *Figures of Speech: American Writers and the Literary Marketplace from Benjamin Franklin to Emily Dickinson* (Knopf, 1989). He edited *Darwinism and the American Intellectual* (Dorsey, 1968) and has coauthored *Freedom and Crisis: An American History* (Random House, 1974).

ABBREVIATIONS

CW   *The Collected Works of Ralph Waldo Emerson*. Ed. Robert Spiller, Alfred Ferguson, et al. Cambridge, MA: Belknap Press, Harvard University Press, 1971– .

EL   *The Early Lectures of Ralph Waldo Emerson*. Ed. Stephen Whicher et al. 3 vols. Cambridge, MA: Belknap Press, Harvard University Press, 1960–72.

EJ   *Emerson in His Journals*. Ed. Joel Porte. Cambridge, MA: Belknap Press, Harvard University Press, 1982.

JMN   *The Journals and Miscellaneous Notebooks of Ralph Waldo Emerson*. Ed. William Gillman et al. 16 vols. Cambridge, MA: Belknap Press, Harvard University Press, 1960–82.

L   *The Letters of Ralph Waldo Emerson*. Ed. Ralph L. Rusk and Eleanor M. Tilton. 9 vols. New York: Columbia University Press, 1939–94.

LJE   Emerson, Ellen Tucker. *The Life of Lidian Jackson Emerson*. Ed. Delores Bird Carpenter. Boston: Twayne Publishers, 1980.

LMF   *The Letters of Margaret Fuller*. Ed. Robert N. Hudspeth. 5 vols. Ithaca: Cornell University Press, 1983– .

W   *The Complete Works of Ralph Waldo Emerson*. Ed. Edward Waldo Emerson. 12 vols. Centenary Edition. Boston and New York: Houghton Mifflin Co., 1903–4.

PREFACE

After an initial period of hagiographic veneration, followed by a backlash of reaction, Emerson and his writings have for several decades enjoyed renewed critical appreciation. In the 1970s, prompted by Stephen Whicher's earlier emphasis on the "tragic" Emerson and Jonathan Bishop's subsequent attention to Emerson's literary craft, readers increasingly called into question the traditional representation of Emerson's texts as cockeyed-optimistic proclamations in impenetrably lapidary prose and paid attention instead to their artistic merit and deeper resonances. In the 1980s and '90s, we have come even more fully to understand both the multivalent harmonies of Emerson's work and the beauties and complexities of its rhetoric. We have also in recent years allowed Emerson to wear a variety of mantles, some of which may seem contradictory (Transcendentalist and pragmatist, prose stylist and orphic poet, theorist and prudential Yankee, social commentator and withdrawn intellectual), finally realizing the truth of his own remark, "I am not the man you take me for."

With its heightened recognition of Emerson's importance, contemporary scholarship follows the lead of a long line of American thinkers and writers. As Stanley Cavell has taught us, Emerson is *the* founding figure in the American philosophical tradition. Henry Thoreau, William James, George Santayana, John Dewey, Arthur Lovejoy, Henry Aiken, William Gass, Cornel West, and Cavell himself have all struggled to win a blessing from the Necessary Angel of Concord. Emerson has also provided a powerful impetus for American poets, whether by attraction or repulsion. Harold Bloom has focused on Emerson as "ghostly father," especially for such writers as Walt Whitman, Wallace Stevens, and A. R. Ammons. A list of Emerson's progeny would go on to include Emily Dickinson, Robert Frost, Marianne Moore, Hart Crane, Charles Olson, and others. Social thinkers also return again and again to Emerson, as the late Yale president A. Bartlett Giamatti's condemnation of Emerson's influence on American culture attests. Finally, American fiction writers have paid a different sort of attention to

Emerson, both representing him directly and creating characters who are recognizably disciples of the sage. Such figures, whether of veneration or derision, make their way variously into the work of Melville, Hawthorne, Alcott, Twain, Howells, James, Cather, Santayana, and Ellison.

It seems that all of us – students, scholars, writers, cultural commentators, political scientists – continue to be pursued by this ex-Unitarian minister turned lecturer, essayist, diarist, philosopher, and poet who helped provide the vocabulary that enables us to think about who we are and what we might become. Indeed, as we approach the bicentenary of Emerson's birth in 2003, the pace of interest in his writing is likely to gain still more momentum. So this seems a good time to offer a guide and companion to Emerson studies. Ours embodies the research and reflections of a baker's dozen of seasoned Emersonians, all of whom have challenged themselves either to cast a new light on familiar topics or to strike out into less familiar territory.

Thus, for example, Phyllis Cole demonstrates that the family milieu that nurtured Emerson – and in particular the presence of his aunt Mary Moody Emerson – had far more to do with the work he produced than we would have expected, especially given Emerson's own strong belief in the singularity of individual genius. Along similar lines, Julie Ellison turns her attention to the conditions of Emerson's life as a writer who mainly worked at home – in the midst of a household run by his wife and daughters and regularly frequented by other children, friends, collaborators, and relatives. How, she asks, did these relationships and presences affect (the *affective* traditionally being coded "female") Emerson's stance as an abstract thinker? How do they influence the way we respond to Emerson's writing and especially to "Experience" – the great meditation freighted with its allusion to the death of Emerson's five-year-old son?

Other new approaches to Emerson in this collection include a reading of *Essays, First Series*, by Albert von Frank that focuses on the subversive and unsettling strategies embedded in that text, as well as a fresh look at Emerson on the Lyceum platform by Jackson Wilson that emphasizes the nimble dance Emerson regularly performed wherein the meeting of conventional audience expectations was offset by controversial critical sallies. Robert D. Richardson leads us through a topic – Emerson and "Nature" – that seems so self-evident as scarcely to demand attention; but he manages to provide an unusual twist to a familiar subject. David Robinson lucidly explores the always tangled history of the Transcendental movement. And Catherine Tufariello revisits the question of Emerson's influence on Whitman and Dickinson without resorting to Harold Bloom's model of influential "anxiety"; rather, she focuses on enabling strategies employed by the two poetic ephebes to transform their mentor from antagonist to facilitator. Robert Weisbuch surprises us with a treatment of Emerson vis-à-vis England and Europe that places the American author in a "post-colonial" posture. Jeffrey Steele investigates the alternately icy and steamy world of Transcendental "friendship" with an eye to revising our sense of Emerson's relations with Fuller and Thoreau. And in strongly argued essays, Robert Milder and Michael Lopez reframe views of Emerson's political ideology and the shape of his writing career that have been in place for a long time – Milder by conceiving of a "radical" Emerson, Lopez by reconsidering what it means to view *The Conduct of Life* as Emerson's "mature" wisdom. Finally, the editors of this collection reopen the questions of Emerson's place as a figure in American culture and his achievement as a poet.

The *Cambridge Companion to Ralph Waldo Emerson* is not intended to exhaust its subject or even, in the end, to provide conventional instruction. Rather, following Emerson himself, its aim is provocation. Describing his own aspirations as a lecturer, Emerson once wrote in his journal: "I said I will agitate others, being agitated myself." Similarly, the authors of these essays would like to inspire a sense of renewed excitement about Emerson's perpetually inexhaustible presence. Recent literary theory encourages readers to appreciate texts for their lack of closure and to explore in them whatever is most suggestive, inconclusive, and evolving. Emerson's work seems to thrive in this critical and analytical environment, inviting, as it always does, our active engagement. This collection, designed for a wide range of audience, participates in and, we hope, furthers the contemporary interest in a multifaceted and unresolved Emerson – one who, more and more, reminds us of his own Sphinx's "unanswered question."

For support toward the completion of this volume, the editors thank Anne Sanow and Phyllis Berk, of Cambridge University Press; Bucknell and Cornell Universities, for research grants; student assistants Kristen Hawley, Diana Leech, and Sean Teuton; Myrna Treston, secretary of the Bucknell Department of English; Jeannette Little, Administrative Assistant in the American Studies Program at Cornell; and their families. Heather White prepared the index.

Joel Porte
Saundra Morris

CHRONOLOGY OF EMERSON'S LIFE

1803   May 25: born in Boston
1811   May 12: father dies, age 42
1812   Enters Boston Public Latin School; begins writing poetry
1817   Enters Harvard College
1820   Begins keeping a journal, a practice that will continue into the 1870s
1821   Graduates from Harvard; teaches in Boston at his brother William's school for girls
1822   Continues to teach; publishes essay on "The Religion of the Middle Ages" in *The Christian Disciple*
1825   February: admitted to Harvard Divinity School; studies interrupted by eye trouble; teaches in Chelmsford
1826   Teaches in Roxbury and Cambridge; October 10: approbated to preach; lung trouble; November: voyages south to improve health
1827   June: returns to Cambridge; December: meets Ellen Tucker
1828   Brother Edward becomes deranged; December 17: Emerson engaged to Ellen, who is already ill with tuberculosis
1829   Ordained junior pastor of Boston's Second Church (Unitarian); September 30: marries Ellen
1831   February 8: Ellen dies, age 19
1832   Increasing ill health; decides he can no longer serve communion; resigns pastorate; December 25: sails for Europe
1833   Travels to Italy, France, and Great Britain; meets British literati, including Wordsworth, Coleridge, and Carlyle; back in Boston, begins career as lecturer with talks on "natural history"
1834   Continues to preach; spring: receives first half of Tucker inheritance; October: Edward dies
1835   Lectures in Boston on biography; August 15: buys home in Concord; September: marries Lydia Jackson

1836   Completes lecture series on English literature; May: brother Charles dies; July: Margaret Fuller visits; September: *Nature* published anonymously in Boston; October 30: Waldo born; winter: lectures on the philosophy of history

1837   July: receives final portion of Tucker estate; August: Thoreau graduates from Harvard, where Emerson delivers "The American Scholar" before the Phi Beta Kappa Society; fall-winter: lectures on human culture

1838   April: writes letter to President Van Buren protesting displacement of Cherokee people from their ancestral lands; July 15: delivers address at Harvard Divinity School that causes him to be banned from speaking at Harvard for many years; July 24: Dartmouth Oration ("Literary Ethics"); winter: lectures on human life

1839   January: preaches last sermon; February 24: Ellen born; winter: lectures on "The Present Age"

1840   July: first issue of Transcendental journal *The Dial*, edited by Margaret Fuller

1841   March: first series of *Essays* published; spring: Thoreau joins household; November 22: Edith born; winter: lectures on "The Times"

1842   January 27: Waldo dies; Emerson succeeds Fuller as editor of *The Dial*; September: takes walking trip with Hawthorne; December: delivers lecture series in New York, during which his "Poetry of the Times" is reviewed by Walter Whitman

1844   July 10: Edward born; April: last issue of *The Dial*; October: *Essays, Second Series* published

1845   July 4: Thoreau moves to Walden Pond and builds cabin on Emerson's property; winter: lectures on "Representative Men"

1846   December: *Poems* published

1847   October: begins second trip to Europe; away 10 months

1849   Lectures on "Mind and Manners in the Nineteenth Century"; *Nature; Addresses, and Lectures* published

1850   January: *Representative Men* published; July: Margaret Fuller Ossoli, returning from Italy, drowns with her husband and son off Fire Island

1851   Excoriates Massachusetts senator Daniel Webster for supporting Fugitive Slave Law; winter: lectures on "The Conduct of Life"

1853   Mother dies, age 84

1854   Lectures on "Topics of Modern Times" in Philadelphia; heavy lecture schedule throughout the country

1855   Antislavery lectures in Boston, New York, and Philadelphia; July 21: sends letter to Whitman praising first edition of *Leaves of Grass*

1856   August: *English Traits* published

1860   December: *The Conduct of Life* published

1862   Lectures on "American Civilization" in Washington and meets President Lincoln; May 6: Thoreau dies

1864   May 23: attends Hawthorne's funeral

1865   April: eulogizes the slain Lincoln

1866   Lectures in the West; receives Doctor of Laws degree from Harvard

1867   April: *May-Day and Other Pieces* published; named Overseer of Harvard College; delivers second Phi Beta Kappa address ("The Progress of Culture")

1870   Writes preface to *Plutarch's Morals*; publishes *Society and Solitude*; lectures at Harvard on "Natural History of Intellect"

1871   April–May: travels to California by train; meets Brigham Young and John Muir

1872   Speaks at Howard University; July 24: house burns; October: sets out for Europe and Egypt with Ellen

1874   December: publishes *Parnassus*, an anthology of his favorite poetry, which omits Poe and Whitman

1875   December: *Letters and Social Aims* published, edited by James Elliot Cabot

1876   Fall: publishes *Selected Poems* with help of Ellen and Cabot

1882   April 27: Emerson dies of pneumonia in Concord; Whitman visits his grave and observes: "A just man, poised on himself, all-loving, all-inclosing, and sane and clear as the sun."

JOEL PORTE

Introduction: Representing America – the Emerson Legacy

My purpose here is to say something about Ralph Waldo Emerson as a figure in American culture. It was Emerson who, in literary terms at least, really put America on the map; who created for himself the practically nonexistent role of man of letters, and for about a half century – from the golden age of Jackson to the gilded age of Grant – criticized, cajoled, sometimes confused, but mainly inspired audiences in America and abroad. When Emerson died in 1882 he was indisputably a *figure* – for some a figure of fun, but for most one to be spoken of with reverence approaching awe. Matthew Arnold declared that Emerson's was the most important work done in prose in the nineteenth century. Nietzsche called him a "brother soul." One of his disciples, Moncure Conway, likened him to Buddha, and twenty years later William James would pronounce him divine.

Somewhat more equivocal homage was also paid to Emerson in the fiction of the period. In the novels of William Dean Howells he is seen both as the prophet of pie in the sky and the proponent of pie in the morning. In Kate Chopin's *The Awakening*, he helps both to raise and to extinguish the consciousness of the restive heroine as she falls asleep over the *Essays* while plotting her escape from a stifling bourgeois marriage. Most notably, in Henry James's *The Bostonians* the master's spirit appears incarnated in the irrepressible though aged Miss Birdseye, the "frumpy little missionary" who represents a last link with the "heroic age of New England life – the age of plain living and high thinking, of pure ideals and earnest effort, of moral passion and noble experiment." She still burns with the "unquenched flame" of Transcendentalism, and in the "simplicity of her vision," looks to a higher if slightly faded reality: "the only thing that was still actual for her," James avers, "was the elevation of the species by the reading of Emerson and the frequentation of Tremont Temple." He declares her to be "sublime," but gives us reason to wonder about that heroic reading of Emerson through what are memorably described as "displaced spectacles."

I

Somehow, the Transcendental vision had gone askew; the "transparent eye-ball" of Emerson's *Nature* seemed to be clouding over. Soon Henry Adams would call Emerson "naif," and T. S. Eliot would dismiss him as "an encumbrance."

If Emerson seemed old hat to disconsolate intellectuals in the '20s owing to his presumed cosmic optimism, that did not keep ordinary readers from enjoying his aphorisms and apothegms. Bliss Perry's *The Heart of Emerson's Journals* was a best-seller in 1926. But even Perry had to admit by 1931 that Transcendentalism had long since gone out of fashion and that its epitaph was being written in doctoral dissertations. Though Emerson himself was still holding his own among a readership as yet unbesieged by diet books and sex manuals, he was nevertheless steadily receding into a historical past that would soon be virtually nonexistent except to the specialist. Now, too, Emerson has mainly been relegated to the college curriculum and the scholarly monograph (though Melville and Hawthorne are hardly household words). America's "classical" literary figures and their books appear to be largely invisible to the distracted and impatient eyes of what, in some quarters, is described as a "post-literate" society.

I intend to argue, nevertheless, that Emerson continues to nag the American conscience even when its ears are filled with other voices. Emerson did not simply produce stirring lectures, addresses, essays, and poems; he was passionately concerned with cultural analysis and devoted to cultural growth – twin imperatives that informed his total career. Emerson sits at the crossroads in a crucial moment of American history and like his own Sphinx asks the unanswered questions of our collective life – questions about the relative claims of conservatism and radicalism, the establishment and the movement, private property and communism; questions about slavery and freedom, the rights of women, the viability of institutions, the possibility of reform, the efficacy of protest, the exercise of power; indeed he asks perpetually about the meaning of America itself and its prospects among the nations. I offer this very abbreviated catalogue of topics only by way of suggesting that Emerson has strong claims to being considered not merely a Transcendental meditator on the infinitude of the private self but rather an *American* thinker deeply concerned with public issues. No other writer of America's so-called literary renaissance was more immersed in the country's civic culture. "Emerson's roots lay deep in the common soil," Bliss Perry notes; "he represented a significant generation of American endeavor, and . . . was a factor in the social and political as well as the intellectual history of his era."

Why should it be necessary to rehearse what was a commonplace of Emerson criticism more than half a century ago? Because the most persistent critical position taken in the 1960s and 1970s viewed Emerson as all but totally abstracted from his place and time – from what certain much-discussed commentators call "history" and "culture" and "the associated life." "The idea of community was dying in him and his fellows," wrote Quentin Anderson in *The Imperial Self.* "He would not be involved in time, he was not a member of a generation." Along the same lines, Ann Douglas argued in *The Feminization of American Culture* that Emerson, as opposed to Margaret Fuller, led a life of metaphor, substituted eloquence for experience, lived in literature and not in history. Somehow these critics, in Larzer Ziff's phrase, became convinced of Emerson's "turn away from history" – of his having conceived of himself as transcending time and circumstance so that he might, like Marie Antoinette, play at being a shepherd in some primitive Arcadia of the spirit.

But Emerson believed no such thing – except perhaps in his youth when he allowed himself to parrot Fourth of July rhetoric about the "uncontaminated innocence" of America versus the corruptions of the Old World. Even on this occasion – I am citing an 1821 journal entry written when Emerson was 18 – he complains that "it is the misfortune of America that her sudden maturity of national condition was accompanied with the knowledge of good and *evil* which would better belong to an older country." He was *hoping* for "reform and improvement," not making a unilateral declaration of independence from the collective experience of humankind. Boston thought of itself more as the Athens of the West than as the Garden of Eden. When Emerson did cast himself in the role of primal man before the Fall, it was for the purpose of introducing a particular tone of feeling – a momentary sense of release from the malady of the quotidian – into his discourse, not for the purpose of deluding himself and others as to where they actually stood. "Adam in the garden," he wrote in 1839, "I am to new name all the beasts in the field & all the gods in the Sky. I am to invite men drenched in time to recover themselves & come out of time, & taste their native immortal air." Emerson was not thinking of casting off his clothes along with his intellectual baggage and fleeing into the virgin forest to start life over but rather of planning a winter lecture series that would give his audience a sense of refreshment and renewal. A few days after setting down his Adamic entry, Emerson admonished himself to trust his own time, and the lecture series he produced was entitled "The Present Age."

Emerson in fact believed that the best use of history "is to enhance our estimate of the present hour." If he *was* coming out of history it was for the purpose of entering his own era more fully. What Emerson disliked was the notion of some Hegelian dialectic or logic of events that reduces individual experience to a mere moment in an unfolding drama. That was not his definition of freedom. He rejected the notion of history as an iron rule of cause and effect that necessarily determines present conduct – the notion, for example, that we are all totally controlled and circumscribed by descent or inheritance. Men and women *are,* Emerson might say, indubitably because their parents have been; but *what* they are is yet to be seen. Time will devour us unless we master it. Emerson internalized or subjectified history so as to be able to use it, to make it part of his own fiber. He did not step out of history but into it, deciding to make it rather than be made by it. "Every mind must know the whole lesson for itself," he writes, "must go over the whole ground. What it does not see, what it does not live, it will not know." Observing that all history was acted by human spirits and written by human minds like his own, Emerson declared himself competent to interpret the texts that time had transmitted. The way to solve the riddle of the Sphinx is to set yourself up on her pedestal. Thus Emerson insisted that "an autobiography should be a book of answers from one individual to the main questions of the time." Why should we pay attention to what does not concern us? "Shall he be a scholar?" he continues, "the infirmities & ridiculousness of the scholar being clearly seen. Shall he fight? Shall he seek to be rich? Shall he go for the ascetic or the conventional life? . . . Shall he value mathematics? Read Dante? or not? Aristophanes? Plato? Cosmogonies . . . What shall he say of Poetry? What of Astronomy? What of religion? Then let us hear his conclusions respecting government & politics. Does he pay taxes and record his title deeds? Does Goethe's Autobiography answer these questions?" The inference is that it does not, at least not for an American living in the 1840s.

In dealing with Emerson, criticism is always in danger of neglecting the actual record in its density and richness in favor of its own theses – viewing Emerson, for example, as an endless seeker with no past at his back, a sort of Transcendental rocket racing into trackless space and attempting to drag American literature with it. To speak honestly, however, though we are all inextricably wedded to time and the "associated life," we nevertheless have moments, perhaps neither quite in time nor quite out of it, when another sort of experience seems possible. A fit of religious exaltation might be one example, sexual ecstasy another. In such moods, if we were Emerson, we might write *Nature* or "The Over-Soul" or "Bacchus" or "Merlin"; but such an expression could only be partial, never the whole of what we want to say. "I am always insincere," Emerson notes, "as always knowing there are other moods." We may wish to sell all we have and join this crusade against time and change, but Emerson will not allow us to hold him to it. We discover that he is not always the moonshiny man we took him for.

James Joyce was no Transcendentalist but even he allowed Stephen Dedalus to exclaim that history was a nightmare from which he was trying to awaken. With a name like Dedalus it was easy to feel burdened by the past, and the same was true for Ralph Waldo Emerson. The Protestant Reformation was in his blood, even antedating the settlement of America, as was implied by a middle name derived from the Waldensian sect. (The site of Thoreau's hut on Emerson's property was thus an appropriate place for the man Emerson called *"a protestant à l'outrance"* – to the *n*th degree.) Far from refusing to be "a member of a generation," as Anderson claimed, Emerson knew precisely which generation he belonged to – the seventh in a line directly descending from the settlers of the Bay Colony.

American history was family history for him. Peter Bulkeley, "one of Emerson's sixty-four grandfathers at the seventh remove," according to Oliver Wendell Holmes's calculation, was moderator, along with Thomas Hooker, at the famous Cambridge Synod of 1637, and resolved that "an assemblage of females, consisting of sixty or more, as is now every week formed, in which one of them, in the character of principal and prophetess, undertakes to expound the scriptures, resolve casuistical cases, and establish doctrines, is determined to be irregular and disorderly." That resolution was passed in order to deal with antinomian Anne Hutchinson, but Margaret Fuller's "conversations," which Emerson attended with so much pleasure, might also have been labeled disorderly conduct if the authority of the theocrats had not been broken in the continuing Protestant Reformation in America.

Emerson's other forebears had much to do with it. His father William noted with chagrin in his dutiful *Historical Sketch of the First Church in Boston* that his own great-grandfather and grandfathers were zealous supporters of the evangelist George Whitefield, of whom Boston's First Church did not approve. It was therefore natural for Emerson to continue the struggle when his own time came. He characterized his father's generation as belonging to an "early ignorant & transitional *Month-of-March,* in our New England culture," thereby clearly implying that his own Transcendental springtime was the inevitable next step. Although that almost insolent way of describing his father's historical moment scarcely did justice to William Emerson's accomplishments as a liberal Congregationalist – he helped to advance the cause of the arts by joining in the founding of the *Monthly Anthology* and the Massachusetts Historical Society – it does suggest that the young Emerson's own identity consciously emerged from generational conflict. Like his father he had graduated from Harvard College and become pastor of an important Boston church (the Second, not the First); and again like his father he was elected to the Boston School Committee and named chaplain to the state senate. It was all easy, fatally easy, but the identity thus procured was false. It was precisely by stepping into his father's shoes that Emerson had avoided the responsibility of defining and being a member of his own generation, and it was only when he cast himself loose from the church and became a Transcendentalist that he was enabled to think of a generation – in the words of sociologist Karl Mannheim – as a "culture-renewing moment" and not as an "age-group movement."

Nothing was more crucial to Emerson's development than his realization that his generation, his "culture-renewing moment," constituted a new and distinct age. If it in some ways bound him, time also had presented him with an opportunity. He became virtually obsessed with defining his age. As early as 1827 he set down in his journal under the heading "Peculiarities of the present Age" almost a program for his own historical context: "It is said to be the age of the first person singular. . . . The reform of the Reformation . . . Transcendentalism. Metaphysics & ethics look inwards." By the following year at least he had read William Hazlitt's *The Spirit of the Age* and found out more about his destiny. He learned there, for example, that Wordsworth and Coleridge, though members of his father's "age-group movement," were closer to him in their own impulses and aims. They – and especially Wordsworth – were for Hazlitt pure emanations of the "spirit of the age," the *modern* spirit, ushered in and exemplified by the French Revolution. The specter of what Hazlitt called "legitimacy" and the spirit of liberty were locked in a life-and-death-struggle. As early as 1801 the writer and reformer Hannah More suggested presciently that the revolutionary impulse had not only unlocked a force fomenting generational conflict but also raised an awareness about gender that would inform the Zeitgeist for years to come: "Not only sons but daughters," she wrote, "have adopted something of that spirit of independence and disdain of control, which characterizes the time." It was a time for protest and original action, as Emerson knew well enough; but the grip of tradition was strong and this young Jacob found it difficult to wring a blessing from the patriarchal specter with whom he wrestled.

Waldo had been educated to prize his pedigree, though it was his own humor to despise it. And there, close by his side, was his father's sister and surrogate, Aunt Mary Moody Emerson, who frequently spoke of the virtues of Waldo's clergymen ancestors, renowned for their piety and eloquence. He acknowledged all that but chafed under the weighty inheritance, insisting, bravely: "The dead sleep in their moonless night; my business is with the living." His father's spirit, however, both introjected and externalized in Aunt Mary, still walked restlessly abroad and asked to be remembered.

On the title-page of *The Spirit of the Age* Hazlitt had invoked Hamlet – a figure with whom Emerson strongly identified. (Later Emerson would insist that "it was not until the 19th century, whose speculative genius is a sort of living Hamlet, that the tragedy of Hamlet could find such wondering readers.") Hazlitt had begun his chapter on Coleridge by lamenting that "the present is an age of talkers, and not of doers; and the reason is, that the world is growing old. We are so far advanced in the Arts and Sciences, that we live in retrospect, and doat on past achievements." Troubled by such an allegation, Emerson would both echo it and strike out at it on the opening page of his first book, *Nature*: "Our age is retrospective. It builds the sepulchres of the fathers. . . ." The burden of the past – America's religious history as personal imperative – was strong and debilitating for Emerson.

The following year, 1837, in "The American Scholar," he whistled a brave tune as he walked past the old sepulchers, but the bones rattled again and his inner debate revived: "Our age is bewailed as the age of Introversion. Must that needs be evil? We, it seems, are critical; we are embarrassed with second thoughts; we cannot enjoy anything for hankering to know whereof the pleasure consists; we are lined with eyes; we see with our feet; the time is infected with Hamlet's unhappiness – 'Sicklied o'er with the pale cast of thought.' " He did not think that his own visionary gleam was a thing to be pitied. Should he, like Oedipus, put out his eyes because he had offended his father? One year later Emerson delivered his decisive blow against his father's church and profession in the Divinity School "Address" and then, indeed, the bones rattled more strongly than ever. Even friends of his own age were troubled, complaining that though they approved intellectually of his doctrine, their feelings were still bound to the old ways. Emerson replied to one such that he, Waldo, "would write for his epitaph, 'Pity 'tis, 'tis true.' " What could this brave New World Hamlet do when surrounded by so many youthful Poloniuses? He would have to continue striking out even at the risk of wounding them. Emerson's fundamental criticism was that America – or New England at least – had devoted far too much energy to arid theological and ecclesiastical dispute. His patriotism consisted in saying simply this: that the American mind and spirit had better ways to occupy itself.

There can be little doubt that Emerson's personal sense of paralysis and uncertainty during the crucial period when he was forging his new identity colored his thoughts and utterances for many years to come. In Ann Douglas's formulation, "as chief apostle of the emerging cult of self-confidence, Emerson would spend his life in a complex effort to shut out the voices of self-contempt." That is not wrong, but I would shift the emphasis a bit.

Emerson's Hamlet side, so to speak, made him perennially concerned with questions of manliness and potency. As he would come to phrase it in the 1850s, "life is a search after power"; but under his breath one can hear Emerson saying, "our experience in life, though, is too often one of powerlessness." The exercise of power, especially in an American context, troubled Emerson, and this internal debate found its most cogent public expression in his last great book, *The Conduct of Life*. As a compendium of what is usually considered Emerson's most mature and worldly wisdom the book is worth returning to, and one such reconsideration was included in the late A. Bartlett Giamatti's baccalaureate address to the Yale class of 1981.

Still uneasy, I think, about the student revolution of the late '60s and early '70s, President Giamatti characterized Emerson's views as "those of a brazen adolescent" and recommended that they be jettisoned. Echoing Anderson, and others, Giamatti pronounced himself disturbed at what he took to be Emerson's desire "to sever America from Europe, and American culture and scholarship and politics from whatever humankind had fashioned before." He argued that Emerson stood for "self-generated, unaffiliated power." Emerson, he claimed, was a prophet "of the secular religion that was the new America" of his time, and Giamatti's key text was the essay "Power" in *The Conduct of Life*. Here is part of his commentary:

> In the dark pages of that powerful meditation on power, on the eve of the [Civil] War, Emerson amply reflects a view of politics and politicians that is disdainful of the hurly-burly, the compromising and dirtiness of it all. But Emerson makes it clear that he does not share those fastidious views. Those views, he says, are only held by the "timid man"; by the "churchmen and men of refinement," implicitly effete and bookish. Emerson was not for them. He was for the man who is strong, healthy, unfettered, the man who knows that nothing is got for nothing and who will stop at nothing to put himself in touch with events and their force. . . . The "thinkers" Emerson really admires are those with "coarse energy, – the 'bruisers,' who have run the gauntlet of caucus and tavern through the county or the state," the politicians who despite their vices have "the good-nature of strength and courage."

Now *The Conduct of Life* is a manifestly and designedly dialectic exercise, chapter balancing and opposing chapter in the Emersonian mode ("Power," for example, is preceded by "Fate"), and should be read that way. But we may at least test the accuracy of Giamatti's paraphrase by listening to Emerson's words:

> Those who have most of this coarse energy – the "bruisers," who have run the gauntlet of caucus and tavern through the county or the state – have their own vices, but they have the good nature of strength and courage. Fierce and

unscrupulous, they are usually frank and direct and above falsehood. Our politics fall into bad hands, and churchmen and men of refinement, it seems agreed, are not fit persons to send to Congress. Politics is a deleterious profession, like some poisonous handicrafts. Men in power have no opinions, but may be had cheap for any opinion, for any purpose; and if it be only a question between the most civil and the most forcible, I lean to the last. These Hoosiers and Suckers are really better than the snivelling opposition. Their wrath is at least of a bold and manly cast.

We notice that Emerson is not really eulogizing the "bruisers"; indeed he says that "men in power have no opinions, but may be had cheap for any opinion." Though he admires their "strength and courage," he knows that they are "unscrupulous." What appeals to him is their candor and directness: whatever they are, they *are* that honestly. (Emerson would have hugged Harry Truman to his bosom while rejecting the smooth deceit of a Nixon.) Emerson understands that "politics is a deleterious profession," that none come back quite clean from bathing in those murky waters. All high principles are finally compromised in the Washington miasma. The best we can hope for, says Emerson, is men of rough honesty who have no stomach for lying or truckling and will stand boldly for what they want, be it good or bad. They will use what power they can and not dissemble, and we are therefore enabled to meet them on their own grounds. Emerson simply had come to the realization that the exercise of power is the name of the game in politics. "Our people," he writes in his journal in 1844, "are slow to learn the wisdom of sending character instead of talent to Congress. Again & again they have sent a man of great acuteness, a fine scholar, a fine forensic orator, and some master of the brawls has crunched him up in his hand like a bit of paper."

That is the obvious bearing of Emerson's remark in "Power" about "churchmen and men of refinement." Giamatti claims that Emerson is disdainful of them and "not for them." But I believe Emerson was simply articulating his *own* sense of powerlessness – and that of his class – when faced with raw and brutal force. He says, let us observe again, "our politics fall into bad hands, and churchmen and men of refinement, it seems agreed, are not fit persons to send to Congress." They may be fit for pulpits and lyceum halls and college classrooms, as Emerson himself was, but they are not fit for Congress, where the "strong, healthy, unfettered" are the ones who carry the day in the caucus room and senate chamber and must therefore be met by opponents who can deal with them on their own terms. But in the 1845 journal entry on which Emerson drew for this passage in "Power," he concludes by insisting: "Yet a bully cannot lead the age."

It is worth adding, in connection with Giamatti's allegation that Emerson rejected "churchmen and men of refinement," that Emerson had reason enough, by the time he published *The Conduct of Life* in 1860, to feel betrayed by the presumed men of principle of his own class and background. Following Daniel Webster's infamous speech of the seventh of March 1850 in favor of the Fugitive Slave Law, almost a thousand distinguished citizens of Boston, including Oliver Wendell Holmes, Sr., published a letter in support of Webster's position and Emerson was outraged. As the crisis over the Fugitive Slave Law sharpened, Emerson filled his journal with angry denunciations of men of refinement and churchmen who supported what he called the "filthy law." "The fame of Webster ends in this nasty law," he wrote, "and as for the Andover & Boston preachers, Dr Dewey & Dr Sharpe who deduce kidnapping from their Bible, tell the poor dear doctor if this be Christianity, it is a religion of dead dogs, let it never pollute the ears & hearts of noble children again."

After President Fillmore signed the Fugitive Slave Law, Sharpe preached a sermon in which he argued that "free citizens of the United States, living under the protection, and enjoying the benefits of our blessed laws, with all the advantages of the national compact, [cannot] be justified in encouraging poor fugitive slaves to acts of resistance." Such was the climate in which Emerson was writing. "I met an episcopal clergyman," he notes, "& allusion being made to Mr Webster's treachery, he replied, 'Why, do you know I think that the great action of his life?' I am told" – Emerson goes on – "they are all involved in one hot haste of terror, presidents of colleges & professors, saints & brokers, insurers, lawyers, importers, jobbers, there is not an unpleasing sentiment, a liberal recollection, not so much as a snatch of an old song for freedom dares intrude." (It was at this time that James Russell Lowell's vernacular mouthpiece, Hosea Biglow, lamented: "Massachusetts, – God forgive her, – / She's a kneelin' with the rest!") "We have seen the great party of property and education in the country," Emerson was to write, "drivelling and huckstering away, for views of party fear or advantage, every principle of humanity and the dearest hopes of mankind; the trustees of power only energetic when mischief could be done, imbecile as corpses when evil was to be prevented." Emerson was worried in the long run less about the southern Democrats and their doomed cause than he was about the propertied Whigs of the North with their material interests. They, and not the "bruisers," were the real "trustees of power." Can one actually believe, with Giamatti, that Emerson extolled "self-generated, unaffiliated power," when we hear him saying, "The American marches with a careless swagger to the height of power, very heedless of his own liberty or of other peoples', in his reckless confidence that he can have all he wants, risking all the prized charters of the human race, bought with battles and revolutions and religion, gambling them all away for the paltry selfish gain"?

Emerson would have nothing to do with an American civilization, so-called, willing to cover its crimes with cries of manifest destiny and America first. "We have much to learn, much to correct," he writes, "a great deal of lying vanity. The spread eagle must fold his foolish wings and be less of a peacock." "I wish to see America," he continues, "not like the old powers of the earth, grasping, exclusive and narrow, but a benefactor such as no country ever was, hospitable to all nations, legislating for all nationalities. Nations were made to help each other as much as families were; and all advancement is by ideas, and not by brute force or mechanic force." That last clause is essential Emerson and deserves to be heard clearly: "all advancement is by ideas, and not by brute force or mechanic force."

Emerson was a severe critic of an America capable of invading Mexico, oppressing blacks, and denying women equal rights. He was outspoken on all these issues and had to suffer public obloquy for his positions. "Humanity asks," he writes, "that government shall not be ashamed to be tender and paternal, but that democratic institutions shall be more thoughtful for the interests of women, for the training of children, and for the welfare of sick and unable persons, and serious care of criminals, than was ever any the best government of the Old World." America in the New World represented for Emerson at least potentially the noblest hopes of humankind. "It is our part," he notes, "to carry out to the last the ends of liberty and justice." As against the degraded New England voice that would finally proclaim that "the business of America is business," Emerson argued for a different definition: "Trade and government will not alone be the favored aims of mankind, but every useful, every elegant art, every exercise of the imagination, the height of reason, the noblest affection, the purest religion will find their home in our institutions, and write our laws for the benefit of men."

Emerson sat for more than forty years in his study in Concord, subjecting himself to what he calls the "tedious joys" of reading and writing, in order to set his place, his people, his life down on paper. Far from indulging himself in an escape from history or a life of metaphor, Emerson was concerned to represent his experience as fully as possible from the peculiar angle of vision permitted by his inheritance and upbringing. With the blood of the Puritans in his veins and in his head the writings of Plato and Shakespeare and Milton and Goethe, and the Persians and the Indians, and Mme. de Stael, and Wordsworth, and Carlyle, and George Sand, and Thoreau, and Margaret Fuller . . . But why continue the list? Emerson was as well versed in world culture as anyone in his time. He was provincial only in his habits and his residence. Like some immense Moby-Dick of the mind, he strained all this intellectual plankton through himself and it became Emerson – in the process, true enough, taking on some of the white tint and enigmatic quality of his New England–disciplined being. But who would care about an Emerson who was simply another carbon copy of the more genial middlebrow commentators already proliferating in mid–nineteenth-century American letters? The America Emerson represented was a more difficult and rigorous proposition – one, as Melville recognized, that dived deep and sounded into the farthest reaches of heavenly space. Though Melville found himself unable to "oscillate in Emerson's rainbow," he nonetheless pronounced him a "great man."

We may locate Emerson's greatness in the capaciousness of his thought. He could *imagine* anything – including an American republic capable of eating its own filth, politically speaking, and being nourished thereby. Emerson may have been fastidious for himself but he knew that America needed a comprehensive appetite and strong digestive system in order to survive. He was therefore prepared to accept the exercise of raw power not because it pleased him or accorded with his own standards but because it was the expression of something authentic and vital in the American experiment. It was – to use his own figure – the dirty water that sometimes fetched the pump when clean water was not to be had. But it was no more than a way of priming the motor, of getting things in motion. Finally the means could be justified only by the ends they achieved.

The Emerson presented to us by many of his critical commentators has often been little more than a caricature of his complex spirit, and it is therefore not very reassuring to hear Giamatti claim that "you do not have to read the prophet to realize his ideas are all around us." Such a procedure will yield us nothing but a straw man conveniently set up and knocked down for polemical purposes. Emerson lives in the veracity of his words as they jump out from the page – words that continue to speak with authority on the difficult issues that beset both our personal and civic existence. As we approach the two-hundreth anniversary of Emerson's birth, it is worth insisting that the only fit celebration of Emerson's life is a pledge that we will not desert his pages. That was William James's belief, and I want to conclude by citing his own description of how he participated in the Emerson centenary in 1903: "I let R.W.E. speak for himself, and I find now, hearing so much from others of him, that there are only a few things that *can* be said of him; he was so squarely and simply himself as to impress every one in the same manner. Reading the whole of him over again continuously has made me feel his real greatness as I never did before. He's really a critter to be thankful for."

I

DAVID M. ROBINSON

Transcendentalism and Its Times

"The ancient manners were giving way," Emerson recalled in 1867, looking back some three decades to the beginning of the Transcendentalist movement. As he tried to explain the milieu in which his early work emerged with such impact, he concluded that "the key to the period appeared to be that the mind had become aware of itself. Men grew reflective and intellectual. There was a new consciousness" (W 10: 325–26). Emerson wanted to explain the movement's sense of newness, of what many felt to be the initiation of a new era in human history. But now at some distance himself from these earlier hopes, he placed the fervor of this movement in a larger framework of the cycles of human history, part of the necessary and inevitable process of reform and renewal. Transcendentalism represented one of the recurrent periods in which "the party of the Past" and "the party of the Future" collide. "At times the resistance is reanimated, the schism runs under the world and appears in Literature, Philosophy, Church, State and social customs" (W 10: 325). Transcendentalism was thus a moment in history containing both expansive hope and a sense of strife and embattlement, and marked by the emergence of new intellectual categories, new relations among persons and classes, and new ethical and political imperatives.[1]

Emerson dramatized the mood of the period in his lecture on "The Transcendentalist" (1842), portraying the "Transcendentalist" as an aspiring and stubborn youth who is pressed to justify a younger generation's hopes and actions before the skeptical inquiries of the "world," a voice of conventional common sense with a recognizably parental attitude. The Transcendentalist confesses to being "miserable with inaction," but rejects the avenues of engagement that the world offers. "We perish of rest and rust. But we do not like your work." The "world" replies that such paralysis is deadly, and chastens the Transcendentalist with the possibility of irrelevance: "you grow old and useless." But the youth's reply is sharp, centering on the primary duty of absolute honesty. "If I cannot work, at least I need not lie. All that is clearly due to-day is not to lie" (CW 1: 212).

The passage tells us much about the mood of resistance to established conventions and expectations, and the desire for rethinking and remaking, that characterized the movement. Perhaps most importantly, it suggests the underlying sense of hope that fueled its reformist energy. The Transcendentalist feels that a consistent honesty, a refusal to "lie" by taking on work that does not confirm a deep calling, will eventuate in both a changed world and a transformed individual within it. This is a belief with profound social and political implications, and it is also a religious affirmation, reminding us of the movement's roots in the complex background of New England's religious history.

New England religious culture was shaped by the imperatives of the Calvinist theology that its Puritan settlers had struggled to maintain and defend. The doctrines of innate depravity and election to grace were central to Calvinism, emphasizing that human nature was irreparably corrupt, and that certain sinners were "elected" by God for salvation through the atonement of Jesus. Of particular importance was the fact that God did the choosing, and that salvation was a gift of grace; an individual's "work" or character could have no bearing on his or her eternal fate. Yet the implications of these doctrines were contested within the Puritan clergy, making New England Calvinism an evolving and at times quite unstable theology.[2] The Puritans qualified and modified these doctrines in several ways, primarily through ideas about the soul's "preparation" for salvation, but they remained an increasingly problematic element of Puritan theology.[3]

In the mid-eighteenth century a number of ministers in and around Boston began to formulate more liberal and positive views of human nature and to stress the importance of individual piety and ethical practice in the process of salvation. Early signs of the fissure within New England theology were Boston minister Charles Chauncy's sharp dissent in the 1740s from the evangelical revival known as the Great Awakening, a dissent based in part on a suspicion of the intense emotionalism or "enthusiasm" inculcated by the revivalists. Chauncy advocated a more reasoned and ordered faith as an alternative to the revivalists' emotionalism. In his dissent, Chauncy set a direction of thinking that implied a more positive view of human nature, and ultimately a more benevolent interpretation of the nature of God.[4]

The dissatisfaction with Calvinist doctrine among the Boston liberals grew during the eighteenth century, but there was no significant theological strife until 1805, when the liberal Henry Ware was elected in a narrow vote as the Hollis Professor of Divinity at Harvard. Ware's election was strongly opposed by many of the orthodox Calvinists, and the ensuing controversy lasted some three decades, eventuating in the split of some of the oldest of the original Puritan churches, and the formation of the American Unitarian Association in 1825, the denominational umbrella under which the liberals gathered.[5]

The Unitarian Controversy brought one vitally important spokesman to the fore for the liberals, William Ellery Channing, minister of the Federal Street Church in Boston. Channing argued that Calvinist doctrines stunted the moral development of the individual. "It is plain," Channing wrote, "that a doctrine, which contradicts our best ideas of goodness and justice, cannot come from the just and good God, or be a true representation of his character" (Channing, 107). He emphasized the divine potential within every individual, and made his religious teaching center on the necessity and the means of cultivating that divine potential. In an 1828 sermon, "Likeness to God," Channing articulated the concept of the spiritual quality of the self that would come to be one of the hallmarks of Transcendentalism. "To understand a great and good being, we must have the seeds of the same excellence," Channing wrote. "God becomes a real being to us, in proportion as his own nature is unfolded within us" (Channing, 147). This emphasis on a conception of human nature as reflective of God's nature completed the Unitarian rejection of Calvinism, and defined the spiritual life in terms of a continuing effort to cultivate the spiritual resources of the individual.

This program of "self-culture" became the groundwork for a new conception of the religious life which accentuated a process of disciplined intellectual and moral growth, and a deepening sensitivity and capacity for spiritual perception and discernment.[6] Although self-culture as Channing propounded it stressed a continuing process of development rather than an instantaneous regeneration, as was being increasingly preached among evangelical revivalists, he still recognized the importance of religious experience in the soul's spiritual development. "To a man who is growing in the likeness of God," he wrote, "faith begins even here to change into vision. He carries within himself a proof of a Deity, which can only be understood by experience. He more than believes, he feels the Divine presence" (Channing, 147). The younger generation who heard Channing, Emerson among them, responded to both strands of his new conception of the spiritual life: that it was an extended process of gradual inner growth dependent on discipline and careful self-cultivation, and that, within it, one would discover the crucially important confirmation of "experience," a feeling of a "Divine presence" within.

Channing's message and example reached Emerson at a crucial point in his intellectual development, when he was seriously weighing the vocation of the ministry, but hesitating to make a commitment to it. His hesitation arose in part from his lack of self-confidence, but also from a distaste for dry theological reasoning and doctrinal preaching that he associated with ministerial study. Channing offered him instead a model of elegant and inspiring pulpit eloquence akin to poetry. In a mood of self-analysis in 1824, he recorded his divided feelings about entering ministerial study, admitting feelings of inadequacy about his "reasoning faculty." But in compensation, he noted his "strong imagination" and "keen relish for the beauties of poetry," determining to make himself into a different kind of preacher, devoted to the "moral imagination" that had moved him in Channing (*JMN* 2: 238).

Emerson eventually came to see the ministry as too restricted a sphere of endeavor, and after some difficult soul-searching, resigned his pulpit at the Second Church in Boston in 1832.[7] Although he continued to preach in Unitarian pulpits for several years after his resignation, his separation from the ministry allowed him to launch a career as a lecturer, essayist, and poet, incorporating many of his pulpit themes into an expanded vision of the possibility of moral reformulation and spiritual growth for the individual. It was a message that struck a responsive chord in a younger generation hungry for an intensified spirituality.

His first book, *Nature* (1836), was part philosophical treatise, part nature hymn, and part revivalist preaching of a Transcendental variety.[8] Emerson's religious and ethical vision fascinated younger readers engaged in their own project of character formation and identity building, like Henry David Thoreau and Margaret Fuller, both of whom were strongly molded by Emerson's thinking and developed close friendships with him. Like Channing, Emerson became something of an exemplar of new possibilities in American intellectual life. His nondogmatic, spiritually engaged, ethically centered preaching and lecturing helped young Unitarian ministers such as James Freeman Clarke, George Ripley, and Theodore Parker see larger possibilities in their careers in the ministry. To them, Emerson represented the avenue toward the revitalization of the Unitarian movement, which they felt had become hardened into convention and routine.[9] This spirit of restless energy and earnest spiritual aspiration, articulated with both rhetorical brilliance and poetic delicacy by Emerson, characterized the mood of the Transcendentalist movement. Initially an outgrowth of the Unitarianism formulated by Channing under the pressures of the Unitarian Controversy, it spilled over the boundaries of the church, and helped to unlock the literary tastes and ambitions of a generation that could no longer accept the aesthetic starvation of American provinciality.

While the Transcendentalists found themselves arrayed against the mainstream by reason of their aesthetic sensibilities and heterodox spiritual aspirations, they were also profoundly affected by the claims of the reform movements of the day. The 1830s and 1840s were a time of political ferment internationally, with revolutions wracking Europe in the late 1840s, as democratic forces began to challenge the established hierarchical regimes. Tension was building in America as well over the conditions created by the economic inequities that were the result of the industrial revolution. Moreover, the continued existence of slavery in the South was a source of increasing moral outrage and political tension.[10]

As Transcendentalism emerged from its Unitarian roots, it thus became an embattled movement. The simmering controversy between the Transcendentalists and more conservative Unitarians intensified in 1838 when Emerson presented an impassioned case for a religion based on the soul's powers of intuition in an address at Harvard Divinity School. Emerson urged the students not to be bound by the dead formality of the models of preaching available to them. "The soul is not preached," he told them. "The Church seems to totter to its fall, almost all life extinct" (CW 1: 84). This spiritless preaching was linked to a lifeless theology, in which "historical Christianity" rather than a living faith was preached, signified by the reliance on an inflated reverence for the person of Jesus rather than the principles that he stood for. Jesus "spoke of miracles," Emerson explained, "for he felt that man's life was a miracle, and all that man doth, and he knew this daily miracle shines, as the man is diviner." The present-day church, he felt, had lost this sense of immediacy and relevance. "But the very word Miracle, as pronounced by Christian churches, gives a false impression. It is Monster. It is not one with the blowing clover and the falling rain" (CW 1: 81). The New Testament miracles were not the key to religious revelation, Emerson averred, but rather the "moral sentiment" (CW 1: 77) which innately resided within every individual. The prominent Unitarian leader Andrews Norton, who was engaged in writing a detailed scholarly study explaining and defending the authenticity and historical accuracy of the biblical evidences of Christianity, responded to Emerson with an attack on the pantheistic tendencies and predilection for linguistic obscurity that he found in the "new school in literature and philosophy" (Miller, The Transcendentalists 193–96). Norton warned not only against what he felt were theological errors, but also against the social danger the new movement seemed to pose: "They announce themselves as the prophets and priests of a new future, in which all is to be changed, all old opinions done away, and all present forms of society abolished" (Miller, The Transcendentalists 194).

Emerson was both dismayed and angered by Norton's attack, but it increased his visibility as a spokesman for those who were dissatisfied with the current situation in religion and literature, and augmented his already growing authority as a theological innovator and literary experimenter. The Divinity School controversy thus helped to coalesce Emerson's friends and supporters, and make them recognize with new urgency that they were a school or movement. In the late 1830s and early 1840s, they articulated the need for reform and innovation with increasing boldness and commitment.[11]

One important source of the energy of their agenda for change was their growing receptivity to the literary and philosophical models of Europe. Goethe was one of the most important of these European authors, regarded as the great interpreter of the modern age in literature by Emerson, who called him "the soul of his century," a writer who "has clothed our modern existence with poetry" (CW 4: 157).[12] Goethe was championed most prominently by Margaret Fuller, who adopted him as an exemplar of creative genius and praised him despite her feeling that his intellect was "too much developed in proportion to the moral nature," that his life did not, in other words, measure up to the strictest of New England moral standards (Fuller, "Goethe" 2). But for Fuller, Goethe cast the spell that was art, and that was essential in helping her to free herself from the restrictions of her culture. She described her ardent reaction to Goethe's *Elective Affinities* with a sense of the aesthetic receptivity that was a crucial element in the Transcendentalist sensibility. "For myself, I never felt so completely the very thing which genius should always make us feel, that I was in its circle, and could not get out till its spell was done, and its last spirit permitted to depart." While others, Fuller wrote, reacted to it as "an immoral book," she experienced it as the epitome of art. "At last I understood that world within a world, that ripest fruit of human nature, which is called Art" (33–34).

The Transcendentalists responded with similar enthusiasm to the English Romantics, especially William Wordsworth and Thomas Carlyle. Wordsworth's introspective concern with spiritual growth and his sensitivity to nature as the corresponding mirror to the soul were echoed and elaborated in Emerson's *Nature* and Thoreau's *Walden* (1854). Emerson read Carlyle's expositions of new thought and writing in Germany with intensity and eagerness in the early 1830s, seeking him out in Scotland in 1833 to form what would be a lifelong friendship. In discussing his age as one of revolutionary change in "The American Scholar" (1837), Emerson explained the Romantics' concern with ordinary experience as a significant affirmation of the dignity and value of the individual. "The literature of the poor, the feelings of the child, the philosophy of the street, the meaning of household life, are the topics of the time." For Emerson, this sign of "new vigor" in modern literature was a further call to the recognition of daily experience as the formative element in the culture of the soul. It lent authority to a renewal of effort to become more alive to the present moment as the only theater of spiritual development. "Give me insight into to-day, and you may have the antique and future worlds" (*CW* 1: 67).

These influences of modern literature were also supplemented by a wide variety of religious and philosophical influences. The Platonic and Neoplatonic traditions were formative to Emerson's thinking; he included Plato as one of his *Representative Men* in the 1850 volume by that title, and wrote in 1842 that "what are called *new views* here in New England, at the present time, . . . are not new, but the very oldest of thoughts cast into the mould of these new times" (*CW* 1: 201). Seeing himself as an expositor of the Idealist tradition in philosophy, of which Plato was the founder, Emerson defined Transcendentalism as "Idealism as it appears in 1842" (*CW* 1: 201). He also recognized the importance of Immanuel Kant and the German Idealist philosophical tradition to his own work and that of his contemporaries.

Further stimulus came from the newly translated texts of Eastern religion and philosophy, which both Emerson and Thoreau read with eagerness, finding important confirmation for the direction of their thinking. Emerson urged Thoreau to prepare a series of articles on "Ethnical Scriptures" for *The Dial*, and Thoreau was particularly inspired by Hindu philosophy, weaving it through *Walden* as a Scripture whose authority matched that of the New Testament.[13] Emerson also had a particular receptivity to speculative and mystical philosophy, and the work of Emanuel Swedenborg, transmitted in part through his American disciple Sampson Reed, made a strong impression on him in the 1820s and 1830s, helping him to develop the doctrine of the "correspondence" between the mind and nature that is central to *Nature*. In "The American Scholar" Emerson called Swedenborg a "man of genius" whose importance lay in his ability to show "the connexion between nature and the affections of the soul" (*CW* 1: 68). Although he would later criticize him in *Representative Men* for the rigidity of his interpretive categories, it was the connections that Swedenborg made between the inner and outer world that helped to propel Emerson's thinking in the direction of correspondence and what it implied – a seamless, monistically united universe, in which the physical and the mental were corresponding versions of the same reality.[14] Thus while grounded in the complex history of New England theology, especially its latest and most liberal iteration in Unitarianism, the Transcendentalists were also molded by an exotic amalgam of foreign influences, both ancient and modern.

In 1840 the Transcendentalists launched their own periodical, *The Dial*, with Margaret Fuller as the first editor, and Emerson, George Ripley, and Bronson Alcott involved in the planning process. They intended it as the vehicle for the expression of their own thought, and the retransmission of texts and ideas that had been important to them, and they felt that it would speak to a wider audience of young people who were also engaged in the process of cultural and social reform.[15] "No one can converse much with different classes of society in New England, without remarking the progress of a revolution," Emerson wrote in its initial issue. "Those who share in it have no external organization, no badge, no creed, no name. They do not vote, or print, or even meet together." But they are united, he explained, in sharing in the "spirit of the time," one critical of the established patterns and institutions and expressing itself as "a protest against usage, and a search for principles." With *The Dial*, he and his colleagues hoped to "give expression to that spirit that lifts men to a higher platform," a change of thinking and perspective which would also mean a change in habits and actions (Miller, *The Transcendentalists* 249–50).

The Dial may be the most revealing window into both the excesses and accomplishments of Transcendentalism. It was eclectic in the extreme, containing a mixture of reviews, literary essays, theological discourse, political commentary and theory, and translations. One of its contributors, Bronson Alcott, became the focal point of ridicule for critics of Transcendentalism because of the hazy and opaque mysticism of his "Orphic Sayings," a collection of aphoristic expressions of abstract idealism.[16] But the journal gave Emerson's work a wider public notice, confirming that he was not a lone prophet but part of a larger group. It also served him as a means of encouraging the work of several aspiring young writers such as Henry David Thoreau, Jones Very, and Christopher Pearse Cranch. It seems increasingly evident that the most significant contribution of *The Dial* was the experience and confidence it gave to its first editor, Fuller, and the venue it provided her for her critical work on Goethe and her landmark treatise on the rights of women, which she expanded into the book *Woman in the Nineteenth Century* (1845).[17]

The Dial was one of the relatively few signs of institution building among the Transcendentalists, who engaged the public primarily through their writing and lecturing. Several of them, however, continued as Unitarian ministers, making in different ways important contributions to the church. Theodore Parker preached one of the most radical and controversial sermons of the entire Transcendentalist movement, *A Discourse of the Transient and Permanent in Christianity*, as a Unitarian ordination sermon in 1841. Parker called for a new conception of religion that recognized both the historical contingency or transience of its articulation as the Christian dogma and mythology, and the enduring importance of its affirmation of the spiritual nature of humanity. "Looking at the word of Jesus, at real Christianity, the pure religion he taught, nothing appears more fixed and certain," Parker said. "But, looking at the history of what men call Christianity, nothing seems more uncertain and perishable" (Miller, *The Transcendentalists* 262). While Parker remained committed to the ministry, he remained within the Unitarian denomination on uneasy terms, feeling increasingly ostracized for his radically modern views of theology and his deepening political activism.[18]

Frederic Henry Hedge and James Freeman Clarke were committed churchmen and committed reformers, engaged in both preserving the church and helping it adapt to the changes of the modern world. Hedge was a parish minister in Bangor, Maine, during the late 1830s, while Transcendentalism was in ferment in the Boston area, and his experience there combined with his commitment to the church as an institution to temper his theological radicalism. But he remained a committed intuitionist in his religious epistemology, one of the cardinal points of departure in the Transcendentalist movement away from Unitarianism. Clarke worked to establish Unitarianism in the Midwest, taking on a pastorate at a newly formed Unitarian church in Louisville, Kentucky. He later returned to Boston to found the Church of the Disciples in 1841, and remained one of the most prominent exponents of Unitarianism in the nineteenth century.[19]

These efforts at the reform of the church were also accompanied by experiments in educational reform that have a continuing significance to the development of modern educational theories and practice. The concept of self-culture was in essence the pursuit of lifelong education, which stressed introspective self-knowledge, spiritual aspiration, and the development of innate inner resources. Emerson regarded the national lecturing that occupied so much of his career from first to last as a kind of grand educational experiment, in which a committed teacher and motivated student might meet on a ground of common endeavor.[20] Bronson Alcott, Emerson's close friend and intellectual ally, founded the Temple School in Boston, and worked with the belief that the teacher's role was to bring out the innate potential of his students. It was a much more student-centered approach to education than was common in the early nineteenth century. But in part because of growing suspicion of Transcendentalism, and in part because Alcott seemed to broach forbidden topics in his school, he was forced to close it in 1838, and did so with a feeling of deep persecution.[21] Alcott remained a part of Emerson's inner circle all his life, but never regained the sense of direction and purposeful vocation that he had achieved in Temple School.

Margaret Fuller's experience as a teacher at Alcott's school and later at another progressive school, the Greene Street School in Providence, Rhode Island, was formative in the development of her intellectual career. Fuller followed her experience as a teacher by establishing an annual series of "Conversations" for women in Boston from 1839 to 1844. Fuller's "Conversations" were in part modeled on the yearly lecture series that Emerson presented in Boston in the late 1830s, but they emphasized dialogue and the opportunity for self-expression by the women in attendance. Fuller's experience with "Conversations" contributed directly to the arguments she propounded for an expanded sphere of action for women in *Woman in the Nineteenth Century*.[22] Elizabeth Palmer Peabody, another Transcendentalist deeply concerned with educational reform, worked as a teacher and a governess, later opening a school with her sister Mary, and then working with Bronson Alcott in his Temple School, where she transcribed his dialogues with his pupils in *Record of a School* (1835). She later became an advocate of the establishment of kindergarten education in America.

These efforts in publishing, ecclesiastical reform, and educational advancement show the Transcendentalists working in and through the settled institutions of the church and the school to effect progressive change. The Transcendentalists were also involved in more radical attempts to alter the American political and economic system by establishing new alternatives to it. By far the best-known example of this is Thoreau's agrarian experiment at Walden Pond, in which he tested the virtues of strict economy, the study of nature, and the contemplative life. Thoreau's brilliant account of his life in the woods in *Walden* has become an essential American book, not only central to the canon of nineteenth-century American literature, but also a founding text for the modern environmental movement.[23] Thoreau's experiment, however, was a solitary one. Others attempted communal agrarian experiments, the most famous of which is Brook Farm, a commune established by George Ripley in 1840.

Ripley conceived of Brook Farm as a way to combine manual and intellectual labor, and thus to allow members of the commune to integrate disparate aspects of their lives into a more unified and harmonious experience. He also hoped that the experiment would provide a secure and noncompetitive economic environment for its members, and that it would model ways in which class divisions between the laborer and the intellectual might be overcome.[24] Ripley decided that a communal agrarian experiment would address many of these problems and goals, and he tried to persuade Emerson to join Brook Farm. After some thought Emerson declined to do so, feeling that his personal and familial needs and his vocational mission would not be well served by the plan. Though he termed it a "noble &

humane" plan in a letter to Ripley in 1840, he explained that "it has little to offer me which with resolution I cannot procure for myself" (*L* 2: 369).

The grounds of Emerson's refusal, and the competing model of agrarian experiment represented by Thoreau at Walden, suggest an important division among the Transcendentalists over the question of self-reliance and communal organization. Although both Emerson and Thoreau were social critics who endorsed progressive political reform efforts and became persuasive speakers and writers for the antislavery effort in the 1850s, they concentrated their intellectual efforts on the ethical imperatives and moral choices faced by the individual. Another perspective existed among the Transcendentalists, articulated by Ripley, William Henry Channing, and Orestes Brownson, which stressed the importance of communal effort and larger-scale organization for institutional and economic reform. Brownson made the case for such efforts in an 1840 essay, "The Laboring Classes," a critique of the political limitations of the doctrine of self-culture. Brownson saw the nature of labor in the newly industrializing economy as the key to the times, which were marked by "the new struggle between the operative and his employer" (Miller, *The Transcendentalists* 437), and he chided the clerical advocates of self-culture with complicity in maintaining the economic status quo. "In a word they always league with the people's masters, and seek to reform without disturbing the social arrangements which render reform necessary" (439).

Brownson's position was perhaps the most radical among the Transcendentalists, but others were much engaged by versions of "Associationism" that were in the air in America in the 1840s. William Henry Channing, nephew of the prominent Unitarian leader, formed the Christian Union of Associationists in 1842 in an attempt to establish an organized advocacy for politically progressive views within a religious framework. He was also influential as a frequent visitor and unofficial pastor at Brook Farm, which became increasingly immersed in Associationist theorizing after its founding in 1841.[25] Ripley and Channing were particularly interested in trying to enact, in concrete ways, a culture of peaceable, noncompetitive political and economic accord in which individuals might develop to the fullest their own interests and potential within the framework of a supportive and nurturing community.

In 1844 the Brook Farmers decided to endorse the vision of the French political theorist Charles Fourier, who called for the establishment of "phalanxes," communal organizations that were highly systematized in their organization and designation of duties and activities. While it does not seem that Brook Farm ever succeeded in approximating Fourier's rage for order, they did see themselves as part of a wave of important social experimentation, of which Fourier was a leading theorist.[26] But Brook Farm was dealt a disastrous blow when a new building, into which the association had poured much of its resources, was destroyed by fire in 1846.

Between the individualism of Emerson and Thoreau, and the commitment to Associationism represented by Brook Farm, Margaret Fuller presents an interesting compromise, although as she matured intellectually, her thinking developed toward a form of Associationism. Her book on women's rights, *Woman in the Nineteenth Century*, is an extension of Emerson's premises on self-culture to the situation of women, with Fuller arguing that a full range of opportunities should be accorded for women's development and expression. She thus adapted Emersonian individualism to meet the needs of women whose opportunities for full individual growth had been thwarted.[27]

Fuller came to believe that her own best work lay in the direction of wider public education through her writing. She became a correspondent for the *New York Tribune* in 1844, where she wrote on both literature and issues of social reform, and she eventually traveled to Italy, where she became engaged in the Italian Revolution of 1848 led by Giuseppe Mazzini. It was in Italy that Fuller's deepest political commitments were developed, for she saw the Italian cause as one of the great democratic political movements in history, and felt that much was at stake in its outcome. Fuller planned to return to America in 1850, where she would have encountered a political climate that was increasingly highly charged because of the growing antislavery debate. But she died in a shipwreck on her return, a tragedy that cost American society a powerful progressive voice at a crucial moment in its history.[28]

Much of the experimental and reformist energy that had fueled the Transcendentalist movement was absorbed in the political realignment that led into the Civil War, and emerged after its completion. By the middle 1850s, what had been a movement, albeit never a cohesive one, dispersed into a variety of different projects, causes, and careers. In the late 1860s the Free Religious Association was formed, again growing out of a dispute within Unitarianism, and many of the Transcendentalists' interests and commitments were furthered in different forms in the FRA.[29] But the flash point of intellectual and political energy had come in the late 1830s and early 1840s. It was, to borrow a phrase from Emerson, a "flash-of-lightning faith" (*CW* 1: 213), but it was a brilliant flash, and those who experienced it were changed profoundly by it. It stands as one of the most meaningful and consequential of American intellectual movements, the implications of which continue to reverberate in American culture.

NOTES

1   For a discussion of the origins of the Transcendentalist movement, see Miller, *The Transcendentalists*, pp. 16–105; and Packer, "The Transcendentalists," pp. 331–61.

2   On the plurality of views within New England Puritanism, and its changing dynamic, see Gura and Foster.

3   On the development and significance of the Puritan theology of preparation for salvation, see Miller, " 'Preparation for Salvation' "; and Pettit.

4   On the development of Unitarianism out of Puritanism in New England, see Wright, *The Beginnings of Unitarianism in America*, especially his discussion of the reaction of Chauncy and other liberals to the Great Awakening (pp. 28–58).

5   On Ware's election, see Wright, *The Unitarian Controversy*, pp. 1–16. For details on the formation of the American Unitarian Association, see Forman, pp. 30–32.

6   On the development of the concept of "self-culture" in nineteenth-century New England Unitarianism, see Robinson, *Apostle of Culture*, pp. 11–35.

7   For discussions of Emerson's resignation, see Mott, pp. 143–67; and Richardson, pp. 118–27.

8   For discussions of the evolution of *Nature*, and its place in Emerson's development, see Sealts and Ferguson; Porte, pp. 64–82; and Hodder, *Emerson's Rhetoric of Revelation*.

9   For a discussion of the impact of Transcendentalism on church reform in New England Unitarianism, see Hutchison.

10 As Reynolds (*European Revolutions and the American Literary Renaissance*) has shown, American reactions to those European revolutions had a strong impact on the development of American literature in the 1840s and 1850s, including that of the Transcendentalists. See in particular pp. 25–78 and 153–70. For a discussion of Emerson's gradually increasing involvement in the antislavery movement, see Gougeon. Of particular note among the movements of social reform were the Associationist movement, dedicated to reform of the patterns of work and the distribution of wealth, and the women's rights movement, to which Margaret Fuller was an important contributor.

11 The context and reception of the Divinity School "Address," and the impact of the following controversy on Emerson, have been discussed extensively. See as examples of some of the discussion, Miller, *The Transcendentalists*, pp. 157–246; Porte, pp. 91–113; Whicher, pp. 72–84; Packer, *Emerson's Fall*, pp. 121–37; Robinson, "Poetry, Personality, and the Divinity School Address"; and Cayton, pp. 163–90.

12 On Goethe's impact on Emerson, see Van Cromphout.

13 For a detailed discussion of the impact of Hinduism on Thoreau, see Hodder, " 'Ex Oriente Lux.' "

14 For discussions of Emerson's doctrine of correspondence, see Paul, pp. 27–51; Packer, *Emerson's Fall*, pp. 32–41; and Van Leer, pp. 36–45.

15 For the origins and achievements of *The Dial* and its contributors, see Myerson, *The New England Transcendentalists and the Dial*.

16 On the reaction to, and ridicule of, Alcott's "Orphic Sayings," see Myerson, " 'In the Transcendental Emporium.' "

17 Fuller's essay was originally published in 1843 in *The Dial* as "The Great Lawsuit. Man *versus* Men. Woman *versus* Women." For a discussion of its relation to *Woman in the Nineteenth Century*, see Reynolds, "From *Dial* Essay to New York Book."

18 For discussions of Parker's conflict with other Unitarian ministers, see Miller, "Theodore Parker," and Grodzins.

19 For a discussion of the careers of Hedge and Clarke in the context of the "Broad Church" element of nineteenth-century American Unitarianism, see Robinson, *The Unitarians and the Universalists*, pp. 101–6. Hedge's theology is articulated in his *Reason in Religion* (1865).

20 For a discussion of Emerson's career as a "teacher" through his writing and lecturing, see Sealts, pp. 267–76.

21 For further information on Alcott's educational experiments at Temple School, see Packer, "The Transcendentalists," pp. 372–74; and Carlson, "Bronson Alcott's 'Journal for 1838,' " Parts One and Two.

22 For discussions of the significance of Fuller's conversations, see Capper, pp. 290–306; and Simmons.

23 For a discussion of Thoreau in the context of environmental writing in America, see Buell.

24 On the history of Brook Farm, see Rose, 130–61; and Guarneri, pp. 44–59, 170–74, 236–38.

25 On Channing's career and political ideas, see Robinson, "The Political Odyssey of William Henry Channing."

26 For details on the nature of the political discourse at Brook Farm that resulted in the change to Fourierism, see Francis. The rise of the Fourierist movement in nineteenth-century America is recounted in Guarneri.

27 For analyses of Fuller's development of a political ethic from the discourse of Transcendentalism, see Robinson, "Margaret Fuller and the Transcendental Ethos"; Chevigny; Capper, pp. 252–350; and Zwarg.

28 On Fuller's activities in Italy, see Fuller, *"These Sad But Glorious Days"*; Reynolds, *European Revolutions and the American Literary Renaissance*, pp. 54–78; and Von Mehren, pp. 252–351.

29 See Packer's chapter entitled "Diaspora" in "The Transcendentalists," pp. 495–547, for a detailed account of the different directions that the energy of the Transcendentalists took in the 1840s and 1850s. For further information on the Free Religious Association, see Persons; and Robinson, *The Unitarians and the Universalists*, pp. 107–22.

BIBLIOGRAPHY

Buell, Lawrence. *The Environmental Imagination: Thoreau, Nature Writing, and the Formation of American Culture.* Cambridge, MA: Harvard University Press, 1995.

Capper, Charles. *Margaret Fuller: An American Romantic Life. The Private Years.* Oxford and New York: Oxford University Press, 1992.

Carlson, Larry A., ed. "Bronson Alcott's 'Journal for 1838' (Part One)." *Studies in the American Renaissance 1993.* Charlottesville: University Press of Virginia, 1993. 161–244.

———. "Bronson Alcott's 'Journal for 1838' (Part Two)." *Studies in the American Renaissance 1994.* Charlottesville: University Press of Virginia, 1994. 123–93.

Cayton, Mary Kupiec. *Emerson's Emergence: Self and Society in the Transformation of New England, 1800–1845.* Chapel Hill: University of North Carolina Press, 1989.

Channing, William Ellery. *William Ellery Channing: Selected Writings.* Ed. David Robinson. Mahwah, NJ: Paulist Press, 1985.

Chevigny, Bell Gale. "To the Edges of Ideology: Margaret Fuller's Centrifugal Evolution." *American Quarterly* 38 (1986): 173–301.

Forman, Charles C. " 'Elected Now by Time.' " *A Stream of Light: A Sesquicentennial History of American Unitarianism.* Ed. Conrad Wright. Boston: Skinner House, 1975. 3–32.

Foster, Stephen. *The Long Argument: English Puritanism and the Shaping of New England Culture, 1570–1700.* Chapel Hill: University of North Carolina Press, 1991.

Francis, Richard. "The Ideology of Brook Farm." *Studies in the American Renaissance 1977.* Ed. Joel Myerson. Boston: Twayne, 1977. 1–48.

Fuller, Margaret. "Goethe." *The Dial* 2 (1841): 1–41.

———. "The Great Lawsuit. Man *versus* Men. Woman *versus* Women." *The Dial* 4 (1843): 1–47.

———. *"These Sad But Glorious Days": Dispatches from Europe, 1846–1850.* Ed. Larry J. Reynolds and Susan Belasco Smith. New Haven and London: Yale University Press, 1991.

———. *Woman in the Nineteenth Century.* New York: Greeley and McElrath, 1845.

Gougeon, Len. *Virtue's Hero: Emerson, Antislavery, and Reform.* Athens: University of Georgia Press, 1990.

Grodzins, Dean. "Theodore Parker's 'Conference with the Boston Association,' January 23, 1843." *Proceedings of the Unitarian Universalist Historical Society* 23 (1995): 66–101.

Guarneri, Carl J. *The Utopian Alternative: Fourierism in Nineteenth-Century America.* Ithaca: Cornell University Press, 1991.

Gura, Philip F. *A Glimpse of Sion's Glory: Puritan Radicalism in New England, 1620–1660.* Middletown, CT: Wesleyan University Press, 1984.

Hedge, Frederic Henry. *Reason in Religion.* Boston: Walker, Fuller, and Co., 1865.

Hodder, Alan D. *Emerson's Rhetoric of Revelation: Nature, the Reader, and the Apocalypse Within.* University Park: The Pennsylvania State University Press, 1989.

———. " 'Ex Oriente Lux': Thoreau's Ecstasies and the Hindu Texts." *Harvard Theological Review* 86 (1993): 403–38.

Hutchison, William R. *The Transcendentalist Ministers: Church Reform in the New England Renaissance.* New Haven: Yale University Press, 1959.

Miller, Perry. " 'Preparation for Salvation' in Seventeenth-Century New England." *Nature's Nation.* Cambridge, MA: Belknap Press of Harvard University Press, 1967. 50–77.

———. "Theodore Parker: Apostasy Within Liberalism." *Nature's Nation*: 134–49.

———. *The Transcendentalists: An Anthology*. Cambridge, MA: Harvard University Press, 1950.

Mott, Wesley T. *"The Strains of Eloquence": Emerson and His Sermons*. University Park: The Pennsylvania State University Press, 1989.

Myerson, Joel. " 'In the Transcendental Emporium': Bronson Alcott's 'Orphic Sayings' in the *Dial*." *English Language Notes* 10 (1972): 31–38.

———. *The New England Transcendentalists and the Dial: A History of the Magazine and Its Contributors*. Rutherford, NJ: Fairleigh Dickinson University Press, 1980.

Packer, B. L. *Emerson's Fall: A New Interpretation of the Major Essays*. New York: Continuum, 1982.

———. "The Transcendentalists." *Prose Writing 1820–1865*. Ed. Sacvan Bercovitch. Cambridge and New York: Cambridge University Press, 1995. 329–604. Vol. 2 of *Cambridge History of American Literature*.

Paul, Sherman. *Emerson's Angle of Vision: Man and Nature in American Experience*. Cambridge, MA: Harvard University Press, 1952.

Persons, Stow. *Free Religion: An American Faith*. New Haven: Yale University Press, 1947.

Pettit, Norman. *The Heart Prepared: Grace and Conversion in Puritan Spiritual Life*. New Haven: Yale University Press, 1966.

Porte, Joel. *Representative Man: Ralph Waldo Emerson in His Time*. New York: Oxford University Press, 1979.

Reynolds, Larry J. *European Revolutions and the American Literary Renaissance*. New Haven: Yale University Press, 1988.

———. "From *Dial* Essay to New York Book: The Making of *Woman in the Nineteenth Century*." *Periodical Literature in Nineteenth-Century America*. Ed. Kenneth M. Price and Susan Belasco Smith. Charlottesville: University Press of Virginia, 1995. 17–34.

Richardson, Robert D., Jr. *Emerson: The Mind on Fire*. Berkeley: University of California Press, 1995.

Robinson, David M. *Apostle of Culture: Emerson as Preacher and Lecturer*. Philadelphia: University of Pennsylvania Press, 1982.

———. "Margaret Fuller and the Transcendental Ethos." *Woman in the Nineteenth Century. Publications of the Modern Language Association* 97 (1982): 83–98.

———. "Poetry, Personality, and the Divinity School Address." *Harvard Theological Review* 82 (1989): 185–99.

———. "The Political Odyssey of William Henry Channing." *American Quarterly* 34 (1982): 165–84.

———. *The Unitarians and the Universalists*. Westport, CT: Greenwood Press, 1985.

Rose, Anne C. *Transcendentalism as a Social Movement, 1830–1850*. New Haven: Yale University Press, 1981.

Sealts, Merton M., Jr. *Emerson on the Scholar*. Columbia: University of Missouri Press, 1992.

Sealts, Merton M., Jr., and Alfred R. Ferguson, eds. *Emerson's Nature – Origin,*

Growth, Meaning. 2nd. ed. Carbondale: Southern Illinois University Press, 1979.

Simmons, Nancy Craig. "Margaret Fuller's Boston Conversations: The 1839–1840 Series." *Studies in the American Renaissance 1994.* Ed. Joel Myerson. Charlottesville: University Press of Virginia, 1994. 195–226.

Van Cromphout, Gustaaf. *Emerson's Modernity and the Example of Goethe.* Columbia: University of Missouri Press, 1990.

Van Leer, David. *Emerson's Epistemology: The Argument of the Essays.* Cambridge: Cambridge University Press, 1986.

Von Mehren, Joan. *Minerva and the Muse: A Life of Margaret Fuller.* Amherst: University of Massachusetts Press, 1994.

Whicher, Stephen E. *Freedom and Fate: An Inner Life of Ralph Waldo Emerson.* Philadelphia: University of Pennsylvania Press, 1953.

Wright, Conrad. *The Beginnings of Unitarianism in America.* 1955, rpt. Hamden, CT: Archon Books, 1977.

———. *The Unitarian Controversy: Essays on American Unitarian History.* Boston: Skinner House, 1994.

Zwarg, Christina. *Feminist Conversations: Fuller, Emerson, and the Play of Reading.* Ithaca: Cornell University Press, 1995.

2

PHYLLIS COLE

Ralph Waldo Emerson in His Family

Ralph Waldo Emerson's birth into a lineage of New England clergy – seven generations stretching back to the Puritan migration – has long offered food for thought to biographers and historians. To his earliest interpreters, genealogy itself had explanatory value: James Elliot Cabot could claim that Emerson received from his father "the blood of several lines of 'painful preachers.' "[1] Recent scholars have returned to the family not as a blood influence so much as a cultural, psychological, and textual field around Emerson's written work. Most important, his writing itself includes a scrutiny of family heritage. As Emerson commented in 1841, after eight pages of journalizing on his aunt, brothers, and ancestry, "I doubt if the interior & spiritual history of New England could be truelier told than through the exhibition of family history such as this, the picture of this group of M.[ary] M.[oody] E.[merson] & the boys, mainly Charles" (*JMN* 7: 446). The memoir that he proposes here never took full shape, but occasional addresses before and after 1841 drew from the well of family memory, as even more deeply did the ongoing, six-decade record of thought in his journal.

This recurrent fascination with "interior history" amounts to both an important aspect of Emerson's self-characterization and a key to his place in the intellectual traditions of New England. But Emerson was no Hawthorne, brooding over the ancestral dust of his native town, nor a Henry Adams, ironically weighing the privilege and burden of being born with the weight of Beacon Hill upon him. On the contrary, his most famous rhetorical gestures turn away from both tradition and its bearers in the family, not honoring the past even by struggling against it. *Nature* opens by inviting readers to leave their fathers' sepulchers and embrace an "original relation to the universe." In "The American Scholar" young literary men likewise show a restless discontent with paternal precedent, even while fearing new ways "as a boy dreads the water before he has learned that he can swim." And at his most radical, in "Self-Reliance," Emerson declares all family members "deceived and deceiving people" whose life of appearance the seeker of truth must abandon – fleeing the house and writing on the lintels of the doorpost "*Whim*" (CW 1: 7, 67; 2: 41–42, 30). His positive reflections on family origin characteristically came in less formal utterance, sometimes written in the same months as these declarations of independence. Whether in metaphor or autobiography, he spoke of the family with internal conflict.

Fathers in particular provoked antipathy and avoidance. In middle age, Emerson wrote to his elder brother that he hardly remembered their father William, who had died when the boys were eight and ten respectively. What recollections he could offer uncannily echo his earlier language in the "American Scholar." William had been a severe man, who had forced his son to swim in the salt water off a Boston wharf; as a child, Emerson recalled, he had once hidden in fright after hearing his father's voice "(as Adam that of the Lord God in the garden)" calling him to take another sea bath. After William's death, severity receded into mere blankness. "I have never heard any sentence or sentiment of his repeated by Mother or Aunt," Emerson insisted, going on to characterize the man's whole cultural generation as an "early ignorant & transitional *Month-of-March*, in our New England culture" (L 4: 179). From a father's early demise he moved quickly to a father's irrelevance.

Even this memory sketch, however, alludes to the wider family scene which enabled Emerson to venerate as well as to reject his lineage. He does not dismiss the entire family or extended past along with the single figure "father," but names the mother and aunt who have been his genuine nurturers and bearers of tradition. Whether or not Ruth Haskins Emerson and Mary Moody Emerson often recalled their deceased kinsman William, these women raised Waldo and his brothers within a complex multigenerational New England family, keeping sentences and sentiments from the longer family past very much alive. After William's death in 1811, Ruth maintained a fierce loyalty to his wider family and its ministerial calling, far above the merchant careers of her own Boston relatives. Working incessantly as mistress of a boarding house, she succeeded in sending four sons to Harvard. Further, she sought to keep an Emersonian presence at her house in the person of William's younger sister Mary, even though this independent, unmarried woman chafed at domestic responsibility and often bolted. And both women kept their boys in touch with the Emersons' ancestral home in Concord, the "Old Manse," birthplace of William and Mary.

Young Waldo grew up with two links to the Emersons' past, the Concord Manse and Aunt Mary herself. At the Manse he encountered living relatives who only inadequately represented the family, his infirm grandmother

Phebe and her second husband Ezra Ripley, longtime minister to Concord. But Aunt Mary felt no hesitation in declaring the Manse's true greatness to reside with her father William Emerson, chaplain to the Minutemen. He had died of camp fever early in the American Revolution, when Mary was only two; and as a result she, alone among her siblings, had been raised away from Concord in the home of his sister. Mary held a lifelong grievance against her mother Phebe and stepfather Ezra for permitting this "exile," but obsessively glorified the home and father that she had lost. Her sorrow and celebration provided foreground to Waldo's a generation later; in the stories that she told lay the "interior & spiritual history of New England" that he remembered as so potent.

Ralph Waldo Emerson's family memory was highly selective, shaped by a two-generation experience of bereavement and a need to recreate the past as imaginative reality. He could choose male ancestors after his own need and desire, as when in 1834 he settled in to board at the Concord Manse and concentrate on new literary work. "Hail to the quiet fields of my fathers!" he wrote in his journal. "Not wholly unattended by supernatural friendship & favor let me come hither. . . . Henceforth I design not to utter any speech, poem, or book that is not entirely & peculiarly my work" (*JMN* 4: 335). In his very declaration of autonomy and originality he sought the mediation and support of forebears whose friendship he conflated with the divine.

Through his first years in Concord, as Emerson made his antipatriarchal pronouncements in *Nature* and the early addresses, he also found expression for a historic vision that was at once familial, local, and national. In 1835 he prepared a "Historical Discourse" for the town's two-hundredth anniversary, acknowledging his descent from founding minister Peter Bulkeley, celebrating amidst a wider history the piety and heroism of his grandfather Emerson and great-grandfather Bliss. A year later he wrote "Concord Hymn" for the dedication of the Battle Monument near his grandparents' Manse, his words expressing both the evanescence of the deeds transpiring "here once" and the need of sons to redeem past bravery through acts of memory (W 11: 31–97; 9: 139).

Emerson most explicitly named his family resources, however, in a journal passage about originality in the spring of 1837. Amidst a critique of Harvard's "levitical education" and the New England clergy's deadness, he celebrated an alternative, more spirited knowledge made available to his own years of growth by Mary Moody Emerson:

I cannot hear the young men whose theological instruction is exclusively owed to Cambridge & to public institution, without feeling how much happier was my star which rained on me influences of ancestral religion. The depth of the religious sentiment which I knew in my Aunt Mary imbuing all her genius & derived to her from such hoarded family traditions, from so many godly lives & godly deaths of sainted kindred at Concord, Malden, York, was itself a culture, an education.

The passage goes on to recount tales of these sainted male ancestors, then returns to the female teller of tales and immediate source of religious culture for him. The prayers that Aunt Mary wrote for him to read at family devotions still sound in his ear "with their prophetic & apocalyptic ejaculations," Waldo confessed; "and when years after, I came to write sermons for my own church I could not find any examples or treasuries of piety so high-toned, so profound, or promising such rich influence as my remembrances of her conversation & letters" (*JMN* 5: 323–24). Through Mary, Waldo had access to these distant and heroic fathers; and in her own depth of "religious sentiment" lay an example that remained actively before his mind in these rebellious days of early Transcendentalism.

The live oral tradition that Mary conveyed to her nephews reached back to the early eighteenth century, to two sets of her grandparents and one of great-grandparents. Even though the family's giving of names like Bulkeley and Waldo recalled more distant forebears, very little concrete knowledge of them apparently remained by the nineteenth century. But with each of the "sainted kindred at Concord, Malden, and York," all of them men and ministers, two generations of widows and daughters had preserved memories of individual character. "Concord" meant grandfather William Emerson, but also Daniel Bliss, the preceding town minister and father of William's wife Phebe; "Malden" referred to grandfather William's father Joseph Emerson, and "York" to Samuel Moody, father of Joseph's wife Mary. Women had sustained this patriarchy – originally through intermarriage, at last through memory; and as a result, their descendant Ralph Waldo Emerson lived in significant relationship with New England's religious past.

This circumstance deserves scrutiny as today readers locate Emerson and Transcendentalism in history. Forty years ago Perry Miller claimed the continuity of a visionary and ecstatic mode in New England religious thought, from its original Puritanism through Jonathan Edwards in the eighteenth century to Emerson in the nineteenth. His thesis has proven both influential and controversial, its connecting links apparently elusive. The complicating factor is that New England's Puritan tradition began to divide in the 1740s, when a Great Awakening of emotionally charged conversions swept the American colonies. Edwards and his evangelical followers, from a base in the Connecticut Valley, defended "affections" or emotions as the center of religious experience, while in Massachusetts Bay the liberals of Boston and Harvard College opposed Awakening, arguing for a religion of reason and virtue instead. Boston-born Emerson, though rebelling against the reasonable religion of his father and college by celebrating visionary feeling, seems to stand on the other side of a cultural and geographical divide from the theologically orthodox Edwards tradition. Even Perry Miller responded to critics by disclaiming the "mystical pretension" of direct descent from Edwards to Emerson, as if ideas could migrate from the Connecticut Valley to Harvard Divinity School.[2]

But if other forms of cultural memory than the public institutions of pulpit and seminary are taken into account, no journey from Valley to Bay is necessary to link these major writers and moments of vision. The eighteenth-century Emersons and their in-laws – an identifiable, not mystical, clerical alliance of eastern Massachusetts with strong Harvard affiliations – stood in the significant minority of their region, supporting the Awakening even as Harvard turned against it. They publicly endorsed Edwards's major theological works, hosted evangelist George Whitefield's divisive preaching, and offered fervent sermons for the conversion of their respective towns. None of the three kinsmen whose ministry coincided with the Awakening was obscure, but all played a role in its colony-wide history; moderates Samuel Moody and Joseph Emerson worked to control the chaos as well as to sustain the spirit that revival engendered, while the more radical Daniel Bliss was himself a source of chaos, requiring outside settlement by men like Moody and Emerson. A generation later William Emerson of Concord was triple heir of their allegiances, preaching a memorial sermon when Whitefield died in 1770.[3]

Most important, this evangelical fervor survived in certain lines of the Emerson family, even though all four of the "sainted kindred" had died by the Revolution's early days. William Emerson, eldest son of the Concord chaplain, grew up under the influence of his stepfather Ripley and post-Revolutionary Harvard to become a leading Boston liberal; writing the history of his church, he knowingly aligned himself against his ancestors Emerson, Moody, and Bliss.[4] But Mary Moody Emerson, daughter of the chaplain, had not been raised in the same household as her brother and of course was excluded from Harvard. Instead she grew up with the Malden family, formed by the lingering culture of Awakening and the memories of her Aunt Ruth. Fifteen years later, after her brother William's death, Mary nurtured Waldo and his brothers in the knowledge of this tradition. With the family saints that Mary was "so swift to remember," Waldo affirmed, came a piety of heart that through life called him to solitude amidst the crowd of his modern friends: "Not praise, not men's acceptance of our doing, but the Spirit's holy errand through us, absorbed [these ancestors'] thought" (*JMN* 7: 443–44).

In this characterization Emerson was at once evoking his ancestors' creedal belief and his own, institutionally unaffiliated search for inspiration. Embracing the Holy Spirit's inner "errand" to the soul did not make him an evangelical, like his contemporaries who advocated mass revival and orthodoxy. But in declaring himself free from Unitarianism, the institutional outgrowth of liberal religion that he had known and served, he made room for old saints as well as new prophets of vision. The cultural divide in Puritan tradition proved no barrier to the free play of thought, especially since Emerson found power in his ancestors more as images of fervor than representatives of doctrine.

His ancestral images tell of the Spirit's influence over ministerial lives in vivid and particular terms. Samuel Moody of York, as Waldo remembered him from Mary's anecdotes, exercised a "commanding administration of his holy office." When offended parishioners tried to walk out of church during his sermons, he called after them, "Come back, you graceless sinner, come back!" (*JMN* 5: 323). Such zeal also produced charity, a never-ending supplying of meal to the needs of others. Most of all it endowed Moody the preacher with an eloquence of charismatic authority. Trying in 1835 to explain the power of Edward Taylor, the Methodist preacher to sailors, Waldo wrote, "He is a living man & explains at once what Whitefield & Fox & Father Moody were to their audiences, by the total infusion of his own soul into his assembly, & consequent absolute dominion over them" (*JMN* 5: 5). In this capsule history of soul preaching, the family saint and the newly discovered hero of religious oratory shared equal stature with the Awakening's major evangelist and the founder of Quakerism.

Joseph Emerson of Malden, in Waldo's estimation, excelled in his capacity to live amidst the world without succumbing to it. Mary had told him that when Joseph's house burned down, he stood nearby with friends and sang, "There is a house not made with hands" (*JMN* 5: 323). Every night he prayed that none of his descendants might ever grow rich.[5] Eventually Waldo searched his great-grandfather's manuscript journal for firsthand revelation of character and found such stories confirmed. Joseph told of buying a shay for his family, but after experiencing a series of mishaps in it turned to self-examination: "Have I done well to get me a shay? Have I not been proud or too fond of this convenience? . . . Should I not be more in my study, & less fond of diversions?" Later, with some amusement, Waldo used this case of acute conscience to exemplify the values of the old New England clergy. He did not claim charismatic power for Joseph comparable to Moody's. But Joseph's diary, he reflected, showed a "useful egotism," for Joseph "*experienced* life for his flock," drew upon episodes from personal life and so preached as representative of the community (*JMN* 10: 186–87, 177; *W* 10: 384–85).

Daniel Bliss of Concord was Mary's highest hero of spirit-driven faith, "a flame of fire! All enthusiasm!"[6] It was probably he whose death Waldo remembered from her story. Having lost the power of speech, Bliss still responded when a colleague minister asked for a gesture of Christ's presence; "he stretched up both hands & died" (*JMN* 5: 323). While preparing the "Historical Discourse" for Concord's anniversary, Waldo delved into the public papers of his ancestor's ministry and found the charges brought by orderly townspeople against this "favorer of religious excitement." Accused of pretending in his prayers to Christ-like power of mediation between God and humanity, Bliss responded that he meant only to express the wonder, amidst sin and worthlessness, of representing Christ at all. Waldo quoted the entire response to his Concord audience, claiming for it the breath of "true piety" (*W* 11: 66).

The "Historical Discourse" also contained a discovery of his more immediate forebear, grandfather William Emerson of Concord, first owner of the Manse where Waldo was residing in 1835. "This month remarkable for the greatest events of the present age," he quoted from William's diary of April 1775, found in a trunk of family papers just days before. To Waldo, the understated line offered evidence that his grandfather "saw clearly the pregnant consequences of the 19th April" (*W* 11: 177). In the family lore derived from Aunt Mary, William of Concord both embodied the piety of his Awakening fathers and acted upon it in the Revolution. Nine years earlier, when Concord prepared a memorial to its Revolutionary preacher, Mary had objected to Waldo's proposed wording of the epitaph and proposed her own. Most of all she insisted on naming her father's chief virtue as "enthusiasm," that same fiery quality she attributed to Daniel Bliss. Without enthusiasm, she asked, "what [are] all our hopes in future?"[7] In his Concord oration Waldo downplayed his grandfather's fire but focused on its resulting patriotic vision of American prospects.

In Waldo's retrospective writing, William the patriot remains distinct from the legendary Awakening ancestors, more immediate and therefore more burdensome emotionally. As Mary had raised her nephews, she not only told inspiring tales of her father's heroism, but unremittingly exhorted them as her male surrogates to vindicate his foreshortened life. In years when Edward Everett and Daniel Webster represented the heights of political eloquence, her letters called them to a higher, more Christian oratory of freedom honoring their ancestor's memory. Writing the epitaph of William in 1826, she insisted on its insignificance to any but his grandsons, but dreamed of their bringing future families to learn at his memorial "that the love of our revolution was the love of God" (*Letters of MME*, pp. 209, 216–17). She represented herself in this male-dominated dream as a mere bystander, but in fact was herself the dreamer and urgent conveyor of enthusiasm. Youngest nephew Charles received Mary's most explicitly political exhortation to new Emersonian glory, and at 17 in 1826 he had already vowed in response to vanquish the nation's errors. But to Waldo, amidst urging to greatness in poetry and divinity, she also advanced grandfather William's example; when Waldo expressed interest in Cicero, she held up his own "noble & heroic Ancestor" as the higher standard of eloquence. For his twenty-third birthday she penned a fantasy portraying "Ancestor" in heavenly dialogue with Plato, inquiring of Waldo's failed health and hearing from the Greek philosopher a prediction of future greatness.[8]

Through his years as a student and young minister, Waldo responded to the full intensity of Mary's idealizations with skepticism; and in 1826, as Aunt Mary celebrated the fiftieth anniversary of America's Revolution, he declared his exemption from all requirements to measure up to heroes of the past. "It is my own humor to despise pedigree," he wrote in his journal. "I was educated to prize it. The kind Aunt whose cares instructed my youth (& whom may God reward) told me oft the virtues of her & mine ancestors. They have been clergymen for many generations & the piety of all & the eloquence of many is yet praised in the Churches. But the dead sleep in their moonless night; my business is with the living" (*JMN* 2: 316). At a time when his own future was threatened by tuberculosis, this was a brave declaration for "the living," one which anticipated the opening sallies of Transcendentalism a decade later. But it was not an unequivocal rejection of either aunt or ancestors, only half of an internal dialogue that would continue beyond 1826. Waldo could also look to ancestry for assurance of greatness; two years later he entitled a special notebook "Genealogy" and, alongside one list of generations, added the motto "Bonus sanguis non mentitur," "Good blood does not lie" (*JMN* 3: 356; see "Emerson Family Genealogy").

Eventually Waldo found in particular a way to embrace ancestor William Emerson as both patriot and pietist. In 1835 he recorded, as if from recent conversation, the family story of William's failure to influence dissolute soldiers as a regular army chaplain, but also discovered in personal papers the evidence of vision after the battle in Concord (*JMN* 5: 13; *W* 11: 77). The man's private spirit – his enthusiasm – at last appealed more. "*Autobiography*," he entitled a journal entry several years later, then immediately leaped back two generations to locate a personal forerunner:

My great grandfather was Rev. Joseph Emerson of Malden. . . . I used to hear that when William, son of Joseph, was yet a boy walking before his father to church, on a Sunday, his father checked him, "William, you walk as if the earth was not good enough for you." "I did not know it, sir," he replied with the utmost humility. This is one of the household anecdotes in which I have found a relationship. 'Tis curious but the same remark was made to me, by Mrs Lucy Brown, when I walked one day under her windows here in Concord.   (*JMN* 9: 46–47)

In this consciously adopted "household anecdote," Waldo chose his own version of ancestor, not a martyr to the American Republic but a son with

Emerson Family Genealogy

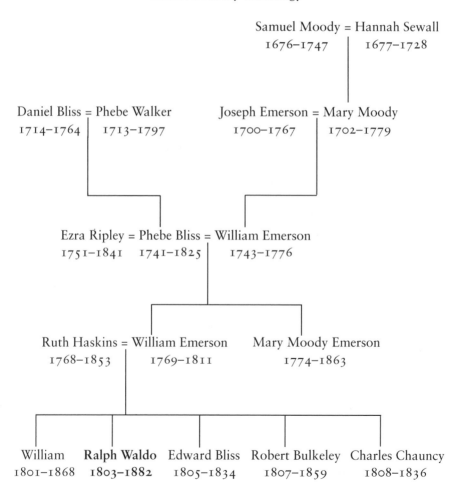

his head in heaven. Indeed he was resolving the paradox of simultaneously rejecting the model of "fathers" and reverencing their example, for here the ancestor most like himself was a son choosing to disregard a father's advice. Father Joseph had charged William with pride, but William's mild answer declared his state instead to be humility, passivity before the Spirit's leading.

That leading remained a vital theme in Waldo's mind through his years of early, most individualistic authorship. In the 1837 journal passage on "ancestral religion," after explicitly naming his forebears' qualities as Mary had made them known, he returned to a vital series of related thoughts on the present moment: first recording his son Waldo's baptism by step-grandfather Ripley; then inserting a passage from the book of Proverbs, "Where there is no vision, the people perish"; and finally offering a scathing critique of a young minister (Ripley's junior colleague Barzillai Frost) who had made a mere show of instruction "without one single real & penetrating word" (*JMN* 5: 323–25). The last part would be incorporated into his declaration against pulpit formalism in the Divinity School "Address," where he sought freedom from the strictures of Christian doctrine, but also looked explicitly to the Christian past for vital preaching of the soul. "Where," he asked, "shall I hear words such as in elder ages drew men to leave all and follow, – father and mother, house and land, wife and child?"(*CW* 1: 85). He himself knew such words more as attributed to Aunt Mary's saints than as heard in the churches of his own day.

Waldo often recognized Mary Moody Emerson's power in his life as a voice of the religious past, but his representations diminished her influence as well. Mary "instructed my youth," he wrote at 21 in 1825, distancing her from the present moment of new adulthood (*JMN* 2: 316). In fact her influence was far from over. Preparing to preach a year later, he implored her to "suggest the secret oracles which such a commission needs" by continuing her uniquely provocative letters. By 1837 he embraced rather than rejected Mary's ancestral tradition, but still identified her chiefly as an influence over childhood through the transmission of stories about the past. Even while adding that the memory of her own prayers, letters, and conversations had inspired his sermon writing, he failed to recall her language as an influence *contemporary to* the sermons. Waldo understood his own capacity for silently absorbing the influence of others. Five months later he named Mary among his chief "benefactors," on a list otherwise comprised of young male contemporaries, but admitted his preference for taking all such gifts "as we take apples off a tree without any thanks" (*L* 1: 171;

JMN 5: 323–24, 385). Over the years Waldo had picked many apples from Mary's tree. She was his chief elder, a living source and partner in thought rather than a mythic image from the past.

He suppressed the extent of her influence because it was so central, not only as his religious grounding but also as a source of the impulses and ideas of Transcendentalism. Mary was Waldo's precursor in Harold Bloom's sense, a predecessor against whom the young writer must struggle even amidst influence, though Bloom referred to the fathers of literary tradition rather than to letter-writing aunts.[9] But Waldo himself took Mary's writing as part of intellectual as well as family history. Even while remaining silent about her influence on him, he gave extraordinary attention to characterizing her mind. Hers was a "representative life," Waldo wrote, marking "the precise time when the power of the old creed yielded to the influence of modern science and humanity." To passionate piety she had joined "the fatal gift of penetration" and thus become a skeptic. Rereading her letters, he discovered not only piety but "genius," that key word of Romanticism. Her language followed organic form, "liberal & manifold as the vegetation from the earth's bosom, or the creations of frost work on the window!" To illustrate her genius he quoted one letter celebrating the day and the balm-of-gilead tree when she had been left delightfully alone by church-going relatives (*W* 10: 399; *JMN* 7: 442–44). Though Waldo did not own the affinity, this scene was closer in spirit to the Divinity School "Address" than to the Great Awakening of Mary's ancestors.

Mary's intellectual independence had begun to emerge by the time of her nephew Waldo's birth, in New England's cultural "Month-of-March"; and students of the nephew will benefit from a fuller sense of the aunt. Raised in considerable poverty by women on the margins of her clerical family, Mary had become a precocious religious seeker and intellectual by early adolescence in the late 1780s. Self-taught beyond the rudiments of literacy available to girls in post-Revolutionary Malden, she read voraciously in the few books available, fiction and poetry as well as divinity. Mary hardly knew her Concord siblings until brother William, as a Harvard student, came visiting in nearby Malden. She instantly loved him – and discovered from his conversation that her favorite book, known in an old copy without cover or title page, was Milton's *Paradise Lost*. Books, friends, and family status soon became more available with her move back to Concord after 17 years' absence. Resentful of the domestic chores expected by her mother and stepfather, Mary nonetheless expanded as a young woman and a thinker. She began keeping a journal and exchanging letters with brother William and their mutual friend Ruth Haskins. By her early twenties in the mid–1790s, Mary was declaring to both of them, in urgently intellectual if inconsistently literate language, her personal vow to seek spiritual perfection (*Letters of MME*, pp. 13–20).

Rather than conducting this search solely on the ground of evangelical piety, her Malden heritage, Mary was by then a daughter of Concord's new liberalism as well. By passing between family homes she had also crossed between religious cultures; on her stepfather's and brother's bookshelves she found not Jonathan Edwards but English rationalist Samuel Clarke, who proved God's existence on the post-Newtonian grounds of his presence in physical time and space. For life, Mary called Clarke her "first master." By the first decade of the nineteenth century, if not before, she had also read and embraced Edwards. But her "Almanack," or journal, focused on the English Enlightenment thought then shaping Boston Unitarianism, Richard Price's Christian Platonism and Joseph Butler's arguments for analogy between human and divine life. It was Mary rather than Waldo who first lived out a double affinity for the two religious cultures that Emerson family history straddled. Later she wrote that she had always been a "deistical pietist," seeking absorption in "the sole idea of an all-surrounding God alone."[10] The old creed yielded in Mary because she was reading across antagonistic traditions, and even more because the very reading presumed a laywoman's independence of ministerial authority. Mary revered her clerical forefathers, but read, thought, and wrote on her own.

Still an enthusiast, seeking God in moments of joyful consciousness, she found revelation in the mind's intuitions and nature's phenomena as well as in the Bible. Proto-Romantic English poetry had religious authority with her, especially Edward Young's *Night Thoughts*, which witnessed God's omnipresence in the nighttime stars and argued for spiritual ascent through a power of solitary mind explicitly named "imagination." Though Young's aspiring souls were all male, and she was full of doubt as a self-educated woman, Mary wrote toward such power in her Almanack. Confiding her inability to respect Malden's boring minister in 1804, she recorded her internal worship at her grandfather's old meetinghouse: "I trod on air – I danced to the music of my own imajanation. . . . It is well no one knows the frolick of my fancy, for they would think me wild unless they knew me." A total eclipse of the sun in 1806 allowed for even fuller ecstasy: "The appearance was unexpected so exquisite a light I cannot describe – the winds were hushed as if in awe – the birds screamed – the stars glowed – with what rapt devotion did I view my Maker's hand" (Almanack, Nov. 7, 1804; June 17, 1806 [ms.]).

William Emerson of Boston, Mary's brother, also observed the eclipse of 1806, but as a member of a Natural Philosophy Society in collective pursuit of empirical knowledge. Sister and brother were both children of the American Enlightenment, both allied to Boston Unitarianism, but with widely divergent sensibilities. William had found his calling in the creation of a new social order; from First Church Boston he promoted rational accomplishment and eschewed enthusiasm. He and Mary supported each other personally but agreed about nothing. She castigated his devotion to the world and urged imitation of their noble forebears; he charged that her "imagination, all fascinating and balloon like as it is," had carried her away from correct judgment. Yet as editor of Boston's first literary journal, the *Monthly Anthology*, William made room for several pseudonymous essays by Mary that could not have pleased his own taste. In one she defended the imagination as a "sensitive pioneer" allowing women's ascent to heavenly abodes; in another she argued that human minds could "infer the operation of infinite wisdom" by analogy to the working of natural law in the life of plants. Throughout William's publication, no other writing anticipated the themes of Transcendentalism as fully as these essays.[11] By celebrating solitude, nature, and imagination, Mary was not only crossing between traditions but also charting new territory.

The fundamental disagreement between William and Mary Emerson explains why, after his death in 1811, she rarely quoted his sentences to nephews. Far from contemptuous of her brother, Mary mourned his death deeply, having for the second time in life lost the male relative who had bestowed quasiclerical status upon her. She did not so much suppress his voice in the years of their education as assert her own, attempting to raise "the boys" so as to fulfill a potential greatness lost to two successive male generations. Later, Waldo recalled that he had once attributed omniscience to his aunt, continuing to remember the sentences of Shakespeare, Milton, and Antoninus as she had quoted them (*JMN* 13: 413; 16: 80). A "favorite" of Mary's along with younger brother Charles, Waldo found a teacher in her unlike those available at Boston Latin. By the time he was a student at Harvard, she was writing of the poetic vocation that might be his. "If I were a Poet this night would inspire me," she began one letter, going on to supply the words and vision that such a poet might feel; in another she moved from fanciful descriptions of springtime to quoting Mark Akenside on the poet's ability to "behold and love / What [God] beholds and loves" (transcribed in *JMN* 1: 333–34).

The vision that Mary offered, in prose by turns halting and rapturous, had grown directly from her earlier devotion to a God revealed in nature and imagination. By 1820 she knew Wordsworth's prophetic sense of the poet's vocation and, along with Mme. de Staël, had embraced "enthusiasm" as a "God within us" for modern poets as well as religious believers. She had evolved into Romantic consciousness, but now, lacking the authorial confidence she had fleetingly known in Waldo's infancy, offered it privately to him rather than writing for publication. The philosophical sources that her letters urged on Waldo in the early twenties – Price and Mme. de Staël, Berkeley and Plotinus, even Hindu devotion – argued an idealism beyond the Scottish Common Sense school taught at Harvard. As a senior, he appropriated her quotation from Mme. de Staël in an essay that won second prize in Harvard's Bowdoin competition. But he omitted Mary's own rhapsodic language of experience in the same letter: "We love nature – to individuate ourselves in her wildest moods; to partake of her extension, & glow with her coulers & fly on her winds; but we love better to cast her off and rely on that only which is imperishable."[12] It would take at least 10 more years for Waldo to articulate such an individuation of soul, at once an embrace and an apocalyptic casting off of nature.

As early as 1821 he began gathering fragments toward such a vision, transcribing her letters, including the sentence on nature, into his new journal as the utterances of "Tnamurya" (*JMN* 1: 334). This anagram for "Aunt Mary," with its sound of Eastern mystery, named his pious elder as a prophetess. Mary has sometimes been called Waldo's "muse," and she did enact the role of female inspirer of male creativity. But instead of muse he named her "Cassandra," "weird woman of her religion," "idolater of Nature," all epithets from pagan lore connoting powerful access to primal forces (*L* 1: 104, 133; *JMN* 1: 49). When he wrote a "letter to Plato" voicing his own skepticism, she wrote back *as* Plato, uniting Greek idealism with Christian redemption in a heaven that allowed the continued expansion of all souls (*JMN* 2: 246–49, 250–52; *Letters of MME*, pp. 185–89). "She described the world of Plato . . . & all the ghosts, as if she had been mesmerized, & saw them objectively," he later recalled (journal "MME 3": 287 [ms.]). It was her powerful if unfinished language that kept him transcribing letters into his journal. Though simultaneously immersed in many books, he directly invoked her aid, "curious to know what living wit (not perverted by the vulgar rage of writing a book) has suggested or concluded, upon the dark sayings & sphinx riddles of philosophy & life" (*L* 7: 125).

This "living wit" shaped both Waldo's entry into the Unitarian ministry and his eventual body of thought after resigning from it. He requested her aid in the spring of 1824, just a month before dedicating his studies to the church in admiration of William Ellery Channing's eloquence (*JMN* 2: 237–38). If the Unitarian founder was quite geniunely Waldo's model preacher, Mary was his active source. He once more invoked her "secret oracles" two years later after receiving letters epitomizing her proto-Transcendentalist views. One, arguing for the human capacity to know God within consciousness, ended with Mme. de Staël's requirement that

God's priests offer "secret memoirs of the soul" from their own experience. Another responded in misspelled but provocative terms to his request for a definition of poetry, describing the Wordsworthian poet as a priest able to enter the "sanctom santorium of nature – where there is a perpetual millennium" (*Letters of MME*, pp. 214–15, 217–18). Meanwhile Waldo, as he emerged from the shadow of illness in the summer and fall of 1826, wrote to her of discovering his own "springs of wonder," opting for a philosophy based on sentiment rather than "bare reason" (*L* 1: 171, 170, 174). Approved as a preacher, Waldo went on to a ministerial career that reflected only a portion of such intensities. Not until *Nature* and the Divinity School "Address" would he fully articulate his experience of wonder, discover a millennium within nature, or call for a new preaching of the soul.

Mary's partnership in Waldo's thinking always coexisted with argument, but not, as generations of interpreters have assumed, argument between the polar opposites of Romantic intuitionism and Calvinist orthodoxy. From the mid–1820s on, even while reaching agreement about grounding faith on the experience of "God within," Mary disputed Waldo's turn away from Christ as the enabler of that experience. Never through two decades of subjective and naturalistic celebration had she wholly abandoned an older strain of faith relying on grace and its biblical revelation of a divine mediator. In 1828, even while admitting her perplexity about the nature of Jesus and her preference to be "absorbed in the sole idea of an all-surrounding God alone," Mary still argued that Waldo's preaching should invoke "the miracle power of the name of the Savior" (journal "MME 2": 228 [ms.]; *Letters of MME*, p. 226). Kantian philosophy made matters even worse in her view, proceeding from the "within" only to an idea rather than a reality of God (Almanack, August 19, 1829 [ms.]). Increasingly she found her heroes in Plato and Jesus rather than in the new European philosophers of mind.

When Waldo, no longer willing to administer the Christian communion rite, proposed resigning from the ministry, Mary resisted passionately. She confessed her attachment to his preaching in Boston, near the ashes of his ancestors: "It may be that the short lives of those most dear to me have given couler to the hopes of one minister remaining to be enrolled with Mathers & Sewalls of that venerable City." She had lost in succession the father and brother who would have established her own vicarious place in the Massachusetts ministry, and now she was about to lose one last opportunity. But a later defense of his resignation revealed as well her part in his thinking. "Others," she wrote to Charles, "may be led to prize more the symbols of an everlasting feast. . . . And he himself free from ties to forms & instruction may find the Angel who can best unite him to the Infinite –

may find in the religion of a solitary imajanation that nearer to the heart" (*Letters of MME*, pp. 314, 320–21).

When Waldo returned to Concord two years later to initiate a career of writing from original perception, fragments of the Emerson family gathered as well. Ruth Haskins Emerson accompanied her son and kept house at the Manse for now-widowed Ezra Ripley. Charles visited constantly from Boston and anticipated settling with his Concord fiancée Elizabeth Hoar. And Mary Moody Emerson rejoined the group from her upcountry farm in Maine, eager to have a say in the informal "symposium" of conversation that immediately began. Soon she recoiled from the young heresies that she had helped bring into being. Nature's voice, she wrote, whispered of weariness and desire for transformation; its voice within her lamented, "I . . . cannot aid the creatures wh[ich] seem my progeny – myself." But Waldo still felt the force of his elder's words, recording her comment on Coleridge's sense of prayer or on Herschel's "mighty facts" about the stars. "A good aunt is more to the young poet than a patron," he stated.[13] A live family group as well as a consciousness of deceased "fathers" supported him as he orated to Concord of its history and began writing *Nature*.

Indeed this manifesto of Transcendentalism, when finally published in September 1836, inscribed within it an oblique sense of the Emerson family. It was a family lamented rather than present. Charles had died of tuberculosis that May, so cutting short Waldo's hope of a shared life in Concord. Waldo acknowledged his brother's influence, grieving in his journal, "The eye is closed that was to see Nature for me, & give me leave to see" (*JMN* 5: 152). Finally he transformed this loss *to* vision in the pages of *Nature*. At the end of the chapter "Discipline," making a crucial transition to "Idealism," he characterized the love of "withdrawn" friends as a source of sweet wisdom within. But this passage, often called a "farewell to Charles,"[14] comes within a longer development of thought including the history of a debt-ridden widow and her orphaned sons of genius. As Waldo argues, all the accompanying "forms, male and female" which surround the growing soul provide it insight into "the power and order that lie at the heart of things," even though each one "bears the marks as of some injury; is marred and superficially defective" (*CW* 1: 28–29, 24). Most of all this passage describes Mary, Waldo's irascible, unfinished oracle. Unlike Charles, she had not died in 1836. Instead, her grief at his death was so intense, and her quarrels with Waldo had so escalated, that she abandoned Concord that summer and fled back to Maine. Waldo completed *Nature* in her absence – and incorporated into it a philosophical idealism, Romantic enthusiasm, and "apocalypse of mind" that were hers as well as his.

Mary continued, usually from a distance, to comment upon Waldo's career in a complex language itself revealing their kindred spirit. Receiving a copy of *Nature*, she wrote back, "Some of it is invaluable to the lover of nature. Yet the solitary admirer of the Author's youngest pen little thought that when his plumes were grown he would like some other classical kind set fire to his gentle nest." Instinctively resuming her own vocabulary of solitude and nature worship, she was calling Waldo a phoenix burning its earthly nest in self-propelled ascent to heaven. She herself, she went on, planned not to "burn a straw of the eyrie," but rather maintain the old terms of faith (*Letters of MME*, p. 374). Through the 1840s she often returned to reading from the personal and historical past, finding Jonathan Edwards her best authority on a subject she phrased in verbal form, "the love of being universally." At the end of 1849, however, she could also record her excitement at rereading *Nature*, which offered new force in its ability to "reveal idealism" and explain "this wonderfull universe wh[ich] astonishes the profoundest thinking phi.[losopher]" (Almanack, Mar. 31, 1841, Dec. 7, 1849 [ms.]). She never acknowledged her own role in its inception.

In these same years Waldo proposed his project of compiling an Emersonian "history of New England." After filling many pages of his journal with quotations and musings toward a memoir of Charles, he realized that his center was Mary's transmission of piety and skepticism *to* Charles and (implicitly) himself. As years of journal writing continued, however, he did not return to his brother and commented only sporadically on more distant ancestors. Mary herself represented the family heritage in his mind, and he sought to gather and transcribe her scattered papers. First he filled a specially entitled journal of excerpts from her letters to himself and his brothers, then only in the 1840s began to receive sections of the Almanack, eventually filling three more thick volumes with her language. Still the tribute waited many more years, until after Mary's death. Only in 1869, himself now beginning to fail mentally, did Waldo present a lecture primarily made up of readings from her letters and Almanack. He entitled it "Amita," Latin for "aunt," but in it revealed very little of the history implied by this family title. None of the ancestral materials were included, very little of her writing that prefigured Transcendentalism, and almost nothing on her relationship to him and his brothers. "It was the privilege of certain boys to have this immeasurably high standard indicated to their childhood," he concluded.[15] The family history embedded in *Nature* had really said more.

Ralph Waldo Emerson's family history still, however, remains a powerful text scattered through his journals. Some of the late transcription of Mary's Almanacks produced his most telling thoughts on her place in the profound changes of consciousness within that history. Her entry of March 7, 1830, located Mary at the birthplace of Daniel Bliss in the Connecticut Valley. "There, in that house," she wrote and Waldo transcribed, "was born one who was connected with my condition, Rev. D. Bliss. Would he had dropt his fiery mantle on my cold spirit!" Like a female Elisha she wished to receive the gift of prophecy from Elijah. Instead, Mary continued, she would wrap herself in plain garments and hide her flawed self in solitude: "Enthusiasm [is] a delight, but may not always be a virtue. . . . Yesterday the stillness of soul in app[ointmen]t day [was] better than all. Wondrous state of man, – never so happy as to be annihilated." The text was Mary's expression of a spiritual journey undertaken apart from Waldo. Waldo made it his own and completed the history by adding his own comment to the transcription: "This is good Buddhism" (journal "MME 2": 10–12 [ms.]). Through his family tradition had come an enthusiasm of Protestant prophecy that, both before him and through him, turned to the East and contemplation.

NOTES

All manuscripts cited in this essay are deposited at the Houghton Library of Harvard University and are quoted with the permission of Houghton and the Ralph Waldo Emerson Memorial Association. Mary Moody Emerson's Almanack is in bMS Am 1280.235 (338), her letters in bMS Am 1280.226, grandfather William Emerson's sermons in bMS Am 1280.235, father William Emerson's letters in bMS Am 1280.226, Ralph Waldo Emerson's journals "MME 1-4" in bMS Am 1280H 146–49, Charles Chauncy Emerson's letters in bMS Am 1280.220 and 226, Ellen Emerson's "What I Can Remember of Stories of Our Ancestors" in bMS Am. 1280.235.

1   *A Memoir of Ralph Waldo Emerson*, in W 13: 7; *JMN* 7: 446.
2   "From Edwards to Emerson," in *Errand into the Wilderness* (Cambridge, MA: Harvard University Press, 1956), p. 184.
3   William Emerson, "On the Death of Mr. W[hitfield] who died on Sabbath Morning 6 O'Clock September 30th [1770]" (ms.). For contemporary evidence of the support that Samuel Moody, Joseph Emerson, and Daniel Bliss gave to Edwards and Whitefield, see Cole, *Mary Moody Emerson and Her Family*, ch. 1.
4   William Emerson, *Historical Sketch of the First Church in Boston* (Boston: Munroe & Francis, 1812), p. 190; *JMN* 7: 443–44.
5   Ellen Emerson, "What I Can Remember of Stories of Our Ancestors Told Me by Aunt Mary Moody Emerson" (ms.).
6   Ellen Emerson, "What I Can Remember" (ms.).
7   *Letters of Mary Moody Emerson*, ed. Nancy Craig Simmons (Athens: University of Georgia Press, 1993), p. 210. Hereafter cited as *Letters of MME*.
8   For the conversation with Charles, see *Letters of MME*, pp. 166, 180–81, 190–

92, and Charles Chauncy Emerson–MME Jan. 30, 1826 (ms.). For Waldo, *Letters of MME*, p. 156, and MME, "Waldo's Birthday," in Almanack, n.d., folder 42 (ms.).

9   Bloom, *The Anxiety of Influence: A Theory of Poetry* (New York: Oxford University Press, 1973), p. 122.

10 Almanack, Sept. 20, 1840, recalling Clarke; Dec. 16, 24, 1810 on Edwards; 1847 recalling Price; Nov. 5, 1804 on Butler (ms.). Ralph Waldo Emerson, journal "MME 2": 228 (ms.).

11 William Emerson–Ruth Haskins Emerson, June 16, 1806 (ms.); *Letters of MME*, p. 54; William Emerson–MME, April 10, 1806 (ms.); *Monthly Anthology* 1 (July 1804), 456–57; 1 (Dec. 1804), 646.

12 MME–William Emerson[3], Nov. 1, 1819 (ms.); Almanack, March 1815. *Letters of MME*, pp. 143–45, 152–60, 139; cf. RWE, "The Present State of Ethical Philosophy," reprinted in Kenneth W. Cameron, *Transcendental Climate* (Hartford, CT: Trandscendental Books, 1963), pp. 14–16.

13 Charles Chauncy Emerson–Elizabeth Hoar, Sept. 21, 1834 (ms.); Almanack, [Oct. 12, 1834], folder 17 (ms.); *JMN* 4: 353, 371; 5: 36.

14 Cf. B. L. Packer, *Emerson's Fall: A New Interpretation of the Major Essays* (New York: Continuum, 1982), ch. 2.

15 Journals "MME 1–4" (ms.)., "Amita" (ms.); W 10: 432. In its posthumous published form the lecture was entitled "Mary Moody Emerson" (*W* 10: 397–433). See also his poetic rendition of passages from the Almanack, "The Nun's Aspiration," in W 9: 253–54; cf. Ralph H. Orth et al. (eds.), *Poetry Notebooks of Ralph Waldo Emerson* (Columbia: University of Missouri Press, 1986), pp. 876–77.

GUIDE TO FURTHER READING

Evelyn Barish. *Emerson: The Roots of Prophecy*. Princeton: Princeton University Press, 1989.

Mary Kupiec Cayton. *Emerson's Emergence*. Chapel Hill: University of North Carolina Press, 1989.

Phyllis Cole. *Mary Moody Emerson and Her Family: An Interior History*. New York: Oxford University Press, 1998.

3

ROBERT MILDER

The Radical Emerson?

I INDIVIDUALISM RECONSIDERED

There must be a Revolution. Let the revolution come. . . .

Emerson, 1838[1]

Emerson has been called many things, but except by theological stalwarts outraged by the Divinity School "Address," "radical" has seldom been one of them. Disposed by taste and training to the rule of gentlemen, he was appalled by the Jacksonian rabble even as he saw it impelled by a feeling of human worth much like his own. Emerson's practical politics were instinctively conservative; the political coloring of his writings is harder to assess. It was once commonplace to observe that the literary Emerson had no politics at all and little sense of history as progressive or teleological. Nature and the Soul were timeless; only the outward costumes and idioms changed. More recently, Emerson has been historicized by embedding him within an American world "poised," as Carolyn Porter has said, "on the verge of the most accelerated capitalist development in modern history."[2] Surely no contemporary registered the new economic forces more acutely than Emerson did. Yet if the Emerson of the 1940s and '50s was construed as loftily indifferent to the currents of the age, the Emerson of the 1980s and '90s has been portrayed as ideologically captive to them.[3]

To speak of a "radical" Emerson is necessarily to speak of a historical Emerson. In the fullest sense, this means crediting Emerson with the complex social being we implicitly claim for ourselves as figures enmeshed in history and deeply constructed by it yet capable nonetheless of what Giles Gunn calls "thinking across culture," or placing new and potentially oppositional valuations on the terms "culture itself provides."[4] Far from a mere symptom or signpost of history, Emerson was himself a historical thinker, conscious of the age both microhistorically in its immediate events and macrohistorically as these assumed significance within the kind of epochal analysis advanced in other frameworks by Tocqueville and Marx. It

49

is scarcely to the point that Emerson's reading of history, like Marx's, ultimately proved wrong. The more pertinent question is whether in 1840 Emerson had grounds for believing he was right. To situate Emerson as a potential radical is not simply to reconstruct the exteriors of his historical world, but to understand how and why the perceived tendencies of the age might have seemed (if only illusively) to present a special set of opportunities and boundaries.

Even with this historical caveat, the notion of a "radical" Emerson is problematic. We refer for convenience to "Emerson," but in truth the superabundance of primary material makes it nearly impossible to fashion a reading of Emerson that is neither reductively schematic nor inclusively vague. Robert E. Burkholder argues sensibly for historical periodization as a means of sifting this embarrassment of riches and bringing some portion of it to relative coherence[5]; yet even within the period 1836–1844, Emerson's Transcendental heyday, there is no univocal or settled "Emerson" any more than there is a univocal or settled "America." Some of Emerson's most familiar writings, moreover, are only marginally pertinent to his "radicalism." *Nature* predates his open ideological involvement with the times. So, to a surprising degree, does *Essays, First Series,* published in 1841 but quarried from lectures and journals of the 1830s, and nowhere more anachronistic than in its opening essay, "History," whose basic *a*historicism sits oddly with the dynamic meliorism of the more contemporaneous "Circles."[6] Emerson's radical period, if so it may be called, is a four-year subphase of his high Transcendentalist career bounded on one side by the Panic of 1837 and on the other by his 1841–42 lectures on "The Times." Commentators addressing a later Emerson will necessarily find a different Emerson. Sacvan Bercovitch is right, for example, in referring to Emerson's "unabashed endorsements from 1842 to 1850 of what can only be called free enterprise ideology,"[7] though to initiate discussion of Emerson and capitalism in 1842 is like beginning *Hamlet* in the middle of the third act. Finally, despite the commendable impulse to narrow topical inquiry within an already narrowed biographical and historical period, Emerson's political stance cannot be separated from his epistemology and metaphysics on one side and from his sense of vocational possibilities on the other. The old spurious division between what Cary Wolfe calls Emerson "the transcendentalist trying to make his break and his peace with the religious tradition" and Emerson the "social and cultural critic" diagnosing Jacksonian America[8] is not to be healed by directing attention from one side of the problem to the other. Emerson's framework for interpreting the age was his understanding of three centuries of post-Reformation history, and his sense of what practically needed to be done was shaped by his estimate of what lay in himself as a speaker and writer to do.

Emerson's major production during the years of his "radicalism" was the course of lectures he delivered in Boston every winter with the exception of the 1840–41 season. Explicitly or not, his subject in each of these annual performances was the Soul in relation to the tendencies of the present age, which he scanned with the attention of a latter-day millennialist looking for signs of the second coming. The lectures are philosophical and establish the broad historical context for revolutionary change, but they are not themselves manifestos of commitment or appeals for a following. The drama of engagement and proselytism is enacted more centrally in four of the occasional addresses of the period – the Address on Education (1837), "The American Scholar" (1837), "Man the Reformer" (1841), and "The Young American" (1844) – and in the 1841–42 lectures on "The Times," which together trace Emerson's journey from social revolutionary (after his fashion) to liberal accommodationist (also after his fashion).

In considering these texts as potentially radical it is useful to recall Marx's distinction between "philosophers," who "have only *interpreted* the world," and activists like Marx himself who wish fundamentally and swiftly "to *change* it."[9] No tinkerer with the social order, the radical is committed to a root-and-branch overhaul, typically through physical force (since entrenched interests seldom yield power voluntarily) yet alternatively, perhaps, through something resembling a "paradigm shift." In *Criticism and Social Change* Frank Lentricchia raises the possibility of this second form of radical action when he asks whether "a literary intellectual" can "do radical work *as* a literary intellectual" through an enterprise of thought and cultural persuasion.[10] Citing Kenneth Burke's distinction "between 'education as a function of society' and 'society as a function of education,'" Lentricchia describes the scholar's task as "the production of knowledge to the ends of power and, maybe, of social change. . . . [W]hat human beings have made, they can and will unmake and then remake and remake again."[11] It would be difficult to find a vision of social renovation closer to Emerson's own at the height of his reformism. "We are to revise the whole of our social structure, the state, the school, religion, marriage, trade, science, and explore their foundation in our own nature," Emerson proclaimed in "Man the Reformer," adding, "What is a man born for but to be a Reformer, a Re-maker of what man has made . . . ?"[12]

On the issues of gender, race, and class that have become indices of political definition, Emerson was a hesitant or tardy reformer at best. While acknowledging that true genius is androgynous, he was disabled by his own personal and vocational anxieties about manliness from doing justice to the nascent feminist movement, though he could ambivalently admire at least one of its proponents, Margaret Fuller. The question of slavery vexed him further because his distaste for the character and methods of the early abolitionists was coupled with embarrassment before his antislavery friends and with moral guilt. Starting with his 1844 address "Emancipation in the British West Indies," Emerson did become "a concerned, sometimes frustrated, but always committed social activist . . . very much involved with, and interested in, the abolition of slavery."[13] His engagement with abolition, however, coincided with his general *dis*engagement from sweeping cultural reform. What Len Gougeon refers to as his "silent years" on slavery (1838–44) were precisely the years of his sharpest attacks on capitalism, and it was partly his despair about an incipient millennium that led him at once to an accommodation with the overall structure of society and to a protest against its more egregious abuses. On class, Emerson had least to say beyond Romantic sentimentalizations of the poor and recurrent attempts (more uneasy than callous) to reconcile their sufferings with cosmic optimism. He himself had been a poor boy – his widowed mother took in boarders – and he came to terms with his early wants and humiliations through an adult belief in the moral compensations of genteel hardship. The deserving poor were strengthened by their schooling in necessity, while the indolent or vicious reaped as they sowed.

The chief reference point for Emerson's radicalism is not gender, race, or class but his relationship to a phenomenon that manifested itself variously in economics, politics, philosophy, and literature, and that impressed contemporary observers for better or worse as the leading characteristic of the age: the emergence of the individual. In calling for a dismantling of the remains of established privilege, the ruling Jacksonians of the 1830s sought a political and economic unburdening of the private self designed, as the *Democratic Review* announced in its inaugural issue of 1837, to "abolish all artificial distinctions, and, preventing the accumulation of any social obstacles to advancement, . . . permit the free development of every germ of talent, wherever it may chance to exist."[14] In Europe, Marx could object that North American liberty was "the liberty of man regarded as an isolated monad withdrawn into himself" and disposed "to see in other men, not the *realization,* but rather the *limitation* of his own liberty."[15] In a nation, however, where talent seemed widely distributed, where land was abundant, and where capitalism had only begun to show its harsher face, individualism was a progressive creed founded not on the biological model of proto-Darwinian struggle but on a Newtonian one in which the "floating atoms" of society would "distribute and combine themselves" harmoniously once the meddling hand of government were removed.[16] Even feminist and abolitionist critics of the liberal order rarely challenged its political and philosophical premises, only its hypocritical exclusions. As Margaret Fuller wrote, "We would have every arbitrary barrier thrown down. We would have every path laid open to Woman as freely as to Man. Were this done, and a slight temporary fermentation allowed to subside, we should see crystallizations more pure and of more various beauty."[17] Frederick Douglass, too, demanded no more for blacks than an open and fair competition with whites in which individuals of both races might rise or fall according to their talents and strength of character.

By 1848 a liberalism understood as "universal participation in the opportunities" held out by the United States had come to form the conceptual boundary of political discourse.[18] The issue for Americans of the 1830s and '40s was not whether the nation would go the way of individualism but what sort of individualism it would have. The recent argument that all individualisms are ultimately expressions of the capitalist ethos is deeply ahistorical so far as it minimizes bitter mid-nineteenth-century contentions for power in favor of a late-twentieth-century ideological Manichaeanism in which the only alternative to entrepreneurialism is some form of collectivism – all rival individualisms, however antimaterialist, amounting finally to capitalistic fellow travelers. Thus Sacvan Bercovitch in *The American Jeremiad* could present Emerson the putative reformer as "reaffirm[ing] the basic tenets of [middle class] culture" and Thoreau the village anarchist as "safeguard[ing] the values that undergird" Concord life even as he pilloried its merchants and market-oriented farmers.[19]

More recently, Bercovitch has refined his argument by distinguishing between "individualism" (laissez-faire acquisitiveness) and its humanistic opposite, "individuality," a belief in the "absolute integrity, spiritual primacy, and inviolable sanctity of the self."[20] Emerson himself tried to resist such a distinction, preferring to believe that material and spiritual development (properly related) were complementary aspects of full selfhood. The "individuality" Bercovitch presents as "a Utopian rallying point against liberal ideology,"[21] was, for Emerson, neither Utopian nor antiliberal; it was a contender for the very definition of "liberal," and the strength of its claim rested on a historical teleology that seemed to augur its imminent triumph. Where free-trade Democrats found their origins in Thomas Paine and Adam Smith, Emerson, who saw "the present aspects of our social state" as having "their root in an invisible spiritual reality" (CW 1: 167), situated Jacksonian laissez-faire within a centuries-long effacement of the institutional church and state. As early as 1827, when John Quincy Adams was president and Transcendentalism yet unborn, Emerson noted the "Peculi-

arities of the present Age," by which he meant a constellation of developments in art, religion, ethics, metaphysics, and political economy whose
shared quality was the dissolution of traditional bonds and the progressive
liberation of human consciousness. "The reform of the Reformation" (*JMN*
3: 70), Emerson called this greatest of human projects, which had begun
not with Jefferson in 1776 but with Martin Luther in 1517, and which now
seemed ready to complete itself in an age of democratic individualism that
was the culmination of history. Even the excesses of the age – its materialism and leveling antiintellectualism – could be seen as symptoms of a transition state in which individuals felt their powers before they understood
their proper aims. "There is a historical progress of man," Emerson began
the "Human Culture" lectures of 1837–38:

> The modern mind teaches (in extremes) that the nation exists for the individ-
> ual; for the guardianship and education of every man. The Reformation con-
> tained the new thought. The English Revolution is its expansion. The Ameri-
> can Declaration of Independence is a formal announcement of it by a nation
> to nations, though a very limited expression. . . . The Vote, – universal suf-
> frage – is another; the downfall of war, the attack upon slavery, are others.
> The furious democracy which in this country from the beginning of its his-
> tory, has shown a wish . . . to leave out men of mark and send illiterate and
> low persons as deputies, . . . is only a perverse or as yet obstructed operation
> of the same instinct, – a stammering and stuttering out of impatience to
> articulate the awful words *I am*.[22]

With its boundless space, democratic polity, and absence of confining
traditions and social structures, America took its place within Emersonian
teleology less as a distinct nation than as a set of enabling conditions for
the prototypical triumph of the self. "It seems to me," Emerson observed
in 1837, "that Circumstances of man are historically somewhat better here
& now than ever. That more freedom exists for Culture" (*JMN* 5: 437). By
"Culture" Emerson meant self-culture, or the unfolding of the individual
according to endogenous laws of growth. In broad outline his ideal was not
far removed from that of Americans generally, whose "sense of their national identity depended," as Rush Welter has said, "not on the degree to
which they had escaped from the human condition, . . . but on the opportunities for full manhood that American institutions peculiarly afforded
them."[23] The difference between Jacksonian and Emersonian individualism
lay in the construction they gave to "full manhood" – for Jacksonians, a
development of human faculties along the lines of the known, save for
whatever innovations democracy might bring; for Emerson, the emergence
of a not wholly imaginable consciousness that would make for a new
heaven *on* a new earth.

Whether or not such a vision counts as radical depends partly on one's willingness to grant the possibility of a metamorphosed self and partly on one's reading of the late 1830s and early '40s as plausibly encouraging such a belief. What critics of Emerson disparage as his "transcendence" – a leap beyond the actualities of the social moment to a qualitatively different future – is precisely the kind of historical intuition that characterized Hegel's man of greatness, an important model for Emerson (as later for Marx) in his "ability to perceive" and "courage to espouse the inevitable next step in the Soul's historic march."[24] All revolutionaries are "Utopians" in this Hegelian sense. The test of a radical vision is not whether it is historically fulfilled or seems to posterity ever to have been realizable, but whether it had a credible basis in *contemporary* apprehensions of reality.

No one in America studied the "signs of the times" more closely than Emerson, whose journals of the 1830s and early '40s are a seismometer of the tendencies of the nation. Immersed in history, Emerson unavoidably misread history, yet his misreading is itself historical not merely as a function of his "implication" in Jacksonian ideology but as a rendering of how history might have appeared to a keen and sanguine mind extrapolating from the past and extending its visible logic to the future. What in hindsight appears the onrush of the nation toward laissez-faire capitalism seemed to the actors themselves a moment of cultural self-definition poised between competing individualism and therefore competing destinies, with the balance tipped markedly but not irrevocably toward materialism. In such circumstances, changing the world meant changing established conceptions of the world and dissociating notions of manhood from the commercial success to which they had become attached.[25] This is the end Emerson proposed for himself in a journal entry of April 1834, which might stand as an epigraph to his work of the next decade:

> Men are convertible.... They want awakening. Get the soul out of bed, out of her deep habitual sleep, out into God's universe, to a perception of its beauty & hearing of its Call and ... your prosy, selfish sensualist [originally, "selfish Capitalist"] awakes a God & is conscious of force to shake the world. (*JMN* 4: 278)

It is telling that Emerson should have written "selfish Capitalist," then thought better of it. Throughout most of his career Emerson was ambivalent toward capitalism, regarding it on one side as the economic manifestation of contemporary individualism and on the other as the gravest threat to individualism. His choice of "selfish" (a moral category) over "Capitalist" (an economic one) suggests that his root quarrel was not with entrepreneurialism per se but with the groveling materialism that accompanied it.

So conceived, the issue assumed an ethical rather than a socioeconomic cast, and the paradigm for revolutionary activity became a secularized analogue to religious conversion. Unitarian reform had typically centered upon moral rather than institutional change. What distinguished Emerson's call to the soul and gave it a potentially radical edge was his vision of a mode of being qualitatively different from commonsense ethicism. The future, as Emerson imagined it, rested on a full-scale reorganization of consciousness even more transformational than Christian conversion because it led individuals beyond the orthodoxies of Scripture and the example of Jesus to a terra incognita of spiritual being that promised to remold traditions and social institutions.

Using his annual lecture series as a secular pulpit, Emerson gave himself to preaching what he later described as the "one doctrine" that informed all his work, "namely, the infinitude of the private man" (*JMN* 7: 342). What prevented him at first from extending his sermon to society at large was the absence of a clear historical opening, for while the movement of the centuries unmistakably heralded the triumph of the soul, the immediate signs of the times pointed in the opposite direction, to the consolidation of capitalist materialism. Frustrated by the incongruence between macrohistory and microhistory – God's plan for the self and His plan for the community – Emerson could exalt the individual only by extricating him from society and denying any collective progress. "There is in [society] an incontrovertible brute force and it is not for the society of any actual present moment that is now or ever shall be, that we can hope or augur well," he wrote in the "Philosophy of History" lectures of 1836–37. "Progress is not for society," he added: "Progress belongs to the Individual" (*EL* 2: 176).

Though sometimes taken as a characteristic opinion, Emerson's disparagement of history was itself a historically circumstanced judgment that the Panic of 1837 would soon reverse. By signaling, as it appeared, the death throes of the capitalist order – "Society has played out its last stake" (*JMN* 5: 331), Emerson announced almost gleefully in May 1837 – the Panic seemed to invite a total reconstruction of social life much as the Depression would for Edmund Wilson, who saw the "economic chaos" of the nation as the "symbol" of a broader "crisis of human culture" and the prelude to "a new order" that would raise competition "from the animal plane of acquisition to the human plane of cultural creation."[26] The collapse of materialist America laid bare for inspection the long-standing cultural bankruptcy that Emerson and Wilson had felt even amidst the nation's prosperity, and it bid them come forward during the interregnum to help refound America on a humanistic ideal of selfhood that, in Wilson's words, would "release the energies of man to spiritual and intellectual endeavor."[27]

Delivered in August of the Panic year, "The American Scholar" is Emerson's entrance into history as a radical seeking not simply to reinterpret the world or even, in outward Marxian fashion, to change it, but to change it *by means of* reinterpreting it. In its sections on nature, books, and action (the three "influences" on the scholar), the address is a locus classicus for Emersonian theories of the relation of the soul to the world. What distinguishes it from Emerson's earlier writings is its contextualization of the scholar's activity within a historical situation that Emerson confronts directly in its opening and closing paragraphs and indirectly through its entire rhetorical structure. Although politically a success, the America Emerson portrays is a cultural and moral failure given to a low materialism and content to take its thought and art from Europe. The scholar is neglected, even dishonored. So far as he is indolent or timid, moreover, the scholar dishonors himself and is heavily to blame for the nation's cultural barrenness as well as for his own disrepute.

The achievement of "The American Scholar" is to begin with the scholar's condition of effeteness and marginality and perform a Copernican revolution which makes him the center of a vital order that the newly awakened American materialist rallies to join. The conversion of the "prosy, selfish sensualist" Emerson had envisioned in 1834 is rhetorically enacted in the oration for an audience of literary youths well prepared by idealism and vocational inclination to respond to its appeal. Scorned by practical men during his long years of preparation, the scholar, in Emerson's mythology, dives deep into himself, discovers truth, and finds to his astonishment that his former detractors now "drink his words because he fulfils for them their own nature. . . . The people delight in it; the better part of every man feels, This is my music: this is myself" (*CW* 1: 63). Expanding on his vignette of the scholar's triumph – a dramatized "proof" of conversional possibility – Emerson draws its widest lesson and proceeds to show how and why a cultural revolution can be inaugurated:

> Men such as they are, very naturally seek money or power; and power because it is as good as money. . . . And why not? for they aspire to the highest, and this, in their sleep-walking, they dream is highest. Wake them, and they shall quit the false and leap to the true, and leave governments to clerks and desks. This revolution is to be wrought by the gradual domestication of the idea of Culture. The main enterprise of the world for splendor, for extent, is the upbuilding of a man. (*CW* 1: 65)

Though visionary rather than concretely programmatic, Emerson's words had a timeliness for his listeners, thanks to the impression fostered by the Panic that America's "emphatic & universal calamity" (*JMN* 5: 331) was, like Wilson's Depression, symptomatic of a broader cultural crisis felt particularly by the young, disenchanted with the world of their elders but paralyzed by hyperconsciousness and unable to project a personal or collective future. Relating the scholar's work more nearly "to the time and to this country" (CW 1: 66), Emerson evokes this cultural void and recasts it as an auspicious historical opportunity – an "age of Revolution; when the old and the new stand side by side, and admit of being compared; when the energies of all men are searched by fear and by hope; when the historic glories of the old, can be compensated by the rich possibilities of the new era" (CW 1: 67). As an augury of this future, Emerson cites the Romantic exploration of "the near, the low, the common" (CW 1: 67) that accompanied and poeticized the emergence of political democracy and attracted literary youths with its generous promise. The appeal, implicit at first but open and impassioned by Emerson's peroration, is for the young to align themselves with the spirit of the age and against the world of their fathers, which has demeaned the ideal of human development to a smug materialism that now, with the Panic, has failed even in its own terms.

Beneath its account of *"Man Thinking"* (CW 1: 53) and its plea for cultural independence, "The American Scholar" does for its audience what all ideological manifestos undertake to do; it rearranges social facts so as to provide (as Alvin W. Gouldner said of ideology generally) "a 'map' of 'what is' in society; a 'report' of how it is working, how it is failing, and also of how it could be changed"; and thus an exhilarating "call to action" embedded in "a world-referencing discourse that presumably justifies that call."[28] The functional coordinates of Emerson's map are IS and OUGHT TO BE (a critique of the present from the standpoint of a spiritual/social ideal), WAS and WILL BE (a reading of historical design), WE and THEY (an opposition of progressive and resistant forces), and HOW (a vision of change focusing on the activity of the scholar). For sympathetic youths who heard or read the oration (Thoreau, for one), its reconceptualization of the social moment had the appeal of a secular religion, with the convert reoriented toward communal life, animated by a new sense of values, possessed of a new cultural language, and committed to new actional ends.[29]

Ideologies may be "interlinked ideas, symbols, and beliefs" used to legitimate and maintain a culture,[30] but they may also be weapons of insurgent groups aimed at dislodging it. From "The American Scholar" through "Man the Reformer" (1841), Emerson ranged himself with disempowered literary intellectuals seeking to capture America for the ideal of "culture." "The Movement" and "The Establishment," Emerson called the rival parties, whose struggle for prominence (tipped always toward the Movement, he then felt) was the defining fact of history (EL 3: 187).

Any historical period, Raymond Williams observed, is a dynamic interplay of "dominant," "residual," and "emergent" forces.[31] As Emerson reconfigured the times in "The Present Age" lectures of 1839–40 – his main attempt not simply to examine "the present . . . for the seeds of the future" (*EL* 3: 182), as his editors remark, but to ideologize the present so as to *create* the future – he focused exclusively on those emergent "elements which are new and operative and by their activity now detaching the future from the past and exposing the decays of the corpse they consume" (*EL* 3: 187). Individualism seemed to him the foremost tendency at work, but in the transitional America of the 1830s it had expressed itself, materially, in a rampant commerce that had usurped the spiritual ends of life, and, intellectually, in a habit of "analysis" that had eroded the social "ties and ligaments" of the past without creating a mythos for the future (*EL* 3: 189). In so defining "the present age," Emerson has set the terms for the epochal task to be done: "Born in an age of calculation and criticism we are to carry it with all its triumphs and yield it captive to the Universal Reason" (*EL* 3: 199). The means to this revolution – as to all great revolutions, Emerson believed – was a reinscription of perceived reality to be accomplished by some new paradigm giver, himself an instrument of historical design: "He who shall represent the genius of his day; he who shall, standing in this great cleft of Past and Future, understand the dignity and power of his position so well as to write the laws of Criticism, of Ethics, of history, will be found an age hence neither false nor unfortunate, but will rank immediately and equally with all the masters whom we now acknowledge" (*EL* 3: 200).

In nothing is Emerson seemingly less radical than in his conviction that the source and agency of social change is the human mind. The actional corollary of his position – the antithesis of Marxian cultural materialism, in which thought is the reflection, not the cause, of social organization – is revolution-by-consciousness. Because "history and the state of the world at any one time [are] directly dependent on the intellectual classification then existing in the minds of men" (*CW* 2: 184), Emerson would argue in "Circles," the condition for transforming "the entire system of human pursuits" (*CW* 2: 184) is transforming human minds. So stated, Emerson's idealism seems loosely Platonic, but it can also be seen as anticipating contemporary ideas about the power of discourse to mold collective mentalities and thereby condition social praxis. Even Marx observes that "the materialist doctrine that men are products of circumstances and upbringing, and that, therefore, changed men are products of other circumstances and changed upbringing, forgets that it is men who change circumstances and that it is essential to educate the educator himself."[32] The struggle Emerson saw occurring in Jacksonian America was between competing cultural languages (or "educations") with their relative assignments of value and consequences for living. If "cultures, however dominant, are never completely hegemonic" but contain "spaces" allowing the formulation of alternative visions,[33] such spaces seemed particularly large in the still unsolidified world of 1830s America. It was here, in these areas of cultural possibility widened by the Panic to a "great cleft of Past and Future," that Emerson's scholar found his historical occasion and public calling.

"Educating the educator" was the core intention of Emerson's "Sermon[s] to Literary Men" (*JMN* 5: 164) of 1837–38 – the Address on Education, "The American Scholar," and "Literary Ethics" – whose audience was not the American materialist so much as the class of intellectuals who would serve as missionaries to him. A contemporary analogue might be Frank Lentricchia's sermon to modern activist scholars, *Criticism and Social Change,* which contends that their "potentially most powerful political work as university humanists must be carried out in . . . what [they] are trained for," criticism and pedagogy, rather than in direct political activity.[34] By way of a pragmatism that views "truth" in Jamesian terms as the capacity of beliefs to put us in productive touch with experience and impel us to act upon the world, Lentricchia comes around to a variety of neoidealism that reempowers literary intellectuals by assigning them a version of the work Emerson assigned himself in the late 1830s: to remythologize history and the present age so as to subvert an established value-laden account of reality (capitalist hegemony) and replace it with a humanistic alternative.

Was the Emerson of 1837–41 radical or merely self-deluded and in unwitting complicity with the forces he opposed? Emerson's editors note that the years of his revolutionary idealism were ones "when it did not seem quite impossible that the hour had come round at last for the great Soul within to awaken and assume its long-delayed sovereignty" (*EL* 2: xii). All failed revolutions look quixotic (or worse) in retrospect, and how we judge Emerson depends heavily on our willingness to reenter history and imagine the times as the participants themselves had ground to imagine them. Even with hindsight, as Raymond Williams remarks, "it is exceptionally difficult to distinguish between those [emergent tendencies] which are really elements of some new phase of the dominant culture . . . and those which are substantially alternative or oppositional to it" – this in addition to the large middle-range of "works and ideas which, while clearly affected by hegemonic limits and pressures, are at least in part significant breaks beyond them, which may again in part be neutralized, reduced, or incorporated, but which in their most active elements nevertheless come through as independent and original."[35] Being "historical" in the most empathetic sense means trying to reconstruct the social moment in all its lived ambiguity. It is to understand how the Emerson of these years could at once be radical in light of the perceived "signs of the times" and quasi-radical in light of subsequent historical developments: proto-modern in his discourse-centered idea of cultural transformation and provincially Romantic in his neglect of the material resistances in society and the institutional changes needed to counter them.

II DISUSING CAPITALISM

So deep is the foundation of the existing social system that it leaves no one out of it. . . . All men have their root in it. You who quarrel with the arrangements of society, and are willing to embroil all, and risk the indisputable good that exists, for the chance of better, live, move, and have your being in this, and your deeds contradict your words every day. For as you cannot jump from the ground without using the resistance of the ground, . . . so you are under the necessity of using the Actual order of things, in order to disuse it.

CW 1: 189

Partly through Emerson's ideological patterning of the shared but inchoate feelings of a literary generation, Transcendentalism evolved in the later 1830s from a spiritual ferment among young, well-educated New England Unitarians into a locus for potentially counterhegemonic activity. Converts found work in a variety of enterprises from utopian experiments (Brook Farm, Fruitlands, Walden) to reformist causes of one kind or another to missionary labors in the benighted West. Emerson himself, the center of the movement, remained aloof from practical reforms, preferring for reasons of temperament and talent the insulated role of podium speaker. By 1839, though still in his middle thirties, he had begun to feel old and without "enthusiasm" or "resources for the instruction & guidance of the people when they shall discover that their present guides are blind" (JMN 7: 239). He had taken his measure and concluded that he was "no hero" (JMN 7: 182), nor could he reconcile the transformational project as grandly conceived with the reformist opportunities that immediately presented themselves. No particular action seemed commensurate with or even significantly contributive toward the revolutionary end in sight. His quarrel with capitalism intensified as he came to see its selfishness as inherent and irremediable, but as the Panic receded the old economic system seemed firmly reentrenched. Contemporary enthusiasm for reform was broader and deeper than ever; the political signs of the times (the Whig victory in 1840, for example) were inauspicious, however, while the economic signs (symbolized by the emergence of the railroad) pointed to a more rampant capitalism rather than a tempered one.

Emerson's movement toward an accommodation with "the Actual order of things" in the 1840s is as complex and problematic as his earlier "radicalism" had been, and it demonstrates once again the intimate connection between his social thought, his metaphysics, and his ongoing crisis of vocation. The unconscious root of his position, here as before, was his estimate of the current phase of his own life pilgrimage – spiritually, of the ebbs and flows (now mostly ebbs) of visionary power, writ large in his changing conception of individual destiny; vocationally, of the way in which his private situation accorded with the age's so as to invite or preclude certain actional possibilities. Would he become the heroic lawgiver he had prophesied in "The Present Age" or was his role to be that of a John the Baptist preparing for some lawgiver-to-come? Though flourishing best in solitude and free from the burden of prophecy, he worried "what right" the "man of genius" had "to retreat from work & indulge himself" (*JMN* 7: 384). "I make haste to speak lest I be found unworthy of my office," he wrote in September 1840, having been reminded by friends that he was not his own man but "a public & sacred property which it were profane in [him] to hinder in its effect or to degrade to base uses" (*JMN* 7: 400).

Aware that his characteristic role was indeed to "speak," Emerson devoted himself in the early 1840s to literary activities: to the *Essays, First Series* that he was writing "as a sort of apology to my country for my apparent idleness" (*JMN* 7: 404) and to the newly launched Transcendentalist quarterly, *The Dial*, which he envisioned not as "a mere literary journal" but as one with "a more earnest aim" such as "the times demand of us all" (*JMN* 7: 388). By addressing a variety of contemporary issues – "Government, Temperance, Abolition, Trade, & Domestic Life" (*JMN* 7: 388) – *The Dial* would lay the groundwork for the revolution of mind that would prompt a revolution in society. In practice *The Dial* was "poor & low & all unequal to its promise" (*JMN* 7: 406); but even if the journal had been better than it was – and his own contributions worthier of the lawgiver's standard – Emerson could not have avoided wondering whether writing of any sort was sufficient at a time when reform movements "had never such scope" (*JMN* 7: 403) and when George and Sophia Ripley were pressing him to make good on his idealism by joining them at Brook Farm. Although communalism of any sort was anathema to Emerson, it troubled him to turn the Ripleys down – on grounds, moreover, that involved a humiliating confession of his maladaptation to social life and his private self-uncertainties.[36] At the opposite pole – radical individualism – stood

Emerson's young disciple, "my brave Henry" Thoreau (*JMN* 7: 201), whose spartan life was an object lesson in self-reliance at once inspiring to Emerson in its manly integrity and tacitly reproachful of his own middle-class comfort.

A sense of moral uneasiness bordering on shame haunts Emerson's letters and journals of late 1840–41, a period that might be described as his "crisis of complicity." In spurning Ripley's invitation to Brook Farm, Emerson did penance by citing his loosely formulated plans for private reform; he wanted, he told Ripley, to "acquir[e] habits of regular manual labor," to "ameliorat[e] or [abolish] in my house the condition of hired menial service," and to transform his "manner of living" so that it might "be honest and agreeable to [his] imagination" (*L* 2: 370). At about the same time (December 1840), he wrote his brother William of plans to "find house room for Mr Alcott & his family under our roof" (*L* 2: 371) – a communitarian project that fell through later in the winter, to be replaced by the more modest and symbiotic arrangement that brought Thoreau to live with him in April 1841. The millennial spirit Emerson did so much to create came home to roost in the early 1840s in a disquietude about social and economic inequality and a conviction that even the "retired scholar," as he self-satirically punned in "The Present Age," must align his daily life with his ideals.

The most significant product of this mood is "Man the Reformer," delivered in Boston in January 1841 and published in *The Dial* the following April. The premise of the address is the intrinsic immorality of capitalism – "a system of selfishness" actuated not by a "law of reciprocity; much less by the sentiments of love and heroism," but by principles of "distrust, of concealment, of superior keenness, not of giving but of taking advantage" (*CW* 1: 148) – an immorality chargeable to those who quietly thrive under capitalism as well as to capitalists themselves. In part Emerson may have been thinking of his own practice of selling tickets for his winter lectures or of the investment income from his first wife's estate that underwrote his literary career and was a source of anxiety in the early days of the Panic. But he was also aware of how all citizens were "implicated" (*CW* 1: 147) in an economic system that "reaches into the whole institution of property, until our laws which establish and protect it" become themselves an expression and instrument of "selfishness" (*CW* 1: 148). The logic of his position leads him to repudiate not simply the marketplace but the basic capitalist means of production – the factory system with its division of labor and its cornucopia of manufactured goods that panders to "the taste for luxury" (*CW* 1: 153) and depraves the national character. "Why needs any man be rich?" he asks: "It is better to go without [the conveniences of life], than to have them at too great a cost. Let us learn the meaning of economy. . . . Can anything be so elegant as to have few wants and to serve one's self . . . ?" (CW 1: 154–55).

The example of young Thoreau, whom he cites in all but name, pervades "Man the Reformer" and serves Emerson in subtle and contradictory ways that reveal much about the layered purposes of the address. As his own energies began to wane, Emerson drew strength from the cadre of idealistic youths that gathered around him, assuming the role of mentor (with deep ambivalence) and assigning them the work of practical renovation he found unsuited to himself. As the champion of the rising generation, Emerson could celebrate and vicariously share in its reformist enthusiasm and quiet his uncomfortable feeling that in "late years" he "skulk[ed] & play[ed] a mean, shiftless, subaltern part much the largest part of the time" (JMN 8: 10). If the renunciations of Thoreau seemed to chide him for his compromises with capitalism, their challenge could be met by endorsing and rhetorically incorporating Thoreau. Thus Emerson puts the case of a hypothetical youth (patterned on Thoreau) "so unhappy as to be born a saint, with keen perceptions, but with the conscience and love of an angel," who must "get his living in the world" but "finds himself excluded from all lucrative works; he has no farm, and he cannot get one; for, to earn money enough to buy one, requires a sort of concentration toward money, which is the selling himself for a number of years, and to him the present hour is as sacred and inviolable as any future hour" (CW 1: 149). So eulogized, Thoreau becomes a vehicle not only for assailing capitalism but for aligning Emerson, its economic beneficiary, firmly against it. Emerson also has praise for Ripley's Brook Farm (unnamed but identifiable), which he uses to illustrate the idea "that every man ought to stand in primary relations with the work of the world" (CW 1: 152). Having co-opted Thoreau's and Ripley's reproofs to him (real or imagined) by assimilating the core of their positions, Emerson establishes his radical sympathies and can now, on the ground of declining "to be absurd and pedantic in reform," disavow the reformers' "extravagant" withdrawal "from the advantages of civil society" (CW 1: 155). His alternative is a new order to be realized not through visionary communalism (Ripley's solution), prickly individualism (Thoreau's), or class struggle (Orestes Brownson's; "The Laboring Classes," published in the summer and early fall of 1840, was also on Emerson's mind) but through the spiritual transformation he comprehends in the word "love" (CW 1: 158–59).

Is Emerson's "love" a radical prescription or a guilt-driven evasion? It would be truest to say it is both at once, just as "Man the Reformer" is both wildly optimistic and soberly resigned. By portraying a universal complicity with capitalism from which only a Ripley, a Thoreau, or a Brownson is free, Emerson has made reformist action a matter of such eccentricity as to justify the thoughtful man's detachment. Yet Emerson's argument is more than an elaborate self-apology. If "Man the Reformer" comes only "to the *edge* of class analysis," as Sacvan Bercovitch has said, it is not because Emerson "never really gave serious thought to social reorganization"[37] but because his model for such reorganization – religious conversion – led him to think in phenomenological rather than institutional terms. By "love" Emerson means nothing less than an Edwardsean "benevolence toward being in general" resulting from the upwelling of spirit that is the Transcendentalist equivalent to grace. "We must be lovers, and instantly the impossible becomes possible" (*CW* 1: 158). So, perhaps, it does; yet in framing the issue in such terms, Emerson stakes everything upon a transformation of self unpredictable in its operation and independent of the will, while disparaging lesser reform efforts as piecemeal, mechanical, and inefficacious, much like the Calvinist's "outward works" performed in a state of sin.

In contrast to the millennialism of "The American Scholar" and "The Present Age," "Man the Reformer" shows Emerson divided between an extraordinarily high and totalistic standard of reform and a practical despair about the means and historical chances for achieving it ("I see no instant prospect of a virtuous revolution" [*CW* 1: 149]). His most "radical" social pronouncement, the address is also, paradoxically, his most quietistic. So long as his assessment of the times and his confidence in the soul combined to warrant a hope for epochal change, Emerson could legitimately cast himself as a reformer, however aloof he remained in practical terms. By 1841, however, it began to seem that history had gone astray and, still more perplexingly, that the soul itself was unreliable. "The worst feature of our biography," he wrote in July,

> is that it is a sort of double consciousness, that the two lives of the Understanding & of the Soul which we lead, really show very little relation to each other, that they never meet & criticize each other, but one prevails now, all buzz & din, and the other prevails then, all infinitude & paradise, and with the progress of life the two discover no greater disposition to reconcile themselves. (*JMN* 8: 10–11)

Emerson incorporated this passage nearly verbatim into his December 1841 address "The Transcendentalist," the most widely known lecture of that series on "The Times" that resurveys the social landscape in an effort to discern the course of history. Emerson's foil to "The Transcendentalist" (a species of the Reformer) is "The Conservative," the former taking his stand on man's "indisputable infinitude," the latter on his "incontestable limitations" (*CW* 1: 185–86). Philosophically, the opposition is between Idealism and Materialism, or the power of consciousness and the negations of hard fact; politically, it is between "the two omnipresent parties of History, the party of the Past and the party of the Future" (*CW* 1: 171). Conservative and Reformer are thus personifications of the residual and emergent social forces Emerson had described in "The Present Age," though now the advantage lies, if anywhere, on the side of Conservatism. Social facts have come to assume a new solidity for Emerson, not because material forces are irresistible but because their claim is stubborn and abiding while the spirit's is inconstant. "An idealist can never go backward to be a materialist" (*CW* 1: 202), Emerson proclaims; he can, however, become a skeptic – that is to say, an idealist stranded by the retreat of spirit and compelled in his seasons of drought to acknowledge the force of the Conservative's case.

One might call the Emerson of "The Times" a dialectical thinker, save that a dialectic implies progress through contention. In the early 1840s Emerson is more properly a "dichotomous" thinker oscillating between extremes that never productively clash, interact, and resolve themselves in a higher synthesis. The resounding assertion of ideal against fact, love against selfishness, that had marked "Man the Reformer" has evolved by "The Times" into a battle between two armed camps, one of disenfranchised virtue, the other of entrenched power. Where "The American Scholar" had envisioned a work of proselytism in which the scholar would emerge from his isolation to redeem the sleepwalking materialist, "The Transcendentalist" returns the would-be scholar to the social peripheries, "miserable with inaction" and "perish[ing] of rest and rust" (*CW* 1: 212), wanting both a calling (an adequate work to perform) and a sociohistorical call (a public demand for his labor).

If the scholar has been shunted aside by historical developments, he has also, Emerson realizes, been infected by them. "So deep is the foundation of the existing social system," he writes in "The Conservative," "that it leaves no one out of it. . . . For as you cannot jump from the ground without using the resistance of the ground, . . . so you are under the necessity of using the Actual order of things, in order to disuse it" (*CW* 1: 189). Emerson does not believe that social structures and ideologies are wholly coercive. Conditioned by history and bound to the very institutions he would reform, the scholar can still creatively "disuse" the system when the reign of the Understanding is broken by some "new influx of light and power" (*CW* 1: 204). Such moments of influx have become increasingly rare, however, as the "active soul" ("the sound estate of every man" in "The American Scholar" [CW 1: 56–57]) has shown itself a dependent soul whose estate seems hopelessly probated. The inward fact of the "double consciousness" has thus impressed itself upon the outward world, the contemporary fallowness of the self having left society captive (as it needn't be) to the relentless energies of "things."

It would be a mistake to regard Emerson's social thought as a by-product of his metaphysics or, conversely, his metaphysics as a rarefication of his social thought. Both are homologous expressions of his effort to sustain his optimism in the face of limitation, declining energies, and unmalleable fact – above all, to extract a unified faith from his tragic experience of doubleness.

In this respect, the essay that sheds the most revealing crosslight on Emerson's emergence as a laissez-faire apologist is one that has little directly to do with the social world, "Experience" (1844). The opposition between the Understanding and the Soul dramatized politically in "The Times" through the figures of the Conservative and the Reformer is reenacted in "Experience" under the headings of the seven "lords of life." The challenge facing Emerson is to reconcile worldly sagacity ("We live amid surfaces, and the art of life is to skate well on them" [CW 3: 35]) with the preeminence of the spirit. In *Nature* material laws not only had their analogue in laws of the mind but were themselves moral, converging on humanity (indeed, inscribed *for* humanity) and benignly "disciplining" it in how to live. By 1844 Emerson's universe of anthropocentric law has become a universe of ruthless force whose "darlings, the great, the strong, the beautiful, are not children of our law" (CW 3: 37) but practitioners of force themselves. "I know that the world I converse with in the city and in the farms, is not the world I *think*. I observe that difference, and shall observe it" (CW 3: 48), Emerson concedes with an acquiescence he did not feel. The pressure to heal the division between mind and world generates the argumentative structure of "Experience," but the most Emerson can offer in answer is the wishful "expectation" of a future faith (CW 3: 41). Cosmologically, he is already halfway toward the seething proto-Darwinian world of "Fate," first delivered as a lecture in 1851. Socially, too, he is moving toward the acceptance of a kindred power, laissez-faire capitalism, equally brutal and no less indifferent to short-term casualties but (he needs to believe) ultimately as benign. On all levels, force is king and any reconstituted optimism will have to acknowledge its imperatives and wring what assurance it can from them.

Coinciding with the changes in Emerson's thought in the early 1840s were immense changes in New England society that materially enthroned the calculations of the Understanding. By 1844 (to cite one sign of the times) the experiment in paternalistic capitalism at the Lowell mills had begun to fray as dissident workers organized a reform association to secure a ten-hour day; in the next few years capitalism in the mills would grow increasingly predatory as competition depressed profits and wages at a time when Irish immigration created a surplus of cheap labor. Closer to home, Concord itself was in flux. The opening of the Boston and Fitchburg Railroad in 1844 made the village a suburb of Boston, transforming its "most modern, innovative farmers" into agrarian capitalists shipping their produce to the city.[38] Nationally, continental expansion held the mind of a populace that would elect hawkish James K. Polk in 1844 and presently find itself in a war of territorial acquisition. On all sides the energies of economic growth seemed to rule the day. "Things are in the saddle, / And ride mankind," Emerson wrote in his 1846 "Ode, Inscribed to W. H. Channing." The question was whether Americans would ride or be ridden.

Because history was always the tablet on which Emerson read the will of Providence, fashioning a new optimism meant first reorienting himself to the times. Emerson was not "co-opted" by liberal capitalism so much as he hastened to join it, since aligning himself with the divinely empowered forces of the age was always the condition for a living philosophy. "The Young American" (1844) – Emerson's "battle cry for the new era of industrial expansion and manifest destiny," as his editors call it (CW 1: 217) – is therefore less an apology for laissez-faire capitalism than an attempt like Henry Adams's sixty years later to plot the lines of force that were remaking contemporary society. The difference is that where Adams the ironist would dwell on multiplicity and a vertiginous acceleration of energies without immanent purpose or foreseeable end, Emerson the seeker of unity is at pains to assimilate the new forces to a cosmic and social teleology – to survey history from the perspective of the "over-god" of the Channing ode and, in so doing, to "marr[y] Right to Might."

Like "The American Scholar," which it seems deliberately to invoke, "The Young American" begins with the problem of a national culture, still unrealized by 1844 but now to be created less through the work of poets and thinkers than through the promptings of the continent itself and the enterprise of its people. An index of Emerson's revised stance toward commerce and technology is his attitude toward the railroad, as late as 1839 a dire threat to "the balance of man" (JMN 7: 268) but in "The Young American" a boon even to an aesthetic appreciation of the landscape. The center of the address, however, is Emerson's effort to reach an accord with capitalism. By emphasizing the "anti-feudal power" of trade (CW 1: 229), which displaces the "physical strength" of kings and aristocrats and "installs" the enlightened forces of "computation, combination, information,

[and] science, in its room" (*CW* 1: 233), Emerson can associate capitalism with *"amelioration in nature,* which alone permits and authorizes amelioration in mankind" (*CW* 1: 231). Implicit in his words are the notions that the civic world is part of nature and subject to its processes and that advancement occurs by cooperating with these processes rather than directing them toward immediate human ends. The political corollary to this belief is an almost unmitigated laissez-faire: "Trade is an instrument of that friendly Power which works for us in our own despite. . . . Our part is plainly not to throw ourselves across the track, not to block improvement, and sit till we are stone, but to watch the uprise of successive mornings, and to conspire with the new works of new days" (*CW* 1: 234).

It is hard to say what proportions of ingenuousness, disingenuousness, irony, sarcasm, and moral self-protectiveness or self-rebuke are contained in Emerson's word "conspire": etymologically, "to breathe together"; denotatively, "to act in harmony toward a common end"; connotatively, "to join in secret agreement to do an unlawful or wrongful act or to use such means to accomplish a lawful end."[39] Trade was distasteful to the patrician in Emerson and repugnant to the moral idealist. Did it operate toward a "lawful end"? Emerson sought to persuade himself it did, down to the point of sanitizing short-term history by maintaining, with regard to capital, that even "the most selfish men" were working "against their private interest for the public welfare" (*CW* 1: 232) and, with regard to labor, that the Irish immigrants exploited by the railroad were better off than in the old country, were winning priceless opportunities for their children, and at the very least were being kept from worse activities by their "grim" 15- or 16-hour day (*CW* 1: 225). Yet Emerson had few real illusions about the immediate benignity of free trade. Though self-regulating and apparently inexorable, his world order in "The Young American" is ethical only in the vast teleology of the ages and for the race as a whole. The belief that things would get better ("amelioration") exacted the enormous concession that presently they were worse, and given the character of the instrumentalities Emerson had to "conspire" with (struggle in nature, struggle in the social world), it meant surrendering all hope that the system of temporal life could be harmonized, as in *Nature,* with lingeringly Christian ethics. Emerson's new universe functioned by "a cruel kindness" consistent with almost any amount of human suffering, provided it occurred in consequence of the unimpeded operation of natural laws. Rather than a benefactress of the private self, nature was "a terrible communist, reserving all profits to the community, without dividends to individuals" (*CW* 1: 231).

That Emerson should borrow his trope for nature from the counting-house shows how deeply he had come to imagine Providence as a cosmic entrepreneur whose laissez-faire methods could be as harsh as any railroad builder's. The universal order, Emerson was convinced, tended toward the good; so, too, did the socioeconomic order insofar as the free operation of the laws of trade pointed toward "the sequel of trade" (CW 1: 234), signs of which Emerson professed to see in the "beneficent socialism" springing up in Europe and America (CW 1: 235). What reconciled Emerson to capitalism in "The Young American" was his belief that it was the appointed instrument of the moment and that it would shade into a socialism that was not so much its antithesis as, in its dedication to the possibilities of the self, its logical fulfillment. His persistent disparagement of socialism in the 1840s was directed not against its ends of economic and social justice but against its intrusive effort to hasten the evolutionary process through which nature itself was working toward similar ends. "The revolutions that impend[ed] over society" would and *should* "recompose [it] after a new order, ... destroy the value of many kinds of property, and replace all property within the dominion of reason and equity" (CW 1: 181), but they would do so according to nature's timetable rather than according to man's.

The conflict between capitalism and socialism receded, then, when Emerson came to regard them as sequential macrophases within a three-stage epochal history (feudalism, capitalism, socialism) that loosely parallels Marx's. Emerson's means, however, were not class struggle but an extension of the associational principle toward the largest of associations, the "Community," which "is only the continuation of the same movement which made the joint-stock companies for manufactures, mining, banking, and so forth" (CW 1: 236). A nation without a feudal past, he felt, did not need a revolutionary present to reach a socialistic future. In this belief, Emerson takes his place within a native tradition that includes Edward Bellamy, Herbert Croly, and the early Van Wyck Brooks, all of whom saw America as evolving organically beyond capitalism and realizing its promise in a socialistic order that would universalize and complete the ideal of democratic selfhood.

Intent on the long-term teleology of change, Emerson could be callously dismissive of its short-term casualties – the "outs," as he called capitalism's victims in "The Young American," who he felt had no higher aim than to become "ins" (CW 1: 239; see *JMN* 8: 264). Nonetheless, the problem of inequity was disturbing enough that Emerson could wish it solved once and for all. "If Government in our present clumsy fashion must go on," he wrote in March 1843, "could it not assume the charge of providing each citizen, on his coming of age, with a pair of acres, to enable him to get his bread honestly? Perhaps one day it will be done by the state's assuming to distribute the estates of the dead" (*JMN* 8: 344). Here Emerson seems closer to Orestes Brownson's disbursement of inherited property than to his own rejection of "meddling, eleemosynary contrivances" in "The Young American" (*CW* 1: 231). The virtue of socialism as a ruling order was that it refined the problems of wealth and class out of existence and allowed for an individualism purged of material selfishness. Meanwhile, during the amphibious present when individualism was widely synonymous with material acquisition, capitalism would of necessity rule the day. The role of the scholar at such a time was to understand and applaud nature's chosen means while instructing his myopic contemporaries in worthier ideas of the self and larger historical ends.

The danger of "conspiring" with capitalism, or "using the Actual order of things, in order to disuse it" (*CW* 1: 189), lay in opening oneself to appropriation by the very groups one sought to convert. By the time of "Wealth," delivered as a lecture in 1851 and published nine years later in *The Conduct of Life*, Emerson had become such an apparent celebrant of enterprise as to be widely sought by mercantile societies throughout the East and Midwest. "Why needs any man be rich?" he had asked in "Man the Reformer" (*CW* 1: 154). Man "is by constitution expensive, and needs to be rich,"[40] he replied a decade later in "Wealth." His strategy in such performances was to begin on the level of commodity and lift his audiences by metaphor to the plane of spirit. "I have never seen a rich man," he announced pointedly: "I have never seen a man as rich as all men ought to be, or with an adequate command of nature" (*W* 6: 95). But Emerson's language and philosophical argument commonly mystified his auditors, who took his words, as Mary Kupiec Cayton has shown, for an "endorsement of the existing order" rather than "a subtle indictment of its shortcomings."[41]

At bottom, Emerson the laissez-faire apologist *accords* with capitalism more than he derives from it, deterministically replicates it, or was co-opted by it. What concerned him most in the mid-to-late 1840s was power – power in nature and power as it might belong to humanity. Power had always absorbed him, but in the 1840s and afterward power migrated inexorably from the individual to the race. The prospect of humanity enlarging its area of freedom "as children stand up against the wall and notch their height from year to year" (*W* 6: 30) was his response to a universe whose economy could no longer be imaged by the harmonies of physics, as in 1837, but only by the terrors of biology – "the forms of the shark, the *labrus*, the jaw of the sea-wolf paved with crushing teeth, the weapons of the grampus, and other warriors hidden in the sea," tokens of a "ferocity in the interiors of nature" (*W* 6: 8) that could be embraced only through a meliorist faith that struggle was the chosen instrument of Creation.

It would have been consistent for Emerson to regard economic struggle with the same tough-mindedness he adopted toward biological struggle, but to do so would have been to surrender his belief that experience was inherently moral. Though nature could not be dressed up in the "clean shirt and white neckcloth of a student of divinity" (W 6: 8), it was essential that the entrepreneur be so dressed lest ethics and historical process, the inner world and the outer world, disastrously collide. It was not enough for Emerson to say of society's cruelties, as he said of nature's in "Fate," that "evil is good in the making" (W 6: 8); he needed to affirm a correspondence between "the counting-room maxims" of the material world, the "laws of the universe," and the spiritual economy of the soul (W 6: 125), so that the triumphs of the rich and the failures of the poor derived from "an intellectual and moral obedience" or disobedience to the inscribed structure of reality (W 6: 101). A laissez-faire cosmos might work teleologically with sublime indifference to anthropic values, but unless the *human* realm operated by moral laws, life was intolerably empty and mean. The metaphysical and ethical strains within Emerson's thinking had diverged in ways he preferred not to confront, and his positive celebration of laissez-faire (as opposed to a grim acquiescence to it) was exacted by his need to believe that the moral economy of nature functioned actively on the level of the individual life as well as in the broad sweep of evolution. In an age of increasingly large and predatory commercial combinations, Emerson thus came to reassert the old Protestant correlation between prosperity and righteousness.[42]

To an extent, it was Emerson's detente with capitalism on the revised teleological basis of struggle in nature and struggle in society that allowed his thought to take a new, more pragmatic turn. Having settled the cosmological problem (nature was "cruelly kind") and despaired of the millenarian one (no revolution was imminent), Emerson was free to address the political and social issues that began to claim more of his attention in the mid–1840s and later.[43] Emerson became a reformer, that is to say, when he ceased to be a Re-former. Even so, his orientation in matters of social action was always fundamentally spiritual, and even his most ardently reformist pronouncements were rooted in and accountable to his apprehension of universal law. Thus when Emerson came forth after much prodding to deliver his first major antislavery address, "Emancipation in the British West Indies" (1844), he could argue for abolition only because he had become convinced that "the negro race is, more than any other, susceptible of rapid civilization" (W 11: 141). Humane sympathies, ethical appeals, claims of political justice and inalienable rights were all insufficient; laissez-faire nature "will only save what is worth saving; and it saves not by compassion, but by power. . . . When at last in a race a new principle appears, an idea – *that* conserves it; ideas only save races. . . . But a compassion for that which is not and cannot be useful and lovely, is degrading and futile" (*W* 11: 143–44). The fruit of such thinking may be pragmatic action, but Emerson's "useful," unlike William James's, implies instrumentality within an essentially monistic universe: reform is justified or not according to whether it seems contributory to nature's unfolding design.

In the end, judgments of Emerson's radicalism depend on which phase of his career one is considering and whether the interpreter's concern is with the psychosocial genesis of his ideas or with their congruence with Jacksonian ideology. Within the first context it is useless to observe that Emerson "reproduces the logic of laissez-faire capitalism" or was "co-opted by liberal America" without examining the path by which he came to his vision of the later 1830s and subsequently departed from it; within the second context it has often seemed enough to trace analogies (e.g., Emersonian selfhood is "like" private property) and waive the matter of causal relationship by appealing to notions of "reflection," "implication," "containment," and "ideological hegemony." To understand Emerson in terms of *lived* history is not ipso facto to rehabilitate him as a "radical," but it *is* to complicate and subtilize an issue that has been treated monolithically by those who would put him to one or another political or cultural use. The question of Emerson's radicalism need not and assuredly cannot be settled. It is enough that it serve as an entry point into the ambiguities of his thought and the assumptions about literary/historical method we bring to it.

NOTES

1 *The Journals and Miscellaneous Notebooks of Ralph Waldo Emerson*, ed. William H. Gilman et al. (Cambridge, MA: Harvard University Press, 1960–), V, 466. Hereafter cited in the text as *JMN* with volume and page numbers.
2 Porter, *Seeing and Being* (Middletown, CT: Wesleyan University Press, 1981), p. xiv.
3 See particularly Sacvan Bercovitch, *The American Jeremiad* (Madison: University of Wisconsin Press, 1975); "The Problem of Ideology in American Literary History," *Critical Inquiry* 12 (1986): 631–53; *The Office of the Scarlet Letter* (Baltimore: Johns Hopkins University Press, 1991); "Emerson, Individualism, and the Ambiguities of Dissent," *South Atlantic Quarterly* 89 (1990): 623–62; and *The Rites of Assent* (London: Routledge, 1993). See also Cary Wolfe, *The Limits of American Literary Ideology in Pound and Emerson* (Cambridge: Cambridge University Press, 1993) and "Alone with America; Cavell, Emerson, and the Politics of Individualism," *New Literary History* 25 (1994): 137–57.

4 Gunn, *Thinking Across the American Grain* (Chicago: University of Chicago Press, 1992), p. 1.
5 See Burkholder, "History's Mad Pranks: Some Recent Emerson Studies." *ESQ*, 38 (1992): 231–63.
6 Although "Circles" is "more than half made up of passages written in [Emerson's] journal as early as 1835," its vision of a universe in process – of nature, society, indeed truth itself in fluctional *becoming* – is quite different in emphasis from the vision of *Nature* or the Philosophy of History lectures. Joseph Slater, "Historical Introduction," *Collected Works of Ralph Waldo Emerson*, ed. Robert E. Spiller et al. (Cambridge, MA: Harvard University Press, 1971–), vol. 2, p. xxv. Hereafter cited as *CW* with volume and page numbers.
7 Bercovitch, "Emerson, Individualism, and the Ambiguities of Dissent": 645. Quentin Anderson argues a similar view of Emerson and Whitman in *The Imperial Self* (New York: Alfred Knopf, 1971), pp. 1–28.
8 Wolfe, "Alone with America": 137.
9 Karl Marx, "Theses on Feuerbach," in *The Marx-Engels Reader*, 2nd ed., ed. Robert C. Tucker (New York: Norton, 1978), p. 145.
10 Lentricchia, *Criticism and Social Change* (Chicago: University of Chicago Press, 1983), p. 2.
11 Lentricchia, pp. 1, 11.
12 Emerson, "Man the Reformer" (*CW* 1:156).
13 Len Gougeon, *Virtue's Hero: Emerson, Antislavery, and Reform* (Athens: University of Georgia Press, 1990), p. 19.
14 "Introduction," *The United States Magazine and Democratic Review* I, 1 (1837): 5.
15 Marx, "On the Jewish Question," in *The Marx-Engels Reader*, p. 42.
16 "Introduction," *The United States Magazine and Democratic Review* I, 1: 7.
17 Fuller, *Woman in the Nineteenth Century* (New York: Norton, 1971), p. 37.
18 Rush Welter, *The Mind of America: 1820 to 1860* (New York: Columbia University Press, 1975), p. 123.
19 Bercovitch, *The America Jeremiad*, pp. 184, 186.
20 Bercovitch, "Emerson, Individualism, and the Ambiguities of Dissent": 632.
21 Bercovitch, "Emerson, Individualism, and the Ambiguities of Dissent": 633.
22 *The Early Lectures of Ralph Waldo Emerson*, ed. Stephen E. Whicher et al. (Cambridge, MA: Harvard University Press, 1959–71), vol. 2, pp. 213–14. Hereafter Cited as *EL* with volume and page numbers.
23 Welter, *The Mind of America: 1820 to 1860*, p. 36.
24 Gustaaf Van Cromphout, "Emerson and the Dialectics of History" *Publications of the Modern Language Association* 91 (1976): 56.
25 See David Leverenz, *Manhood and the American Renaissance* (Ithaca, NY: Cornell University Press, 1989), ch. 3.
26 Edmund Wilson to Theodore Dreiser, *Edmund Wilson: Letters on Literature and Politics, 1912–72*, ed. Elena Wilson (New York: Farrar, Straus, and Giroux, 1977), pp. 222, 223.
27 Wilson to Dreiser, p. 222.
28 Alvin W. Gouldner, *The Dialectic of Ideology and Technology* (New York: Continuum, 1976), p. 30.
29 See Gouldner, p. 47. For a discussion of Thoreau and "The American

Scholar," see Robert Milder, *Reimagining Thoreau* (Cambridge: Cambridge University Press, 1995), pp. 13–15.

30 Bercovitch, "The Problem of Ideology in American Literary History": 635.

31 Raymond Williams, *Marxism and Literature* (Oxford: Oxford University Press, 1977), p. 123.

32 Marx, "Theses on Feuerbach," in *The Marx-Engels Reader,* p. 144.

33 Gunn, p. 1.

34 Lentricchia, *Criticism and Social Change,* p. 7.

35 Williams, *Marxism and Literature,* pp. 123, 114.

36 *The Letters of Ralph Waldo Emerson,* ed. Ralph L. Rusk and Eleanor M. Tilton (New York: Columbia University Press, 1939–   ), vol. 2, pp. 368–71, hereafter cited as *L* with volume and page numbers; *JMN* 7:407–8.

37 Bercovitch, "Emerson, Individualism, and the Ambiguities of Dissent": 641, 642.

38 Robert A. Gross, "Concord, Boston, and the Wider World: Transcendentalism and Urbanism," in *New Perspectives on Concord's History* (Concord: Massachusetts Foundation for the Humanities and Public Policy, 1983), p. 112.

39 *Webster's Ninth New Collegiate Dictionary* (Springfield, MA: Merriam-Webster, 1986) p. 281.

40 Emerson, "Wealth," *Complete Works* (Boston: Houghton Mifflin, 1911), vol. 6, p. 85. Hereafter cited as *W* with volume and page numbers.

41 Mary Kupiec Cayton, "The Making of an American Prophet: Emerson, His Audiences, and the Rise of the Culture Industry in Nineteenth-Century America," *American Historical Review* 92 (1987): 613.

42 "Wealth" maintains many of the laissez-faire principles Emerson advanced in the late 1830s, but because the historical and philosophical landscape has changed so dramatically, what had been a progressive, even a potentially radical creed in pre-corporate America has become an effectual prop of the capitalist order. In 1837 free trade was the gospel of the Jacksonian *Democratic Review;* by the time of Emerson's death in 1882, it would belong to social Darwinists like William Graham Sumner.

43 See David M. Robinson, *Emerson and the Conduct of Life* (Cambridge: Cambridge University Press, 1993).

4

R. JACKSON WILSON

Emerson as Lecturer: Man Thinking, Man Saying

In 1833, Waldo Emerson (as he still called himself) gave a talk at the Unitarian chapel in Edinburgh, Scotland. At least one member of the audience remembered it ecstatically:

> The originality of his thoughts, the consummate beauty of the language in which they were clothed, the calm dignity of his bearing, the absence of all oratorical effect, and the singular directness and simplicity of his manner . . . made a deep impression on me. . . . His voice was the sweetest, the most winning and penetrating of any I ever heard.[1]

The enthusiastic auditor might have added that the 30-year-old visiting American speaker did not receive any sort of fee.

Almost four decades later, in the spring of 1872, Ralph Waldo Emerson (as he came to be known in his fame), was giving a lecture in Boston, part of an organized "course" of public talks. It was an old lecture, one he had used many times and had published years before. But that was all right. His audiences, he had learned, seemed to prefer the old lectures. And, in any case, now nearly 70 and suffering from what he cheerfully called "holes in the mind," he was no longer able to write new ones. He also needed to be escorted and watched over by his 33-year-old daughter, Ellen, who sat near him as he read. She was desperately nervous, for she hadn't made Emerson practice the reading, so she waited anxiously to see whether her father could make it through the hour. As she wrote to her brother, Edward:

> Well I sat at the lecture in about as great fear as I was able to bear, lest there should be some terrific crash, for I hadn't heard it beforehand as I ought, and his memory is entirely gone, so that he blithely read the same page twice over. . . . Father has just come home and I have scolded & mourned to him about it and he thinks we shan't have the same trouble again, doesn't feel half as badly about it as I.[2]

And there was something else to cheer up the indefatigable old trouper: the ticket sales for the lecture series had already brought in a very large sum of nineteenth-century dollars, $1,300. "That," Ellen told her brother, "makes Father very happy."

The extraordinary life that lay between these two moments was one of immense intellectual achievement. Emerson became the best-known man of letters that America would produce in the nineteenth century. And he did it by dint of hard work as much as talent. Year after year, he continued to read prodigiously and creatively. He wrote early and often, and then re-wrote and rewrote again. He became truly the master of the distinctive prose style he forged for himself in the 1830s. He came close to living up to the extraordinary ambition he laid down in his journal in 1834, at the outset of his remarkable writing career: "The high prize of eloquence may be mine, the joy of uttering what no other can utter & what all must receive."[3]

But the "uttering" and the "receiving" would be done in a very specific setting, a setting that belonged distinctively to the middle third of the nine-teenth century in the United States. Emerson would write, but he would not exactly fit the recently discovered cultural category of "author." He would make a considerable body of poetry, and would himself work a good deal at defining what it meant to be truly a poet. But that identity – however he might expand and flex it – would never quite fit, either. To call him merely an "intellectual" or a "thinker" misses the point badly – though he did coin the famous definition of the true scholar as "Man Thinking." What he actually *did* for most of his adult life, what gave concrete shape to his career, was the giving of public lectures. More than any other major writer of what came to be called the American Renaissance, he was a creature of the Lyceum, a loose federation of hundreds of local organizations that sponsored regular series of public lectures by traveling speakers. In practice, Ralph Waldo Emerson was not "Man Thinking" but "Man Saying."

It was his lectures that gave Emerson his initial fame, and always pro-vided him with his main source of income. He published volume after vol-ume of essays, but almost all of them had been written first as lectures. As he did his monumental reading, he read (as he put it) "creatively," always with an eye on what he might put to use in the lecture he was at work on. If he kept an elaborate journal, it served him not only as a diary, and not only as a place to put down musings, but as a file of terse axioms and extended paragraphs that might come in handy for some future lecture. And as he wrote and rewrote, he worked always under the pressure of deadlines. His mind was on higher things, on all the stock Victorian sub-jects: God, death, immortality, spirit, nature, and the rest. But his eye was on the clock. The lecture schedules were fixed and demanding. The topics were there in advance, frozen onto printed posters (though he was generally careful to set titles that would leave him plenty of room for maneuver: "Fate," "Human Life," "Hospitality," "Self-Reliance," and the like). He had started out in the 1820s as a minister, with what he called the "terri-fick" obligation to write a sermon every week. But when he began in the 1830s to lecture for his living, the obligation to satisfy the demands of the Lyceum circuit was just as unrelenting. He was a disciplined man, and found that he could give only about 21 hours to writing a lecture, if he wanted to reserve enough time to keep up with the reading and rereading he needed to do for the next topic on the upcoming schedule. So it was within those 21 hours that his "eloquence" had to be carefully shaped. For it was an eloquence aimed at a very particular kind of "uttering," and there were men and women at countless towns along the lecture trail, waiting to decide for themselves whether they "must receive." And the eloquence itself had to be clocked. Like all the hundreds of others who hit the Lyceum trail, he was bound by the 50-minute hour that became a fixed convention. Shakespeare's Puck, Emerson noted, boasted that he could girdle the globe in only 40 minutes. "I," he said, "take fifty."[4]

Lecturing could be a draining career, and the more successful a man or woman was at it, the more draining it could become. "The Lyceum," Emerson complained, "is a terrible tyrant, with long arms that reach from Chicago and Milwaukee to Concord." An invitation to go on a three-week tour to the Middle West, as he described it in the late 1850s, was like a bet proposed by the Lyceum agency: " 'I'll bet you fifty dollars a day for three weeks, that you will not leave your library and wade and freeze and ride and run, and suffer all manner of indignities, and stand up for an hour each night reading in a hall,' and I answer, 'I'll bet I will.' I do it, and win the $900."[5] But he did it, year after year, decade after decade. And in the most practical terms, the lecturing career worked. As his reputation approached its peak, in the 1850s, he was giving about 70 lectures a year in about 50 different towns and cities. In a typical winter "season," he was earning around $2,000 from the talks – more than his income from any other source. This was about four times the annual income of a skilled worker in New England. And things kept improving. In 1866, he was invited to give a series of six lectures, all in Boston, and earned over $900 from them. Two years later, a winter series of talks, again in Boston, netted him $1,600. And this was only part of it. All the while, he continued to make extended tours to the Middle West and even as far as California, and also kept up his faithful trek into upstate New York, where the towns along the Erie Canal had created the concentration of local lyceums known among the lecturers of the circuit as "the Buffalo trail."

For anyone interested in Emerson as a writer, of course, this practical detail of his life is just that: a practical (and antique) detail, with no important bearing on either the content or the form of his essays. For many serious and dedicated readers – and for many literary critics – any suggestion that what Emerson actually did for a living might have had any serious effect on what he wrote and how he wrote it might seem a bit crude and scandalous, a bit like wondering who picked up the check for the Last Supper. But the demands and conventions of lecturing were never very far from Emerson's mind. And for him they meant more than irksome necessity and binding constraint – and more, too, than fees. Lectures meant opportunity as well, the chance to do something that could not be done in mere print. For him, the lecture hall was a highly charged setting that offered extraordinary possibilities. There, where he confronted expectant faces of men and women, he wanted much of them and of himself. And what he wanted was something that could not be gotten outside the lecture hall:

> I will agitate others, being agitated myself. I dared to hope for extacy & eloquence. A new theatre, a new art, I said, is mine. Let us see if philosophy, if ethics, if chiromancy, if the discovery of the divine in the house & the barn, in all works & all plays, cannot make the cheek blush, the lip quiver, & the tear start. I will not waste myself. On the strength of Things I will be borne, and try if Folly, Custom, Convention, & Phlegm cannot be made to hear our sharp artillery.[6]

The public lecture, he thought, was a peculiar opportunity to "try the magic of sincerity, that luxury permitted only to kings and poets."[7] And when he felt failure, he felt it in terms that matched the intensity of his aspirations:

> Alas! alas! I have not the recollection of one strong moment. A cold mechanical preparation for a delivery as decorous – fine things, pretty things, wise things – but no arrows, no axes, no nectar, no growling, no transpiercing, no loving, no enchantment.[8]

For Emerson, working as Man Saying was not just an irksome bit of drudgery necessary to sustain the more genuine and authentic life of Man Thinking. He loved his library, and the scholarly solitude it could give him. But he loved the lectern as well. And in hard reality, it was not the lecturer that supported the thinker; on the contrary, it was Man Thinking who labored to provide Man Saying with the possibilities of moments of "loving" and "enchantment." And if, as a writer, Emerson worked long and hard to develop a style that had arrows and axes, the arrows were to fly and the axes fall out loud, in crowded halls, from his lips and not just from his pen. If his writing style were to be marked by peculiar shiftings from nectar to growlings and back again, it was because that style was the one that might cause real visible cheeks to blush, lips to quiver, and tears to start. The somewhat vague intellectual movement – transcendentalism – with which he became identified was important to him. But whatever transcendentalism might have signified as a body of ideas, its significance to him lay finally in its capacity to produce magical moments of "transpiercing" in the lecture hall.

There was something obviously ministerial about the way Emerson hoped to use the public lecture to bring a sharp artillery to bear on folly and phlegm. And it is tempting to treat his surrender of his own pulpit as nothing more than a choice to take up a secular pastorate. He understood that his listeners had such expectations. "I am," he once said with more than a trace of bitterness as he set about to prepare his next annual series of Lyceum talks, "to indicate constantly, though all unworthy, the Ideal and Holy Life, the life within life – the Forgotten Good, the Unknown Cause in which we sprawl & sin."[9]

But his decision to leave the ministry involved much more than a decision to preach on weeknights rather than on Sunday mornings. Writing essays for public consumption would demand much more than taking a few denominational phrases out of old sermons, so that they could be read in public rather than in church. The prose of the lectern would have to be different from the prose of the pulpit.

When Emerson left the ministry, he did not leave a career only. He left behind a conception of what it meant to be a man of letters. Much of what he would write in the years that followed his break with his own past and his attempt to forge a new future would be a justification of that decision, a justification that would also involve the creation of a new conception of the true nature of the figure he came to call "the Poet," the figure he hoped would share with kings the unique privilege of public sincerity.

The Reverend R. Waldo Emerson was the son, grandson, and great-grandson of ministers. His grandfather Emerson had held the pulpit of the church at Concord. His father was minister of Boston's prestigious First Church. The first semon Emerson ever preached was given in a church presided over by an uncle. He preached his second sermon from his dead father's pulpit. In that same pulpit he gave his first sustained series of replacement sermons after he was licensed to preach. When he was ordained at the Second Church in March of 1829, the ceremony was a tableau of ancestral and institutional continuity. The first ritual step, the "charge" to the new minister, was administered by the man who had married Emerson's grandfather's widow – and who had also charged Emerson's own father 37 years before. The ordination sermon was delivered by an uncle. The "right hand of fellowship" welcoming the new minister to his congregation was offered by the man who had replaced Emerson's father at the First Church.

Emerson had grown up and gone through Harvard College and Harvard's Divinity School with what he called "great expectation." And this expectation had governed his life. In 1824, about to turn 21, he made his understanding of that expectation explicit in his journal: "I deliberately dedicate my time, my talents, & my hopes to the Church."[10] At 21 he might be, as he put it, *legally* a man. But he would not become fully a man until he had a congregation of his own . . . and, it went without saying, until he had a wife. These two expectations were met in 1829, when he was about to become minister of Boston's Second Unitarian Church and to marry Ellen Tucker, the pretty, 19-year-old daughter of a wealthy merchant family. The moment was dramatic:

> My history has had its important days within a brief period. Whilst I enjoy the luxury of an unmeasured affection for an object so deserving of it all & who requites it all, I am called by an ancient & respectable church to become its pastor. I recognize in these events . . . the hand of my heavenly Father. . . . I feel my total dependance. O God direct & guard & bless me."[11]

And so, as he set out on his first career, Emerson thought of his life as one that was happily defined by expectation and continuity. Both his marriage and his ministry, intimately connected in his mind, were not only sanctioned by civil contracts but also legitimated by clear public understandings of his status and its responsibilities.

Sanction and legitimacy were derived, ultimately, from the congregation that gave him its "call." And he had a quite definite idea of what a congregation was. In one of his sermons, he asked, "When we came up this morning to the house of God did we come in savage solitude each from his lonely house a congregation of hermits to whom society is unwelcome?" His answer, emphatically, was no. The congregation was a community, in place before he came to it, and with ties that were finally independent of anything he might bring to it, a community of which he was also a member:

> We have taken sweet counsel together. We do not live for ourselves; we do not rejoice, we do not weep alone. Our lives are bound up in others. Our blood beats in our breasts pulse for pulse with a true accord at the honor & the shame of a hundred other hearts to which God has united us in family or in friendship.[12]

To be a minister, for him, was to take up what he called a "priestly" vocation, to become the moral voice of such a community. It was a career that was emphatically institutional. The ideal congregation was not an audience but an intimate constituency. The pastor did not shepherd a flock of strangers but a company of men and women whose parents he would bury and whose children he would teach. This relationship was manifested concretely in the legal contract that bound the minister to his congregation, with a definite income, in principle for life. The duties were clear and fixed by powerful traditions. He could count his visits to the sick and the grieving; he could keep track of the numbers of people he married or baptized. There were sermons to prepare, and he could carefully number these, too. Having to write one every week might seem pressing. But there were certain well-understood conventions that provided ready texts and frameworks, sanctioned by usage and communal expectation. The speaking tasks were definite and limited, performed for a familiar and continuing audience, done at close range, and for a steady, measured reward.

But within a few years it all came unraveled. Ellen Tucker Emerson died of tuberculosis early in 1831. Then, a little more than a year later, Emerson provoked a crisis with his parishioners by telling them that he was no longer willing to serve communion wine and bread. Many of the church's members wanted to accept his position and keep him, and he probably could have worked out some sort of compromise. But he was clearly intent on leaving not just his congregation but the ministry. The two intimately connected things he had thought made him finally a man – his ordination and his marriage – had been annulled, one by death and one by his own choice.

After many conversations with Emerson, his brother Charles summed up the tension of the moment neatly:

> Now things seem to be flying to pieces, and I don't know when they will again be put together and he [be] harnessed in . . . the labors of a daily calling. . . . I do not doubt he may write and be a fine thinker, all alone by himself; but I think he needs to be dragged closer to people by some practical vocation, however it may irk his tastes.[13]

The question was, now, what was to be the relationship between being a "fine thinker, all alone," and being harnessed to some practical vocation. Emerson himself was vague. "Projects sprout and bloom in my head," he wrote a few weeks after his resignation, "of action, literature, philosophy." And he had mused during the past year that he might "commence author." But his immediate "action" was to take the final months of salary the church had agreed to make him a present of, and use it to go to Europe. When he started for home nine months later, he told himself that the trip had confirmed his "convictions." On the ship back to New York, he was a little more explicit: "I like my book about nature," he said in his journal.

Then he added, with only an ampersand to join the thoughts, "& wish I knew where & how I ought to live."[14] He seemed to be certain about one thing – that he would write a book about nature – and uncertain about the other – how he would live. But the two fell together easily in one sentence exactly because it was clear that the first was part of the answer to the second. He was going to live by writing. But the writing would be aimed directly at the platform. The very first thing he did when he reached New York was to arrange to give a public lecture. It was, in effect, a second ordination.

This choice of a new career was made easier – perhaps made possible at all – by Ellen Tucker Emerson's will. After a little bit of wrangling, her estate was settled in his favor, and the resulting capital of over $23,000 would yield a steady income of about $1,300 a year. It was not quite enough to live on comfortably, since he wanted to be able to take care of his mother and a mentally troubled brother, and intended to marry again. But he could reasonably hope to earn enough from writing and lecturing to supplement the $1,300 a year his inheritance would bring. From this point onward, Emerson's experience would be organized almost entirely around the fact that he was a writer by calling, and that almost all the writing would be destined for his "new theater."

During the next few years, Emerson worked mightily on his lectures. But he also kept at work on the "book about nature." The two things were very closely related. The book, which he published in 1836 under the simple title *Nature*, was really not about nature. It was about his new calling. In the book, Emerson presented what amounted to a justification of his leaving the ministry. But he also drew up a careful portrait of a type of man – the Poet, he called him – that could replace his earlier "priestly" definition of himself. *Nature*, among other things, was an attempt to devise an implicit but convincing curriculum vitae, one that would serve as a legitimate set of credentials for a man who would dare to go to the lectern in a public hall full of strangers and invoke that magic that was the peculiar right of only kings and poets. As a minister, Emerson had had credentials aplenty to testify to the capacity in which he mounted the pulpit: his Harvard degrees, his license, his ordination, his contract with the Second Church. But as a "fine thinker," he had no ready credentials. And his audiences, unlike his congregation, were not a community unless he and his words could make them one.

So he began *Nature* with several pages of narrative, the story of "a man" who made a tense and exhilarating spiritual pilgrimage, a pilgrimage whose outcome would richly entitle him to say, "On the strength of Things, I will be borne," and to work the magic of poets and kings. *Nature*, like most books, had many purposes. But perhaps the most urgent was to create a compelling portrait of a man – the Poet – who had penetrated the deepest mysteries of the world, not through reading and study but through a very special kind of experience, and was now entitled to the "joy of uttering what no other can utter." This figuring of the Poet, whose name ought to be put into quotation marks as "Emerson," was to be Emerson's most enduring creation. It would hover about him all those hundreds of times he would go to a lectern, carefully arrange his manuscript, train his blue eyes on the audience, and begin to turn his rich baritone voice to the task of bringing "sincerity" and "enchantment" to the hall.

This would-be enchanter, this figuring of "Emerson" that emerged from *Nature,* was a type of man very different from the Reverend Waldo Emerson of the Second Church. In fact, the career of this "Emerson" began in a way that knowing readers around Boston would recognize as Emerson's repudiation of the ministry. *Nature* opened with a famous complaint: "Our age is retrospective. It builds the sepulchres of the fathers. . . . The foregoing generations beheld God and nature face to face; we, through their eyes. . . . [W]hy should we grope among the dry bones of the past, or put the living generation into masquerade out of its faded wardrobe?"[15] Emerson's own sepulchered "fathers" had been ministers, of course, and he had for a time dressed himself out of their faded wardrobe. And while he was preparing to resign from the Second Church, he had complained that "The profession is antiquated. In an altered age, we worship in the dead forms of our forefathers."[16]

But the weight of the dead hand of the past, with all its heavy residue of institutions and creeds, fell not just on the ministry but on society at large, on "our age." The pages that followed were to be the story of how a singular and solitary man – sometimes called the Poet, but finally and triumphantly called simply "I" – would escape from the social sepulcher. He would end, for himself at least, the groping among dry bones and he would put off the faded masquerade that ordinary men and women wore. And he would emerge from the experience uniquely qualified to speak on such matters as "Beauty" or "Spirit."

The drama began innocently enough:

> To go into solitude, a man needs to retire as much from his chamber as from society. I am not solitary whilst I read and write, though nobody is with me. But if a man would be alone, let him look at the stars.

But it was clear, even in this innocent-seeming first step in the Poet's pilgrimage, that his spiritual quest must not take place in society but away from it, in solitude. And the reference to "his chamber" was also heavily freighted. It would have been understood by any nineteenth-century reader to mean a "study," and Emerson was making it clear at the outset that the kind of wisdom his figure was seeking could not be found in books. The answers were somehow in the stars.

Emerson took his figure from his chamber and into increasingly perfect solitude. And to him this meant deeper and deeper into nature. And as he progresses, the poet learns that in solitude and in nature he can see what others cannot see and know what others do not know. He climbs a hill and looks out over a stretch of neat New England countryside. He has known it well in social terms, known who owned which farms and woodlots: "The charming landscape which I saw this morning, is indubitably made up of some twenty or thirty farms. Miller owns this field, Locke that, and Manning the woodland beyond." But now in his solitude, he comes to understand that what he is seeing is not land at all, but land*scape,* something spiritual and mysterious, accessible only to the extraordinary eye. It turns out that Miller, Locke, and Manning do not really *have* their property: "But none of them owns the landscape. There is a property in the horizon that no man has but he whose eye can integrate all the parts, that is the poet. This is the best part of these men's farms, yet to this their land-deeds give them no title."

Given his extraordinary eye, the Poet can now see beauty and truth in the most unlikely settings. He crosses an empty, bare, and muddy town common, under a lowering sky. But he begins to experience a kind of mystical ecstasy, gladdening, but almost frightening:

> Crossing a bare common, in snow puddles, at twilight, under a clouded sky, without having in my thoughts any occurrence of special good fortune, I have enjoyed a perfect exhilaration. Almost I fear to think how glad I am.

But the Poet's drama would find its climax in a place of more profound solitude. Emerson took him finally to "the woods," away from city streets, cultivated landscapes, and village commons. He will discover then that the woods are farms of a sort – God's farms. He discovers that the woods are not wild, but a place of "decorum," and he a welcome "guest." He recovers a kind of spiritual childhood, but also soars out of time, out of the confines of "the age" and into the perpetual, the perennial, and the millennial.

> In the woods, too, a man casts off his years, as the snake his slough, and at what period soever of life, is always a child. In the woods, is perpetual youth. Within these plantations of God, a decorum and sanctity reign, a perennial

festival is dressed, and the guest sees not how he should tire of them in a thousand years. In the woods, we return to reason and faith. There I feel that nothing can befal me in life, – no disgrace, no calamity, (leaving me my eyes,) which nature cannot repair.

In these plantations of God, the poet completes his extraordinary enterprise. He becomes mystically at one with Nature. He vanishes into the world, but simultaneously takes the whole world into himself. There is a transaction, in which he loses his private identity, and becomes nothing in order to see all. But in the transaction, he gains spiritual liquidity: his head is "bathed"; "currents" flow through him:

> Standing on the bare ground, – my head bathed by the blithe air, and uplifted into infinite space, – all mean egotism vanishes. I become a transparent eyeball. I am nothing. I see all. The currents of the Universal Being circulate through me; I am part or particle of God.

Whether Ralph Waldo Emerson ever had such mystical moments himself is a difficult and perhaps insoluble puzzle. What mattered, in the end, is that his figuring of "Emerson" had them. For that figure, the ecstatic possession of Nature, the direct, eyes-on experience of the currents of Universal Being, provided the set of credentials he needed. To Emerson's career as a writer and lecturer, they were as essential as his Harvard degrees, his license, and his ordination had been to his first career as a minister. For what he would claim to bring to the lecture hall was not information, not mere knowledge gotten out of books, but his own out-of-the ordinary experience. Out on the Buffalo "trail," reading his very popular lecture on "Self-Reliance," it was essential that he find his "magic" in that "sincerity" that was the peculiar entitlement of poets and kings. It would be not exactly Emerson but the "I" of *Nature* who could say:

> In this pleasing contrite wood-life which God allows me, let me record day by day my honest thought without prospect or retrospect, and, I cannot doubt, it will be found symmetrical, though I mean it not and see it not. My book should smell of pines and resound with the hum of insects.[17]

And when, a few minutes further into "Self-Reliance," he would say of the "true man" that "Where he is there is Nature," the truest referent of "Nature" would be his book about *Nature*.

The figure of "Emerson" that emerged from *Nature* was a radical one. His poet was willing to ask fundamental questions about the three essential institutions of middle-class culture as Emerson knew it: family, church, and property. The poet in the narrative breaks free of every conventional obligation of family – and with it, other forms of "acquaintance." He subverts churches and ministries by becoming himself part and particle of God. And he casts doubt on the meaning of property by trivializing ordinary men's claims to real estate.

But the radicalism was oddly inconsequential. There is a profound difference, Emerson once said, between the "timber of the woodcutter" and "the tree of the poet." He meant, of course, that the poet's tree was somehow spiritually superior. But while the woodcutter might make timber of the poet's tree, the poet could lay only his eye, and not his hand, on the tree of the woodcutter. In his lectures, Emerson was always very careful not to try to persuade his audiences to take any specific actions. He did not ask farmers to surrender their farms in order to possess landscapes. He did not ask others to retire from society and go into nature to pursue the ultimate mysteries of the world. In fact, what he offered his audiences was the powerful suggestion that he had already done these things for them, and that through him and his language, they might vicariously come to know what his poet had come to know immediately. If he had been glad to the brink of fear as he felt uplifted into infinite space, then he could offer them at least a momentary taste of that gladness and that fear.

In any case, the radicalism of the figure Emerson had devised for himself was a radicalism wonderfully suited to the lecture circuit. It invited his listeners to consider, for 50 minutes at least, looking at their world from an unaccustomed and perhaps even shocking new angle of vision. But then, when his lectures were finished, he would board the train for the next town and his audiences could go back to their lives. He could tell them things that might shock them. "As men's prayers are a disease of the will," he could say, "so are their creeds a disease of the intellect." But he would not be in town the next week to meet preachers or deacons or faithful parishioners in the streets. "No law can be sacred to me but that of my nature," he could say on the platform, knowing full well that it would have been another thing altogether to make such a remark to a settled congregation that he would have to meet week after week. "I shun father and mother and wife and brother when my genius calls me," he might tell an audience in Indiana. Next week he would be in Michigan, and would never know whether any family quarrels had erupted.

But of course the magic and the enchantment he wanted to create involved much more than administering a few rhetorical shocks and verbal surprises. He had to begin with what he knew were the expectations of his middle- and upper-middle-class audiences. They were quite literate people, for whom the lecture series might be the central social moment of the long winters of New England and the upper Middle West. They expected to be entertained. They even expected to be taught something. But most of all, he thought, they expected 50 minutes of spiritual uplift. In 1839, with his new career beginning to prosper, Emerson thought with considerable resentment about what his audiences wanted from him:

> I submit to sell tickets again. . . . But what shall be the substance of my shrift [penance; confession]? Adam in the Garden, I am to new name all the beasts in the field & all the gods in the Sky. I am to invite men drenched in time to recover themselves & come out of time, & taste their native immortal air. . . . I am to celebrate the spiritual powers. . . . I am to console the brave sufferers under evils whose end they cannot see by appeals to the great optimist self-affirmed in all bosoms.[18]

What he needed to do was to devise ways of satisfying such conventional expectations without surrendering the quality he strove hardest for – originality. Without originality, there was no hope of genuine magic. Without originality, he could only fall into what (after Plato) he called the "confectionary" mode of public discourse. Without real originality, any cheeks that might blush or lips that might tremble or tears that might fall would be the result of mere showmanship. And so he could not do what some of his fellow lecturers did; he could not thunder, or grow faint with emotion, or even produce a quiver on his own lips, a tear from his own eye. Once, when Emerson offered to attend a lecture his friend Oliver Wendell Holmes was giving, Holmes begged him not to attend because the lecture would be marred by the kinds of stage tricks Holmes thought he had to use. "I entreat you not to go," Holmes told him. "I am forced to study effects. You and others may be able to combine popular effect with the exhibition of truths. I cannot. I am compelled to study effects." And there was the other danger, always present, that he would meet the audience too much on its ground, and too little on his own, creating not magic but only complacent satisfaction. For much of his career, there was not only his own acute conscience to warn him of this tempting chasm, there was also his contrary young friend Henry David Thoreau, who told Emerson often enough that he regretted "that whatever was written for a lecture, or whatever succeeded with the audience was bad."[19]

The problem, then, was how to work with the sanctimonious requirements he thought his audiences brought with them to the halls, but to do it in a way that preserved his sense that he had spoken his own original truths, rather than merely mouthing theirs. And this without the deployment of any obvious "effects," any theatrical sleights that would surely wreck any possibility of genuine magic. In short, the problem was a problem of style. In a measure, the question of style translated itself into a question of oral performance: how, exactly, would he speak? But no clear boundary could be drawn between the style of his performance and the style of his writing. His writing and his platform delivery had to be consistent and mutually reinforcing. The writing had to be an anticipatory echo of the public reading.

Many men and women on the Lyceum circuits had begun to cultivate an extemporaneous delivery (or one that appeared to be extemporaneous, at least). It was the style of preaching that had come to dominate in many Protestant congregations during the great evangelical revivals of the 1820s and 1830s. But Emerson steadfastly refused the temptation. He did so partly because he cared profoundly about precision in language. But it was essential to his style that he read, calmly and with great decorum, and in a rich but evenly controlled voice. He also had a capacity to speak in a voice that sounded to his hearers "gentle" and "sweet." (His very curious courtship of his second wife was conducted mainly in three talks he gave in her town of Plymouth in 1834, just before he wrote her a letter proposing marriage, after they had met only a couple of times at receptions. She had found him in the lectures to be "an angelic being," and accepted the proposal.)[20]

But more than gentleness and decorum were at stake in Emerson's platform style. During the years when he was perfecting his own platform manner, he became fascinated with a locally famous preacher known as "Father" Edward Thompson Taylor, who ran a Methodist chapel for sailors on Ann Street, in Boston's North End. Working always without a written text, Taylor roared away at his congregation of seamen (and pale young Unitarians who came to watch in mixed alarm and envy). He was, Emerson thought, guided by "instincts diviner than rules." And his sermons consisted of "a string of audacious felicities harmonized by a spirit of joyful love." Compared to Taylor, other preachers seemed "puny" and "cowardly": "He shows us what a man can do."[21] Emerson even mused that perhaps he ought to lace his own lectures with a few "Ann Street oaths." In the end, though, he knew that Taylor's style would not be his. He may have lacked the knack, but there was a larger reason. He intended to build an imposing edifice in his work, and Taylor's methods would not give him the result he wanted. "Extempore speaking can be good," he told himself, "& written discourses can be good. A tent is a very good thing, but so is a cathedral."[22] And a cathedral required serenity, control, gravity.

So Emerson worked deliberately to build a kind of tension into his lecturing. He would struggle mightily to find surprising and even shocking things to say to his audiences. Indeed, he would carefully space pithy and challenging aphorisms – though not Ann Street oaths – through the lectures,

and tell his audiences in a hundred different ways that the time had come
to question every assumption, to challenge every received truth, and even
to consider taking down all their social institutions stone by stone. But he
would do this in a carefully disciplined way, always making it clear that he
was sticking close to a finely wrought text, and was a man incapable of
anything that might come close to ranting. In effect, he created a kind of
tightrope for himself, stretched over several sets of paired pitfalls. One was
the danger of cheap "effects" and its opposite, the danger of a coldly mechanical preparation for a coldly mechanical delivery. Another was the
need to make his sentiments urgent and sincere, paired with the danger that
gravity and serenity might fail and he be left with a tent instead of a cathedral. And then there was the need to enrich the lecture with pungent and
gripping lines, lines that could be his "arrows" and his "axes," but to do
so without, in the end, disappointing his audiences' pious expectations of
"nectar." Night after night, winter after winter on the lecture circuit, he
walked this tightrope of his own devising. And, whether they knew it or
not, watching him do this must surely have been one of the principal thrills
his audiences took away from those legendary performances.

But this keen balancing between effect and decorum, between surprising
originalities and the conventions of uplift, between axes and nectar, was
not just a feature of his lecturing style. It folded itself into his writing style
as well. For his writing – most of it, at least – consisted of texts (in a
somewhat old-fashioned sense of the term), texts that were carefully designed to be spoken aloud. And so the writing, too, took much of its energy
from the tensions he generated in the prose between the startling and the
conventional, between the rough and (as he would have said) "manly" edge
it could take on, and the smoother and sweeter stretches of calm with which
he knew how to smooth his writing.

This characteristic of Emerson's prose style can be seen quite plainly in
the most enduring of his lectures – still the most common reader's introduction to his writing – "The American Scholar." It was written for a very
special occasion. But the occasion only magnified and brought into sharper
relief the kinds of stylistic tensions that would be present in all his public
lectures. In 1837, he was invited by Harvard's Phi Beta Kappa Society to
give the commencement address it sponsored every year. Over the years, a
particular subject had become traditional: the scholar in America.

The occasion was of considerable moment for a man with Emerson's
background and personal history. Many alumni members of Phi Beta
Kappa would be there. Most of the faculty would be present. Indeed the
200 or so gowned graduating students would be joined by men of all ages,

filling the aisles. There would even be people standing outside, listening at the windows. The rhetorical situation invited – even demanded – gravity and decorum. And the audience would expect – just as his future lecture audiences would expect – a moment of moral uplift.

But most of the people in the audience also knew that something odd might happen this year. The main business of Harvard was still to prepare young men for the ministry. And now a speaker was coming who had gone through that training, but had then abandoned the very career that was still the most likely choice of any member of the class of 1837 who had been inducted into Phi Beta Kappa. There was a hovering possibility that he might disturb the gravity of the occasion – the kind of possibility that Emerson brought with him to all his lectures, the possibility that was, in fact, one of his principal professional assets.

Emerson understood the dramatic and contradictory components of the occasion, and he knew how to use them well. He would be exquisitely well mannered, not just in his delivery but in his language. But he would also hurl shocking sentence fragments at the audience, like "A thought too bold – a dream too wild." In a smoothly restrained voice, he would read stretches of smoothly restrained prose. But then he would suddenly interject a "transpiercing" plea for "savage nature." He would threaten the solemn formality of the hall with the frightening observation that "out of terrible Druids and Berserkirs, come at last Alfred and Shakspear." He would verge toward Ann Street oaths with words like "bold," "wild," "savage," "terrible" and the like, knowing full well that the weight of such words was doubled and redoubled precisely because the occasion was so formal and the audience so ready for piety and uplift.

And so Emerson prepared a lecture that could serve as a stylistic model for the hundreds he would write, a lecture that exploited the rhetorical balance between the decorous and the "savage." He wrote approvingly of the unsettling new figure of Emanuel Swedenborg, with his "theory of insanity, of beasts, of unclean and fearful things."[23] But he hedged this axe with the nectared assurance that in the end the best culture was still to be sought after in the comforting old names – Chaucer, Shakespeare, Plato, and the rest.

He began in perfect docility, identifying himself with the occasion, the audience, and its usages. "Mr. President and Gentlemen," he said, "I greet you on the re-commencement of our literary year." But, in the space of less than a minute, he was talking about casting usage to the winds, promising that the American scholar's day of "apprenticeship" and "dependence" was coming to an end. But then, swiftly, he dropped back into a reassuring conformity with tradition and its prescriptions: he tranquilly agreed to "accept the topic which not only usage, but the nature of our association, seem to prescribe to this day."

Throughout the lecture, Emerson repeated this kind of maneuver, moving deftly from safe and predictable ground to language that was meant to jolt and even threaten, but then coming to rest again in the familiar and congenial. For example, when he came to his discussion of the relationship between the scholar and nature – about 10 minutes into the lecture – he put himself on a kind of verbal trapeze, swinging between sentences meant to unsettle and sentences meant to calm. He introduced the subject of nature in sentence fragments that might shock any audience familiar with the Old Testament's association of beholding with begetting:

> Every day, the sun; and, after sunset, night and her stars. Ever the winds blow; ever the grass grows. Every day, men and women, conversing, beholding and beholden.

But no sooner did he provoke his audience with this gesture toward what he called the "unintelligible" than he introduced the figure of the scholar, not caught up in the holding and beholding at all, but musing over it, assessing it, and from a very safe distance. "The scholar must needs stand wistful and admiring before this great spectacle. He must settle its value in his mind." Then, a minute later, he was churning the audience again, offering them a picture of a feminized nature infinitely turbulent:

> Far, too, as her splendors shine, system on system shooting like rays, upward, downward, without centre, without circumference, – in the mass and in the particle nature hastens . . .

But what this out-of-control nature was hastening *to* turned out to be quite safe. Nature hastens only to a "mind," cool and assessing. The sentence ended, lamely, ". . . hastens to render account of herself to the mind." "Classification begins," he went on. And it turned out that what the scholar was to do with nature – by classifying – was to discover law, not random "shooting . . . upward, downward." So Emerson made clear, what he had in mind was really something that would lead to astronomy, chemistry, and the other familiar subjects of the curriculum. But then, as soon as he had given this innocent cast to the relationship between the scholar and nature, he swung again toward the misty and dreamlike. All science finally leads to the same conclusion, he said: nature and mind have the same "root." So the true scholar sees that what he shares with nature is a common fundament, which is nothing less than the "soul of his soul." And – just in case anyone did not see that this was a radical idea – he characterized it himself:

"A thought too bold," he insisted, "a dream too wild." But then, to complete the rhetorical circuit, he gently lowered himself and his audience from this carefully framed verbal climax back onto stable ground. Was not their ancient precept "Know thyself"? And was not the current conventional wisdom "Study nature"? Well then, his doctrine of the unity of mind and nature was nothing more than a recognition that these two unexceptionable "precepts" were in fact "one maxim." Solid comfort indeed for an audience that lived off precept and maxim, and for whom a nature in which men and women beheld and were beholden, or a nature that shot rays without center or circumference, might seem an uninvited and unwelcome guest in any lecture hall.

Emerson followed this same strategy throughout the talk – as he would do throughout his career. Again and again, he shifted into phrases that anyone in the audience might suspect *ought* to be shocking, then back out again, into formulas that were amply sanctioned by tradition and usage. He, a manifestly bookish man, told his equally bookish audience that books could be "noxious," both for ordinary people and for scholars. "The sluggish and perverted mind of the multitude" takes its stand on some book. Men of intellect do worse, even. They found colleges, build libraries, form churches, and ordain ministers. Emerson passed his judgment on this tendency in what was probably the most flat-footed sentence he ever spoke: "This is bad; this is worse than it seems." But he still assured them, implicitly, that learning really was legitimate and important – invoking the name of one revered author after another as evidence that his own work was firmly grounded on years of devoted reading.

A little further on, he let fly his most dangerous rhetorical "arrow" by making a rude gesture toward ministers. He set the stage for the gesture by saying that it was common wisdom that men of letters were as unfit for real work "as a penknife for an axe." A penknife was still, of course, a knife used to prepare quill pens, so the image was apt. But the simile also had potentially sexual implications, and Emerson quickly worked them out. He said (as though he were just innocently repeating an ugly but common rumor) that he had "heard" an unpleasant thing about ministers. The rumor was that the clergy are "addressed as women." (There is no way to know, of course, how clearly he pronounced the "a" in "addressed.") He had heard, he said, that ministers were fit to hear only "mincing and diluted speech." Indeed, he went on, "there are advocates for their celibacy." The audience must have strained forward a bit, wondering where such threatening language might lead. But, as it would turn out, Emerson was headed toward a final conclusion in which any minister, any earnest middle-class American audience, would take comfort.

Even this conclusion, though, would involve its own alternation between the shocking and the tame. He began his closing with a radical-sounding condemnation of American culture. The "spirit" of Americans was "already suspected to be timid, imitative, tame." The very air was made "thick and fat" by greed, both in public and private life. "The mind of this country, taught to aim at low objects, eats upon itself." The scholars were no better than the rest of the people; they were "decent, indolent, complaisant." And for young men of talent and promise, for the "thousands" of potential artists, poets, and scholars who were "crowding to the barriers for the career," the result was "tragic." There is no work for any but the decorous and the complaisant." So young men of promise can only be "hindered from action by the disgust which the principles on which business is managed inspire, and turn drudges, or die of disgust, – some of them suicides."

The point could hardly have been more emphatic. He hammered away, even repeating "complaisant" and "disgust" within seconds, as though he were at a loss for words. He went to his own rhetorical limit with this indictment of the business society of his day, of its "avarice" and its disgusting "principles." He surely read his own words calmly, but the words themselves might have been written by some angry prophet who had been "inflated by the mountain winds, shined upon by all the stars of God," and then come down from that mountain to condemn the thick and fat world.

But there was no possibility that he might leave the matter here. He was clearly determined to honor the opinions and mental habits of his audience. So he was bound to end more gently, and in safety, bound to offer a mild, painless cure for the "tragic" social and cultural disease he had just diagnosed. He had no choice but to ask, as he now did, "What is the remedy?" In his answer, he could return his audience to terrain more cultivated than the lexical fens of "avarice," "disgust," and "suicide." And so he did. As a "remedy," he counseled softly, "Patience – patience." He counseled the scholar to take comfort in the fact that he was not alone, for he had the company of "the shades of all the good and great" – presumably the ghosts of Plato, Chaucer, Shakespeare, Goethe, and the rest. He also offered "solace" in terms vague enough to calm any fear that he might recommend a real change in the way scholars actually behaved in the world: he told them to be consoled by "the perspective of your own infinite life." The "work" he offered his audience was as vague as the solace. But to this concourse of ministers, would-be ministers, and might-have-been ministers, it was a most familiar idea of work. Their task, Emerson said, was "the study and the communication of principles." And if this labor could make "good instincts prevalent," they might bring about the "conversion of the world."

Now Emerson had only one brief turn left, one more swing from a hint of anarchy to a resolution in tried formulas. He told his audience they were all "units" – that is, discrete individuals – who could not be lumped together and "reckoned" as a class, a party, or a section. No, they were all separate, private men, each of whom could walk on his own feet, work with his own hands, speak his own mind. But, lest this suggest that he was promoting eccentricity and idiosyncrasy, he invoked two formulas that made it perfectly clear that he was not encouraging private excesses: first, he addressed them familiarly as "brothers and friends"; then he said they would go into the world as independent individuals, "please God." With this benediction securely in place, he finished with a vision of the future admirably designed to leave no doubt as to his own suitability, not only for this lecture and for the coming dinner and its toast to concord, but also for a career lecturing to audiences composed overwhelmingly of morally earnest and earnestly moral middle-class men and women. "A nation of men," he said, "will for the first time exist, because each believes himself inspired by the Divine Soul which also inspires all men."

This careful technique served Emerson and his audiences very well, and for decades. It served his many adoring readers, too. It helps explain how the published lectures could find a place of honor in the staidest libraries of the Victorian middle class, but could also become the highly treasured reading of so violent a critic of middle-class morality as Friedrich Nietzsche. Both Nietzsche and the most adoring and pious Victorian readers were right. Emerson worked diligently to be sure that his work contained both sorts of "wisdom." That was his formula for the "magic" he wanted to work. That, more than any particular and idiosyncratic set of tricks with words, really *was* his style.

NOTES

1   Oliver Wendell Holmes, *Ralph Waldo Emerson* (Boston: 1884), p. 65.
2   Edith E. W. Gregg, ed., *The Letters of Ellen Tucker Emerson*, 2 vols. (Kent, Ohio: 1982), 1: 658.
3   Entry for October 6, 1834, in William H. Gilman et al., eds., *The Journals and Miscellaneous Notebooks of Ralph Waldo Emerson*, 16 vols. (Cambridge, MA: 1960–82). All quotations from these wonderfully edited volumes will be cited as *JMN*, with the volume number and the date of the entry.
4   *JMN* 5: 286 (February, 1837).
5   Quoted in Carlos Baker, *Emerson Among the Eccentrics: A Group Portrait* (New York: 1996), p. 399.
6   *JMN* 7: 338–39 (February 19, 1840).
7   *JMN* 7: 271 (October 18, 1839). *Emerson in His Journals*, ed. Joel Porte (Cambridge, MA: 1982), p. 227.

8 *JMN* 7: 339 (February 19, 1840).

9 *JMN* 7: 271 (October 18, 1839).

10 *JMN* 2: 237 (April 18, 1824).

11 *JMN* 3: 149–50 (January 17, 1829).

12 This sermon was written into Emerson's journal in June of 1827, during his first year as a licensed minister. See *JMN* 3: 91.

13 Quoted in James Elliot Cabot, *A Memoir of Ralph Waldo Emerson*, 2 vols. (Boston: 1895), 1: 174.

14 *JMN* 4: 237 (September 6, 1833).

15 All quotes on the following several pages are (unless otherwise noted), from the "Introduction" and "Chapter 1." The edition I have used is Warner Berthoff, ed., *"Nature"* . . . *A Facsimile of the First Edition* (New York: 1968).

16 *JMN* 4: 27 (January, 1832).

17 "Self-Reliance," in Edward W. Emerson, ed., *The Complete Works*, 12 vols. (Boston: 1903–4), 2: 58.

18 *JMN* 7: 270–71 (October 18, 1839).

19 *JMN* 13: 270 (December, 1853).

20 Ellen Tucker Emerson, *Life of Lidian Jackson Emerson* (Boston: 1984), p. 47.

21 *JMN* 5: 5 (January, 1835).

22 *JMN* 7: 227 (July 7, 1839).

23 All quotations in the following discussion of the Phi Beta Kappa address are taken from the version printed in Robert Spiller, Alfred Ferguson, et al., eds., *The Collected Works of Ralph Waldo Emerson*, vol. 1 (Cambridge, MA: 1971–   ), pp. 52–70.

5

ROBERT D. RICHARDSON, JR.

Emerson and Nature

Explicit or implicit in nearly everything Emerson wrote is the conviction that nature bats last, that nature is the law, the final word, the supreme court. Others have believed – still believe – that the determining force in our lives is grace, or that it is the state – the polis, the community – or that it is the past. More recently it has been argued that the central force is economics or race or sex or genetics. Emerson's basic teaching is that the fundamental context of our lives is nature.

Emerson's definition of nature is a broad one. Nature is the way things are. Philosophically, Emerson says, the universe is made up of nature and the soul, or nature and consciousness. Everything that is *not me* is nature; nature thus includes nature (in the common sense of the green world), art, all other persons, and my own body.

Emerson's interest in nature was more than theoretical. Like his friends Alcott and Thoreau, Emerson was passionately attached to the natural world. "The mind," says Alcott, speaking for them all, "craves the view of mountain, ocean, forest, lake and plain, the open horizon, the firmament – an actual contact with the elements." As a boy, Emerson rambled in the woods and fields outside Boston. As a young man, he thought for a while of becoming a naturalist. As a father, he took his children on nature walks and taught them all the flowers and birds and trees. All his life his interest in nature was rooted in his delight in and close observation of nature. Of one sunrise he wrote, "the long slender bars of cloud float like fishes in the sea of crimson light." Of a particularly fine January sunset, he wrote, "The western clouds divided and subdivided themselves into pink flakes modulated with tints of unspeakable softness; and the air had so much life and sweetness, that it was a pain to come within doors. . . . The leafless trees become spires of flame in the sunset, with the blue east for their background, and the stars of the dead calices of flowers, and every withered stem and stubble rimed with frost contribute something to the mute music."[1]

The decisive moment in Emerson's interest in nature came in 1832, in Paris, when he was 29. He had trained for the Unitarian ministry, and in 1829 became the minister of Boston's Second Church. At about the same time he fell in love with and married a beautiful young woman named Ellen Tucker, who hoped to become a poet. But Ellen died in 1831, after they had been married only a year and a half. This tragic event, together with Emerson's growing interest in science, especially astronomy, led him to question seriously what he called "historical Christianity." In May 1832, he told his congregation, "I regard it as the irresistible effect of the Copernican astronomy to have made the theological scheme of redemption absolutely incredible."[2]

Emerson resigned from his church, gave up his house, sold his furniture, relocated his mother, and sailed for Europe. After an eight-month tour of Italy and a quick trip through Switzerland and France, he found himself in Paris gazing at the vast and wonderful exhibits in the Jardin des Plantes, where he experienced a vocational epiphany. He observed in his journal that "the Universe is a more amazing puzzle than ever as you glance along this bewildering series of animated forms – the hazy butterflies, the carved shells, the birds, beasts, fishes, insects, snakes – & the upheaving principle of life everywhere incipient in the very rock aping organized forms."[3] Not only were the specimens in the exhibits linked to each other, they were also linked to him. Perhaps for the first time since the death of Ellen, Emerson felt an agitated, sympathetic – almost physical – connection with the natural world. He was powerfully stirred. "I feel the centipede in me – cayman, carp, eagle & fox. I am moved by strange sympathies, I say continually 'I will be a naturalist'."[4]

When Emerson returned home and began a new career as a public lecturer, the first subject he took up was science, which he understood as the study of nature. But Emerson never became a scientist, or even a naturalist, not in the semiliterary way Thoreau did, and certainly not in the way his cousin, George B. Emerson, author of a standard botany of Massachusetts, did. Emerson had, however, a daily and a detailed knowledge of the natural world, as his family and friends testified. He taught his children how to recognize the birds by their songs. He knew the names of all the plants; he took daily walks to Walden Pond. He loved the word *lespedeza*, his daughter recalled, and he would say it over and over as a sort of homemade Yankee mantra. Emerson was an avid gardener and orchard keeper. He planted trees to mark his children's birthdays. He grew many varieties of apple, pear, and quince, although he did so with more enthusiasm than skill. His son recalled how the local botanical society launched an inquiry into how Emerson could get such poor results from such splendid stock.

Emerson remained interested in the sciences all his life. He read in geology, astronomy, chemistry, and, above all, botany. He was a friend of Louis Agassiz, who was the leading scientist of his time, and he kept up with new discoveries and controversies. As Dirk Struik, a modern historian of New England's contributions to science, has observed, Emerson's warm interest in science – his hospitable openness to it – was itself a real contribution, because it helped to create an intellectual atmosphere in which there is no necessary gulf between science and the humanities, no structural reason for the existence of the "two cultures" described by C. P. Snow in his famous essay of 1956. What science and the humanities have in common, Emerson argued, is a perennial interest in nature.

The most important result of Emerson's long engagement with nature was the publication in 1836 of the small book he called *Nature*. Its opening paragraph represents a turning point, not only in American literature, but also in his own life. It records the moment when Emerson turned explicitly and self-consciously from biography, history, and criticism to nature for his starting point. Reading the first paragraph of *Nature* has brought about a similar shake-up in many a reader as well. "Our age is retrospective," he begins. "It builds the sepulchres of the fathers. It writes biographies, histories, and criticism." Emerson clears the agenda with a dismissive sweep, pointing out that "the foregoing generations beheld God and nature face to face; we, through their eyes." The question Emerson incites us to ask is "Why should not we also enjoy an original relation to the universe?" The emphasis is on the word *also*. "Why should not *we* have a poetry and philosophy of insight and not of tradition, and a religion by revelation to *us*, and not the history of *theirs?*"[5]

Pursuing his own question, Emerson sets out the main benefits we derive from nature, and from putting nature first. In the chapter called "Commodity," he considers how nature provides the raw material and the energy for everything we build, grow, or eat. Who can fail to be impressed by "the steady and prodigal provision that has been made for his support and delight on this green ball which floats through the heavens?" It was the practical usefulness of nature that Emerson had in mind as he admired a tide-mill, "which, on the seashore, makes the tides drive the wheels and grind corn, and which thus engages the assistance of the moon like a hired hand, to grind, and wind, and pump, and saw, and split stone, and roll iron." And it was a typical leap of imagination for Emerson to draw from this activity his much-repeated injunction to "hitch your wagon to a star," which gains its full force when we see that the emphasis is on the word *your*. But nature as commodity is only the most obvious and most tangible of benefits, and Emerson quickly moves on to the less-material gifts of nature.[6]

In the chapter called "Beauty," he outlines a theory of aesthetics grounded in nature. "Such is the constitution of things, or such the plastic power of the human eye, that the primary forms, as the sky, the mountain, the tree, the animal, give us a delight *in and for themselves.*" Nature provides us our first and most reliable standards of beauty. "Nature is a sea of forms," he says, and "the standard of beauty is the entire circuit of natural forms." This is a fundamental proposition, a given, an "ultimate end." "No reason can be asked or given why the soul seeks beauty," says Emerson. It cannot be explained, but is itself the explanation for other things.

Just as nature provides us with our standard of beauty (Emerson's natural aesthetic can be traced from Henry Thoreau and Horatio Greenough to Frederick Church, Frank Lloyd Wright, and Edward Weston and John Cage), so *Nature* provides us with language and with an explanation of the use of language. Emerson goes further; for him, nature *is* language. "Nature is the vehicle of thought" is his formulation. Certainly for writers – and perhaps for everyone – this is the central chapter of Emerson's central book. To begin with, Emerson shows how "words are signs of natural facts." Not only does "apple" stand for an apple, but most abstractions, when traced to their origins, will be found to have roots in the visible, the concrete, the tangible. *Sierra* means saw, "supercilious" is from the Latin *super cilia,* meaning raised eyebrow. "Experience" goes back to Latin *periculum* and so means something won or snatched from danger. So, as Emerson will say later in his essay "The Poet" (to which the book *Nature* is linked by the underground river of Emerson's interest in language), language is fossil poetry. It is noteworthy that Emerson's ideas about language were picked up in England by Richard Trench and led, perhaps indirectly, to the undertaking of the *Oxford English Dictionary.*[7]

The next step of Emerson's argument is the most difficult, the most philosophically limiting, and, for the writer, the most exciting point. The writer understands, says Emerson, that "it is not words only that are emblematic; it is things which are emblematic." He fills a paragraph with examples. "Who looks upon a river in a meditative hour, and is not reminded of the flux of all things? Throw a stone into the stream, and the circles that propagate themselves are the beautiful type of all influence." What writers understand is "this immediate dependence of language upon nature." What writers do is "this conversion of an outward phenomenon onto a type of somewhat [something] in human life."[8]

What Emerson understood, and what American writers since Emerson have been able to get from him, is the importance of the primary connection between the writer and nature. Emerson puts it with unusual vehemence. "Hundreds of writers may be found in every long-civilized nation, who for a short time believe, and make others believe, that they see and utter truths, who do not of themselves clothe one thought in its natural garment, but who feed unconsciously on the language created by the primary writers of the country, those, namely, who hold primarily on nature."⁹

The essence of language then is imagery. For this reason "good writing and brilliant discourse are perpetual allegories." The reason we love imagery and respond to it is not just that language is a vast river of images, but also that nature itself is the inexhaustible upstream reservoir and source of all the rivers of language. "The world is emblematic," Emerson says. "Parts of speech are metaphors, because the whole of nature is a metaphor of the human mind." Every mind can claim all of nature for its material.[10]

Emerson is an idealist, a believer that process, purpose, or concept precedes and determines product. The most daring, and to a modern reader, the most challenging aspect of Emerson's nature, is his argument that nature teaches him to look beyond nature. To put it more carefully, he says that the beauty and interrelatedness of physical, outward nature leads him to inquire into the inner laws of nature which determine the outer appearances.

"In my utter impotence to test the authenticity of the report of my senses, to know whether the impressions they make on me correspond with outlying objects, what difference does it make, whether Orion is up there in heaven, or some god paints the image in the firmament of the soul?" Conceding that phenomena are real enough whether they objectively exist or exist only in the mind, Emerson pushes on to contend that "it is the uniform effect of culture [education, consciousness] on the human mind, not to shake our faith in the stability of particular phenomena, as of heat, water, azote [nitrogen]; but to lead us to regard nature as a phenomenon, not a substance; to attribute necessary existence to spirit; to esteem nature [that is, external nature] as an accident and an effect."[11]

The distinction Emerson makes here between the inner, invisible *laws* of nature, and the external, visible *forms* of nature is not a new one. The English Romantic poets, especially Coleridge, recognized a similar distinction between *natura naturans* (nature as a collection of active forces and processes) and *natura naturata* (the finished products of nature, natural objects). Perhaps Emerson's greatest contribution was his account of how these two aspects of nature are interrelated. His lifelong endeavor was to show how the laws and processes of nature are part of mind, and to work out the relation between mind and external nature. Emerson was, finally, a naturalist of mental more than of physical facts. Beginning around 1848, he worked on and off for the rest of his life on a project he called "Natural History of Intellect."

Like all thorough romantics, and like the new scientists from Goethe to Lyell and Darwin, Emerson understood that nature is in continuous change or flux. "There are no fixtures in nature," he wrote in "Circles." "The universe is fluid and volatile. Permanence is but a word of degrees." He understood nature to be a process rather than a thing. "Thus there is no sleep, no pause, no preservation, but all things renew, germinate and spring." His view of nature as dynamic also explains his preference for nature over history. "In nature every moment is new; the past is always swallowed and forgotten; the coming only is sacred. Nothing is secure but life, transition, the energizing spirit."[12]

As much as Emerson was committed to the idea that all is flux – an idea he called "the metamorphosis" – and as much as he was committed to the pluralistic, the diverse, and the particular, he also understood that there were laws governing appearances and that things in nature are unified and whole, though not always in obvious ways. "Everything in nature contains all the powers of nature," he wrote in "Compensation." "Every thing is made of one hidden stuff, as the naturalist sees one type under every metamorphosis."[13]

The central point, the pivot of Emerson's understanding of nature, is his conception of the all-encompassing relationship that exists at all times between the mind – understood as a more or less constant, classifying power – and the infinite variety of external nature. He had read Kant and Schelling and was echoing Kant when he wrote in "The Oversoul" that "the sources of nature are in [man's] own mind." He knew Schelling's breathtaking all-inclusive proposal that "nature is externalized mind; mind is internalized nature." In "The American Scholar" Emerson said that "nature is the opposite of the soul, answering to it part for part. One is seal and one is print. Its beauty is the beauty of his own mind. Its laws are the laws of his own mind. So much of nature as he [the scholar] is ignorant of, so much of his own mind does he not yet possess." In "Compensation" he wrote, "each new form repeats not only the main character of the type, but part for part all the details, all the aims, furtherances, hindrances, energies and whole system of every other. Every occupation, trade, art, transaction, is a compend of the world, and a correlative of every other. Each one is an entire emblem of human life; of its good and ill, its trials, its enemies, its course and its end."[14]

This radical and comprehensive connection between nature and mind is the unwobbling pivot, the fundamental condition of most of Emerson's work, and it explains why he can turn to nature for his starting point on virtually any subject. We can touch here only on a few of the most important.

Nature was Emerson's starting point for a new theology. His rejection, in the Divinity School "Address," of organized – or as he called it, historical – Christianity was a protest not against, but on behalf of, religion. Following the Scottish Common Sense philosophers, Emerson argued that the "moral sentiment," which is found in all human beings, "is the essence of all religions." By religion, Emerson means concrete, personal, religious feelings or experience. "The intuition of the moral sentiment is an insight into the perfection of the laws of the soul." Intuition is, for Emerson, like religion, a matter of actual, present personal experience. "It cannot be received at second hand. Truly speaking it is not instruction, but provocation, that I can receive from another soul. What he announces, I must find true in me, or wholly reject: and on his word, or as his second, be he who he may," be he Jesus or Moses, or Paul, or Augustine, "I can accept nothing." Thus revelation must be revelation to me or to you. "Men have come to speak of the revelation as somewhat [something] long ago given and done, as if God were dead." But if there is a God then he is present now in all of us, Emerson believes. "It is the office of a true teacher to show us that God is, not was, that he speaketh, not spake." Emerson is not interested in second-hand revelations, secondhand gospel. For this reason he never refers to the Bible as an authority. He cares about what he calls the "Gospel of the present moment." He rejects the standard Christian chronological concept of history, the idea that there was one creation, that there will be one day of judgment. Religious convictions and feelings, like all others, exist for Emerson only in the present.

Thus he says "there is no profane history . . . all history is sacred." Creation is continuous. Every day is a day of creation. So, too, with the day of judgment. "No man has learned anything until he has learned that every day is judgment day." Noting that the Hebrew word for prophet is also the word for poet, Emerson insists that the modern poet can do for his people what the old Hebrew prophet-poets did for theirs. (Walt Whitman was listening.) The incarnation means God takes on flesh in every person, not just in one. When Emerson writes that "infancy is the perpetual Messiah," he means that the power of the concept of the Messiah is the hope and promise we feel in every infant. Because we live in nature, Emerson believes we can see God every day, face to face. He will have none of the disabling, through-a-glass-darkly dirge of lamentation. As he expresses it in his finest lyric poem, "Days," the days themselves are gods, bringing to each of us gifts according to our capacity to receive. Every day offers us new kingdoms, powers, and glories. It is on our own heads if we settle out of court for a few herbs and apples.[15]

Nature is also Emerson's practical guide to an ethical life. In this he is a modern stoic. He believed, like Marcus Aurelius and Montaigne, that nature rather than tradition or authority or the state is our best teacher. To live in nature means above all to live in the present, to seize the day. "Life only avails, not the having lived," he says in "Self-Reliance." "Power ceases in the instant of repose; it resides in the moment of transition from a past to a new state, in the shooting of the gulf."[16]

Nature for Emerson was a theory of the nature of things – how things are; it was a guide to life, a foundation for philosophy, art, language, education, and everyday living. "Nature is what you may do." It was the green world of gardens and parks, and the wild world of the sea and the woods. Above all, and running through all his thought on the subject, nature was for Emerson the experience of nature. Some of the most often-cited passages in Emerson's writings are accounts of immediate physical experiences. "Crossing a bare common, in snow puddles, at twilight, under a clouded sky, without having in my thought any occurrence of special good fortune, I have enjoyed a perfect exhilaration. I am glad to the brink of fear." Even the famous passage about becoming a transparent eyeball is best understood not as a theory of nature, but as an actual moment of experience, a feeling. Emerson devoted an entire essay to this aspect of nature. It is called "The Method of Nature." To a post-Darwinian reader, the title inevitably suggests a discussion of evolution, or the formation of elements beginning with hydrogen. The essay is, however, about the human experiencing of nature, which is, at its most intense, a state Emerson calls "ecstasy." By ecstasy he does not mean a technical out-of-body experience, but a joyous consciousness of the rich plenitude of existence. He speaks of the "redundancy or excess of life which in conscious beings we call ecstasy." "Surely joy is the condition of life," said Thoreau, and Emerson agreed, saying "Life is an ecstasy." For Emerson the feeling of joy was a state of ecstasy which, in his lexicon, meant nearly the same thing as "enthusiasm," that other key to a fully lived life. "Nothing great was ever achieved without enthusiasm," he said in "Circles," adding that "the way of life is wonderful: it is by abandonment." When we are in this state of heightened awareness, of enthusiasm, of ecstasy, we come as close to the secret heart of nature as we can get. The important thing about your enthusiasm for nature – or for Emerson – is the enthusiasm in you. This is the highest and most valuable teaching of that nature we all agree we cannot do without. As Emerson says in "Illusions," the permanent interest of every person is "never to be in a false position, but to have the weight of nature to back him in all that he does."[17]

NOTES

1   Amos Bronson Alcott, "Report of the School Committee, 1861" in *Essays on Education,* ed. Walter Harding (Gainesville, FL: Scholars' Facsimiles and Reprints, 1960), p. 189. R. W. Emerson, *Nature,* in *Essays and Lectures* (New York: Viking Press, The Library of America, 1983), p. 15.

2   R. W. Emerson, *Journals and Miscellaneous Notebooks,* vol. 4, ed. Wm. H. Gilman et al. (Cambridge, MA: Harvard University Press, 1964), p. 26.

3   Cited in Robert D. Richardson, Jr., *Emerson: The Mind on Fire* (Berkeley: University of California Press, 1995), p. 208.

4   *JMN* 4, pp. 198, 199, 200.

5   Emerson, *Nature,* in *Essays and Lectures,* p. 7, emphasis added.

6   R. W. Emerson, "Civilization," in *Society and Solitude* (Cambridge, MA: Riverside Press, 1904), p. 30.

7   Richard Trench, *On the Study of Words,* 22d ed. (New York: Macmillan, 1900, orig. 1851), p. 5. In earlier editions RWE is not named but is identified as "a popular American author."

8   Emerson, *Nature,* in *Essays and Lectures,* pp. 20, 21, 22.

9   Emerson, *Nature,* in *Essays and Lectures,* pp. 22–23.

10 Emerson, *Nature,* in *Essays and Lectures,* pp. 23, 24.

11 Emerson, *Nature,* in *Essays and Lectures,* pp. 32, 33.

12 Emerson, "Circles," in *Essays and Lectures,* pp. 403, 412–13.

13 Emerson, "Compensation," in *Essays and Lectures,* p. 289.

14 Emerson, "The Oversoul," in *Essays and Lectures,* p. 399; "The American Scholar," in *Essays and Lectures,* p. 56; "Compensation," in *Essays and Lectures,* p. 289.

15 Emerson, "An Address . . ." in *Essays and Lectures,* pp. 76, 79, 88; "The Oversoul," in *Essays and Lectures,* p. 400; "Days," in *Collected Poems and Translations* (New York: Viking Press, The Library of America, 1994), p. 178.

16 Emerson, "Self-Reliance," in *Essays and Lectures,* p. 271.

17 Emerson, "Fate," in *Essays and Lectures,* pp. 949, 963; "The Method of Nature," in *Essays and Lectures,* p. 121; "Circles," in *Essays and Lectures,* p. 414; "Illusions," in *Essays and Lectures,* p. 1122.

6

ALBERT J. VON FRANK

Essays: First Series (1841)

As far as the spiritual character of the period overpowers the artist, and finds expression in his work, so far it will retain a certain grandeur, and will represent to future beholders the Unknown, the Inevitable, the Divine.

Ralph Waldo Emerson, "Art"[1]

Without superstitious reference to the Bible – indeed, without the slightest veneration of any scripture – Emerson yet writes in the tradition of the wisdom literature of the Old Testament, of Proverbs and Ecclesiastes. He is concerned, as the prophets were, with the relation of spirit and human behavior, of right seeing and right living, the perfection of justice, and the power that comes into human beings when they yield to the truth. Too polite and civilized to be a Jeremiah in style, Emerson nevertheless sees his audience as worshiping false gods and as laboring under a compensatory punishment for their general disloyalty to the regime of spirit. His work is restoration. He finds the sacred quarantined in small religious redoubts, calls it out, makes it credible, and broadcasts it lavishly over the landscape. We watch this process in astonishment.

Emerson had offered *Nature* (1836) as a theoretical preface to work, already planned, in the essay form: when he mailed a copy of this manifesto to Carlyle, he called it "an entering wedge . . . for something more worthy and significant."[2] Retrospectively, we may say that *Nature* describes the stance or point of view of the essayist and prepares the audience to accept further reports from that quarter. In this function *Nature* sustains much the same relationship to *Essays* (later called *Essays: First Series*) as Whitman's Preface in *Leaves of Grass* does to the "Song of Myself." The need, in both cases, for some sort of preliminary statement is documented in the bemused and uncomprehending responses of many early reviewers, which in turn are an index of how much Emerson's expression, like Whitman's, posed a real challenge to the conventional thought of the day.

It may be that every valuable book makes report of some world the reader is not already possessed of, but few such books are as deliberate or as self-conscious as Emerson's *Essays* in setting all that is familiar in the world of the reader against the vision of the author. The coherence of the volume can be (and has been) made out in various ways, but it lies most obviously in the promise that Emerson's singular point of view will settle a similar glory on every mundane subject it renovatingly touches, one after another, in successive essays.

Readers today, as in 1841, turn to the opening chapter on "History" with convictions in place as to the meaning of the topic – generally some form of the prejudice that history is, onerously, the factual record of other people's doings in other times in far-off alien places. Emerson shows us that it is just this arbitrary insistence on "othering" that makes for the wearisome impertinence of history as ordinarily received. How was it determined that we have no property in the fortitude of saints or the inquisitiveness of explorers, no share in the courage or willfulness of conquering soldiers? How did we come to decide that we are not ourselves, always, the heroes and victims of the world drama, and rightly entitled therefore to the praise or blame for all that is human? Popular religion in Emerson's day maintained that all individuals were fully represented in that famous first fault of Adam and Eve, but no living individual was held to be similarly implicated in the discoveries of Columbus, say, or Luther or Newton. Yet to Emerson what the human spirit does through its multitude of individual agents cannot be alien or "other" to the observing human spirit. If we are alive, it must be *human* life that we live, so that, in consequence, we never watch anything in history but ourselves. That we respond at all comprehendingly to foreign traits and fates shows that their ground plan has been in us all along – shows us that, as Emerson says in his book's first sentence, "There is one mind common to all individual men" (3).

The modern feeling of unconnectedness or alienation, according to Emerson, has its source in a personal disloyalty to the regime of spirit, in that rebellious mood he calls "skepticism." We *choose* to regard the world as wholly material rather than as an affair of impalpable ideas, meanings, virtues, values, and spirit – and then complain, in T. S. Eliot's phrase, that we "can connect / Nothing with nothing." We come to Emerson's essay already understanding, in our genially concessive way, that history is the record of human accomplishment in time – and yet there is no slightest shock of recognition, no spontaneous sense of affinity. Its facts are a burden. It lies there "behind" us, a useless and unmanageable heap, while the popular metaphors – "dustbin," "dead hand" – eclipse older associations of history with immortality. If Emerson's essay changes our relation to history, gives it life and circulation, puts it in us and around us, it does so by defining "human" in spiritual terms. The regime of spirit is recommended, by implication, as the only ground on which connection, affiliation, and meaning can reasonably be expected to operate at all, and the only basis on which we can possess our history as anything *but* a burden. We say, after this first essay (as after the others): How much finer the world looks from these premises than from my accustomed ones!

If the first essay enlarges the reader by provoking him to occupy the whole range of human history, to dilate to the dimensions of all mankind, the second makes him more personally authentic by teaching him to inhabit himself. "Self-Reliance" is the more dramatic for taking up the case of the self that is intimidated by history and deferential to it, that has not the right relation of identity to circumstance. The indictment of that person leaves no person unblamed.

Where does the self come from? We may doubt that we are born with one, but if we are not, then who learns it, who acquires it? We are so in love with alienation that we think of the self as a secret which for better or worse no other self wholly knows or shares in. We tend therefore to suspect the notion that "there is one mind common to all men," and wonder how, if that were true, we could speak of selves at all. The "one mind" is that which agrees that justice is preferable to injustice, truth to falsehood, courage to fear; it is not any sum total of facts and experiences, but a mere pointing back to a divine origin. This we are born with and it marks us as human. Emerson calls it the soul, which he defines as "light; where it is, is day; where it was, is night" (38). The self is not, as Locke would have it, a compound of what we see; it is, rather, what we see *with*.

Emerson supposes that our individual or biographical selves are works in progress. In the struggle for self-realization, as in other, less important struggles, some events are hindrances and others are furtherances. Our judgments about the phenomena are tutelary, so that, by practice, it should come to be oftener day with us than night. It follows that it cannot matter much what in particular we see, so long as our particular world is bathed in light. Unwrapping the metaphor, then, the great-souled man sees more (has more life) than others (have we not suspected it?), and experience, or life in time, is for all a never-to-be-completed struggle for just this kind of enlargement.

Those whose sight is dominated by or in service to some vision not their own are to that extent colonized and disadvantaged in the struggle for self-realization; they repudiate the great gift of life and kill themselves in their haste to live for others. "Society . . . is in conspiracy against the manhood of every one of its members," as Emerson said (29), because its main business is to enlist you under this banner or that, so as to keep your hands off any banner of your own. "I am ashamed to think how easily we capitulate to badges and names, to large societies and dead institutions" (30). But if we are not content to be colonized by the external requirements of family, church, social position, occupation, and political party – if we are dismayed at the thought of having constantly to negotiate the emergent conflicts of a multitude of incoherent affiliations – where, if not from these sources, are we to "get a life"? Emerson says: From the access that we all have to things timeless and unaccidental, from the original source of life, or the regime of spirit, where, if anywhere, native coherence is, and the home of truth and beauty. If we conform to that, we come into possession of what, by virtue of having it, makes us human, and without which we are "not false in a few particulars, authors of a few lies, but false in all particulars" (32). Self-trust (or self-reliance) is nothing other than an operative belief that the self has an innate capacity in the direction of truth, coupled with the courage to explore it, even at the cost of appearing ridiculous to the neighbors.

If the first two essays consider the relation of the individual to the regime of spirit in word and deed, the next two – "Compensation" and "Spiritual Laws" – take up the nature of the regime itself. "Compensation" begins with a humorously satirical account of the misrepresentation of spirit by a dead (or spiritless) tradition embodied in an orthodox preacher, perhaps the same who is pilloried in "Self-Reliance." The good, says this preacher in Emerson's paraphrase, shall have the same sort of fun in the next world as sinners have in this. Heaven, that is to say, is a delayed recompense for the otherwise unrewarded and insupportable trials of earthly virtue. Emerson sees this popular view not only as a superstition, but (what is really the same thing) as a materialist's understanding of the workings of the spirit.

"Justice is not postponed," says Emerson (60), because the essential moral unity that pervades the universe and comprises its law does not permit accumulations of debits or credits. Accounts are always balanced. To believe otherwise is to believe that effects can be disunited from causes and means and ends divorced. "Has a man gained any thing," he asks, "who has received a hundred favors and rendered none?" (65). Ordinary life – the life of the implied reader – is an inevitably disappointed search for advantages in a world of rigorous polarities; against the "absolute balance of Give and Take" (67), we search for a preponderance of Take, only to find in the end that our gains, at best, about equal our losses. But the self that engages in this selfish game also overlooks it and is instructed and improved by it, by victories and defeats in equal measure. For such gains in wisdom and virtue there is no penalty, because we have moved out of the realm of addition and subtraction, out of circumstance altogether, and into the realm of authentic life and real being. "In a virtuous action, I properly *am*" is Emerson's psychologically credible way of asserting the divine identity of man (71).

The astonishment belonging to any good reading of Emerson's essays is an effect of the utter antagonism between his positions and the corresponding positions of popular Christianity, and, simultaneously, of the degree to which Emerson is felt to have the better of the argument. "Spiritual Laws" offers another good example. Just as the reader of "History" thinks he knows what history is, so the conventionally religious reader of "Spiritual Laws" thinks of law as something imposed from above by a powerful alien deity to keep our criminal nature in check. But in Emerson's thought law and nature are not opponents, but expressions each of the other. Law is not laid on the world as a punitive afterthought but is the necessary idea from which creation in all its beauty and balance first springs. Law is simply the nature of a thing (as science was then showing), and the law of a self is the nature or character of that self, "a method, a progressive arrangement, a selecting principle" (84). Spiritual laws, therefore, are not hidden or occult or past finding out: although they are, to be sure, about as intrinsic as anything can be, they do nothing from day to day but announce themselves.

The regime or rule of the spirit makes the Christian's willful struggle against nature look pointless, even harmful. Children, Emerson observes in one example, should not be coerced (against their nature) to attend Sunday School, but should be taught in response to questions as they naturally arise (79–80). Force and discipline betray an anxious conviction that nature is somehow illegal, a renegade from God. The more faithful gesture is to suppose that nothing is at last outside the government of God, and that if the world has traps and dangers in it, these teach circumspection and arm the soul. Do not hate nature, Emerson advises, but accept it, and above all accept the nature of your own character, which is also a spiritual law, one that will organize the world to your private perception.

In the essay on "Love," Emerson is as cool and general as Jesus or Socrates on the same subject. He pretends that he might have written differently had he been younger, and while he hopes in his belated manner to say nothing "treasonable to nature," still he must apologize beforehand. His announced purpose is to make an essay toward "that inward view of the law, which shall describe a truth ever young and beautiful, so central that it shall commend itself to the eye at whatever angle beholden" (100). The emphasis on the "law" of love is variously appropriate at this point, but the charm and gaiety that Emerson tries to import by allusion to the circumstantial evidence of romance fights a losing battle against the gravity of the larger point, which is that in love, as in other things, the world is constantly emptying out into memory. Bodies teach the insufficiency of bodies, persons the insufficiency of persons. The compensation is the positive degree of the same case: that no event more conducts us to a permanent and ideal beauty than the episodes of love that nature gives us.

"Friendship," the next essay, finds its difference from the preceding not in gender or in temperature, but in the distinction between private and public. Friends are the public complement of the self, which makes them at once a high privilege and a problem. They are not for decoration or diversion, but belong instead to the main line of life – this because, in their standing violation of one's privacy, friends promise an education (in the root sense of a "drawing out"). In "Self-Reliance," Emerson had said that "Nothing is at last sacred but the integrity of your own mind" (30), yet in an equal friendship one gratefully finds this unity, this sacred integrity, distributed into an audience for purposes of circulation.

Emerson's thinking here about the relation of self and other seems to reflect an underlying preoccupation with the conditions of communication in the author/reader relationship. Writing at just the moment when authorship was becoming professionalized and indiscriminate, Emerson would not abandon the belief that communication, at its best and most efficient, is the momentary joining of a single mind with one other. As a preacher and as a lecturer, he had learned to let himself be overheard and to fit his speech only to such a sensibility as he understood and felt connected to – that is to say, in the main, his own. Just as we never speak to all of the many who might be listening, neither (as Emily Dickinson said) do we think or live to such a public crowd, but always to the few who elect themselves by the quality of their receptive concern: to our friends, that is, known and unknown. Whatever else he or she may be, a friend is an ideal reader, an encourager of "sincerity," and a recipient of "letters" (as he or she several times appears in the essay). The affection that subsists between friends is indistinguishable from the joy of unencumbered, truthful communication – or of spiritual circulation – predicated on a similarity of natures. If it were not in some sense true that "There is one mind common to all individual men," communication of any sort would be at a standstill; yet, of course, if the proposition were true in the very simplest sense, communication would not have arisen in the first place.

Emerson's vaunted mysticism amounts to little more than a consistent belief in the reality of ideas, yet those who were made uncomfortable by the challenge of Emerson's idealism found they could dismiss him with a charge of specious otherworldliness. When Hawthorne met Emerson in Concord a year after the publication of *Essays,* he called him "that everlasting rejecter of all that is, and seeker for he knows not what"[3] – as though Emerson's thought had unfitted him for life in this present world. It was a not uncommon suspicion, and yet, for what it's worth, Emerson led in Concord a more sociable, better circumstanced, and more materially competent life than Hawthorne ever did. If, like Hawthorne, we begin to wonder whether a transcendentalist might perhaps be too moonshiny to see that his rents are paid and his larder filled, we have only to read "Prudence," the seventh essay, to have our doubts allayed.

A modern reader will scarcely know what "prudence" is – or rather what it meant before America's consumer culture turned it into a silly, purely negative virtue, hovering somewhere between caution and timidity and hinting at failure. (Nowadays, prudence is what puts the credit card between the blades of the scissors.) Yet in 1841 Emerson could define it, uncontroversially, as "the art of securing a present well-being" (141), and while he understood that it was not the very highest quality a person might have (remarking that it was "the virtue of the senses" [131]), still he supposed it could not be absent from character in its fullest development.

That awareness belongs to Emerson's revision of the popular notion of genius, which, by attributing improvidence and eccentricity to it, slanders the higher life and makes it unattractive. The inspired poet going mad in his garret, neglected by the world he neglects – the "man of genius, of an ardent temperament, reckless of physical laws, self-indulgent," who regards his "transgressions of the laws of the senses" as trivial compared to his devotion to his art (137) – these are disordered souls, not heroes. Common sense (a map of traps and promises) and a thorough and accurate knowledge of the world in all its beauty and vulgarity are not optional components of genius. Every petty success at becoming more comfortable in the world, even the most elementary and ordinary, whether by the rich man or the poor, implies mastery of some law; every failing, a violation of some law. To be prudent is simply to be attentive to the nature of things (that is to say, to know their laws) in a universe that is from its foundation legal and symbolic. Because there is nowhere that law does not penetrate, human actions all have value, all have significance: "The good husband finds method as efficient in the packing of firewood in a shed, or in the harvesting of fruits in the cellar, as in Peninsular campaigns or the files of the Department of State" (134). No one who means to live fully can afford to be a "rejecter of all that is," but, as Emerson said in "Self-Reliance," must rather "accept the place the divine Providence has found for you; the society of your contemporaries, the connexion of events" (28).

Emerson admits that there is a pathology in trifling and an unworthiness in many accustomed acts. But what makes any such action blameworthy? It is not the deed itself, but always the variable matter of its meaning, its spiritual counterpart or place in consciousness, that has value and invites judgment. Collecting firewood may be an occupation for the hands (and trivial enough so considered), but it may also be, at will, an occupation for the spirit, as when we see through the act to a world fitted to our comfort and uses, or when we see that the art of stacking cordwood has laws of its own. Whether an act is primarily an affair of the senses or an affair of the senses and spirit in union is determined by consciousness, by a registering of the generalized or symbolic meaning of the act. Emerson laments the divergence between prudence and poetry, and redefines and revalues the former by asserting its intrinsic connection with the latter.

Prudence serves to put us in good circumstances, the better to establish our power in the world; but as no virtue is quite sane by itself, but flourishes in company, so the highest prudence is a multiplier of connections to phenomena and their laws, to matter and to spirit. Understood as Emerson understands it, prudence is a homely virtue that makes the lowest parts of life continuous with the highest, makes them royal and poetic, as surely as a sensual greed and selfishness make them empty, literal, and disconnected.

We begin to recognize in Emerson's essays the fundamental and recurring gesture of restoring the circularity that is interrupted when spirit (meaning) is ignored by a practically skeptical, practically materialist culture. The underlying problem against which *Essays* is written is the same as that which opens Emerson's 1843 poem "Blight":

> Give me truths;
> For I am weary of the surfaces,
> And die of inanition.[4]

Essays is a book for a world in which history is arid, men are washed-out images of deferred or absent authority, virtue is held to be disadvantageous, laws are disbelieved and dishonored, love is personal aggrandizement, friends are appurtenances, prudence is mere Yankee shrewdness, and nothing quite means enough to make life worth persisting in. Emerson shows us a desiccated two-dimensional world by adopting the ironic perspective of its missing third dimension ("virtue is Height," he says [40]). Like Ahab, Emerson finds it necessary to "strike through the mask," though, unlike Ahab, he expects to find on the other side (indeed, does find) an indicated and predicted realm of spirit – not formed in fright, as Melville supposed, but consonant with the beauty, balance, and benevolence of all the violated creative laws.

Melville thought this was too good to be true and characteristically preferred to look instead to nature's sublime antagonism. Struggle was Melville's way, as yielding was Emerson's. And yet when we look at *Essays* as a work of satire – nearly a jeremiad – we are made forcibly aware that a profound sense of an evil to be opposed runs through the whole. In "Heroism" the reader is at last admonished that his training "must not omit the arming of the man. Let him hear in season that he is born into the state of war" (148).

The heroes of the modern media are generally the first who arrive at the scene of an accident. We marvel as they put themselves in peril to save the helpless. We are with them from the start, and in our instant approval we become ourselves vicarious heroes – at the trifling cost of a newspaper. The Emersonian hero is a different thing altogether – magnanimous, but not selflessly so. He is the opponent of an evil which few recognize besides himself and so acts without seconds or helpers. Because "Heroism works in contradiction to the voice of mankind" (149), the hero as Emerson defines him is more apt to be accused and scorned than applauded. Indeed he is a good deal closer to Ahab than to any more modern figure, for the hero, we are told, "finds a quality in him that is negligent of expense, of health, of life, of danger, of hatred, of reproach, and knows that his will is higher and more excellent than all actual and all possible antagonists" (149). The hero's defiant act is the ultimate test of self-reliance and its highest use.

Heroism is attractive (as literature attests) because it prefers an idea to the kinds of material interests that a common prudence respects. Why should a heroic act seem beautiful? Because it gives back to the universe its proper order; because it connects our trivial "common life" to its unconsidered third dimension and makes spirit again "master of the world" (149). Emerson clarifies his definition by recourse to the negative case, touching briefly on the comedy of the unheroic life:

> Yet the little man . . . works [at life] so headlong and believing, is born red, and dies gray, arranging his toilet, attending on his own health, laying traps for sweet food and strong wine, setting his heart on a horse or a rifle, made happy with a little gossip, or a little praise, that the great soul cannot choose but laugh at such earnest nonsense. (149)

We see in the heroic act that our lives can have extension beyond the grocery store into realms of eternal justice. Heroism and the search for signification are indivisible. The hero delivers himself and us from "nonsense"; he is the redemptive bringer of meaning.

So, the parallel with Ahab has its limits after all. While Emerson's essay makes for consistently interesting reading as a gloss on *Moby-Dick,* the fact is that Emerson and Melville had very different views regarding the nature of the evil to be confronted. Without trying to develop their contrasting ideas, it might be enough to suggest that Emerson had got over his shock and disappointment at the fall of man and Melville hadn't. Having insisted (in "History") on a share of the general glory of humanity, he cannot arbitrarily withdraw from the general shame. But how coolly and with what sense of justice he takes it:

> The violations of the laws of nature by our predecessors and our contemporaries, are punished in us also. The disease and deformity around us, certify the infraction of natural, intellectual and moral laws, and often violation on violation to breed such compound misery. A lockjaw, that bends a man's head back to his heels, hydrophobia, that makes him bark at his wife and babes, insanity, that makes him eat grass; war, plague, cholera, famine, indicate a certain ferocity in nature, which, as it had its inlet by human crime, must have its outlet by human suffering. Unhappily, no man exists who has not in his own person become, to some amount, a stockholder in the sin, and so made himself liable to a share in the expiation. (147–48)

Evil, for Emerson, is the attempted negation of the permanent laws of the universe, and when such violations become routine and pass for orthodoxy (as, for example, in the slavery issue) the rebuking hero exposes himself even to martyrdom, as did the abolitionist editor Elijah P. Lovejoy, the one contemporary hero referred to by name in the essay (155). The allusion to the recently dead Lovejoy makes it clear how pointedly Emerson is redefining heroism for an emerging generation of romantic reformers, young men who had a choice to make between the middle-class comforts of a professional life and that promising figure they cut at first "of a youthful giant who is sent to work revolutions" (153). The antislavery agitation of the 1840s and '50s needed heroes, prompt, fearless, and committed in their idealism: Emerson's commanding influence with the younger generation made him one of the most efficient manufacturers of precisely these combatants.[5]

"God will not make himself manifest to cowards," says Emerson in the next essay, "The Over-Soul" (174). The statement is a typically effective use of tautology for emphasis: divine revelation is a process of hero making, not of intimidation; conversely, the way to close with God is to have no fear, but perfect faith instead. Having determined that the universe is nothing to be afraid of; that God is good and not malevolent; that the permanent laws are the reign of God and the only evil lies in resistance to them; –

having assented to all this and seeing that one's assent proceeds from a substantial congruence between self and universe (that these are one, after all, and not two, at once the subject and object of revelation), then fear, suspicion, doubt, division, and resistance depart, we yield ourselves to "the perfect whole," and live just to that extent with God.[6]

Emerson doesn't soften this "hard saying," which is core doctrine for the whole book. He knows that readers will balk at this proposition and so he is elaborately concerned to raise and meet objections. He concedes, for example, that no one has ever achieved this transcendental state of illumination or soul-fullness (though Jesus, he allows, came closest). It is not an ecstatic state because it is not a going out of the self, but rather the self's utterly complete realization, the imaginary end point of coming-to-be. In fact, Emerson is a great deal more interested in the real process – which we can and do know – than in its conceptually important but thoroughly imaginary finish.

That we do in fact know this process allows us to project or imagine its fulfillment as a theory of human progress:

> There is a difference between one and another hour of life, in their authority and subsequent effect. Our faith comes in moments; our vice is habitual. Yet there is a depth in those brief moments, which constrains us to ascribe more reality to them than to all other experiences. For this reason, the argument, which is always forthcoming to silence those who conceive extraordinary hopes of man, namely, the appeal to experience, is forever invalid and vain. (159)

Blight and blindness may be the average of human experience in history, yet the fact that we are still, from moment to moment, vehicles and inlets of truth, that we are vulnerable to superiority and invaded by goodness, that we recognize and honor these transient glimmers of a better way of being, proves our title to a perfect estate. We become heroes (or real or self-reliant individuals) by submitting in emergencies to this perfect and most impersonal version of ourselves. "I, the imperfect, adore my own Perfect," says Emerson (175), deploying yet one more of his stunningly adequate synonyms for God.

In "Circles," Emerson proposes to show that "there is no end in nature" (179), that circulation, not arrival – growth and onwardness, not perfection or stasis – is the lord of life. We may (as we do and must) worship and adore what is above us, but life is never more than a movement toward. There is always more elevation, always more completion. "Our life is an apprenticeship to the truth that around every circle another can be drawn" (179). Thus it is a clear misreading of "The Over-Soul" to suppose that

Emerson advocates any ultimate transcendence or that he is guilty of some misestimation of human potential in naming a condition that none can achieve.

The tribute paid in "Circles" to growth and aspiration feels like a new note, as though Emerson were just now discovering the organic implication of his views, but we soon see that it contradicts nothing earlier said and conclude that the sense of novelty is an effect of emphasis merely, showing again how the author's particular acts of attention renovate whatever falls in the field of vision. Our lives, he says, are ever-expanding, self-propagated circles, large or small according to "the force or truth of the individual soul" (180). These are the worlds we invent and inhabit. The only failing is the acceptance as final and adequate of some particular extension we have attained. "Thus far and no further" is the voice of conservatism, which disguises coagulation and death as peace and contentment. "But if the soul is quick and strong it bursts over that boundary on all sides and expands another orbit on the great deep, which also runs up into a high wave, with attempt again to stop and to bind" (181).

The leading implication of all this (not lost on the younger generation who were Emerson's most devoted readers) is that to affirm life is to be a perpetual revolutionary, a consistent opponent of all agreements that anything is ever settled. The essay itself reflects this stance in Emerson, deriving as it does, by way of a lecture entitled "The Protest," from his confrontation with the defenders of orthodoxy in the Divinity School "Address," who were pained by the young man's intimation that Jesus was not now and always "the last word."[7] So here in "Circles," he says:

> Christianity is rightly dear to the best of mankind; yet was there never a young philosopher whose breeding had fallen into the Christian church, by whom that brave text of Paul's, was not specially prized: "Then shall also the Son be subject unto Him who put all things under him, that God may be all in all." Let the claims and virtues of persons be never so great and welcome, the instinct of man presses eagerly onward to the impersonal and illimitable, and gladly arms itself against the dogmatism of bigots with this generous word, out of the book itself. (185–86)

Essays was in 1841, as it now is, a manual of self-defense for young persons against the tyranny and authority of age. "I unsettle all things" (188).

One could wish that the book had ended with the sublime "Circles," which more than touches on all the topics earlier named, and with an effect as of inscribing a circle round them. It is the last of the really striking essays in this first collection, though the final two, "Intellect" and "Art," have other and higher work to do than to eke out the meager symmetries of 12. They are concerned with the problematic implications of two ideas set forth most clearly in "Circles": first, that the act of dissolving or unsettling (or, as we might say, resisting arrest) is the very sign of life, and, second, that truth is a "flying Perfect" (179), always to be pursued, never to be attained. Without the further elaboration of these concluding essays, it might seem that we have the arts of negation and rebellion at command – so that the world "may at any time be superseded and decease" (183) – while we yet lack all assurance that we can improve on the old plan. (Hence Hawthorne's conservative doubts.)

"Intellect" considers the act of taking apart, as "Art" considers the putting together. Both (to their hurt) are cast almost as formal scientific investigations into the structure of the mind, or as attempts, as Emerson says, to sketch "a natural history of the intellect" (193). In the first, thought is described as the universal solvent. Certain natural substances, such as fire or water, dissolve certain other substances, such as wood or salt, but only thought resolves everything into itself. "The intellect pierces the form, overleaps the wall, detects intrinsic likeness between remote things and reduces all things into a few principles" (194). In other words, thought opposes the massing of the universe in material objectivity, resists the limitation of form, and mediates for persons between appearance and reality. It does, in its ceaseless, ever-unsatisfied activity, what it is said, in "Circles," persons should do. The "taking apart" function of thought, if destructive, is not therefore negative, but is a continuous affirmation of reality. "The making a fact the subject of thought, raises it" (194).

The link between "Intellect" and "Art" is the distinction, in the former essay, between this dissolving thought and "the intellect constructive," or "Genius" (198). Emerson's injunction at the end of *Nature* to "Build, therefore, your own world,"[8] was an invitation to the reader to trust, or to rely on, his own genius, not as an artist in the usual sense, but as the central figure in his own worldview. This constructive faculty is universal (if the talents of the reporter/artist are not) and is engaged alike by those who love the truth and those who love repose. The former "will keep himself aloof from all moorings and afloat" (202), while the latter, the conservative, will early find some good-enough system and settle himself there forever. The constructive feats of the lover of truth are the tentative, ever-finer shapes the world assumes in consciousness, according to those revelations we are positioned to receive and which we successively acknowledge as we yield to them.

"Art" provides a large definition that, unsurprisingly, subsumes *Essays*. It is the function of art to separate out various particularities (or topics) and so offer them to the attention of an audience as to affirm the fit and sacred relation of those trivial particularities to infinitude. Nothing makes this possible in the first place but the underlying unity of nature which must express (and so forever represents) all in each. The creative way of art is the creative way of nature, affording endless circulation from instance to ideal and back again: "What is a man but nature's finer success in self-explication?" (209).

"Art is the need to create," says Emerson (215), but if the product is at last only beautiful objects, it misses circulation and so misses its calling: "Nothing less than the creation of man and nature is its end" (215). Here again is the indictment of the reader's familiar world, in which art is the *end* of creation and stands sequestered in museums, patronized by a certain class in devoted hours, and held apart from life for contrast or rebuke: "Now men do not see nature to be beautiful, and they go to make a statue which shall be" (217). This decadence is another form of conservative limitation or boundary drawing, partly expressed in the distinction, which Emerson rejects, between the fine and the useful arts (218). Because art is properly and naturally coextensive with life, it cannot be made into a deer park and fenced without attracting young Shakespeares to steal from it: art pushes out into the common life and by affirming the connection between that life and perfect and complete life does indeed connive at the creation of man and nature.

In 1841 and frequently since, *Essays* has been faulted for its lack of clarity, by which is usually meant its lack of rigorous and definitive logic, and on essentially that score Emerson is denied the title of philosopher. In certain obvious ways, however, the chapters of *Essays* are discrete, cooperating exercises in definition, remotely modeled on early Latin School writing assignments in which the young Emerson had been encouraged to expand on such topics as "Eloquence" or "Solitude." He seems never to have been without a sense of the shortcomings of the rationalist lexicography of Samuel Johnson and the entire nineteenth-century age of dictionaries, which offered to make meanings by a policy of enclosure and a policing of boundaries, as though one might arrive at a spiritual essence (or meaning) by driving life off like water from a solution.

The ordinary pattern of definition is art in museums and religion in churches (correlative to Johnson's idea of having language, definitively, in a book). Selves define themselves by trimming more commonly than by expansion. We know history as history because it fills up the past: to add "for us" is the antidefinitional gesture that seeks to solve the world and smuggle banished life back in. *Essays* is about these transliminal gestures, which announce that we live less between walls after all than in an atmosphere of conductivity, open in every direction. Because that atmosphere *is* the regime of spirit, and because "all works of the highest art . . . are religious" (213), Emerson's stance in this book is, by definition, prophetic.

NOTES

1   *The Collected Works of Ralph Waldo Emerson,* vol. 2: *Essays: First Series,* ed. Joseph Slater, Alfred R. Ferguson, and Jean Ferguson Carr (Cambridge, MA: The Belknap Press of Harvard University Press, 1979), p. 210. Subsequent quotations are from this volume and will be cited parenthetically.

2   *The Correspondence of Emerson and Carlyle,* ed. Joseph Slater (New York: Columbia University Press, 1964), p. 149.

3   Nathaniel Hawthorne, *The American Notebooks,* ed. Claude M. Simpson (Columbus: Ohio State University Press, 1972), p. 357.

4   *Ralph Waldo Emerson: Collected Poems and Translations,* ed. Harold Bloom and Paul Kane (New York: Library of America, 1994), p. 111.

5   I develop this point at length in *Anthony Burns and the Revolution of 1854* (Cambridge, MA: Harvard University Press, 1998).

6   For the concept of yielding to the perfect whole, see the poem "Each and All," written between 1834 and 1837, in *Collected Poems,* p. 9–10.

7   See Joel Porte, *Representative Man: Ralph Waldo Emerson in His Time* (New York: Oxford University Press, 1979), p. 91, and B. L. Packer, *Emerson's Fall: A New Interpretation of the Major Essays* (New York: Continuum, 1982), pp. 132–33.

8   *The Collected Works of Ralph Waldo Emerson,* vol. 1: *Nature, Addresses, and Lectures,* ed. Robert E. Spiller and Alfred R. Ferguson (Cambridge, MA: The Belknap Press of Harvard University Press, 1971), p. 45.

7

JEFFREY STEELE

Transcendental Friendship: Emerson, Fuller, and Thoreau

In the 1830s and '40s, Ralph Waldo Emerson, Margaret Fuller, and Henry David Thoreau engaged in a prolonged series of meditations and dialogues on the meaning of friendship. At key moments, each writer decided that fundamental issues of human development could not be articulated without taking into account the role of friends. But Transcendentalist models of individuation cannot be completely reconciled with theories of social relationship; for the demands of self-reliance, especially the intuition of the "divine" depths of the self, often pull one out of the social orbit into an intense introspection. As a result, Transcendentalist discussions of friendship often emerged in response to moments of crisis (whether encounters with death, separation, or personal misunderstanding) that laid bare the specter of isolation underlying their theories. This tension (between friendship and isolation) poignantly dramatizes one of the paradoxes of Transcendentalist literary expression: its central subject matter – profound moments of imaginative and spiritual intensity – could only be described in retrospect, from the vantage point of someone who had passed through and remembered the experience.

Although Emerson, Fuller, and Thoreau reflected on friendship throughout their lives, several important phases stand out in their discussions of the topic. Emerson's reflections on friendship culminated in his 1841 essay on "Friendship," included in *Essays: First Series*. During the fall and winter of 1840–41, as Emerson was finishing this essay, he and Margaret Fuller (seven years his junior) engaged in a prolonged and important debate on the meaning of friendship, especially as it impinged on their own relationship to each other and their circle of mutual friends (Samuel Ward, Anna Barker, and Caroline Sturgis). Fuller's most important writings on friendship, found in her 1840–41 essays and letters, grow directly out of this context and can be best understood as a response to Emerson. Fourteen years younger than Emerson, Thoreau joined the conversation late. His long meditation on friendship in the "Wednesday" section of *A Week on*

the Concord and Merrimack Rivers appeared in 1849, eight years after
Emerson's influential essay. Throughout the 1840s up to 1852, Thoreau's
journals are filled with discussions of friendship, many of them written in
response to the personal conflicts that eventually distanced him from his
companion and mentor, Emerson. While they shared a number of themes
with Emerson, Thoreau's private reflections made painfully visible the internal tensions of transcendental friendship – a difficult, albeit noble, ideal.

Throughout his career, Emerson wrestled with the problem of friendship.
"Friendship is something very delicious to my understanding," he reflected
in an early journal; "Yet the friends that occupy my thoughts are not men
but certain phantoms clothed in the form & face & apparel of men by
whom they were suggested & to whom they bear a resemblance" (*JMN* 2:
25). Recognizing the value of social being, he realized the potential conflict
between the demands of affection and the intellectual world in which he
longed to dwell. On the one hand, Emerson saw friendship as an expansion
of being. "The faculties," he observed, "are not called out except by means
of the affections" (*JMN* 4: 271); "our intellectual and active powers increase with our affections" (*CW* 2: 113). But on the other hand, he frequently defined the benefits of friendship in terms that suspended the phenomenal world of human emotions. "Most persons exist to us merely or
chiefly in relations of time & space," he considered; "Those whom we love,
whom we venerate, or whom we serve, exist to us independently of these
relations" (*JMN* 5: 61). "That which is individual & remains individual in
my experience is of no value," he noted elsewhere in his journals; "What is
fit to engage me & so engage others permanently, is what has put off its
weeds of time & place & personal relation" (*JMN* 7: 65). But such an
idealized definition of friendship – what we might call "transcendental
friendship" – threatened to turn Emerson's friends into "phantoms" who
merely reflected the eternal laws he intuited within.[1]

A fundamental instability characterizes Emerson's view of friendship, for
it is nearly impossible to reconcile an idealized model of individual being
with an appreciation of human fallibility. Constructing a model in which
friendship "must not surmise or provide for infirmity" (*CW* 2: 127), Emerson often found it difficult to respond fully to the sense of imperfection
and crisis that led some of his friends to draw on his emotional support. As
a result, he could not completely reconcile the intractability of real persons
with his idealized image of human potential. Rarely does Emerson's characterization of friendship maintain an equal plane. The first sign of inferiority in one's friend threatens the relationship. In the face of one's "greatness," he argues, the "crude and cold companion . . . will presently pass
away," since "true love transcends the unworthy object, and dwells and

broods on the eternal" (*CW* 2: 127). Finding few equals in his social circle, Emerson was forced to reflect soberly that friendship "cannot subsist in its perfection" (*CW* 2: 121). The consequence of such observations was that friendship, in his conception, tends to become an imaginary relation that defines an ideal harmony rarely realized on earth. "I please my imagination more with a circle of godlike men and women variously related to each other," he commented in "Friendship,"

> and between whom subsists a lofty intelligence. . . . In good company, the individuals merge their egotism into a social soul exactly coextensive with the several consciousnesses there present. (*CW* 2: 121–22)

But such a utopian ideal of community, realized at rare moments, depended upon the acquiescence of all parties to a merger in which all shared equally in the Oversoul, meeting on "a higher platform" in which they could reveal their godlike natures (*CW* 2: 126).

As a result of such tensions in Emerson's thought, some critics have echoed Margaret Fuller's accusation that Emerson's theories prevented him from accepting the flaws of his friends. "I felt that you did not for me the highest office of friendship," Fuller once complained to Emerson, "by offering me the clue of the labyrinth of my own being."[2] But Emerson founded his model of being, as Fuller herself realized at other times, not on the image of the labyrinth but rather on an image of infinite power that expressed itself in privileged moments of insight. The awareness of personal friction that motivated Fuller's complaint threatened to perpetuate the very sense of blankness against which Emerson constantly struggled. In opposition to such limitation, he labored to maintain the sense of "in-streaming causing power" (*CW* 1: 43), which he saw as the foundation of the "active soul" (*CW* 1: 56). At times, he felt that the demands of personal relations seemed to reinforce the "conspiracy" of society against "the manhood of every one of its members" (*CW* 2: 29) – a social noise that drowned out the divine inspiration emerging from deep within.

But we must not forget that *Essays: First Series* contains both "Self-Reliance" and "Friendship." For all of his prophetic insistence upon "the infinitude of the private man" (*JMN* 7: 342), Emerson never relinquished the claims of friendship. Indeed, the two conceptions – self-reliance and friendship – despite their antithetical appearance are intimately connected in Emerson's thought. "Isolation must precede society," he reflects; yet the "office of conversation is to give me self-possession" (*JMN* 7: 175, 176). Emerson needs a concept of social being (manifested in his idea of conformity in "Self-Reliance") to define the value of personal independence. Conversely, true friendship reveals the depths of the individual self through a process that "dwells and broods on the eternal" lying beneath our flawed exteriors (*CW* 2: 127). Meeting on an eternal plane, true friends – in Emerson's vision – unlocked the divine potential that each carried within. But such a sublime view of social relations carried with it the risk of perpetual disappointment. "Who is capable of a manly friendship?" he asked himself in 1835. The answer: "Very few. Charles [Emerson's younger brother] thinks he can count five persons of *character*" (*JMN* 5: 38). The inevitable conclusion, he later observed in "Friendship," was a theory that excluded most social relations:

> The higher the style we demand of friendship, of course the less easy to establish it with flesh and blood. We can walk alone in the world. Friends, such as we desire, are dreams and fables. But a sublime hope cheers ever the faithful heart, that elsewhere, in other regions of the universal power, souls are now acting, enduring, and daring, which can love us, and which we can love.   (*CW* 2: 125)

The challenge confronting Emerson was "not to negate the personal but rather to adjust it to the universal."[3] This enterprise was exacerbated by two major sources of personal conflict: 1) the death of loved ones, and 2) moments of social crisis that threatened to isolate him.

In its first phase, Emerson's vision of friendship was precipitated by the dynamic of mourning.[4] Friends revealed their full value when they were withdrawn. The most difficult realization, which he most fully expressed later in his career in essays such as "Experience," was that a "plaint of tragedy" attaches "to persons, to friendship and love" (*CW* 3: 33). An elegiac note runs throughout Emerson's discussions of friendship, dating back to the deaths of his first wife Ellen in 1831 and his younger brother Charles in 1836. Within a month after Charles's death, Emerson had "transmuted" the image of his brother into his "archetype for friendship."[5] In his journal, he recorded the nucleus for the following passage, printed later that year in *Nature*:

> When much intercourse with a friend has supplied us with a standard of excellence, and has increased our respect for the resources of God who thus sends a real person to outgo our ideal; when he has, moreover, become an object of thought, and, whilst his character retains all its unconscious effect, is converted in the mind into solid and sweet wisdom, – it is a sign to us that his office is closing, and he is commonly withdrawn from our sight in a short time.   (*CW* 1: 28–29)[6]

Some readers have seen in such passages a chilling expediency, reflecting the idea that a friend is no longer needed once his meaning has been absorbed. In an extreme statement of this position, Stephen Yarbrough has argued that "Emerson places no value on friendships for their own sakes," since he views friends as "a kind of commodity . . . something for a soul to use to further its own growth."[7] Certainly, some of Emerson's comments seem to incline in that direction; for example, the following passage from "Friendship": "Is it not that the soul puts forth friends, as the tree puts forth leaves, and presently, by the germination of new buds, extrudes the old leaf?" (CW 2: 116).

But a more generous view locates in such observations a stoic reflection of the vicissitudes of life. Since "our reality is dynamic . . . always sundering, always involved in death" (in the words of George Sebouhian), even the most tragic losses must become the source of wisdom.[8] "We cannot part with our friends. We cannot let our angels go," Emerson later observed in "Compensation":

> We do not see that they only go out, that archangels may come in. We are idolaters of the old. We do not believe in the riches of the soul, in its proper eternity and omnipresence. We do not believe there is any force in to-day to rival or re-create that beautiful yesterday. . . . And yet the compensations of calamity are made apparent to the understanding also, after long intervals of time. . . . The death of a dear friend, wife, brother, lover, which seemed nothing but privation, somewhat later assumes the aspect of a guide or genius; for it commonly operates revolutions in our way of life, terminates an epoch of infancy or of youth which was waiting to be closed. (CW 2: 72–73)

The austerity of this viewpoint reflected the real losses in Emerson's life. By the time it was published in 1841, he had lost his father, first wife, and two brothers.

In 1836, almost three months after Charles's death in May, a new epoch opened in the history of Emerson's friendships: Margaret Fuller, after several years' urging by mutual friends that they should meet, finally commenced a three-week visit with the Emersons on July 21.[9] Fuller traveled to Concord from Groton (in western Massachusetts), where she was living with her mother and her younger siblings. In October 1835, her father Timothy, who had retired from Congress, died of cholera. Like Emerson, Fuller when they first met was mourning the death of a beloved relative, whose passing left a significant void in her life. While Emerson searched for replacements for his lost brother, Fuller eventually came to see in Emerson a substitute for her departed father (a part he was reluctant to play).[10]

Their friendship was further complicated by Emerson's marriage the previous September to Lydia Jackson, his second wife (whom he renamed "Lidian"). At the time when Emerson and Fuller first met, Lidian – "not a woman who took pregnancy lightly" – was six months pregnant with the first of the couple's four children.[11] (Emerson had no children from his first marriage.) Despite the awkwardness of Fuller's timing and unfavorable first impressions, she managed to charm the household, so that within a week Lidian was able to exclaim in a letter, "We like her – she likes us."[12] But in future years, Fuller's periodic visits with the Emersons became a source of annoyance for Lidian, who came to resent the time that her husband spent with a woman possessing such intellectual and emotional gifts. It seems significant that the "period of the electric, idealized relationship of Emerson with Fuller roughly coincided with Lidian's childbearing years – from October, 1836, when Waldo was born, to July 10, 1844, Edward's birth."[13] One of the unresolved questions in both Emerson and Fuller scholarship is the extent to which their friendship was shaped by nineteenth-century gender roles that influenced Emerson's reactions both to his wife and to his female friends.

From the beginning, Fuller challenged Emerson's conception of himself, primarily – it seems – because she embodied a style of being that he admired but could not completely fathom. "She disturbed his equanimity," Harry Warfel once observed, "as no one else had done, except possibly Aunt Mary Moody Emerson."[14] In contrast to those of Emerson's other acquaintances, Fuller's intellectual depth and emotional complexity resisted being turned into a thought, a touchstone of one epoch in his life. "All natures seem poor beside one so rich," Emerson later observed about her in an 1843 journal"; "We are taught by her plenty how lifeless & outward we were. . . . Beside her friendship, other friendships seem trade" (*JMN* 8: 368). Emerson's superlatives have seemed to substantiate Carl Strauch's groundbreaking study, which focused critical attention upon the possible romantic connection between Emerson and Fuller.[15] But such speculation has deflected attention from the overlapping relationships existing in their circle of friends. Fuller brought into Emerson's orbit a new set of concerns and a new circle of acquaintances who later provided "the raw material of his essay on friendship."[16] From 1836 to 1841, the majority of Emerson's reflections on friendship (recorded in his journals and letters) focused on the lives of Fuller and a close-knit set of friends introduced to him by her: Samuel Ward, Anna Barker, and Caroline Sturgis.

By the time Emerson had completed his essay "Friendship" late in 1840, each of these persons had become a close friend, shaping his vision of friendship and social relations in general. Since Fuller also counted Ward, Barker, and Sturgis among her intimates, both Emerson's and Fuller's meditations on friendship developed in response to events in a shared social circle. Especially important for their relationship was the complex emotional aftermath of the betrothal and marriage of Samuel Ward and Anna Barker.[17] Both Emerson and Fuller considered Ward (whom they called "Raphael" because of his artistic talent) one of their closest intimates. In 1839, Fuller had formed a romantic attachment with Ward – a relationship that was shattered by the arrival of the beautiful Anna. When Ward and Barker announced their engagement in October 1839, shock waves reverberated through the Emerson-Fuller circle, especially as Emerson and Fuller realized that the impending nuptials would significantly alter their relationship to each other and their closest friends.

Initially delighted with this "chronicle of sweet romance" (*JMN* 7: 273), Emerson gradually realized over the next year that the marriage of Ward and Barker (which took place October 3, 1840) threatened to isolate him from a man he came to address as a "brother." Eight months after Ward's marriage, for example, he exclaimed that "I am very far from consenting to be forgotten by you, and in my lonely woods I see you and talk with you so often, that it seems to me that through some of the fine channels which inform fine souls, you must sometimes feel the influence."[18] Judging from the tone of Emerson's correspondence, his feelings for Ward seem to have grown stronger *after* the marriage, since it is not until October 1841 that he addresses him as "My dear Sam," instead of the formal "My dear Sir" and less affectionate "My dear friend" of earlier letters.[19] Given the significant financial and social differences between Ward and Emerson, this shift is striking.[20] This might be partially explained as a displaced effect of his attraction to the beautiful and wealthy Anna Barker, whose entrance into his circle elicited one of the memorable passages later used in his essay on "Friendship": "A new person is ever to me a great event" (*JMN* 7: 259). Missing from the published essay is the continuation of the journal entry in which Emerson recorded his first impressions: "I enjoyed the frank and generous confidence of a being so lovely, so fortunate, & so remote from my own experiences" (*JMN* 7: 259). Emerson's changing relationship with Samuel Ward, as well as his "powerful but ambivalent response to Barker's magnetism," were additional factors complicating his vision of friendship during this period.[21]

The Ward-Barker relationship was an even more intense emotional shock for Fuller, since it represented the loss of two people she deeply loved.[22] After she learned of the engagement, Fuller's letters to Samuel Ward expressed a deep sense of betrayal and emotional entanglement. "You love me no more – How did you pray me to draw near to you!" she lamented in September 1839.[23] But Fuller's feelings for Ward were complicated by her relation to Anna Barker, "that eldest and divinest love," she wrote Caroline Sturgis, describing Anna as "my beloved" who "has returned to transcend in every way not only my hope, but my imagination."[24] Several years later, in her 1842 journal, Fuller looked back at the emotional turmoil of 1839–40 in the following terms:

> Many things interested me at the time which are not worth writing about, but nothing fixed my attention so much, as a large engraving of M[m]e Recamier in her boudoir. I have so often thought over the intimacy between her and Me de Stael. It is so true that a woman may be in love with a woman, and a man with a man. . . . It is regulated by the same love as that of love between persons of different sexes, only it is purely intellectual and spiritual, unprofaned by any mixture of lower instincts. . . . how natural is the love of Wallenstein for Max, that of Me de Stael for de Recamier, mine for Anna Barker[.] I loved Anna for a time I think with as much passion as I was then strong enough to feel.[25]

Emerson seems to have understood Fuller's attraction to Barker and to have shared her coded language. Although the evidence is not absolutely conclusive, it is striking that he repeatedly referred to Anna Barker, in his 1839 letters to Fuller, as Récamier (using the same historical analogy that Fuller later used in her journal).[26] If this is a tacit acknowledgment of Fuller's attraction to Barker, theories of Emerson and Fuller's love for each other are greatly complicated.

Thus, the immediate context of Emerson and Fuller's most fervent discussion of friendship was not solely their own relationship to each other but also their mutual realization that the Ward-Barker engagement represented a shared emotional crisis.[27] Emerson's August 29, 1840, letter to Fuller reveals a great deal of tact on the matter:

> But ah! my friend, *you* must be generous beyond even the strain of heroism to bear your part in this scene & resign without a sigh two Friends; – you whose heart unceasingly demands all, & is a sea that hates an ebb. I know there will be an ardent will & endeavor on their parts to prevent if it were indeed possible & in all ways to relieve & conceal this bereavement but I doubt they must deal with too keen a seer and a heart too thoroughly alive in its affections to cover up the whole fact with roses & myrrh.
>
> (*L* 2: 327–28)

During the ensuing months, as the October wedding approached, both Emerson and Fuller attempted to sort out for themselves and each other the effects of this event.

By the fall, the impending marriage of Ward and Barker precipitated many of the most important moments in Emerson and Fuller's complicated debate on the meaning of friendship. Attempting to counteract her sense of abandonment, Fuller turned to Emerson for emotional support, attempting – it seems – to secure from him a declaration of friendship (if not love) that was not forthcoming. "But did you not ask for a 'foe' in your friend?" Fuller asked Emerson in late September; "Did you not ask for a 'large formidable nature'? But a beautiful foe, I am not yet to you. Shall I ever be?"[28] As a response, the following passage from Emerson's journals has been interpreted by many readers as referring to Fuller:

> Sept. 26. You would have me love you. What shall I love? Your body? The supposition disgusts you. What you have thought & said? Well, whilst you were thinking & saying them, but not now. I see no possibility of loving any thing but what now is, & is becoming; your courage, your enterprize, your budding affection, your opening thought, your prayer, I can love, – but what else? (*JMN* 7: 400)

Such passages have motivated a great deal of biographical speculation, seeming to support the contention, advanced by Carl Strauch among others, that Emerson's theories of friendship grew out of a romantic confrontation with Fuller culminating in her declaration of love.[29] But it misrepresents their complex relationship to reduce it to a possible romantic encounter, especially when we consider that both Emerson and Fuller shared great emotional ambivalence over the expression of what Fuller in her 1842 journal termed the "lower instincts." In the texts of both writers, expressions of personal passion were quickly sublimated into highly wrought idealizations of beloved others. Thus Emerson, in the journal entry just cited, concludes that he can love Fuller's "courage," "enterprize," "thought," and "prayer," but not her "body."

The word "prayer" is especially revealing, given the "mighty changes" that Fuller sensed were taking place in her "spiritual life" during this period.[30] "All has been revealed, all foreshown yet I know it not," she continued in this letter to Caroline Sturgis; "Experiment has given place to certainty, pride to obedience, thought to love, and truth is lost in beauty." "All things I have given up to the central power, myself, you also," she wrote Emerson a few days later.[31] Undergoing a profound emotional and spiritual crisis, Fuller appealed to Emerson for both emotional support and theological confirmation of her most impassioned insights. Thus, she was hurt and shocked when he viewed her deepest inspiration as personal idiosyncrasy. Earlier in the letter cited above, she complained:

> How often have I said, this light will never understand my fire; this clear eye will never discern the law by which I am filling my circle; this simple force will never interpret my need of manifold being.[32]

Emerson's correspondence with Caroline Sturgis confirms the theological
dimensions of his debate with Fuller over the meaning of friendship. Complaining to her that "there are new sects in heaven who teach an occult
religion," he reiterated his demand that "true energy" be "divine by the
tests that it is humane, loving, universal" (L 2: 346–47). "How rarely can
a female mind be impersonal," Emerson had observed in his journal a
month after his 1836 meeting with Fuller, "S[arah]. A[lden]. R[ipley]. is
wonderfully free from egotism of place & time & blood. M[argaret].
F[uller]. by no means so free with all her superiority" (JMN 5: 190). In
Emerson's terms, Fuller's concern with specific events and personalities was
theologically suspect, as well as an inadequate foundation for a theory of
friendship. In his view, "every personal consideration that we allow, costs
us heavenly state" (JMN 7: 528).

Emerson's demand that friendship be "free from egotism of place & time
& blood" deeply troubled Fuller, as it has disturbed some of her readers
since, because it seems to omit human imperfection from the equation.
Emerson, we might conclude, judged himself and his friends by a standard
so high that few human beings could match it. The consequence of such
views was the charge (which persists to this day) that Emerson exhibited
emotional coldness. Both Sturgis and Fuller seem to have exacerbated his
sense that he lacked their emotional warmth. After an 1838 visit from
Sturgis, for example, he reflected that "twice she engaged my cold pedantic
self into a fine surprise of thought & hope" (JMN 7: 15). The next year, in
response to Fuller's charge that he "always seemed to be on stilts," he
observed: "Most of the persons whom I see in my own house I see across a
gulf. I cannot go to them nor they come to me. Nothing can exceed the
frigidity & labor of my speech with such" (JMN 7: 301). In his correspondence with Fuller, he was aware of a "prison" of "temperament," forcing
him to "deal courteously with all comers, but through cold water" (L 2:
239). As Fuller and Emerson's debate over friendship intensified in late
1840, she eventually charged him with "inhospitality of soul," causing the
observation from Emerson that "nothing would be so grateful to me as to
melt once for all these icy barriers" (JMN 7: 509).

For Emerson, characterizations of his temperament and relationships so-
lidified the fluidity necessary for the release of the divine energies bonding
together ideal friends. Thus, he complained to both Fuller and Sturgis that
their interpretations of his temperament exacerbated his sense of isolation.
(Ironically, a decade later, Thoreau felt similarly threatened by Emerson's
limiting characterization of their friendship.) "I ought never to have suffered you to lead me into any conversation or writing on our relation, a
topic from which with all persons my Genius ever sternly warns me away,"

Emerson complained in the October 1840 letter to Fuller that terminated their debate on the nature of friendship:

> I was content & happy to meet on a human footing a woman of sense & sentiment with whom one could exchange reasonable words & go away as-sured that wherever she went there was light & force & honour. . . . Touch it not – speak not of it – and this most welcome natural alliance becomes from month to month, – & the slower & with the more intervals the better, – our air & diet. A robust & total understanding grows up resembling nothing so much as the relation of brothers who are intimate & perfect friends with-out having ever spoken of the fact. But tell me that I am cold or unkind, and in my most flowing state I become a cake of ice. I can feel the crystals shoot & the drops solidify. It may do for others but it is not for me to bring the relation to speech. Instantly I find myself a solitary unrelated person, destitute not only of all social faculty but of all private substance. (*L* 2: 352)

Arguing for an unexamined intimacy, the intellectual comradeship of "brothers" (a term that recalled his strong bond with his dead brother Charles and which was echoed in his correspondence with Samuel Ward), Emerson defended an impersonal model of friendship that recognized nei-ther sexual nor personal differences. On the universal plane of Oversoul, in which "one blood rolls uninterruptedly an endless circulation through all men" (*JMN* 7: 268), such differences seemed irrelevant. Although personal isolation was a real possibility that, at times, haunted Emerson, the impos-sibility of totally satisfying "contact with men" was compensated for by "the impersonal God" illuminating his heart (*JMN* 7: 301).

Margaret Fuller, of course, was not content with the elimination of either personality or sexual difference from her conception of friendship. For she was acutely aware that Emerson's assertion of an unarticulated fraternal bond between them mystified the gendered inequality of their positions, since they met as intellectual but not as social or economic equals. As a result, she accepted Emerson's conclusion that there is a fundamental "dif-ference in our constitution," leading to their using a "different rhetoric . . . as if we had been born & bred in different nations" (*L* 2: 353). But her interpretation of this difference took her in a much different direction. In her most important analyses of friendship, Fuller considered carefully the differences between male and female styles of friendship. In her unpublished "Autobiographical Romance," as well other 1840–41 writings, she sug-gested that the most fulfilling friendships for women were often with other women. Read within the context of the Emerson-Fuller friendship, such texts become an important critique of the unexamined gender privilege of Emerson's position.

In the midst of their debate over friendship, Fuller complained to Caroline Sturgis of Emerson's "tedious attempts to learn the universe by thought alone."[33] In her eyes, he had idealized friendship into a relationship that transcended personal feeling – a vision (Fuller wrote William Henry Channing) that she found ennobling but an imperfect representation of "our manifold nature."[34] A sticking point for Fuller was the issue of personal limitation. "We are not merely one another's priests or gods," she exclaimed in her letter to Channing,

> but ministering angels, exercising in the past the same function as the Great Soul in the whole of seeing the perfect through the imperfect nay, making it come there. Why am I to love my friend the less for the obstruction in his life?[35]

In "the tales of chivalry," she adds, should Amadis reject the "brother of his soul" if "he be mutilated in one of his first battles"? Spenser's Britomart, in the *Faerie Queene,* "does battle" to free Artegall from the "enchanter's spell," laboring to free him "from the evil power." Such friends, Fuller concludes, "are always faithful through the dark hours to the bright"; they do not turn away at the sign of personal limitation.

Elsewhere in her discussion of friendship, Fuller argues that the most equal friendships exist between women, who are able to meet on an equal plane (as opposed to the gender inequalities structured into male-female friendships). In her posthumously published "Autobiographical Romance," she depicts her first important female friend (the Englishwoman Ellen Kilshaw) as the doorway to a "whole region of new life."[36] Such friends, she argues, "not only know themselves more, but *are* more for having met, and regions of their being, which would else have laid sealed in cold obstruction, burst into leaf and bloom and song."[37] In contrast to Emerson's unidirectional model of friendship (which stresses the benefits derived *from* one's friends), Fuller presents a reciprocal model of friendship in which *both* parties are enlarged by the relationship. "The soul environs itself with friends," Emerson observes in "Friendship," "that it may enter into a grander self-acquaintance or solitude" (CW 2: 116–17). Fuller, in contrast, observes that – in the most intimate friendships – "both seem to rise."[38]

Fuller's most important and extended discussion of friendship occurs in her 1842 essay in *The Dial,* "Bettine Brentano and Her Friend Günderode." Ostensibly a discussion of members of Goethe's circle, this essay reads like a coded analysis of the differences between Fuller's relationships with Emerson and her female friends. Fuller's basic strategy is to measure Bettine Brentano's friendship with Goethe (recorded in the 1837 volume *Goethe's Correspondence with a Child*) against her friendship with the canoness

Karoline von Günderode (dramatized in the fictionalized correspondence that Fuller translated and published in 1842). Bettine's friendship with Goethe, in Fuller's eyes, was flawed by their "unequal" position. As a result, she found herself in a position of idolizing the distant, but unresponsive, Goethe, who manifested only the "cold pleasure of an observer" – a characterization that echoes Fuller's complaint of Emerson's "coldness" in her 1840 letters.[39] In contrast to the hierarchical relationship of Bettine and Goethe, Fuller praises the friendship of Bettine and Günderode, whose lives exist on a more equal plane.[40] Without the "inspiration" of such an intimate friend, Fuller asserts, our "thoughts stretch out into eternity and find no home."[41] The friend, in these terms, sustains "the aspiration of [one's] nobler nature"; for, in "true intimacy," we find the

> harmonious development of mind by mind, two souls prophesying to one another, two minds feeding one another, two human hearts sustaining and pardoning one another![42]

But such relationships, she observes, are very rare. Often, only "one party keeps true to the original covenant" and is forced to wander among the "tombs of . . . buried loves."[43]

Margaret Fuller's observations on friendship call into question theories (like those of Emerson) that attempt to analyze friendship in gender-neutral terms. One's friendships, she argues, are always complicated by social position. Thus, the unequal position of women in nineteenth-century society greatly complicates their relationships with men and even with other women. Although she idealizes friendship, Fuller is unable to share Emerson's conviction that friends lead us to a realm of ideal truth. Social relationships, in her analysis, exist in a phenomenal realm shaped by economic, political, and ideological interests. As a result, the relationships of true friends (such as the women friends Fuller idealizes) take their meaning in relation to various specific social contexts. We see this linkage most clearly in the ways, during Fuller's lifetime, in which models of female friendship and "sisterhood" became linked to political reform movements, such as the female moral-reform societies that were emerging in New York.[44] By the time she published *Woman in the Nineteenth Century* in 1845, Fuller's understanding of social being fundamentally challenged any theory of transcendental friendship.

Like Fuller, Henry David Thoreau found that Emerson's theories of friendship did not do full justice to the complexities of human relationships. Although he shared Emerson's tendency to idealize friendship, Thoreau paid more attention to the intractability of others. "We must accept each other as we are," he observed in his essay on friendship in *A Week on the*

Concord and Merrimack Rivers; "I could tame a hyena more easily than my Friend. He is a material which no tool of mine will work."[45] According to David Suchoff, such passages represent Thoreau's construction of a model of meaning that departed radically from Emerson's belief in the "correspondence" between the mind and nature. "Friendship," in Thoreau's text, "will symbolize the quest for meaning as a complex relationship to a fundamental absence."[46] This absence extended to Thoreau's friendships; for, by the time he published *A Week* in 1849, his friendship with Emerson had become strained.[47] During the previous decade, Thoreau had lived in the Emerson household, built his cabin on Emerson's land at Walden Pond, been the recipient of Emerson's assistance in the publication of his writing, worked as the tutor for the children of Emerson's brother, and been deeply influenced by his ideas. It has been argued that Thoreau's relationship with the older Emerson verged on "identification" with his famous mentor.[48] But as Thoreau began to individuate himself as a thinker and writer, it became increasingly difficult for him to accept Emerson's "condescension" and "assumption of discipleship."[49] As a result, many of Thoreau's most important statements about friendship reflect a retrospective understanding of the ways in which transcendental friendship might fail.

At times, Thoreau realized, friends spoke different languages. "As our constitution our geniuses are different – so our standards," he observed in one of his journals, "and we are amenable to different codes."[50] Such a recognition of difference allowed Thoreau to muse, in one of his most striking journal reflections, that friends are

> eternally strange to one another. . . . They are like two boughs crossed in the wood, which play backward and forwards upon one another in the wind, and only wear into each other, but never the sap of one flows into the pores of the other, for then the wind would no longer draw from them the strains which enchanted the wood. They are not two united, but rather one divided.[51]

Like Emerson, Thoreau recognized the combative and antagonistic aspects of friendship. But instead of drawing him deeper into the Oversoul, such moments of crisis reminded him of the evanescent and fragile quality of human relationships. In his experience, the world of "actual persons" rarely matched the domain of the "ideal friend."[52]

But the recognition of personal and constitutional differences did not prevent Thoreau from constructing a model of friendship as rarefied as Emerson's. Language, he believed, could never capture the subtle play of love and faith that constituted true friendship. "The language of Friendship," he noted in *A Week*, "is not words but meanings. It is an intelligence above language."[53] "All that has been said of friendship is like botany to flowers," he noted in his journal. "It can never be recognised by the understanding. It cannot be the subject of reconciliation or the theme of conversation even between friends."[54] Hoping to be related to his friend "by the most etherial part of our natures alone," Thoreau described friendship as a "mystic relation," as the meeting of "essences."[55] In his eyes, the very act of discussing friendship "profanes" an ideal relationship that must be based on mutual trust; for friendship "can never be talked about."[56] At the moment that one "makes a theme of friendship," it "is always something past" and "descends to merely human relations."[57] Even the act of praising a friend, by articulating what should remain inexpressible, would "sunder him from myself."[58] In these terms, Thoreau's self-conscious discussions of friendship in the late 1840s increasingly signaled his distance from the transcendental ideal they expressed. Having experienced the failure of his friendship with Emerson and others, he was able to measure the ways in which transcendental friendship might be destroyed.[59]

Ultimately, Thoreau's model of friendship depends upon a hermeneutic of faith, in which the relationship between friends must be based upon "generosity," "nobleness," and "trust."[60] Friendship, in these terms, involves the "exercise of the purest imagination and the rarest faith," for it is a relationship "without confession."[61] "The only ledge I can rear the arch of Friendship from," Thoreau insists, "is the ground of infinite faith – If you have lost any of your faith in me – you might as well have lost it all."[62] The result of such assumptions was that transcendental friendship for Thoreau (as for Emerson and Fuller) took on tragic dimensions at moments when personal disagreements motivated analyses of relationships in crisis. "Ah I yearn toward thee my friend," Thoreau lamented in an 1851 journal, "but I have not confidence in thee. We do not believe in the same God. I am not thou – Thou art not I."[63] Later in the same entry (which most likely refers to Emerson), he observed that "Ever and anon there will come the consciousness to mar our love – that change the theme but a hair's breadth & we are tragically strange to one another."[64] Thoreau was affronted by what seemed like Emerson's failure to understand his writing and his motives (for example, his dual commitment to both ideal truth and practical knowledge). Like Fuller, Thoreau felt that – at key moments – Emerson should have understood and appreciated the individual needs of his character. But such demands lay bare the fundamental instability of transcendental friendship, which required in friends an unshaken faith in each other's nobility of thought and character – a demand that often contradicted individual demands for social recognition.

Investing their highest dreams of human development in each other, all three writers eventually found that few others could match the expansive scope of their ideals. Emerson (like Fuller and Thoreau) hoped that the meeting of friends allowed the "deity" in each to "cancel the thick walls of individual character, relation, age, sex, & circumstance" (*JMN* 7: 212). But the dilemma faced by these writers was that their emotional commitments to each other could not be separated from the phenomenal world in which they dwelled. Recognizing the ways in which the "intellectual and active powers increase with our affections" (*CW* 2: 113), none of the three could envision a stable model of friendship in which the demands of affection and intellect did not contradict each other. We see this in Emerson's account of the "two elements that go to the composition of friendship" – "Truth" (associated with absolute sincerity) and "Tenderness" (*CW* 2: 119, 120). "Every man alone is sincere," Emerson reflected; "At the entrance of a second person, hypocrisy begins" (119). This hypocrisy or "dissimulation" results in part from the emotional demands of the other – demands that mirror the "thick walls of individual character, relation, age, sex, & circumstance." Put another way, theories of transcendental friendship made it impossible to be faithful both to one's ideas and to one's feelings.

In Emerson's essay "Friendship," the final certitude was the immediate intuition of the "soul." From the divine perspective of the soul, even the most intimate friend belonged to "the vast shadow of the Phenomenal"; for the friend was "not my soul, but a picture and effigy of that" (*CW* 2: 116). As a result, a "friend . . . is a sort of paradox in nature":

> I who alone am, I who see nothing in nature whose existence I can affirm with equal evidence to my own, behold now the semblance of my being in all its height, variety and curiosity, reiterated in a foreign form.   (*CW* 2: 120)

Ultimately, there was no way out of this epistemological impasse, since Emerson analyzed friendship through dualistic categories that valued thought over feeling, intuition over perception, universal truth over worldly phenomena. But if the existential texture and emotional richness of friendship are missing in Emerson's discussions, they are replaced by an expression of friendship's ideal – a relationship of mutual recognition so perfect that it could never be fully realized on earth.

NOTES

1   Stephen Yarbrough, for example, argues that "Transcendental friendship is, first of all, an idealized relationship, something to be approached, not attained, and if attained, not sustained." "From the Vice of Intimacy to the Vice of

Habit: The Theories of Friendship of Emerson and Thoreau," *Thoreau Society Quarterly* 13.3/4 (July/Oct. 1981): 63.

2   *The Letters of Margaret Fuller*, ed. Robert N. Hudspeth, 6 vols. (Ithaca & London: Cornell University Press, 1983–94), 2: 159.

3   Mary E. Rucker, "Emerson's 'Friendship' as Process," *ESQ* 18.4 (1972): 247.

4   George Sebouhian, "A Dialogue with Death: An Examination of Emerson's 'Friendship,' " *Studies in the American Renaissance* 1989: 221–22.

5   Robert D. Richardson, Jr., *Emerson: The Mind on Fire* (Berkeley, Los Angeles, & London: University of California Press, 1995), p. 224.

6   The original journal passage is found in *JMN* 5: 174.

7   Stephen R. Yarbrough, p. 66.

8   Sebouhian, p. 221.

9   Charles Capper, *Margaret Fuller: An American Romantic Life* (Oxford & New York: Oxford University Press, 1992), p. 187.

10 For example, in her letter of Sept. 29, 1840, to Emerson, Fuller wrote: "Then indeed, when my soul in its childish agony of prayer, stretched out its arms to you *as a father*, did you not see what was meant by this crying for the moon . . . ?" (*Letters* 2: 160, my italics.)

11 Marie Olesen Urbanski, "The Ambivalence of Ralph Waldo Emerson Towards Margaret Fuller," *Thoreau Society Quarterly* 10.3 (July 1978): 28.

12 Capper, pp. 187–88.

13 Urbanski, p. 28.

14 Harry R. Warfel, "Margaret Fuller and Ralph Waldo Emerson," *Publications of the Modern Language Association* 50 (June 1935): 591.

15 Carl F. Strauch, "Hatred's Swift Repulsions: Emerson, Margaret Fuller, and Others," *Studies in Romanticism* 7.2 (Winter 1968): 65–103.

16 John Bard McNulty, "Emerson's Friends and the Essay on Friendship," *New England Quarterly* 19 (1946): 391.

17 Dorothy Berkson, " 'Born and Bred in Different Nations': Margaret Fuller and Ralph Waldo Emerson," in Shirley Marchalonis, ed., *Patrons and Protégées: Gender, Friendship, and Writing in Nineteenth-Century America* (New Brunswick, NJ, & London: Rutgers University Press, 1988), pp. 8–10.

18 *Letters of Emerson to a Friend* (Boston: Houghton Mifflin, 1899), p. 33.

19 Eleanor M. Tilton, ed., *The Letters of Ralph Waldo Emerson, Volume Seven 1807–1844* (New York: Columbia University Press, 1990), p. 476.

20 In "The Emerson-Ward Friendship: Ideals and Realities" (*SAR* 1984), David Baldwin observes that "the differences in their income and occupational heritage placed them in separate groups. The Ward family was a member of Boston society; Emerson's was not" (p. 300).

21 Berkson, p. 9.

22 Berkson comes very close to unraveling the ways in which the Ward-Barker engagement complicated Fuller's life. She asserts: "While Fuller's response to the marriage was also highly charged, this is not surprising, since she had once apparently thought of Ward as a lover, and since Anna Barker was one of a number of women with whom Fuller had had (and continued in Anna's case to have) intense relationships of the sort Carroll Smith-Rosenberg has documented" (p. 11).

23 Fuller, *Letters* 2: 90.

24 Fuller, *Letters* 2: 93.
25 *The Essential Margaret Fuller*, ed. Jeffrey Steele (New Brunswick, NJ: Rutgers University Press, 1992), pp. 22–23. Mme Jeanne-Françoise Récamier (1777–1849) was known for her literary salon; Mme de Staël (1766–1817, née Anne Louise Germaine Necker) was a French author remembered as a theorist of Romanticism and for her novel *Corinne* (1807).
26 Carl Strauch notices the reference, without making the connection (p. 86).
27 Additional factors complicating Emerson and Fuller's friendship during this period were her editorship of *The Dial* and their different responses to the Brook Farm utopian community, which Fuller (but not Emerson) joined for a while.
28 Fuller, *Letters* 2: 160.
29 Strauch, p. 70. In similar terms, Marie Olesen Urbanski argues that Emerson's and Fuller's "explosive" emotions culminated in "some kind of sexual confrontation" (pp. 30–31).
30 Fuller, *Letters* 2: 158.
31 Fuller, *Letters* 2: 160.
32 Fuller, *Letters* 2: 159.
33 Fuller, *Letters* 2: 170.
34 Fuller, *Letters* 2: 214.
35 Fuller, *Letters* 2: 214.
36 *The Essential Margaret Fuller*, p. 39.
37 *The Essential Margaret Fuller*, pp. 40–41.
38 *The Essential Margaret Fuller*, p. 41.
39 *The Essential Margaret Fuller*, pp. 61–62.
40 Bettine's friendship with Günderode was tragically terminated by Günderode's suicide (after her rejection by Friedrich Creuzer). In contrast to this dysfunctional male-female relationship, Fuller locates in her bond with Bettine the best qualities of friendship. See Renate Delphendaehl, "Margaret Fuller: Interpreter and Translator of German Literature," in Marie Mitchell Olesen Urbanski, ed., *Margaret Fuller: Visionary of the New Age* (Orono, ME: Northern Lights, 1994), p. 93.
41 *The Essential Margaret Fuller*, p. 66.
42 *The Essential Margaret Fuller*, p. 67.
43 *The Essential Margaret Fuller*, pp. 66–67.
44 Barbara J. Berg analyzes the genesis of these societies in *The Remembered Gate: Origins of American Feminism* (Oxford & New York: Oxford University Press, 1978).
45 Henry D. Thoreau, *The Illustrated **A Week on the Concord and Merrimack Rivers***, ed. Carl F. Hovde, William L. Howarth, and Elizabeth Hall Witherell (Princeton, NJ: Princeton University Press, 1983), pp. 283–84.
46 David B. Suchoff, " 'A More Conscious Silence': Friendship and Language in Thoreau's *Week*," *English Literary History* 49 (1982): 684.
47 Useful discussions of the strains in their relationship are found in Joel Porte, *Emerson and Thoreau: Transcendentalists in Conflict* (Middletown, CT: Wesleyan University Press, 1966); Paul Hourihan, "Crisis in the Thoreau-Emerson Friendship: The Symbolic Function of 'Civil Disobedience,' " in *Thoreau's Psychology: Eight Essays*, ed. Raymond D. Gozzi (Lanham, MD: University Press

of America, 1983); and Robert Sattelmeyer, "Thoreau and Emerson," in *The Cambridge Companion to Henry David Thoreau,* ed. Joel Myerson (Cambridge & New York: Cambridge University Press, 1995).

48 Hourihan, p. 113.
49 Porte, p. 98.
50 Henry D. Thoreau, *Journal,* ed. John C. Broderick, Robert Sattelmeyer, et al., 4 vols. to date (Princeton, NJ: Princeton University Press, 1981–), 4: 314.
51 Thoreau, *Journal,* 1: 236–37.
52 Thoreau, *Journal,* 3: 98.
53 Thoreau, *A Week,* p. 273.
54 Thoreau, *Journal,* 2: 87–88.
55 Thoreau, *Journal,* 3: 19, 40, 29.
56 Thoreau, *Journal,* 2: 380.
57 Thoreau, *Journal,* 3: 193.
58 Thoreau, *Journal,* 2: 45.
59 Porte observes that "The history of many of Thoreau's Transcendental friendships is the sadly predictable tale of the painful disparity between the real men he tried to befriend and the ideal they offered him instead" (p. 103).
60 Thoreau, *Journal,* 2: 88.
61 Thoreau, *Journal,* 2: 380.
62 Thoreau, *Journal,* 4: 312.
63 Thoreau, *Journal,* 4: 137.
64 Thoreau, *Journal,* 4: 137.

8

JULIE ELLISON

Tears for Emerson: *Essays, Second Series*

I wonder if I am the only reader of Emerson who weeps over the death of his son in 1842. I have never heard anyone else confess to this reaction, although the story of how Emerson's "Experience" refers to Waldo Emerson's death is told briefly by Emerson himself, in the willfully perverse third paragraph of the essay. Then it is narrated repeatedly by twentieth-century scholars and critics, who treasure this moment as the most dramatic autobiographical reference in Emerson's published prose:

> In the death of my son, now more than two years ago, I seem to have lost a beautiful estate, – no more. I cannot get it nearer to me. If tomorrow I should be informed of the bankruptcy of my principal debtors, the loss of my property would be a great inconvenience to me, perhaps, for many years; but it would leave me as it found me, – neither better nor worse. So is it with this calamity: it does not touch me: something which I fancied was a part of me, which could not be torn away without tearing me, nor enlarged without enriching me, falls off from me, and leaves no scar. It was caducous. I grieve that grief can teach me nothing, nor carry me one step into real nature.... Nothing is left us now but death. We look to that with a grim satisfaction, saying, there at least is reality that will not dodge us.   (*CW* 3: 28–29)

The story of Waldo's death, referred to even here through the paradoxical claim that the author has failed to mourn, is not only told, but illustrated in recent publications. The photograph of the handsome five-year-old with a fierce, open gaze haunts readers of Gay Wilson Allen's *Waldo Emerson* and of Joel Porte's *Emerson in His Journals*, readers of Volume 3 of the new *Collected Works (Essays, Second Series)*, and readers of Dolores Bird Carpenter's edition of Ellen Tucker Emerson's manuscript biography of her mother, *The Life of Lidian Jackson Emerson*. The history of this photographic image confirms the "evanescence and lubricity of all objects, which lets them slip through our fingers then when we clutch hardest," as Emerson laments in "Experience" (*CW* 3: 29). "In the October, I should

140

think it was, of 1841 came the first travelling daguerreotypist to Concord," Ellen recalled:

> Mr. John Thoreau [Henry David Thoreau's brother] offered to take Waldo to have his daguerreotype taken. It needed in those days a blaze of sunlight which made Waldo frown; otherwise it was good. . . . Ten years later, when daguerreotyping had advanced and the plates were much smoother and better, Mother had Waldo's copied, and the copy I still have. We had both it and the original till Edward [Edward Waldo Emerson, born in 1844] who was accustomed only to photographs and little knew the nature of the daguerreotype, seeing it dusty, removed its glass and wiped it with a soft cloth. He was dismayed to find no trace of Waldo left, only a bare silver plate.
>
> (*LJE* 85)

A sentimental reaction to Emerson's essay today tells us something about the demographics of the professoriate, increasingly populated by scholarly parents like myself. Our reactions are shaped by the domestic economies in which we participate when we simultaneously write and parent in the 1990s – and by a national debate throughout the decade about identity politics and the relationship between policy and care. Although domesticity and sentimentality do not inevitably go together, the intricate relationship between work and family revealed by the widespread influence of feminist approaches to literary history encourages the transference of emotional conventions from one set of practices to the other. Furthermore, feminism has modified the practices of academic writing so that it is no longer unthinkable for critics contributing to scholarly volumes such as this one to admit to weeping over the children they encounter in their work. This change has been accompanied by a surging interest in autobiography, confession, and other forms of personal narrative, both in academic fields and in American culture generally. The revisionist sentimentalizing of public life makes the sensitive man family-friendly in the discourses of advertising, politics, and religion.

This may be the reason that scholars are now so absorbed in the cultural contribution of emotional expression. In the early eighteenth century, sentiment was associated with male civic virtue in dominant Anglo-American cultures, not with life in the home. But in antebellum America, as in Britain during the same period, domesticity and sentiment were conflated, so that tender feelings and family life were connected – without, however, severing the relationship between liberal politics and emotional susceptibility. I have talked with many students and colleagues, mostly women, about our shared susceptibility to the erasure, suffering, or death of children in the sentimental and domestic fiction of the nineteenth century, most memorably in novels such as Charles Dickens's *Dombey and Son* (1848), Susan Warner's *The Wide, Wide World* (1850), Harriet Beecher Stowe's *Uncle Tom's Cabin* (1852), and Louisa May Alcott's *Little Women* (1868–69). In addition to our newfound susceptibility to the death of fictional children, we are drawn to the biographies of writers like Mary Shelley, who lost three young children, and of Margaret Fuller, who died in a shipwreck off Fire Island after first witnessing the drownings of her husband and son. Even as one over-identifies with these narratives, one analyzes how the dynamics of mourning are inseparable from judgments about the value of domesticity, of mothering, and, I would argue, of fathering. In fact, the point of naming dead children, fictional and real, is to summon up our emotions *as critical readers*, for it is often the information available to the scholar that turns the true stories of children's deaths into something to weep over. We ask, under what *critical* circumstances does "Experience" become a story over which readers may shed tears? In Emerson's own day, what was the role of convention or cultural habit in allotting expressions of grief to various genres – essays, letters, and poems? What domestic divisions of labor led to the variety of written responses to Waldo's death by Emerson and those close to him? What does the essay's composition tell us about masculine domesticity in the nineteenth century?

"Experience" leads us to expand our questions about the literary response to domestic loss to include the problem of occasional writing in general. Most of Emerson's essays resist their connections to specific personal or public events, while his other writings – journals, poems, lectures – frequently embrace these occasions. In what sense is "Experience" an *occasional* essay, meaning one "arising out of, required by, or made for, the occasion" (*Oxford English Dictionary*)? And how does its occasional character illuminate the domestic scene of Emerson's literary production?

In January 1842, five-year-old Waldo Emerson came down with scarlet fever on a Monday and died the following Thursday night. Emerson sums up his concept of serial reality at the very beginning of "Experience": "Where do we find ourselves? In a series, of which we do not know the extremes and believe that it has none" (CW 3: 27). One measures Emerson's career in terms of series: lecture series; *Essays, First Series;* and *Essays, Second Series.* Death also constitutes one of the fundamental serial realities of Emerson's career. His father died when he was eight; his first wife died after 18 months of marriage in 1831; his adult brothers, Edward and Charles, died in 1834 and 1836, respectively; and then Waldo in 1842.[1] Repetitive traumas are certainly not the sole source of Emerson's romance with repetition or with notions of the series. The popularity of the series in antebellum America has at least as much to do with the literary marketplace as with biographical factors. Nonetheless, in "Experience," the word "series" refers both to recurring loss and to the emotionally and cognitively dissociated states of mind, the "evanescence and lubricity" that accompany it. And as one examines the writings linked to "Experience," they, too, begin to constitute a series, the nonprogressive rewriting so characteristic of Emerson's mode of production.

The texts surrounding Waldo's death draw our attention to the relationship between literature and paternity. Patsy Yaeger has made the case for a revised understanding of literary fathers. She zeroes in on the often-suppressed history of the body as it is registered in the material and sexual meanings that frequently evade us in familiar texts. Readers, she argues, should attend to

> the ways in which the father's . . . desire and libidinal body are ever-present in literary and cultural texts, but as themes that are disguised, as contents under pressure. . . . [I]n the course of uncovering this invisible father, [feminist critics] have also begun to refigure him, to make him visible, vulnerable, carnal. We must . . . reconstruct this father as a contactable, masterable, libidinal body, as a being who can be anatomized, fragmented, shattered – or cherished – as someone who no longer operates from an abstract and transcendental realm.[2]

Since Emerson is a poet of "abstract and transcendental" realms, Yaeger's project of embodiment seems especially well suited to his work.[3]

Addressing the textual effects of a child's death forces us to see the writer as father in the context of the household and to see domesticity as a social system. Gillian Brown has joined the history of domesticity to the history of selfhood in the concept of "domestic individualism." She stresses the importance of notions of property and the family in constituting nineteenth-century views of the person. Domesticity "inflects" individuality, she proposes, and reveals a self that is continually developing its "properties" in relation to "the process of ownership and production." The domestic individual strives toward a sense of self-possession that depends both on feelings about the house and the objects and people that fill it, and on views of the market that arrange labor, money, and things outside the home. "Domestic processes" caused individuals both to identify with and to separate themselves from nineteenth-century capitalism: "In . . . the cohabitation of the individual with the economic, material conditions and mental states . . . coalesce."[4]

When Emerson likens the death of his son to the loss of "a beautiful estate, – no more" and to sudden "bankruptcy," he is drawing on long-standing notions of a father's property in his children. He feels that his relation to his son should be, but somehow is not, experienced by him as different from his alienated relation to land and money (CW 3: 29).[5] The relative remoteness of economic fact compared to family bonds confirms a pattern observed by Gillian Brown: affectionate investments in family members become meaningful by virtue of their difference from the domain of the market economy, even while conceptions of ownership are shared by both. Near the end of "Experience," Emerson critiques the sentimental position as one in which bodily integrity, signifying one's control over feeling, is put in jeopardy. "The life of truth," he states (or rather, wishes), "is not the slave of tears, contritions, and perturbations." He dramatizes sentimental risk through one of his characteristic allegories of the swimmer in trouble: "a sympathetic person is placed in the dilemma of a swimmer among drowning men, who all catch at him, and if he give so much as a leg or a finger, they will drown him" (CW 3: 47). Self-loss in the affective realm is likened to slavery in the domain of labor: one should own one's emotions as one does one's effort.

Gillian Brown focuses on such shifting connections between possessions, domestic responsibilities, "right feeling" (40), and "property relations in a market society" (43) as these are dramatized in nineteenth-century novels. What would it mean to apply Yaeger's reassessment of the embodied father and Brown's exploration of the domesticated individual to the Emersonian essay – a genre that he shaped in nervous relation or resistance to novels? The discourse of the essays is without determinate characters and settings, but the essays are fascinated with character, effort, fraught encounters among or within human subjectivities, and the dynamics of ownership and appropriation. Emerson's essays have been both praised and castigated for their impersonal obsession with the self.[6] In recent years, however, critics have sought to connect both the essays and the author to the social, material world, to the economy of lecture tours and paying audiences, to the class tensions of antebellum Boston, to the politics of antislavery and abolition.[7] To link a biographical event (Waldo's death) to the family culture of work and feeling, and then to read the essays as texts composed in negotiation with and out of resistance to both paternal and national occasions, is a strategy consistent with the new referentiality of Emerson studies and of literary studies in general.

Of Waldo Emerson's death we possess an involved textual record. Lidian Jackson Emerson, Emerson's wife, wrote a number of letters on the subject, still unpublished; later she lent these to the young Transcendentalist Charles King Newcomb for use in a story eventually published in The Dial, "The Two Dolons." In this bizarre tale, a child at one with nature accepts sacrificial death at the hands of an inspired hermit in a Greek tunic – a savage rewriting of the child's relationship to nature celebrated in Emerson's elegy for Waldo, "Threnody" (*JMN* 8: 179; *L* 3: 55–56, 66–67; *The Dial* 3.1, July 1842, 112–23). Her daughter drew on these letters, as well, in writing *The Life of Lidian Jackson Emerson*. Another set of written responses consists of Ralph Waldo Emerson's journal entries and the letters that spread news of the child's death, along with his correspondents' ongoing answers. These brief records of the early fluctuations of mourning contain language that later emerges fully developed, but generically divided, in "Experience" and in Emerson's elegy, "Threnody." The daily sense of domestic loss becomes the theme of "Threnody"; the inability to feel and the chaos of perception mark the origin of "Experience." Two themes are paramount in these letters and journal entries: the association of the child with domestic *topoi*, or signifying places, and the way he represents Emerson's connection to social life, which, once severed, leaves the author suddenly undomesticated or unhoused: "with him has departed all that is glad & festal & almost all that is social even, for me, from this world" (*L* 3: 8). The imagery for which "Experience" is most renowned pervades the letters where the child's final "breath" turns facts to air:

> He gave up his innocent breath last night and my world this morning is poor enough. . . . Shall I ever dare to love any thing again. Farewell and Farewell, O my Boy!

> Alas! I chiefly grieve that I cannot grieve; that this fact takes no more deep hold than other facts, is as dreamlike as they; a lambent flame that will not burn playing on the surface of my river. Must every experience – those that promised to be dearest & most penetrative, – only kiss my cheek like the wind & pass away?
> (*L* 3: 8–9)

The passages that honor Waldo's place in the family's "daily economy" form catalogues of objects and persons, the acquisitions blessed or mediated by the child:

> What he looked upon is better, what he looked not upon is insignificant. . . . [T]he landscape was dishonored by this loss. For this boy in whose remembrance I have both slept & awaked so oft, decorated for me the morning star, & the evening cloud, how much more all the particulars of daily economy; for he had touched with his lively curiosity every trivial fact & circumstance in the household, the hard coal & the soft coal which I put into my stove; the wood of which he brought his little quota for grandmother's fire, the hammer, the pincers, & file, he was so eager to use; the microscope, the magnet, the little globe, & every trinket & instrument in the study; the loads of gravel on the meadow, the nests in the henhouse and many & many a little visit to the doghouse and to the barn.
> (*JMN* 8: 163–64)

Never I think did a child enjoy more. He had been thoroughly respected by his parents & those around him & not interfered with; and he had been the most fortunate in respect to the influences near him . . . his Aunt Elizabeth . . . Mary Russell . . . Henry Thoreau . . . Margaret Fuller & Caroline Sturgis . . . his Grandmother.   (*JMN* 8: 164–65)

Coleridge, who seldom lived with his wife and children but who composed some of the definitive romantic poems on domestic fatherhood, dramatized himself poetically as the writer in residence.[8] Emerson, who did most of his writing at home, rarely refers to this fact. But in "Threnody," begun by Emerson in the weeks after Waldo's death, the speaker zeroes in on "my empty house" (line 9) and names over the "daily haunts" of the missing boy.[9] The discourse of mourning joins the discourse of domesticity: "I had the right, few days ago / Thy steps to watch, thy place to know." Here the "right . . . / . . . to know" expresses the epistemological privilege of the parent; his property in the child takes the form of knowledge, and his loss takes the form of painful ignorance. The daily observation of the father at home yields up a catalogue of vacated paths and places which, like the journal entries, reveals the groundedness of the child in the social and familial place:

> The ominous hole he dug in the sand,
> And childhood's castles built or planned . . .
> The poultry-yard, the shed, the barn, –
> And every inch of garden ground
> Paced by the blessed feet around . . .
>   (*CPT* 119, lines 87–91)[10]

That almost every detail of the poem refers to specific memories of Waldo is confirmed by Emerson's journals and Ellen Tucker Emerson's account of her family's household life. A long section of the poem, for example, concerns Waldo's walk to school, the subject of numerous anecdotes (*LJE* 90–91): "The school-march, each day's festival, / When every morn my bosom glowed / To watch the convoy on the road" (*CPT* 118, lines 58–60). As with other children who become culturally significant within an adult circle, Waldo Emerson had been the focus of close attention and admiration. The last letter Emerson wrote before Waldo fell ill quoted one of the boy's *bons mots* (*L* 3: 5). But posthumously, Waldo was both more intensely domesticated and more fully transcendentalized than he had been in life.

In the next lines of the poem, the author-father is positioned at his study window and passersby admire the procession in the street. This section also refers to the peculiarly spiritual quality that "took the eye" of Waldo's adult admirers. Waldo Emerson's delighted performance of brotherly leadership is construed as a sign of poetic vocation and ethical purity:

> The little captain innocent
> Took the eye with him as he went;
> Each village senior paused to scan
> And speak the lovely caravan.
> From the window I look out
> To mark thy beautiful parade . . .
>   (*CPT* 119, lines 71–76)

While this would seem to be a representation of specifically fatherly witness, Emerson composed "Threnody" in dialogue with others. Margaret Fuller, outside the immediate family, mourned Waldo the longest. Her highly self-conscious relation to the idea of the radiant, moral child arises out of the complex dynamics of her relationship with Emerson. This relationship was at its most intense between the founding of the Transcendentalist periodical *The Dial* in 1840 and its cessation in 1844. Fuller edited the magazine until 1842, when Emerson took it over, but the enterprise was collaborative throughout. As Christina Zwarg shows in her analysis of the Emerson-Fuller relationship, Fuller's influence on Emerson was equal to or greater than Emerson's on Fuller.[11] Fuller's witty and demanding letters to Emerson are rich in interpretive feedback; she works hard at beaming Emerson's emotional style and intellectual habits back at him in a challenging tone. In the letters she writes after Waldo's death, mourning becomes interactive.[12]

Fuller carried on a number of friendships in the tones of visionary passion and metaphysical elaboration, and her response to Waldo is consistent with her other communicative investments. She not only registers her own passion for the child, but also characterizes him as the mediator between herself and Emerson. The boy becomes the messenger who had once visibly enacted the openness and affection that Emerson was too inhibited to display. When Waldo died, she lost the amplified access to the father that he had provided. One year after his death, in the winter of 1843, Fuller dreamed of him. In her dream the boy announced that his name was now Charles, presumably a link to Emerson's brother, who had died in 1836 (*LMF* 3: 114). In January 1844, she wrote Emerson on the second anniversary of Waldo's death, a few months before the last issue of *The Dial* appeared. Waldo's power to mediate her connection with Emerson is still a live issue. She understands the aura of withdrawal she had always resented in him as a sign of persistent grief, and she herself mourns – as a blow to her friendship with Emerson – the palpable social loss of the child's com-municative presence:

> [T]o me this season can never pass without opening anew the deep wound. I do not find myself at all consoled for the loss of that beautiful form which seemed to me the realization of hope more than any other. I miss him when I go to your home, I miss him when I think of you there; you seem to me lonely as if he filled to you a place which no other ever could in any degree.[13]
>
> ... I think of him a great deal and feel at this distance of time that there was no fancy, no exaggeration in the feelings he excited. His beauty was real, was substantial. I have all his looks before me now. I have just been reading a note of yours which he brought me in the red room, and I see him just as he looked that day, a messenger of good tidings, an angel.
>
> (*LMF* 3: 175–76)

The following summer, after admiring the Hawthornes' beautiful infant daughter – who, as Herbert has shown, herself carried a substantial burden of cultural mystique with her into adulthood[14] – Fuller referred again to the subject of "*mein herzens kind*" ["child of my heart"]. In addressing Caroline Sturgis, a close mutual friend, she emphasizes her own history of "pure" attachment and repeated loss. In her splendid closing cadences, Fuller prays to be liberated from mourning through a contest in which sublimity defeats demonic sentiment:

> Father, thou hast taught me to prostrate myself in the dust, even with my brow in the dust and *ask to be taught*. Yes, teach me, and wash by age-long flood of truth from my being each atom over which these demons of time can assert their power.
> (*LMF* 3: 218–19)[15]

Fuller's is the opposite of Emerson's similarly oceanic lament in "Experience" over the way grief makes us feel remote from the object of mourning:

> An innavigable sea washes with silent waves between us and the things we aim at and converse with. Grief too will make us idealists. In the death of my son, now more than two years ago, I seem to have lost a beautiful estate, – no more. I cannot get it nearer to me.
> (*CW* 3: 28–29).

Grief makes both Fuller and Emerson "idealists," but for Emerson idealism presents an "innavigable" buffer to conversation. New England romantic idealism, these confessions suggest, both practices and criticizes sympathy.

As Sharon Cameron has powerfully argued, "Experience" is "an elegy, an essay whose primary task is its work of mourning." Although in "Experience" "dissociation replaces tears" in the speaker's sensations, he nonetheless "knows that tears are the particular experience from which dissociation will protect him." The difficulty with the essay, then, as Cameron notes, is that "it supposes the loss of affect rather than the loss of the son to be the primary object mourned."[16] Despite the contribution her reading makes to our understanding of the essay, Cameron's narrow focus on "Experience" in isolation from related texts blocks a more inclusive view of the mourning process. Fuller's claim to tears in her letters and Emerson's own testimony to felt daily pain in "Threnody" suggest that "Experience" registers a psychological difference from those texts but also a key difference of *genre*. The division of labor between the crises of cognition and subjectivity that comprise "Experience" and the domestic emotions performed in "Threnody" reflects a habit of splitting up emotional "work" by assigning some processes to philosophical speculation and others to participatory or contagious sentiment. This distribution of feelings among genres gives quite different social meanings to essays, speeches, and treatises, with their defenses against sensibility, and to novels, poems, and family letters, which self-consciously dramatize sympathy. The effect of these generic divisions can be schizophrenic. Emerson says he cannot grieve in one place ("Experience") but can, and does, in another ("Threnody"). Of course, I am stating these differences in a way that is far too binary. Focusing on the logic of feeling in the Emerson household shows how truly difficult and tenuous these distinctions between public and domestic, speculative and sentimental modes can be.

In a recent *New Yorker* cartoon, a couple are standing at their front door. The befuddled-looking husband in suit and tie carrying a briefcase is obviously about to leave for the office. The caption reads: "Wait a minute. Where am I going? I'm a writer."[17] This man has temporarily forgotten that writers work at home, and the cartoon calls attention to that lapsed assumption. As in so many families of male writers, during the day Emerson was in but not of the household, though his correspondence shows him to be constantly involved in hiring servants, negotiating finances, and sustaining family networks. Lidian Jackson Emerson, who overcame her own strong resistance to a domestic career when she became Emerson's second wife,[18] cared for the children along with female servants and others; she also protected the space and time allotted to Emerson's writing. The boundaries of the writer's study were not impermeable: children, other family members, and guests entered often. Emerson heard the sounds of domestic activity, saw it through the window, recorded it in his journal, and sought it out on his walks.[19] The writer's room was thought of as a separate sphere within the household, a space for the imagination within the domestic economy but one through which the winds of family moods and actions blew.

Emerson had a good deal to say on the subject of domesticity. Barbara Ryan has recently demonstrated that he had mixed feelings about the poli-

tics of household work and about servants. He alternated between pleasure
in Lidian Emerson's management, irritation both with her and with servants, and an appreciation of the dehumanizing effects of housework. His
1838 lecture "Home" was followed in 1843 by "Domestic Life," collected
in *Society and Solitude* (1870). Done too compulsively or for the wrong
reasons, housework "oppresses women," he writes in "Domestic Life": "a
house kept to the end of prudence is laborious without joy" (*W* 7: 109). As
Ryan explores the relationship between Emerson's ambivalence about servant labor and his shift to public support of abolitionism in his speech
"Emancipation in the British West Indies" (1844), she concludes: "His
greatest imaginative leap was to see what most domestic employers refused
to consider: that waged domestic service was not wholly different from
Southern slavery." Emerson periodically struggled to avoid a reclusive domesticity and felt guilty about excluding servants from the family community, partly, Ryan shows, because of his appreciation of "the conceptual
proximity of waged and chattel service."

Contemporary advice books distanced husbands from household labor
and laborers, and some books of this kind explicitly justified domestic service performed for intellectuals. Without servants, the author of one such
manual urged, "they would not have time to preach and write books, and
spread knowledge and religion."[20] Despite – or perhaps because of – this
justification, male writers were increasingly writing about the homely circumstances of writing, thus actively foregrounding the relation between
domesticity and composition. The family was both impossibly distracting
and a rich source of literary inspiration and subject matter.

Emerson developed his own version of the double function of domesticity
set forth by Gillian Brown. He understood that material reality and economic decisions are fully bound up with a sense of self: "I am not one thing
and my expenditures another. My expenditure is me" ("Domestic Life," *W*
7: 107). But this attitude tended to coexist with the claim that the self's
mental powers should dematerialize the idea of home. Home becomes an
idea or attitude. "The spirit . . . is at home in law," he pronounces: "the
more inward the principle of association is the more permanent it will be."
Home is dematerialized and turned into a serial condition, a state of mind
that works against commitments to daily materiality: "it is the effect of this
domestication in the All to estrange the man in the particular." Emerson
concludes the lecture on "Home" with an account of how we become sentimental about our children. He explains parental emotion as caused by the
encounter between the universal child and specific epistemological opportunity: "A child, – every child, is infinitely beautiful; but the father alone
by position and duty is led to look near enough to see and know" (*EL* 3:

29, 31, 32). The father looking through the window at his son in "Threnody" acquires his "right to know" – and his right to write – from his domestic "position." At the same time, that "position" can be retailed in lectures and essays only in the form of an idea. When Emerson comes to write about the death of Waldo, epistemological location – the home as the place in which the child was known – takes on new value as the stimulus of both memory and forgetting.

Doubtless, male and female authors have composed their works in residential spaces for centuries. When I talk about male authors establishing themselves at home, I mean how they come to *write about the domestic conditions of their writing,* or about their own lives within the family. William Wordsworth, who dated his poetic vocation from the moment when he set up independent housekeeping with his sister, Dorothy Wordsworth, established the paradigm of the doubly sequestered writer in collaboration with her.[21] Coleridge imagined this scenario in some detail in advising young men with literary aspirations in *Biographia Literaria.* Don't be a professional writer, he warns. Do your writing after dinner, at home. Return from practicing your profession "at evening, to your family, prepared for its social enjoyments. . . . Then, when you retire into your study . . . the social silence, or undisturbing voices of a wife or sister will be like a restorative atmosphere, or soft music which moulds a dream without becoming its object."[22] The author is protected within and by the house from public life, then protected once again from the distracting incursions of domestic activity by further retreat to the study.

My own father was a writer who worked at home, and my first poem, written at the age of six, began: "Be as quiet as a mouse. / There's a writer in the house." My mother conscientiously policed the door to his office – part of the basement in one house, over the garage in another. On the occasions when I was invited in, the room had a messy grandeur, even an odor, all its own. While my father withdrew in order to write, many of the articles produced in that withdrawal were genial, even sentimental, pieces on family life: genre scenes of his mother, who worked at the canteen in Chicago's Union Station during World War II; my sisters' dancing school; my Swedish baby nurse; my co-op nursery. A hundred and fifty years before women claimed "a room of one's own" – Virginia Woolf's brilliant figure for the writer's domestic economy – and long before my own family tried to negotiate the pitfalls of residential composition, middle-class men like Emerson and his romantic predecessors worked hard to establish themselves at home. When this retreat fails to buffer the writing process sufficiently, other forms of escape into solitude may be necessary. Emerson spent nights in Boston at the Parker House Hotel before giving a lecture "that he might shut himself up alone with his lecture and write uninter-rupted" (*LJE* 145). My father stayed in a motel if he was having trouble meeting a deadline. This pattern of the writer's room – which one finds variations of in Hawthorne's prefaces, Melville's *Pierre,* and Longfellow's poem "The Children's Hour" – corrects too-facile references to domesticity and private life as female spheres. And it provides a context for Woolf's revisionist claims for the female author who responds to an *existing* mas-culine desire for the room within the house.

So far I have probed the links between domesticity and authorship in order to make sense of the way Emerson responds, in prose and verse, to the "occasion" of Waldo's death. To explore the meaning of occasional writing for Emerson and his contemporaries further, it is necessary to factor in politics – party politics, reform or protest movements, and ideological debates. The relationship in Emerson's work among these three terms is particularly complex in the early 1840s, the period when most of *Essays, Second Series* was composed. His antislavery speeches, one of which he excluded from *Essays, Second Series,* are not separable from his theory of domesticity or from the history of his domestic experience. Emerson had been swayed by the notion that domesticity is antithetical to politics. Ac-cording to Wordsworth's widely disseminated model, politics is to domes-ticity as burnout is to recuperation. For British Jacobins of the 1790s, po-litical exhaustion came about through sympathy for the French Revolution. The Wordsworthian cure for a radical's fatigue combined rural retirement and domestic affections, which together made possible a restored connec-tion to feeling.

The intuition that political opinions are incompatible with art, which still operates strongly today, was not peculiar to Wordsworth, Coleridge, or Emerson. Rather, such nervousness about the public place of the aesthetic invites us to question more closely a whole range of nineteenth-century negotiations between literature and politics. What changes in political ex-perience took place as political engagement became accessible to educated middle-class men and women? What was the economy or periodicity of "the cause" as played out in cycles of publicity, debate, legislative process, and reaction? Was there an emerging notion of political effort that had qualities distinct from other forms of work? Did the culture of individual-ism cause people to feel that they possessed scant supplies of energy and passion available for the common weal? Or did reformist communities so highly value intense bonds within the group that they seemed to wipe out other affiliations or induce a subsequent "recovery" phase of personal pri-vacy? The notion that radicalism tires itself out through the exhaustion of its adherents – as opposed, say, to being defeated in contests with other political positions or changing in response to altered circumstances – emerged then. It is still with us as "burnout," which has become an understandable response to any intensive, sustained engagement.

Gillian Brown has supplied us with the link between individual solitude and domesticity, and shows how they combine to generate writers' resistance to perceived market domains.[23] Taking her argument one step further, we can conclude that, under certain conditions, the perceived fusion of the reading public with the market made domesticity more highly valued as an anticommercial *and* antipublic sanctuary. If both the market and politics are viewed as eminently social, then economic and political forms of collective behavior become conflated with one another. When the recoil toward individualism is a defense against the social, then distaste for the social registers skepticism toward both political participation and market entanglements. It is not simply politics that comes to seem tiring, therefore, but social life itself.

Stephen Whicher introduced into Emerson studies the now too-well-known dichotomy "Freedom or Fate," terms for self-determining experience and everything which is not self-determined, respectively. This opposition is bound up with the related dualism of artistic individualism versus social involvement and is commonly used to differentiate between the "early" and "later" phases of Emerson's career, as well.[24] Nowhere is it more important to resist the artist-versus-society doublet, however, than in exploring the relationship between domesticity and politics.

For the better part of the twentieth century, Emerson was thought to have been wholly committed to the view that individualism preserved the imagination from the wasting effects of reform movements. In 1840, he turned down an invitation to join Brook Farm, the utopian community in Roxbury: "to join this body would be to traverse all my long trumpeted theory . . . that a man is stronger than a city, that his solitude is more prevalent & beneficent than the concert of crowds" (*JMN* 7: 407–8). His diatribe against reformers in "Self-Reliance" (1841) castigates the politics of sympathy and calls the reformer "home" even while defining home as the place where the family no longer holds sway over genius:

> I am ashamed to think how easily we capitulate to badges and names, to large societies and dead institutions. . . . If an angry bigot assumes this bountiful cause of Abolition, and comes to me with his last news from Barbadoes, why should I not say to him, "Go love thy infant; love thy woodchopper: be good-natured and modest: have that grace; and never varnish your hard, uncharitable ambition with this incredible tenderness for black folk a thousand miles off. Thy love afar is spite at home." . . . I shun father and mother and wife and brother, when my genius calls me. I would write on the lintels of the

door-post, *Whim*. . . . I tell thee, thou foolish philanthropist, that I grudge the dollar, the dime, the cent I give to such men as do not belong to me and to whom I do not belong. . . . [T]hough I confess with shame I sometimes succumb and give the dollar, it is a wicked dollar which by and by I shall have the manhood to withhold.   (CW 2: 30–31)

Activism on behalf of suffering others "a thousand miles off" is proof of a false relation to home. But being at home is a false relation to the family itself. The connoisseur of the inability to feel, Emerson reclaimed selfhood in order to oppose expenditures of emotion in vicarious or mediated relations. This tendency emanated from early nineteenth-century Unitarian culture, too, which established its difference from protestant orthodoxies largely through its emphasis on noncoerced human particularity.[25]

Emerson's political experience was intensely domestic. From his undergraduate years at Harvard to the end of his writing career, Emerson was pressured to take public political stands, and that pressure came above all from family members. Len Gougeon's exhaustive account of Emerson's relationship to the abolitionist movement documents the strong antislavery commitments of Emerson's brother, Charles; of his Aunt Mary Moody Emerson, after her own conversion to the cause in 1835; and above all of his second wife, Lidian, a staunch and early abolitionist who joined forces with the well-organized Women's Anti-slavery Society of Concord, founded around the time of her marriage to Emerson in 1835. Thoreau's family also was involved in this and other local initiatives. In 1844, Elizabeth Hoar, Charles's fiancée before his death, and her father, Samuel Hoar, Emerson's neighbor, journeyed to South Carolina to represent Massachusetts in investigating charges that black sailors on Massachusetts ships were being illegally seized.[26] Members of Emerson's family defined themselves in terms of their opinions on elections, legislation, and judicial decisions, as well as on a wide range of social reforms espoused by voluntary organizations. Politics, we must conclude, did not come at Emerson from a civic realm distinct from family affairs, but from within the home circle itself. Domestic authorship, in sum, involved manifold degrees and kinds of privacy and publicity. Writing at home produced an elaborate web of relationships experienced as both familial and political.

Emerson prefaced his essay "Politics" with a gnomic motto that revives a georgic relation between the home farm and the republican state. It proposes a Jeffersonian scenario, a world in which "the statesman ploughs / a furrow for the wheat," and ends with this quatrain: "When the Church is social worth, / When the state-house is the hearth, / Then the perfect State is come, / The republican at home."[27] The sociable household politics of these closing lines suggests the kind of familial polity that surrounded Emerson. When in "The American Scholar" (1837) he urged "the gradual domestication of the idea of culture," he celebrated not only the notion of "the private life of one man" but also, almost against his will, an idea of integration according to which public culture and private life interact in symbiotic "domestication" (CW 1: 66).

At the same time, Emerson is continually queasy about anything involving large numbers of people, including his own career as a lecturer. He was bemused, embarrassed, even disgusted when contemplating group living (Brook Farm), reform movements ("New England Reformers"), and humanity in its racially defined masses.[28] In "Politics," written not long before the onset of Emerson's more committed antislavery statements, he cannot decide whether he most dislikes politics because it is too personal or because it is not personal enough. "Parties of principle, as, religious sects, or the parties of free-trade, of universal suffrage, of abolition of slavery, of abolition of capital punishment," he complains, "degenerate into enthusiasms" and are "perpetually corrupted by personality" (CW 3: 122–23). But then he punningly criticizes taxation for irritating citizens by collecting resources for impersonal "public ends" that "look vague and quixotic" by virtue of their remoteness: "A man who cannot be acquainted with me, taxes me; looking from afar at me, ordains that a part of my labor shall go to this or that whimsical end" (CW 3: 125–26).

As Gougeon demonstrates, Emerson was always antislavery in his personal views and became decisively and publicly linked to the abolitionist position in 1844. In the 1850s, Emerson spoke out repeatedly in public forums on behalf of abolitionist actions, including violent resistance to the Fugitive Slave Act and support for John Brown's raid on Harpers Ferry. These addresses were in some cases lost or unpublished, and hence absent from the canon of Emerson's works for many years. His speech given on the annual observation of West Indian emancipation was composed as he was starting to decide on the shape of *Essays, Second Series*. Scholars now think that this much-publicized address marked the turn to a more historically informed and concrete focus than is apparent in Emerson's earlier writings.[29] When his publisher informed him that the planned volume was too short, Emerson thought of adding this speech, which would have made a startling contrast to "Politics." But instead he included the more detached and bemused lecture "New England Reformers" (CW 3: xxiv–xxx).[30] The contrast between commitment to and detachment from the abolitionist cause apparent in the speech on West Indian emancipation and "New England Reformers" suggests that Emerson's statements on politics display a generic divide not dissimilar to the split between the ability and the inability to mourn expressed in the difference between the poem "Threnody" and the essay "Experience." His antislavery speeches – referred to by one editor as his "guerilla lectures" and destined by him for a planned "Book of Occasional Discourses" – set forth a pragmatic, activist politics.[31] The lectures that he revised for publication as "essays," by contrast, were suspicious of civic actions. Emerson might well have asserted about his essays, as Heather McHugh does about her poems, "they're about / how nothing is about, they're not / about about."[32] For him, therefore, the essay fosters the avoidance of political reference and the "address" – like the elegy – signals the willingness to engage in overtly occasional discourse.[33]

I concur with Cameron's view of "Experience," except insofar as it addresses *only* "Experience":

> "It does not touch me," Emerson says of grief at the beginning of the essay, but the lament turns to defiance at the end of the essay, where grief is the subject that cannot be touched. If the conversion I am describing savages the idea of reconciliation – to the child's death, to everything death represents – this is in keeping with the rest of the essay, which, like some science-fiction manifesto, insists definitionally on the isolated, the alien, the rootless, the excluded.[34]

All the qualities Cameron summarizes in her conclusions about the psychology of mourning apply to so many of Emerson's essays, early and late, that the question needs to be extended from "How does 'Experience' theorize and enact grief?" to "What is the relationship between domestic ground and the essay's serial flow?"

"Experience" is not typically understood as one of Emerson's explorations of domesticity, as "The Poet" is not regarded as dealing with grief, though it may well do so. Nonetheless, "Experience" negotiates constantly with familial, social life. In a complex paragraph midway through the essay, Emerson acknowledges the "small mercies" of "company" for one, like himself, who is "expecting nothing" and therefore is "full of thanks for moderate goods." Influenced by sociable contacts, "I am grown by sympathy a little eager and sentimental," he confesses, drawing on such moments to "give . . . reality" to the world's "vanishing meteorous appearance" (*CW* 3: 36). Resting for a while in "the temperate zone," "the middle region of our being," he arranges the "succession of mood or objects" so that domesticity and old-time religion (associated with Lidian Jackson Emerson) are contiguous to the poet's solitary "pulses" (39), as in fact his study was contiguous to household economy: "In the morning I wake and find the old world, wife, babes and mother, Concord and Boston, the dear old spiritual world, and even the dear old devil

not far off" (CW 3: 32). In the "equator of life," "thought . . . spirit . . . poetry" keep domesticity in full view (CW 3: 36).

At the end of this long paragraph, Emerson acknowledges our nostalgia
for being deeply grounded, envying "Indians, trappers, and bee-hunters"
for what seems to be their paradoxically more profound domestic connection with earth and place: "We fancy that we are strangers, and not so
intimately domesticated in the planet as the wild man, and the wild beast
and bird." But in fact "wild" creatures and the people who track them
"have no more root in the deep world" than the suburban author "and are
just such superficial tenants of the globe." Emerson first permits domesticity
to share the realism of the "mid-world," then deconstructs domesticity,
showing the local life of the body to be as slippery and subjective as the
dreams of the poet (CW 3: 37). By the very end of "Experience" – its
anticlimax – Emerson has reestablished the hierarchical split between mundane domesticity and elevated isolation: "We dress our garden, eat our
dinners, discuss the household with our wives, and these things make no
impression, are forgotten next week; but in the solitude to which every man
is always returning, he has a sanity and revelations, which in his passage
into new worlds he will carry with him" (CW 3: 49).

The more devastating turn away from the home comes a few pages earlier, however, after Emerson's exposition of the "Fall of Man" into conscious subjectivity. The "Fall" consists of the knowledge that we see "me-
diately" through "subject-lenses" and discover that the "great and crescive
self . . . ruins the kingdom of mortal friendship and love" (CW 3: 44). Emerson embraces the self, with all its mobility and partiality, as the temporary
ground of vision. This barren ground, the "bleak rocks" of one of the most
famous passages in Emerson's writing, becomes the point from which he
can resist tears, sympathy, and social engagement. Mourning is permitted
to return here but it is tearless, resolutely unsentimental and antinovelistic:

> And yet is the God the native of these bleak rocks. That need makes in morals
> the capital virtue of self-trust. We must hold hard to this poverty, however
> scandalous, and by more vigorous self-recoveries . . . possess our axis more
> firmly. The life of truth is cold, and so far mournful; but it is not the slave of
> tears, contritions, and perturbations. It does not attempt another's work, nor
> adopt another's facts. . . . I possess such a key to my own, as persuades me
> . . . that they also have a key to theirs. A sympathetic person is placed in the
> dilemma of a swimmer among drowning men, who all catch at him, and if he
> give so much as a leg or a finger, they will drown him. . . . Charity would be
> wasted. . . . A wise and hardy physician will say, *Come out of that,* as the
> first condition of advice.

In this our talking America, we are ruined by our good nature and listening on all sides. (CW 3: 47)

In the genre of the essay, Emerson fretfully resists sentimental genres such as elegiac poetry, the domestic novel, and abolitionist advocacy. He refuses to participate in the child's deathbed scene as it was narrated in nineteenth-century fiction, in visible grieving as it was choreographed in contemporary rituals of mourning, or in the dramatization of pain and sympathy that characterized much antislavery discourse. "Experience" in particular and Emerson's essays in general are largely constituted by this unsteady resistance to the occasion. Essays are the textual equivalent of the writer's study, where the desire for solitude competes with familial crises. In other kinds of writing – poems, letters, journals, speeches – Emerson sympathizes with social and domestic events. But his most ambitious works, the volumes of collected essays, celebrate the escape from the occasion while honoring the loss of mourning itself.

NOTES

1 B. L. Packer, *Emerson's Fall: A New Interpretation of the Major Essays* (New York: Continuum Press, 1982), pp. 48–57. James M. Cox, "R. W. Emerson: The Circles of the Eye" in *Emerson: Prophecy, Metamorphosis, and Influence*, ed. David Levin, English Institute Essays (New York: Columbia University Press, 1975), pp. 71–72, 74–75, cited by Packer.
2 Patricia Yaeger and Beth Kowaleski-Wallace, eds. *Refiguring the Father: New Feminist Readings of Patriarchy* (Carbondale and Edwardsville: Southern Illinois University Press, 1989). Yaeger, "The Father's Breasts," p. 19.
3 Indeed, the philosopher Stanley Cavell, without any conscious reference to feminism, also reads "Experience" partly in these terms. Tracing the connection between death and "male birth," he concludes by "taking the essay's idea of itself as pregnant to be declared in the passages that relate the son now dead to the writer-father's body." *This New Yet Unapproachable America* (Albuquerque: Living Batch Press, 1989), pp. 98–105, passim, and pp. 103–104.
4 Gillian Brown, *Domestic Individualism: Imagining Self in Nineteenth-Century America* (Berkeley: University of California Press, 1990), pp. 1–2, 9–10.
5 Joel Porte, *Representative Man* (New York: Oxford University Press, 1979), pp. 247–52. Porte discusses Emerson's financial management and economic status, especially in the context of the Panic of 1837 and the ensuing depression.
6 Impersonal, not least because Emerson knew himself to be physically and socially inhibited; he wished, as much as possible, to be saved from bodily embarrassments: involuntary laughter, excessive appetite, affectionate display. Julie Ellison, "The Laws of Ice: Emerson's Irony and 'The Comic,'" *ESQ* 30 (2nd Quarter 1984): 73, 76–77.

7 Anne C. Rose, *Transcendentalism as a Social Movement, 1830–1850* (New Haven: Yale University Press, 1981).

8 The cultural prestige Waldo had attained among a small group of relatives and close associates reminds one of the status accorded to Hartley Coleridge, who starred as a magical child in his father's poems, especially in "The Nightingale: A Conversation Poem." Hartley's value was enhanced by Coleridge's feelings of guilt after the infant death of his second son, Berkeley, while the poet was away on his German sabbatical. Yaeger, "The Father's Breasts," in Yaeger and Kowaleski-Wallace, *Refiguring the Father: New Feminist Readings of Patriarchy*, pp.13–15.

9 *Emerson: Collected Poems & Translations*, ed. Harold Bloom and Paul Kane (New York: The Library of America, 1994), pp. 117–24, hereafter cited as *CPT*.

10 Ellen Tucker Emerson recalls the link between walking the grounds and her father's rituals of naming, although the anecdote she tells takes place long after Waldo's death: "After breakfast [on Sundays] we usually went out into the garden with Father and visited its trees, then out into the pear-orchard and not seldom this round took all the time before church. It was a most domestic and happy progress from tree to tree. . . . Father told us all about each tree and we talked to him, and when fruit was ripe we picked it up and ate as we went." To some of the trees Emerson gave occasional names, such as "The thirty-seven Approbation-Tree," to commemorate the number of "Approbations" awarded to Edith Emerson's rival for her teacher's approval (*LJE* 119–20).

11 Christina Zwarg, *Feminist Conversations: Fuller, Emerson, and the Play of Reading* (Ithaca: Cornell University Press, 1995), ch. 8, "Emerson's Scene before the Women."

12 In her chapter on "Mourning the Dead: A Study in Sentimental Ritual," Karen Halttunen explores nineteenth-century mourning ritual in terms of the double binds it creates for the American middle class. While Halttunen's discussions of the tension between emotional authenticity and genteel performance marked an important step in studies of sentimental culture, I would urge a more multidimensional history of mourning that includes the potential for self-conscious reflection on the social costs and benefits of idealization by its participants. Her middle-class mourners and performers end up looking rather like caricatures of the genteel impulse. *Confidence Men and Painted Women: A Study of Middle-Class Culture in America, 1830–1870* (New Haven: Yale University Press, 1982). See also Neil L. Tolchin, *Mourning, Gender, and Creativity in the Art of Herman Melville* (New Haven: Yale University Press, 1988). Related discussions of mourning include: Evelyn Barish, *Emerson: The Roots of Prophecy* (Princeton: Princeton University Press, 1989), ch. 2, "Parents"; Margaret Morganroth Gullette, "Why Children Die in Contemporary American Fiction," *Michigan Quarterly Review* 31.1 (Winter 1992): 56–72; Judith Walzer Leavitt, "Under the Shadow of Maternity: American Women's Responses to Death and Debility Fears in Nineteenth-Century Childbirth," *Feminist Studies* 12.1 (Spring 1986): 129–54; Larua S. Smart, "Parental Bereavement in Anglo-American History" *Omega* 28 (1): 49–61; E. Michael Thron, "The Significance of Catherine Wordsworth's Death to Thomas De Quincey and William Wordsworth," *Studies in English Literature* 28 (Autumn 1988): 559–67.

13 Here Fuller directs an ironic feminist comment at the patriarchal lineage she is helping to construct: "I hope you will have another son, for I perceive that men do not feel themselves represented to the next generation by *daughters,* but I hope, if you do . . . that Waldo will always be to us your eldest b[o]rn, and have his own niche in our thoughts, and have no image intruded too near him."

14 T. Walter Herbert, *Dearly Beloved: The Hawthornes and the Making of the Middle-Class Family* (Berkeley: University of California Press, 1993), pp. 156–58, 169–83, 218–24, 281–83.

15 Fuller also writes to a mutual friend, William Henry Channing, probing the nature of imaginative affection and the problem of "meeting" one's imaginative objects. Her sense of Waldo's value as a representation of beautiful ideas is clear, and is compatible with her maternal feelings. In this passage she echoes a piece of family lore about Waldo recorded later by Ellen Tucker Emerson: "He had been, Mother thought, much like other children till he was nearly five. Then he seemed wiser and more angelic all the time" (*LJE* 85). "Five years he was an angel to us, and I know not that any person was ever more the theme of thought to me. As I walk the streets they swarm with apparently worthless lives, and the question will rise, why he, why just he, who 'bore within himself the golden future,' must be torn away? His father will meet him again; but to me he seems lost, and yet that is weakness. I *must* meet that which he represented, since I so truly loved it. He was the only child I ever saw, that I sometimes wished I could have called mine" (*LMF* 3: 42–43).

16 Sharon Cameron, "Representing Grief: Emerson's 'Experience,' " *Representations* 15 (Summer 1986): 25, 18, 24.

17 *New Yorker* 27 June–4 July 1994: 102.

18 Ellen Tucker Emerson reports her mother's memory of responding to Ralph Waldo Emerson's proposal: "She shut her eyes while she told him that she foresaw that with her long life wholly aside from housekeeping she should not be a skillful mistress of a house and that it would be a load of care and labour from which she shrank and a giving up of an existence she thoroughly enjoyed and to which she had become exactly fitted, and she could not undertake it unless he was sure he loved her and needed her enough to justify her in doing it" (*LJE* 48).

19 Moncure Conway, a future biographer of Emerson, found himself in the thick of domestic interaction when he visited Concord in 1853: "Emerson received him in the library. 'On learning that I . . . had come to Concord simply to see him, he called from his library door, 'Queeney!' Mrs. Emerson came, and I was invited to remain some days.' Conway replied that he must return to the college that evening, and apologized for taking up his host's time, but Emerson seemed to have time for everyone, including his children, who came in to report on their experiences of the morning. Edith said a man next door had accused a woman (probably a servant) of stealing something, and she had struck him in the leg with a corkscrew. Her father said, 'He insinuated that she was a rogue, and she insinuated the corkscrew into his leg.' " Gay Wilson Allen, *Waldo Emerson: A Biography* (New York: Viking Press, 1981) p. 571.

20 Barbara Ryan, "Emerson's 'Domestic and Social Experiments': Service, Slavery, and the Unhired Man," *American Literature* 66.3 (September 1994): 489.

21 Kurt Heinzelman, "The Cult of Domesticity: Dorothy and William Words-

worth at Grasmere" in *Romanticism and Feminism,* ed. Anne K. Mellor (Bloomington: Indiana University Press, 1988), pp. 52–78. Alan Liu, *Wordsworth: The Sense of History* (Stanford: Stanford University Press, 1989), ch. 6, "The Tragedy of the Family."

22 *The Collected Works of Samuel Taylor Coleridge,* Bollingen Series 75, vol. 7 (Princeton: Princeton University Press, 1983): *Biographia Literaria,* ed. James Engell and Walter Jackson Bate, 1, pp. 224–25.

23 Gillian Brown explores sentimental novels and literary markets in *Domestic Individualism,* ch. 5, "Anti-sentimentalism and Authorship in *Pierre.*"

24 Stephen E. Whicher, *Freedom and Fate: An Inner Life of Ralph Waldo Emerson,* 2d ed. (Philadelphia: University of Pennsylvania Press, 1971).

25 Len Gougeon, *Virtue's Hero: Emerson, Antislavery, and Reform* (Athens: The University of Georgia Press, 1990), pp. 41–49.

26 Len Gougeon, *Virtue's Hero,* pp. 27–28, 37, 75, 92–93.

27 See Michael T. Gilmore, *American Romanticism and the Marketplace* (Chicago: University of Chicago Press, 1985), ch. 1, "Emerson and the Persistence of the Commodity," on Emerson and agrarian ideals.

28 Julie Ellison, "The Edge of Urbanity: Emerson's *English Traits,*" *ESQ* 32 (2nd Quarter 1986): 96–109, addresses related questions in sections on "The British Animal," "Race," and "Mechanism."

29 Len Gougeon, *Virtue's Hero,* pp. 82–85.

30 Len Gougeon, *Virtue's Hero,* ch. 1, "Abolition and the Biographers."

31 Len Gougeon, *Virtue's Hero,* p. 293.

32 Heather McHugh, "20–200 on 747" in *Shades* (Middletown, CT: Wesleyan University Press,1988), p. 3.

33 What does it mean to say that "Experience" is or is not "about" the death of Waldo Emerson? Everything we know about the composition of the essay points to its origin in Emerson's letters and journal entries in response to that event. But at the same time it shares much common ground with "The Poet," which opens *Essays, Second Series,* with "Experience" coming second. "The Poet," while originating in a lecture of the same title delivered in Emerson's series on "The Times" in the winter of 1841–42, was almost wholly a new composition begun in the spring of 1842 following Waldo's death. Because these two adjacent essays are so distinct in mood, "The Poet" is never read by critics as a text arising from this trauma. "The Poet" performs imaginative volatility, resistance to the arbiters of taste, and free association on the margins of social life. "Experience" inquires into permanent dissociation and rarely, if ever, accelerates to sublimity or pleasure. Still, the language of "Experience" relies on the imagery of speed, flow, and metamorphosis used in "The Poet," and vice versa. "The Poet" and "Experience," both written in the aftermath of loss, echo the earlier essay, "Circles," published in *Essays, First Series* (1841). "Circles" fully articulated a serial ontology ("Every ultimate fact is only the first of a new series") and validated notions of discontinuity, mood, and the surface ("Our moods do not believe in each other") (CW 2: 181, 182). I have not discussed "The Poet" in the present essay because I have dealt with it at length elsewhere. See *Emerson's Romantic Style* (Princeton: Princeton University Press, 1984), ch. 5.

34 Sharon Cameron, "Representing Grief: Emerson's 'Experience,' " p. 37.

9

CATHERINE TUFARIELLO

"The Remembering Wine": Emerson's Influence on Whitman and Dickinson

In a journal entry of 1859, Emerson expressed satisfaction at having successfully imbued would-be students with the doctrine of self-reliance:

> I have been writing & speaking what were once called novelties, for twenty-five or thirty years, & have not now one disciple. Why? Not that what I said was not true; not that it has not found intelligent receivers but because it did not go from any wish in me to bring men to me, but to themselves. . . . This is my boast that I have no school & no follower. I should account it a measure of the impurity of insight, if it did not create independence.[1]

This passage offers a glimpse of a precursor's perspective on the problem of literary influence. Instead of expressing anxiety about receiving influence, or, for that matter, an anxious desire to be influential, Emerson boasts (albeit perhaps ambivalently) of having declined to exert a personal influence on others that might have warped them from their own orbits. Throughout his writings, Emerson represents himself as an experimenter, a questioner, a seeker, rather than a guide or a sage. His resistance to influencing others protects his own independence as well as the self-sufficiency of his readers. As though concurring with Emerson's private musings, Walt Whitman wrote in a late review of Emerson's books, published in his *Complete Prose Works* of 1892, "Who wants to be any man's mere follower? lurks behind every page. No teacher ever taught, that has so provided for his pupil's setting up independently – no truer evolutionist."[2] The only way to be a true disciple of Emerson, as Whitman recognized, is to be unlike him.

Despite Emerson's own conviction that he was without literary heirs, he is commonly regarded as the literary father of the two greatest nineteenth-century American poets, Walt Whitman and Emily Dickinson. The formal and personal contrasts between these two poets, who never met or read each other's work – between Whitman's wavelike lines and Dickinson's lapidary ones, his tireless self-promotion and her rigorous reticence – are more obvious, at first glance, than their affinities. Yet both, for the most part, rejected the iambic pentameter of canonical English verse, adapting instead the folk forms of Biblical psalms and church hymns; both were autodidacts and omnivorous readers; both wrote poems figuring the poet as a solitary spider spinning "Continents of Light" out of the "vacant vast surrounding" of America.[3] They were unknowingly linked, as well, by being steeped in the writings of Emerson, who represents a bridge between these two most inventive of his contemporary readers. His lectures, essays, and poems comprise an invisible filament, a "yarn of pearl," as Dickinson calls the spider's web, stretching from her fascicles, the packets of poems that she bound together in a kind of private self-publication, to the public and repeatedly revised *Leaves of Grass*.

Whitman and Dickinson also shared Emerson's characteristically American insistence on literary self-reliance and his resistance to acknowledging influence. Anticipating by several years the barbaric persona of "Song of Myself," who aggressively repels all influences emanating from "the spectres in books," Whitman reminded himself in an early notebook to "make no quotations and no reference to any other writers."[4] Yet Whitman's notebooks are filled with free renderings, in his own words, of his eclectic reading. Dickinson's quotations from favorite writers – whether Shakespeare or Elizabeth Barrett Browning, Keats or Emerson – were rare tributes, and rarely exact. She, too, was wary of even the appearance of possible influence. In a letter to Thomas Higginson, she noted that she had marked a line in one of the poems she enclosed, implying that it was because she had later encountered a similar phrase or figure elsewhere: "I marked a line in One Verse – because I met it after I made it – and never consciously touch a paint, mixed by another person."[5] Yet Dickinson did not relinquish or revise the line: "I do not let go it, because it is mine."

Whitman learned to "let the words go," as Emerson had recommended in his attack on rote memory in "Self-Reliance," and through paraphrase made the ideas that he encountered in books his own; Dickinson, like Jacob striving with the angel on Peniel, took hold of words and would not let go until she had blessed them with her own particular finish or inflection, tint or slant. In the last sentence of her final letter to Higginson, written shortly before her death in 1886, she misquoted Genesis 32, making Jacob refuse to let his divine adversary go, not until the angel grants, but until Jacob himself confers, a blessing: "Audacity of Bliss, said Jacob to the Angel 'I will not let thee go except I bless thee' – Pugilist and Poet, Jacob was correct" (L #1042). Simply by substituting "I" for "Thou" as the subject of "bless" and "thee" for "me" as the object, Dickinson makes Jacob, her figure for the poet, more powerful than his divine muse – much as, with an

"Audacity of Bliss" equal to hers, Whitman blesses his own soul in "Song of Myself," or Emerson's poet blesses the forbidding Sphinx.

Genesis 32 is, of course, for literary critic Harold Bloom the locus classicus of literary *agon,* the Oedipal battle for dominance between poetic fathers and their sons. Shorn of its connotations of generational combat, Bloom's wrestling metaphor is a resonant one for Whitman, and even (unlikely as it may seem) for Dickinson, who in her playful epithet for Jacob so naturally pairs "Poet" with "Pugilist." Whitman and Dickinson were creative readers of the best, Emersonian kind, and in their different ways both took up arguments with Emerson. But their debates with prior writers were more pleasurable, less melancholy, than Bloom's theory allows – more like a game, or even an erotic encounter, than like a battle to the death. There is no room, in the grim struggle for immortality between poetic "ephebes" and the oppressive fathers whose places they would usurp, for jokes, for play, for intoxication, for the green world in which Whitman loafs on the grass with his soul or the "Inns of Molten Blue" from which Dickinson ecstatically reels, both of them inebriated, as Emerson said that a true poet should be, by the mere act of breathing. Ultimately Whitman's gymnast's struggle, with Emerson as with his own readers, is as much a lover's embrace as a wrestler's hold, and Dickinson wrestles less with the shades of individual "precursors" than with language itself, often with Emersonian wit and whimsy. In reading Emerson, both imbibed "the remembering wine" of "Bacchus," a "joyful juice" that allows those who drink it to see a familiar world as though for the first time. And both, in their own poems, remember him – for, as Dickinson's misquotation of Jacob reminds us, it is really the later poet who can bestow, through allusion, the blessing of memory.

For all three writers, reading was a stimulus both to flights of transcendence and to deepened self-knowledge. Emerson himself provided an apt metaphor – an alternative, like the spider's web, to the familiar genealogical one – for literary influence generally and for the role he played in the poetic development of Whitman and Dickinson when he wrote, in *Representative Men,* "Other men are lenses through which we read our own minds."[6] Looking through the lens of Emerson's words, Whitman and Dickinson each honed their distinctive and very different ways of seeing.

I greet you at the beginning of a great career, which yet must have had a long foreground somewhere, for such a start.

On July 21, 1855, after reading the gift copy of *Leaves of Grass* sent to him by the unknown author, Emerson wrote the most famous thank-you letter in American literature. In his prediction Emerson proved prescient, though the "great career" was mainly posthumous, and though Whitman must sometimes have remembered with bitterness the thrilling prophecy that he stamped in gold (without Emerson's permission, and to his annoyance) on the spine of the second edition. But what of the "long foreground" that Emerson assumed must lie behind the extraordinary poems – behind the frontispiece sketch of the anonymous author with his slouched hat, open shirt, and challenging stare? The mystery of Walter Whitman, Jr.'s, metamorphosis, at age 36, from itinerant reporter, pulp novelist, and poetaster into Walt Whitman, major poet, has tantalized students of American poetry ever since. In his letter, Emerson seems to recognize *Leaves* as a response to his own calls for a new American poetry: "It meets the demand I am always making of what seemed the sterile and stingy nature, as if too much handiwork, or too much lymph in the temperament, were making our western wits fat and mean." He may well have wondered, as many others have since, exactly what role his own writings played in the "long foreground" that gave birth to *Leaves of Grass* – "a nondescript monster," he would write in an 1856 letter to Thomas Carlyle, "which yet has terrible eyes & buffalo strength, & was indubitably American."

When he wrote his letter of greeting, Emerson could not have known that Whitman's first literary ambition, as C. Carroll Hollis and others have noted, was not to be a poet but to be, like Emerson, a lecturer or "wander-teacher." Whitman's notebooks from the later 1840s through the 1850s include proposed itineraries for "Walt Whitman's Lectures" ("strong live addresses directly to the people, North and South, East and West"), lists of possible titles for unwritten lectures, stage directions to himself on the fine and not-so-fine points of elocution (Whitman instructs himself to declaim one passage "*fiercely* and with screaming energy"), and drafts for advertisements or publicity posters, with the admission price 10 to 15 cents.[7] It is often impossible to determine whether Whitman originally intended to incorporate many of the loosely rhythmic, fragmentary prose passages in his early notebooks into a poem or a lecture.[8] "Pictures," an important precursor poem to *Leaves of Grass*, includes "Ralph Waldo Emerson, of New England, at the lecturer's desk lecturing" in its expansive catalogue of formative images, and Emerson was among the great men, along with Voltaire and Elias Hicks, whom Whitman considered as a subject for a lecture of his own (*WWW* 34).

It is worth asking, then, why Whitman gave up his original ambition and chose to publish poetry instead of delivering lectures. Hollis's explanation is that Whitman, despite his fantasies to the contrary, had no gift whatever for public speaking. On the rare occasions when Whitman did give a public address, he was in the habit of submitting anonymous "reviews" of his own platform performances to local newspapers before he had even left New York. Though Whitman extolled his own "interior magnetism" and "vocal perfection," more objective reviewers were less than enthusiastic. When he delivered a poem, infelicitously titled "After All, Not to Create Only" (later "Song of the Exposition"), on opening day of the National Industrial Exhibition in New York in 1871, several papers reported that only a few in the audience of several hundred could hear him, both because of his weak projection and the background din of exhibits being constructed, and the *Tribune* published a parody that began,

Who was it sang of the procreant urge, recounted sextillions of subjects?
Who but myself, the Kosmos, concerned not at all about either the effect or the answer.

(In the guise of an anonymous New York correspondent, Whitman published his own version of the speech's reception in the Washington *Chronicle*; in it, five hundred workmen paused with tools in hand to listen, and the enthusiastic audience numbered two to three thousand.)[9] It was really Emerson who possessed the rich baritone and compelling stage presence that Whitman liked to claim for himself, and his dream of a lyceum career brought him into direct competition with Emerson.

Emerson's talent as a lecturer may have been as instrumental as Whitman's lack of it in the process of Whitman's poetic self-fashioning. He could, after all, have decided to publish essays instead of turning from oratory to poetry. Although Emerson wrote poetry throughout his life and published two volumes of verse, he often expressed unease about claiming the status of poet. In both *Nature* and the essay "The Poet," he presents himself as the transcriber of the song of "a certain poet" or "my orphic poet," rather than as the originator of that song. In addition to his own self-doubts, Emerson was vulnerable to the charge that his own poetry, while innovative for its time, fell short of the vision that he had so eloquently articulated in "The Poet" of a new and experimental American poetics. Emerson's prose was praised as poetic and his poetry (often unfairly) criticized as prosaic, while Whitman was having little success as either a conventional poet or a lecturer. But by redefining himself from would-be orator to oratorical poet, Whitman was able, instead of playing Emerson's imitator or adversary, to play Christ to his John the Baptist – a transformation Emerson himself facilitated by the prophetic role he had adopted in the essay and lecture "The Poet." By casting parts of his undelivered lectures into lines, emphasizing and enhancing the rhetorical repetitions and parallelisms that were already latent in the notebook versions, Whitman was able to assimilate and transform the ideas and the style of the man whom he credited with bringing him from a simmer to a full creative boil.

A crucial stage in the long process of Whitman's evolution from an omnivorous reader into the poet of *Leaves* was his practice of composing prose paraphrases of the writers whom he admired. Whitman's notebooks reflect his lifelong habit of putting the ideas of others into his own words – a habit that continued to shape his published prose and his poetry.[10] Such was his practice in the long, untitled prose essay that introduced the first edition of *Leaves of Grass*, a work of prose as generically liminal and provocative as the poems that followed.

Though the form of the Preface, as it has since come to be called, struck nineteenth-century readers as unorthodox, its content placed Whitman squarely in Emerson's school. Full of paraphrases of "The Poet," the essay has often been cited as the text in which Whitman's indebtedness to Emerson is most embarrassingly apparent. Juxtaposing it with "The Poet" indeed yields striking parallels: Emerson's "America is a poem in our eyes" becomes "The United States themselves are essentially the greatest poem"; Emerson's "Poets are thus liberating gods" becomes "The attitude of great poets is to cheer up slaves and horrify despots"; Emerson's catalogue of the facts of American life that "are yet unsung" becomes in the Preface a similar enumeration of the qualities of "the common people" of the United States, who are "unrhymed poetry" awaiting "the gigantic and generous treatment" they deserve; and Emerson's epithet for the poet, "the reconciler, whom all things await" becomes in Whitmanian paraphrase "the arbiter" and "the equalizer."

Even passages that seem straightforwardly derivative, however, are sometimes more revisionary than they appear. For example, Whitman's claim that the poet "incarnates [his country's] geography" alludes simultaneously to Emerson's "[America's] ample geography dazzles the imagination, and it will not wait long for metres" and to his central idea of the poet as representative man. Yet Whitman's "a bard is to be commensurate with a people," his paraphrase of Emerson's "the poet is representative," is followed by a long, loose, and detailed geographic catalogue, first of American rivers and lakes, then of indigenous trees, then native birds. The poet becomes more than an exemplary man; he is transformed into a colossus striding across the American continent, his image reflected in the "blue breadth" of lakes, a giant whose stature finds its formal analogue in the sweeping comprehensiveness of Whitman's catalogue. It is as if Whitman set out to illustrate and exemplify Emerson's prophecy that the imaginatively dazzling "ample geography" of America would soon find a new poetic form of commensurate plenitude and breadth. Whitman's recounting of the aspects of American life deserving poetic commemoration self-reflexively claims the "gigantic and generous" stature that he calls for. The catalogue reads like an Adamic prose poem, as Whitman fluidly, if a bit frenetically, reels off names: "the inland sea of Virginia and Maryland and the sea off Massachusetts and Maine and over Manhattan bay and over Champlain and Erie and over Ontario and Huron"; "the growths of pine and cedar and hemlock and liveoak and locust and chestnut and cypress and limetree and cottonwood"; "with flights and songs and screams that answer those of the wildpigeon and highhold and orchard-oriole and coot and surf-duck and redshouldered hawk and fish-hawk and white ibis." This kind of paraphrase, at least for a reader familiar with "The Poet," reads like a concrete illustration and exemplification of an oracular Emersonian pronouncement. And in fact, one of the *Oxford English Dictionary*'s definitions of paraphrase is "a practical exemplification of or commentary upon some principle, maxim, etc.," a definition that counters the usual association of paraphrase with summary and abstraction. Often Whitman responds to an Emerson axiom, or aphorism, with one of the trademark catalogues of particulars that would become so familiar to readers of *Leaves of Grass*.

Perhaps the richest revision of Emerson in the Preface is Whitman's allusion to his famous defense of organic form: "For it is not metres, but a metre-making argument, that makes a poem, – a thought so passionate and alive, that, like the spirit of a plant or an animal, it has an architecture of its own, and adorns nature with a new thing. The thought and the form are equal in the order of time, but in the order of genesis the thought is prior to the form" (*E and L* 450). Whitman's paraphrase of this moment is a breathless elaboration, structured on the accretions of coordinate words and phrases called polysyndeton:

> The poetic quality is not marshalled in rhyme or uniformity or abstract addresses to things nor in melancholy complaints or good precepts, but is the life of these and much else and is in the soul. The profit of rhyme is that it drops seeds of a sweeter and more luxuriant rhyme, and of uniformity that it conveys itself into its own roots in the ground out of sight. The rhyme and uniformity of perfect poems show the free growth of metrical laws and bud from them as unerringly and loosely as lilacs or roses on a bush, and take shapes as compact as the shapes of chestnuts and oranges and melons and pears, and shed the perfume impalpable to form. (*CPSP* 11)

Syntactically, the passage is structured much like Emerson's: "It is not x, but y," not form, but something else – for Emerson, the poem's idea or "argument," for Whitman, an intangible animating principle, the "poetic quality" – that makes a poem a poem. The first sentence is a rough paraphrase of Emerson's distinction between genuine poetry and mere verse, no matter how artfully polished. The evolutionary metaphor of rhyme as a plant dispersing seeds recalls Emerson's famous metaphor for the mortal poet disseminating his immortal poems: the "agaric," in accordance with nature's prudential economy, shaking out its spores. Yet Whitman's version of the organic theory of poetry is followed not by a single unifying metaphor or analogy, but, once again, by a list of specific examples. Whitman elaborates the metaphor of organicism central to Emerson's essay and to Romantic theories of poetry, particularizing it and investing it with sensory appeal. The minicatalogues of poetic conventions, flowers, and fruits seem to proliferate of their own accord, as the grammar of the passage enacts the natural burgeoning and efflorescence it describes. Whereas Emerson had written that "poems are a corrupt version of some text in nature, with which they ought to be made to tally," Whitman takes Romantic organicism farther, as though rejecting the idea that poetic language has fallen from natural perfection. With its lush imagery and paratactic expansiveness, this passage could easily be recast as free verse and titled "Improvisation on a Theme by Emerson." The proliferation of concrete examples, at once illustrating and revising more abstract, epigrammatic sentences from "The Poet," anticipates the more complex and creative modes of paraphrase-as-exemplification that come into play in Whitman's poetry.

The Preface shows the potential rhetorical force of prose restatement, but it was in his poetry that Whitman's gift for paraphrase achieved genius. At key moments in "Song of Myself," Whitman's longest and most ambitious poem, he enacts passages from "The Poet." Whereas the prose allusions to Emerson's essay are earnest and discursive, if not always coherent, the poetic ones are dramatic and playful. For example, the poem's opening page recalls Emerson's advice that the hopeful poet should avoid artificial stimulants: "The sublime vision comes to the pure and simple soul in a clean and chaste body" (*E and L* 460). Whitman, of course, celebrates every inch of his body as clean and chaste, even when masturbating or embracing prostitutes. Emerson continues, "So the poet's habit of living should be set on a key so low and plain, that the common influences should delight him. His cheerfulness should be the gift of the sunlight; the air should suffice for his inspiration, and he should be tipsy with water" (*E and L* 461). Whitman meditates on the contrast between indoor and outdoor spaces, characteristically summoning up Emerson's spirit without reinvoking his words:

Houses and rooms are full of perfumes . . . the shelves are crowded with perfumes,
I breathe the fragrance myself and know it and like it,

The distillation would intoxicate me also, but I shall not let it.
The atmosphere is not a perfume . . . it has no taste of the distillation . . . it is
　odorless,
It is for my mouth forever. . . . I am in love with it,
I will go to the bank by the wood and become undisguised and naked,
I am mad for it to be in contact with me.　　　　　　　　　　　(*CPSP* 27)

Intoxicated with the act of breathing, the speaker rejects the artificial stimulation of perfume, his substitution for Emerson's "wine and French coffee," in favor of literal "inspiration." The opposition between "houses and rooms" and unhoused nature represents for Whitman the opposition between Europe and America, female and male, the dead past and the living present. Emerson is Whitman's ally and champion as he seizes the mantle of the long-awaited American bard, lusty, robust, and supremely fit for the present moment.

　By dramatizing passages from Emerson's essays, turning discursive axioms into performative utterances, Whitman used the ordinarily prosaic act of paraphrase to create poetry. And when Whitman "performs" passages from Emerson's essays in his own poetry, shifting from the third person to the lyric "I" and from descriptive to performative language, something uncanny happens: the hierarchy that normally obtains between an earlier text and a later one, an original text and a paraphrase, is inverted, and the earlier text comes to sound, in retrospect, like a paraphrase of the later one. This process occurs when, for example, the persona of "Song of Myself" undergoes a climactic transformation. Throughout the poem the speaker has been assuming the identities of a series of others, becoming by turns a runaway slave, an injured fireman pulled from the wreckage of a burning building, an "old artillerist" reliving his fort's bombardment, a handcuffed convict, a cholera patient, and finally a beggar. But then this pattern of interaction with the world is abruptly, imperatively broken: "Somehow I have been stunned. Stand back! / . . . I discover myself on a verge of the usual mistake" (*CPSP* 70). The speaker never explicitly tells us what the mistake in question has been, but its nature becomes clear in the course of the following lines, as he is transformed from a helpless fellow sufferer into a modern Christ, a worker of miracles: "To any one dying . . . thither I speed and twist the knob of the door, / Turn the bedclothes toward the foot of the bed, / Let the physician and the priest go home" (*CPSP* 73). The speaker has learned that it is not enough simply to express sympathy with the suffering and the dying; it is necessary to do something to alleviate their pain. And he is more than up to the task, becoming literally an inspiring, life-giving force: "I dilate you with tremendous breath. . . . I buoy you up" (*CPSP* 73).

This moment of realization and self-empowerment enacts a passage from "Self-Reliance." A few pages after he contrasts children who "painfully recollect the exact words" of their teacher with those few adults mature enough to "let the words go," Emerson deplores the infirmity of human sympathy: "We come to them who weep foolishly, and sit down and cry for company, instead of imparting to them truth and health in rough electric shocks, putting them once more in communication with their own reason" (*E and L* 276). Despite its temporal priority, Emerson's sentence reads like a paraphrase of the relevant section from "Song of Myself," a summary of the theme or gist of Whitman's poem. The phrase "in rough electric shocks" even sounds to twentieth-century ears more as if it were written by Whitman than by Emerson, aptly capturing the brusque "tough love" of Whitman's secular miracle worker: "You there, impotent, loose in the knees, open your scarfed chops till I blow grit within you" (*CPSP* 72). His recognition of his power to inspire summons forth, as if by magic, an audience for the poet's words. For it is after his metamorphosis from fellow sufferer into miracle worker that Whitman's future disciples – who did not yet exist when he composed the poem – make their first appearance as an "average unending procession" following him down the open road. Whitman's relationship with Emerson is imbricated with his alternately aggressive and tenderly seductive love affair with his readers, and his poetry derives much of its urgent energy from his imagined encounters with readers and literary predecessors alike.

In "Democratic Vistas," Whitman followed Emerson, as Thoreau had done in the "Reading" chapter of *Walden*, by defining the process of reading as creative contention with the author rather than the passive absorption of his ideas: "[T]he process of reading is not a half sleep, but, in highest sense, a gymnast's struggle . . . the reader is to do something for himself, must be on the alert . . . the text furnishing the hints, the clue, the start or framework" (*CPSP* 992; my ellipses). Though strenuous, the reader's struggle is also pleasurably erotic, its purpose not to dominate or destroy the adversary but to win his blessing. In the most famous stanza of "Song of Myself," Emerson is the angel from whom Whitman wrests a blessing of his own vision and his own words:

I believe in you my soul . . . the other I am must not abase itself to you,
And you must not be abased to the other.

Loafe with me on the grass . . . loose the stop from your throat,
Not words, not music or rhyme I want, not custom or lecture, not even the best,
Only the lull I like, the hum of your valved voice.

I mind how we lay in June, such a transparent summer morning;
You settled your head athwart my hips and gently turned over upon me,
And parted the shirt from my bosom-bone, and plunged your tongue to my bare-
stript heart,
And reached till you felt my beard, and reached till you held my feet.

Swiftly arose and spread about me the peace and love and knowledge that pass all
the art and argument of the earth;
And I know that the hand of God is the elderhand of my own,
And I know that the spirit of God is the eldest brother of my own,
And that all the men ever born are also my brothers . . . and the women my sisters
and lovers,
And that a kelson of the creation is love;
And limitless are leaves stiff or drooping in the fields,
And brown ants in the little wells beneath them,
And mossy scabs of the wormfence, and heaped stones, and elder and mullen and
pokeweed.

This passage, by now so familiar and yet still so wonderfully strange, is
Whitman's profession of his poetic creed, of the first principles or articles
of faith on which the rest of the poem depends. Many readers have detected
Emerson's presence here in the word "transparent," a key word that reap-
pears throughout Emerson's prose writings. Whitman's mystical vision is
refracted through Emerson, who had lamented in *Nature* the division between body and soul that Whitman, in this passage, claims to heal: "The
ruin or blank, that we see when we look at nature, is in our own eye. The
axis of vision is not coincident with the axis of things, and so they appear
not transparent but opake" (*E and L* 47). According to Emerson, it is only
during rare and privileged moments of vision, and only for the wise, that
"the universe becomes transparent, and the light of higher laws than its
own, shines through it" (*E and L* 25). On a transparent summer morning,
Whitman consummates Emerson's uncelebrated union between self and
soul, body and spirit, mind and world.

Of course, the most memorable appearance of the word "transparent" in
Nature is in Emerson's own privileged moment of vision, and it is that
moment – the startling, comical apotheosis of the American sublime – that
Whitman's insight literally revises, sees again. The most famous sentence in
Nature, and perhaps in all of Emerson's writings, is not a prophecy, a
description, or a prescription, but a performance: "I become a transparent
eye-ball; I am nothing; I see all; the currents of the Universal Being circulate
through me; I am part or particle of God" (*E and L* 10). This remarkable,
notoriously outlandish image would inspire Christopher Cranch's carica-

ture of Emerson as an enormous eyeball precariously balanced on spindly legs. For Whitman, it proved a provocation to more radical revision than literalization or hyperbole. Whitman's usual strategy of dramatizing descriptive passages from the essays will not work when, as here, Emerson's own language is so spectacularly performative. Signaling his Emerson subtext with a single word – the word that, for both, was shorthand for the poetic privilege of seeing the world permeated with the light of truth – Whitman counterposes his own mystical experience with the one in *Nature*. Emerson's epiphany begins at twilight, under a clouded winter sky; Whitman's comes on a clear morning in June, like a bolt from the blue. Emerson stands on bare ground, his "head bathed by the blithe air, and uplifted into infinite space"; Whitman reclines on a bank, his body in contact with the grass. Emerson experiences a mystical oneness with the Universal Being; Whitman experiences oneness with himself and, ultimately, a fraternal kinship with everything in nature and every other human being. Not only do the circumstances and the substance of these visions differ markedly, but as Kenneth Price has pointed out, so do their aftermaths.[11] Emerson's visionary experience results in his becoming an impersonal lover of "uncontained and immortal beauty," even as consciousness of the people with claims on his personal love becomes "a trifle and a disturbance" (*E and L* 10). For Whitman, on the other hand, oneness with God and nature is not opposed to human kinship; rather, one leads to the other.

The differences between the two epiphanies are reducible to literal differences of vision. Whereas Emerson gazes upward at the stars and outward at "the tranquil landscape" and "the distant line of the horizon," Whitman's eye is drawn downward, his gaze so acute that he can see the brown ants beneath the leaves in the field. He finds beauty not in constellations or receding vistas but in the common shrubs and weeds underfoot, in homely "elder and mullein and pokeweed"; not in the perfect circle of the horizon but in the zigzagging rails of the wormfence, covered with patches of moss. He sees a natural world saturated with sexual energy, substituting "limitless" leaves, humorously tumescent or limp, for Emerson's "infinite space." He implies that Emerson's emphasis on vision, the most cerebral and distancing sense, is incomplete without a celebration of the more carnal pleasures of touch, taste, smell, and sound. In Whitman's epiphany, the ethereal wine of Emerson's vision – the sweet cordial of the air that Emerson breathes just before he evanesces into spirit – is transmuted into an earthier "joyful juice," an ejaculate filling the break between the embrace and its aftermath[12] as it will spill out again, more explicitly, in a later passage of the poem: "Something I cannot see puts upward libidinous prongs, / Seas of bright juice suffuse heaven" (*CPSP* 52). Whitman pulls the transparent, transcendent Emersonian soul, yearning toward the infinite and chary of human relations, back into the solid and perishable body, where it belongs.

Ultimately, however, Emerson is at least as much a presiding genius or male muse as an antagonist in Whitman's longest poem, in which a self-conscious refusal to invoke female muses leads to this story of how the speaker became a poet – by, to borrow a phrase from Dickinson, telling his soul to sing. Emerson's complex dual role as Whitman's competitor and muse derives both from Whitman's sexuality and from their shared nationality. As an American poet in an age rife with literary nationalism, Whitman is in a more sympathetic relationship to Emerson than he could be either to an English Romantic like Wordsworth or to an English contemporary like Matthew Arnold. In *Notes and Fragments*, which is full of critical and competitive notes on the lives of great European poets, novelists, and philosophers, the notes on Shakespeare read like a rough sketch for a Whitmanian *Representative Men*; among his jottings is the reminder, "See Emerson's Shakespeare" (*NF* 87). By disparaging "the courtly muses of Europe" and promoting self-reliance, Emerson encouraged Whitman's literary ambitions, and by celebrating Emerson as a representative American writer, Whitman elevates himself. Thus, Emerson is never simply an adversary for Whitman; he is always also an ally.

Given that, all his life, Whitman's strongest erotic attachments were to other men, it is not surprising, yet critical to a full understanding of his responses to Emerson, that his muse is male, a mirror image of himself. The soul seduces him not with custom, rhyme, or lecture (the latter a word that Whitman would surely have associated with Emerson), but with pure sound, the sound of the human voice without the words: "Only the lull I like, the hum of your valvèd voice." More than a decade earlier, as a young reporter for the New York *Aurora*, Whitman had attended Emerson's lecture on "The Nature and Powers of the Poet" and immersed himself in that voice as in an aria at one of the operas he loved. In this passage, he dramatizes how he became a poet and found his own. Like David's lyre, the soul accompanies his song, and, like the Psalmist, he addresses his soul imperatively: "[L]oose the stop from your throat." (Perhaps he is also addressing the former Walter Whitman, the unsuccessful lecturer.) Rather than being silenced or preempted by the penetration of the "tongue," or voice, of the other whom he claims as part of him, he rises from the grass able to call forth and embrace the reader as he has been embraced.

Unlike Whitman, Emily Dickinson could not easily find in Emerson's call for an American poet, with its masculine aesthetics, a prophecy of her own advent. Despite Emerson's qualified sympathy for the cause of women's rights, it does not seem to have occurred to him that the poet whom he sought might turn out to be a woman. Emerson associates the poet, the "namer and sayer," both with Adam and with the Son of the Trinity, and his metaphor for the poetic process is both sexually and theologically male; the end of poetry is that "thought may be ejaculated as Logos, or Word" (*E and L* 466). It is thus not surprising that feminist critics have tended to emphasize the oppressiveness, for Dickinson, of Emerson's poetic vision.[13] In such readings Emerson becomes Dickinson's poetic father, the literary analogue of the formidable Edward Dickinson, whom she had to combat to attain her own poetic identity. But although literary critics may refer for convenience's sake to "the Emersonian tradition," in fact Emerson's legacy is, by his own design, a contradictory and capacious one, and Emily Dickinson was another of his students who, against the odds of her gender, succeeded in setting up independently.

If anything, Dickinson's literary independence exceeded Whitman's. Whereas Whitman capitalized on the personal (albeit sometimes ambivalent) friendship that he established with Emerson, Dickinson twice passed up the opportunity to meet him in person. During a lecture tour in 1857, Emerson stayed at the Evergreens with Emily's brother Austin Dickinson and his wife, Sue Gilbert. Invited to a tea in his honor, Dickinson declined to emerge from her father's house for the occasion – and this was years before she had become completely reclusive. Twelve years later, when Thomas Higginson tried to persuade her to make a visit to Boston ("You must come to Boston sometimes? All ladies do"), holding out as an incentive an upcoming reading by Emerson to be followed by a meeting of the local "Woman's Club," Dickinson simply did not respond, and Higginson had to come to her for their long-deferred meeting (L #330a). Yet her refusal was not because she lacked appreciation for Emerson's writings. A girlhood friend, Emily Fowler Ford, remarked that Dickinson was immersed in Emerson's essays in the mid-1840s, more than a decade before he made this visit to Amherst, and in 1850 Benjamin Newton, her father's law apprentice and Dickinson's beloved "Tutor," had given her a copy of the 1847 *Poems*, in which each marked their respective favorites. She remained a reader of Emerson throughout her life and was deeply affected by his death in April 1882.

Why, then, did Dickinson refuse these invitations? A note that she sent to Sue after Emerson had left Amherst offers a clue. Sue remembered that Emily had written to her, "It must have been as if he had come from where dreams are born?" In one of her poems about the pleasures of reading, Dickinson used the same phrase about a personified "Antique Book," who brings news of past centuries "As One should come to Town – / And tell you all your Dreams – were true / He lived – where Dreams were born – ."[14] Emerson had come to Dickinson's town, bearing his lecture on "The Beautiful in Rural Life," to tell her that all her dreams were true, but she preferred to get her enchantment from his books: "His presence is Enchantment – ," she says of the book in the poem, "You beg him not to go." Emerson's physical presence could not compare, for her, with the companionship of his essays and poems. Dickinson's relationship to him was to be purely through the medium of the written word, the medium that – as her many poems about reading books and receiving letters attest – was for her more vital and intimate than speech. She treated Emerson the visiting celebrity with the composed indifference with which the queenly soul receives, or rather refuses to receive, the emperor kneeling at her doorstep in "The Soul selects her own Society – ."[15] But if she would not cross the "low gate" of her father's house to pay homage to Emerson the man, the "Valves of her attention" were receptive to his poetics and his words. Indeed, in declining to sit at the feet of the writers who preceded her, she resembles Emerson, whose writings encouraged her to respond to past literature in this self-reliant way.

Yet it is difficult not to wish that Dickinson, even if unwilling to meet Emerson in person, had sent her poems to him. Surely he would have recognized the extraordinariness of her gift as infallibly as he recognized the genius of the unknown author of *Leaves of Grass*. When it came to poetry, they were kindred spirits. Dickinson shared Emerson's passion for poetry as a stimulus to rapture, a "daily Bliss" (Dickinson) or "daily joy" (Emerson) that is meted out all too parsimoniously in the rest of life. And despite the challenges posed by her gender, she responded enthusiastically to Emerson's conception of the poet. "I taste a liquor never brewed" (P 214), for example, is an exuberantly facetious literalization of the same passage that Whitman dramatizes at the beginning of "Song of Myself," Emerson's prescription that candidates for the exalted position of American bard should eschew all stimulants but water and air. Dickinson obediently presents herself as an ecstatic "Inebriate of Air" and "Debauchee of Dew," "Reeling – thro endless summer days – / From inns of Molten Blue!" The opening line weds the intoxicating water of "The Poet" with the celestial wine of "Bacchus": as Emerson calls to the god for "wine which never grew / In the belly of the grape," Dickinson declares that she has already partaken of her own immortal nectar, an unbrewed beer that never foamed from "Tankards scooped in Pearl – ." Under its influence she ascends higher and higher, on invisible wings of fancy, "Till Seraphs swing their snowy Hats – / And Saints – to windows run – / To see the little Tippler / Leaning against the –

Sun – ." Her mixing of Christian and classical allusions is also reminiscent of "Bacchus." This unfallen female Icarus far outsoars the "winged man" of "The Poet," who makes extravagant promises but who finally disenchants (*E and L* 452). Leaning, unsinged, against the sun and hailed by seraphs, Dickinson tells Emerson that she is one of "the few who received the true nectar" (*E and L* 460), a celestial tour guide who will not disappoint. The poem affirms both Emerson's vision of the American poet and her own aptness for the role, as Dickinson implicitly claims, with whimsical and witty confidence, to be the poet for whom Emerson has long looked (among American men) in vain.

Emerson's association of poetry with play appealed to her just as much as the high lyricism and vatic apostrophes of "The Poet." One of her favorite poems seems to have been "The Humble-Bee," from which Dickinson – who rarely quoted other poets – quoted three times in her letters. In his famous nursery rhyme, Isaac Watts, whose hymns so influenced the form of her poetry, used the "little busy bee" as an emblem of industriousness, a Franklinian avatar of the Protestant work ethic. But Dickinson sided with Emerson in associating bees with indolence and freedom. The "humble-bee" is, like Dickinson's enchanted book, a courier from another world, an "animated torrid zone" who brings news to New England of "Indian wildernesses" and "Syrian peace," much as her hummingbird delivers "the mail from Tunis" in a single morning. While Emerson's bee is an "Epicurean of June" (a phrase that might easily have come from Dickinson's pen), her bees are swashbuckling "Buccaneers of Buzz" (P 1405). Travel is indeed a fool's paradise, when such exotic wonders arrive every day at the door of the patient poet.

Like Whitman, Dickinson affirmed Emerson's central belief that it is the special mark of poetic genius to be able to find the sublime hidden in the trivial and the familiar, to extract the attar of the marvelous from common flowers. But she implicitly rejected the organic metaphors for poetry that pervade *Nature* and that so appealed to Whitman. Language itself plays the primary role, in Dickinson's poetics, that nature plays for Emerson. When Emerson suffered from eye trouble in the early 1830s, he was, although one of his symptoms was an inability to read, most concerned about being shut out from the sight of nature. Thus he becomes, in the opening chapter of *Nature*, all sight, and expresses confidence that – with one crucial caveat – the woods can heal him of any ill: "There I feel that nothing can befall me in life, – no disgrace, no calamity, (leaving me my eyes,) which nature cannot repair" (*E and L* 10). When Dickinson was diagnosed with an eye ailment, she was most afraid of being exiled from the world of books, writing to Joseph Lyman, a family friend, "Some years ago I had a woe, the only one that ever made me tremble. It was a shutting out of all the dearest ones of time, the strongest friends of the soul – BOOKS." When her doctor forbade her to read, "He might as well have said, 'Eyes be blind,' 'heart be still.' "[16]

Even Emerson's appetite for reading seems almost pallid next to the Keatsian sensuality of Dickinson's, after the physician's prohibition was finally lifted. Of reading Shakespeare again, she wrote, "I devoured the luscious passages. I thought I should tear the leaves out as I turned them." How different is the young Emerson's emphasis, in a brief journal entry of December 1835: "In Shakespear I actually shade my eyes as I read for the splendor of the thoughts" (*EJ* 145). Reading is the long-anticipated reward of Dickinson's recovery; Emerson's association of Shakespeare with a glorious yet potentially blinding sun supports the theory that his perplexing inability to read may have been, as some scholars have suspected, partly psychological. (Indeed, perhaps his opening words to Whitman, with their oddly negative phrasing – "I am not blind to the worth of the wonderful gift of 'Leaves of Grass' " – are really a defensive disclaimer, i.e., "I am not blinded by it.") For Dickinson, it is not the universe that appears transparent in moments of supreme poetic vision, but words that suddenly become, under the writer's gaze, as luminous as gems. "Sometimes I write one," she confided to Lyman, "and look at his outlines till he glows as no sapphire" (*Lyman Letters,* p. 78).

Conversely, nature is not a text for Dickinson, a repository of symbols waiting to be deciphered by the inspired poet. In her canon nature is as unfathomable a mystery as God. Even in her most benign maternal aspect, she does not communicate with human beings but "Wills Silence – Everywhere – " (P 790). Nature is distinguished by two central facts, that she endures and does not speak:

> We pass, and she abides.
> We conjugate Her Skill
> While She creates and federates
> Without a syllable.   (P 811)

Dickinson emphasizes nature's constant motion, which cannot be captured by clumsy human efforts to "conjugate" her, to make her "Skill" an object. The verbs denoting her actions, "creates" and "federates," are intransitive in this poem. Nature's business is not to serve, or to serve as an object for, human art or aspirations. For Emerson – the Emerson of *Nature,* anyway – nature's true function is, if man only knew it, to bear him, like the humble donkey on which Christ rode, to the heavenly Jerusalem of new perception. His present alienation from nature is due to an error in vision, to an inability to perceive his right relation to the world. When Dickinson gazes at

nature, often what she sees is not transparency but a deeper opacity. This
happens in Poem 1175, "The Lightning is a yellow Fork," which begins,
like some of Dickinson's other nature poems, with a domestication of nature that quickly turns uncanny:

> The Lightning is a yellow Fork
> From Tables in the sky
> By inadvertent fingers dropt
> The awful Cutlery
>
> Of mansions never quite disclosed
> And never quite concealed
> The Apparatus of the Dark
> To ignorance revealed.

The opening lines might have been used to introduce a nursery rhyme, one
designed to tame this awesome force of nature for the comfort of children.
But the homespun, proverbial definition of lightning only enhances the
strangeness of the second stanza, as lightning, instead of penetrating the
night, makes the darkness darker. The clanging "Cutlery" of celestial man-
sions is not cozy but "awful," and what is revealed to human ignorance in
sporadic flashes from above is not the light of higher laws shining through
the visible world, but "The Apparatus of the Dark."

In her only explicit statement about the relationship between nature and
art, Dickinson wrote to Higginson late in her career, "Nature is a haunted
house – but Art – a house that tries to be haunted" (L #459a). For Emerson,
man is haunted by the intuition of a lost oneness with nature; the waving
boughs gesture, however obscurely, to him, and hint of kinship. For Dickinson, nature is haunted by a foreignness that cannot be exorcized. "What
mystery pervades a well!" (P 1400) reads like a response to Emerson's
Nature. As if anticipating Frost's "For Once, Then, Something," the
speaker ponders what might reside in the depths of the well and, like Frost's
speaker, has difficulty seeing past her own surface reflection:

> What mystery pervades a well!
> That water lives so far –
> A neighbor from another world
> Residing in a jar
>
> Whose limit none have ever seen
> But just his lid of glass –
> Like looking every time you please
> In an abyss's face!

In another short lyric about the relationship between art and nature, Wallace Stevens's "Anecdote of the Jar," the humble human artifact, merely by its presence, imposes order on the wilderness that surrounds it. Dickinson's jar, the well, does not tame the water it contains, which remains fathomless and inscrutable, "a neighbor from another world." Here we have a playful Dickinsonian redaction of Emerson's *I and the abyss,* but with the opposition between them collapsed: the abyss's depths and the speaker's reflected face are the same; the abyss is within the self. The bemused tone turns a tinge acerbic in the penultimate stanza:

> But nature is a stranger yet;
> The ones that cite her most
> Have never passed her haunted house,
> Nor simplified her ghost.

Very likely Emerson is implicated here, as Margaret Homans has surmised, among "the ones that cite her most."[17] Nature is not a text, Dickinson implies, to be cited in support of inevitably reductive human arguments or interpretations. Punning on "sight" with "cite," Dickinson also criticizes the appropriative vision that is the obverse of Emerson as transparent eyeball, self-abnegatingly dilated to the circulations of the Oversoul. In the final chapter of *Nature*, titled "Prospects," Emerson predicts that one day nature will be fully subjected to the human will. For Dickinson, nature has its own spirit or "ghost," independent of human desire. Nature remains a stranger both despite and because of human complacency, including the complacency of men like Emerson who believe that they can know nature. Dickinson drives home that central point with a final paradox:

> To pity those that know her not
> Is helped by the regret
> That those who know her, know her less
> The nearer her they get.

The opposition that I have been drawing between Dickinson's and Emerson's respective views of language and nature, of words and the world, should not be insisted upon too strenuously. At times Emerson shows a keen consciousness of nature's intransigence to human designs and obliviousness to human desires. In "Threnody," for example, his elegy for his young son Waldo, he rejects the pathetic fallacy much as Dickinson does in "I dreaded that first Robin, so" (P 348) and other poems of grief. Whereas elegies traditionally assert the sympathetic mourning of nature for the one who has died, Emerson inverts this convention to lament nature's failure to reflect his own pain: "The morrow dawned with needless glow; / Each snowbird chirped, each fowl must crow"[18] (*CPT* 119). Going a step further, Dickinson not only fails to find, but refuses even to seek, conventional forms of consolation. Comparable poems about bereavement in her canon are uncompromising, wearing what Emerson calls "the blasphemy of grief" like a badge of honor, the thorny crown of "The Queen of Calvary" (P 348). Thus when Emerson acknowledges human alienation from nature and even from experience, he sounds a good deal like Dickinson.

If Dickinson was skeptical of Emerson's primary analogy between human language and the natural world, she embraced other aspects of his poetics – for example, his observation that individual words are fossil poems. Marked in her copy of Emerson's *Essays: Second Series* are these sentences from "The Poet": "Day and night, house and garden, a few books, a few actions, serve us as well as would all trades and all spectacles. We are far from having exhausted the significance of the few symbols we use. We can come to use them yet with a terrible simplicity. It does not need that a poem should be long. Every word was once a poem" (*E and L* 455). It is easy to see why Dickinson, whose outward life was so circumscribed but whose sense of the pleasures and powers of the poetic word was so keen, would have read these sentences as if they were addressed to her personally. In the same passage of the essay, Emerson mentions the dictionary as an inspired, or inspiring, text: "Bare lists of words are found suggestive, to an imaginative and excited mind." Perhaps Dickinson was thinking of this passage when she told Higginson that during a time of great grief and isolation, her "Lexicon" had been her "only companion" (L #261). As Whitman's signature trope is the act of "letting the words go," Dickinson's is the act of laying claim to words – of appropriating, interrogating, testing, redefining them.

Much has already been written about Dickinson's adoption and redefinition of key words from the discourse of American transcendentalism, and particularly from the essays and poetry of Emerson: ecstasy, experience, skepticism, consciousness, nature, beauty, circumference. Such words typically do not function, however, as gestures of deference to his genius or as embodiments of his authority. She helps herself to Emerson's vocabulary in a spirit neither of filial reverence nor of filial rebellion, but with an insouciant boldness truly Emersonian. While Dickinson was influenced, for example, by the circle symbolism so pervasive in Emerson's work, she also gave "Circumference" her own spin. In the summer of 1862, the most prolific year of Dickinson's poetic career, she wrote to Higginson, "My Business is Circumference – " (L #268). She thus alluded to having chosen, like Emerson, a poetic vocation over religious orthodoxy. Jesus' declared calling was to go about his Father's business; Dickinson's vocation is not to go about Emerson's business but to form her own orbit, however elliptical. For both Emerson and Dickinson the circle is a symbol, not of static perfection, but of continual change and outward movement; not of divine stasis, but of human seeking. For Emerson, the circumference created by the expression of each new genius must be ruptured to make way for the next, for "around every circle another can be drawn" and "every ultimate fact is only the first of a new series" (*E and L* 403, 405). Though each circle marks a limit, it also generates the next, as concentric ripples spread from a stone tossed in a pond. Emerson thus prepares the way for Dickinson's re-inflection, in which "Circumference" no longer signifies a boundary, but the moment of its violation. The poet is an explorer on the farthest verge of human experience, mapping moments of doubt and skepticism, imaginatively crossing the boundary between life and death, recording extreme psychic states, from despair and the threat of madness to ecstasy. In the final lines of one of her circumference poems, Dickinson voyages "Out upon Circumference / Beyond the Dip of Bell" (P 378). Instead of enclosing her protectively under its dome like a delicate instrument beneath a bell jar, the bell's parabolic curve launches her outward. To be "beyond the Dip of Bell" is to be outside of the comforts of received religion, an infinitesimal speck in infinite space.

Much as Emerson himself redefined Coleridge's "Reason" and "Understanding" to suit his own purposes, Dickinson covets, and takes possession of, words that stimulate her imagination wherever she may find them. In the same letter to Higginson in which she announced her poetic business to be "Circumference," she used another "Emersonian" word as well: "When I state myself, as the Representative of the Verse – it does not mean – me – but a supposed person" (L #268). Dickinson reacts here to an apparent lapse that Higginson had made, in his previous letter, into the biographical fallacy, stressing the disjunction between her own identity and the fictive "I" of her lyrics. One would think that of all the words in the Transcendentalist lexicon, the word "representative," so empowering for Whitman, would most resist appropriation by a woman poet. In nineteenth-century America the word was, in poetry as in politics, gendered male.[19] Dickinson could not aspire to be one of Emerson's exemplary men, who would translate the particulars of American culture and politics into universality. By saying that she "states" herself as "Representative of the Verse," Dickinson plays on the word's political context, as though calling attention to her own redefinition. Behind her verb is the United States, and behind her striking epithet the House of Representatives to which her prominent lawyer father, Edward Dickinson, was elected in 1852, but which included none of her sex. She was, in a sense, a Representative of the House to which, in her early thirties, she confined herself. Whereas Whitman responds to *Representative Men* by constructing a capacious yet unitary poetic voice that purports to embrace and speak for every reader, Dickinson speaks on behalf of the poem itself.

Dickinson can be seen as defending herself against the maleness of Emerson's exemplary poet by speaking, as Emerson himself did, "thorough a thousand voices," each the voice of a fictive speaker or "supposed person." Although Emerson's essays seem on the surface to be the discourse of one man, Barbara Packer and others have noted that Emerson actually takes on many personae – speaking as Orphic poet, idealist, calm and genial rationalist, objector to his own theories, antinomian, optimist, extreme skeptic. In his poetry, he assumes the voices of nature, the sea, a pine tree, the Sphinx, a squirrel, the muse, or his fictional poet Saadi; Dickinson adopts the voices of a wounded soldier, a wife, a queen, a boy, a fly, a religious skeptic, a young girl who has died. In the same letter to Higginson in which she claimed the title Representative of the Verse, she included a poem clearly speaking in the voice of a "supposed person," "Success is counted sweetest" (P 67). In 1878 this poem, the only one that Dickinson published outside of a newspaper in her lifetime, was solicited by Helen Hunt Jackson for an anthology titled *A Masque of Poets,* which challenged readers to deduce the anonymous authors. Several reviewers attributed "Success," as the editors titled it, to Emerson.[20]

Yet to some late-twentieth-century readers, Dickinson's poem, in which a dying soldier "comprehend[s] the nectar" of victory better than the victors, has seemed a bitingly satiric denial of the doctrine of "compensation":

Success is counted sweetest
By those who ne'er succeed.
To comprehend a nectar
Requires sorest need.

Not one of all the purple Host
Who took the Flag today
Can tell the definition
So clear of Victory

As he defeated – dying –
On whose forbidden ear
The distant strains of triumph
Burst agonized and clear!

Emerson opens his essay "Compensation" with a critique of a sermon by a preacher who had argued that although there is no justice on earth, the faithful Christian can expect heaven to bring a deferred reward for good behavior, compounded by the pleasure of seeing the evildoers who prospered in life get their just deserts. "The blindness of the preacher," Emerson concludes, "consisted in deferring to the base estimate of the market of what constitutes a manly success, instead of confronting and convicting the world from the truth" (*E and L* 286). For Emerson, justice is done in this world: Every gain brings with it a corresponding loss, and every loss a gain. Dickinson pushes this Emerson axiom to its extreme (but not, I think, absurd) conclusion, asserting that success is truly defined only by those who fail, comprehended by them in the very bitterness of defeat. The victors taste the "nectar" of success, savoring its sweetness, but the immediacy of their experience is shallow next to the privation of the defeated, who plumb the word to its depths and whose knowledge is at once more conceptual – in normal usage, one "comprehends" abstractions, not nectars – and more profound.

Emerson might indeed, as Albert Gelpi has remarked, have found Dickinson's recurrent theme of "sumptuous Destitution" morbid, but in fact it is a radical outgrowth of his own temperate precept of compensation, bred to withstand the more arid climate of her verse. At the end of "Compensation," Emerson recuperates life's losses by noting that even the most terrible suffering brings, in time, a countervailing enlargement of the self. In "Success is counted sweetest" Dickinson tests this claim, as she so often does, by placing it under pressure – in this case, the extreme pressure of the moment of death. The soldier suffers a fatal wound; the remainder of his life, which must compensate him for that ultimate loss, is compressed into the few minutes when he lies dying. Can any gain in knowledge, the poem compels us to ask, serve as a compensation for death?

If the poem clearly satirized Emerson's philosophy of compensation, it would probably not have been mistaken for his own work; if it were clearly a straight illustration or explication of Emerson, it would not open itself so readily to an ironic reading. In fact, the tone is irresolvedly ambiguous, and I suspect that its indeterminacy of tone, as much as its form or theme, led readers of *A Masque of Poets* to ascribe it to Emerson.[21] It is not clear how we are to respond to the declared victory of the dying soldier – any more than it is clear how we are to read the poet's declaration, in "The Sphinx," that " 'the joy that is sweetest / Lurks in stings of remorse' " (*CPT* 7). In "Compensation," Emerson had insisted, "Every sweet hath its sour; every evil its good" (*E and L* 287), but of Waldo's death he would later write in his journal, "I comprehend nothing of this fact but its bitterness" (*EJ* 280). Precariously balanced between the calm optimism of the first sentence and the utter hopelessness of the second, the tone of a famous sentence from the journals, written a few weeks later in April 1842, is as indeterminate as Dickinson's "Success" or his own "The Sphinx": "I am *Defeated* all the time; yet to Victory I am born" (*EJ* 283). These words can communicate opposite meanings depending on the tone in which they are uttered; they can be made to convey human resilience in the face of grief, or the bitterest despair. They might also serve as a fitting epigraph for Dickinson's poem.

Emerson liked to keep readers guessing, and Dickinson too knew that "the Riddle we can guess / We speedily despise – " (P 1222). After his one meeting with Dickinson, Thomas Higginson responded to her as to a riddle whose answer eluded him, writing afterward to his wife, "She was much too enigmatical a being for me to solve in an hour's interview" (L #342b). Not surprisingly, "The Sphinx" was one of the titles that Dickinson marked in her copy of Emerson's poems, and her own poems sometimes read like attempts to out-riddle the Sphinx of Concord. Among them is "It sifts from Leaden Sieves" (P 311), her response to one of Emerson's finest poems, "The Snow-Storm." Natural description was a familiar nineteenth-century poetic genre, and the description of a snowstorm was an inevitable subject for a poet living in New England. A comparison of the two poems shows what different ways there were of seeing, in Dickinson's phrase, "New Englandly."

"The Snow-Storm" consists of blank verse divided asymmetrically into two verse paragraphs of 9 and 19 lines (*CPT* 34). The first part describes the arrival of the snow from the perspective of those whom it shuts indoors. The "whited air" veils everything external to the "housemates" who sit companionably by a blazing fire, secluded from visitors, "In a tumultuous privacy of storm" (it was this line, perhaps the poem's most felicitous, that Dickinson quoted in a letter). The furious roaring of the wind outside the house enhances the domestic intimacy within. In the blank space between the first part and the second, the storm stops. The second section opens with an apostrophe to the reader, an invitation to emerge from the house and observe the creative transformations wrought by the storm: "Come see the north wind's masonry." The wind is a "fierce artificer," a natural architect at once savage and whimsical: "Mockingly, / On coop or kennel he hangs Parian wreaths." Decorating chicken coops and dog kennels with sculptures from ancient Paros, filling up the farmer's lane until it is finally impassable, crowning the gate with a "tapering turret," the storm writes *Whim* upon the lintel of human industry and pragmatism. The north wind is an artist who envelopes and exaggerates the shapes of everyday things, giving a rural village the distorted look of a dream landscape. By making ordinary chores impossible, "the mad wind's night-work" enforces a fresh look at a familiar world. "The frolic architecture of the snow" has the freedom, spontaneity, and unexpectedness that Emerson attributed to the best human art.

Emerson's north wind represents the artist generally, but he is also a poet figure. The oxymoron "fierce artificer" is echoed in the final line, when the storm leaves behind a paradoxically "frolic architecture." Both phrases distill Emerson's sense, expounded at length in the essay "The Poet,"of the way that poetry combines wildness and craft, that a seemingly chaotic spontaneity can create form and beauty. And at the core of that beauty, unseen as the grain of sand at the center of a pearl, can be the poet's own suffering. Once the storm has passed, "A swan-like form invests the hidden thorn." In legend, swans were said to sing, with heartbreaking beauty, shortly before they died, and thus came to be figures for the bard. A beautiful poem about grief, like "Threnody" (its title the Greek word for a dirge), invests the poet's pain with form and meaning, thereby provisionally transforming it. But the thorn is still there, and in that sense, the mad wind is a deceiver, an illusionist. In the essay "Illusions," snow represents all of the phantasms and fallacies that blind mankind from birth: "On the instant, and incessantly, fall snow-storms of illusions" (*E and L* 1123). The reappearance of the sun, near the end of "The Snow-Storm," heralds the evaporation of that seemingly solid "frolic architecture." And perhaps the companionable but generic "housemates," the nameless sighing farmer kept from his tasks, are no more real. At the end of "Illusions," the false belief that he is part of a mass of other people yields to an exemplary man's recognition that he is really in solitude with the gods: "And when, by and by, for an instant, the air clears, and the cloud lifts a little, there are the gods still sitting around him on their thrones – they alone with him alone" (*E and L* 1124). That recognition of the soul's radical aloneness with God, or the gods, pervades the poetry of Emily Dickinson, and constitutes one of her deepest affinities with Emerson.

Dickinson liked to borrow the subjects of published poets, giving her own rendition of what crickets in summer sound like or a snowstorm looks like. Next to Emerson's, Dickinson's vision of a New England snowstorm seems, at first reading at least, almost childlike in its simplicity. Emerson's complex syntax, frequent enjambments, and Latinate diction contrast with Dickinson's series of short, end-stopped, declarative sentences. Whereas Emerson announces his poem with the title, Dickinson invites us to identify the unnamed "it" – that is, to guess the riddle:

It sifts from Leaden Sieves –
It powders all the Wood.
It fills with Alabaster Wool
The Wrinkles of the Road –

It makes an Even Face
Of Mountain, and of Plain –
Unbroken Forehead from the East
Unto the East again –

It reaches to the Fence –
It wraps it Rail by Rail
Till it is lost in Fleeces –
It deals Celestial Vail

To Stump, and Stack – and Stem –
A Summer's empty Room –
Acres of Joints, where Harvests were,
Recordless, but for them –

It Ruffles Wrists of Posts
As Ankles of a Queen –
Then stills its Artisans – like Ghosts –
Denying they have been.

Unlike Emerson's poem, Dickinson's does not record a human encounter with nature. There is no "inside" in which to retreat from the storm, no household or larger community (however unreal), no human beings at all. The poem opens fancifully, depicting the snow first as flour or confectioners' sugar that sifts from gray clouds and powders the trees, then as a cosmetic that gradually erases "the Wrinkles of the Road." The comparison of snow with wool would have been familiar to her from Psalm 147: "He giveth snow like wool: he scattereth the hoarfrost like ashes." But Dickinson modifies "wool" with hard and chilly "Alabaster," a white marble used in funerary monuments. Gazing down at the sleeping Desdemona, Othello says that he will "Not scar that whiter skin of hers than snow / And smooth as monumental alabaster" (V.ii.6–7). Desdemona will soon be dead, and the landscape in Dickinson's poem is similarly corpselike, a body being prepared for interment. The snow is not a cosmetician after all, but a mortician, rendering nature's face pale, still, and featureless: "It makes an Even Face / Of Mountain, and of Plain – / Unbroken Forehead from the East / Unto the East again – ." The landscape's "Even Face" recalls the "even feet" of the marching angels in another poem, identical in their "Uniforms of Snow" (P 126). In both poems, whiteness, snow, and evenness converge to suggest, disturbingly, the obliteration of individual distinctions. Yet if the storm is vaguely sinister here, it again turns whimsical at the end, draping lacy ruffles around prosaic fenceposts, much as, in Emerson's poem, wreaths of Parian marble festoon the chicken coop. In the final line, "Denying they have been" echoes Emerson's "Retiring, as he were not" – the storm stops as if it never was, as if the snowflakes had been so many ghosts. (In an earlier version, the unnamed agent of the storm "stills his Artisans – like Swans" – a strange simile unless Dickinson had "The Snow-Storm" in mind.) Dickinson's riddle crystallizes the paradox of a New England snowstorm, which is at once playful and potentially dangerous, and which renders the landscape both deathly and beautiful.

All riddles describe something while withholding its name. Folk riddles typically are full of paradoxes, and like Dickinson's poem they often take common, natural things as their subjects – snowflakes, an egg, a spider, a cobweb, a firefly, a cloud. Dickinson's riddle shares a solution with this ancient one, quoted by Richard Wilbur in his essay "The Persistence of Riddles":[22]

> White bird featherless
> Flew from Paradise,
> Pitched on the castle wall;
> Along came Lord Landless,
> Took it up handless,
> And rode away horseless to the King's white hall.

The poem's perplexing negations – a bird without feathers, a landless lord who picks up the bird without hands and rides away without a horse – challenge the reader to reach, by an imaginative leap, the new interpretation (that the bird is not really a bird, though it flies; that Lord Landless is not a human ruler but the sun; and so on) that will make sense of them. By comparison, Dickinson's riddle seems easy. Yet in the third stanza, the middle of the poem and presumably also of the storm, the storm's agent suddenly becomes indistinguishable from its object: "It reaches to the fence, / It wraps it rail by rail / Till it is lost in fleeces." At this point, the solution seems a bit less certain than before, and the reader might well be as "lost" as the pronoun's shifting antecedents. In Dickinson's poems, the commonest and most primal words in English – grief, love, death, immortality, sunlight, snow, poetry – become riddles whose ambiguous pronouns give the unnamed signified a resonance and mystery beyond what the noun itself could convey.

By not naming the referent explicitly, she also opens up a space for the reader to substitute alternate answers to the obvious one. *Death* is one possible substitution, as we have seen, but so is *poetry*, for which Dickinson sometimes used snow as a metaphor. "It sifts" passes Dickinson's own reader-response definition of poetry, quoted by Thomas Higginson: "If I read a book and it makes my whole body so cold no fire ever can warm me I know that is poetry" (L #342a). Her poem is the product of a mind of winter that not even Emerson's radiant fireplace could warm. Unlike Stevens's snow man, her speaker cannot be said to see, with chilly objectivity, "nothing that is not there," for the scene is filtered through an idiosyncratic human consciousness that only Dickinson could create. But the speaker does see "the nothing that is," the emptiness of a denuded landscape that is all the more vacant because it still holds the shape of human presence and summer's plenty, "A blanker whiteness of benighted snow," as Frost says in "Desert Places," "With no expression, nothing to express."[23] While the speaker of Frost's poem projects his human loneliness out onto nature, the "supposed person" who represents Dickinson's verse refuses to hear misery in the sound of the wind or to see loneliness in the swirling snow. She remains an enigma, withdrawn – like the unnamed agent of the storm or like Emerson's own poet Uriel – behind the snow's "celestial Vail."

Returning to Emerson's metaphor, cited at the beginning of this chapter, we can conclude that Dickinson saw the world very differently, through the lens of his words, than Whitman did. If we exchange Emerson's metaphor from *Representative Men* – that we learn to see ourselves through the lenses of other men – with a similar one from "Experience," he was perhaps not so much a lens as a source of light, filtered by each of them through the very differently ground and colored lenses of the self: "Thus inevitably does the universe wear our color. . . . As I am, so I see" (*EL* 489). Dickinson sees the Emerson of reticence, Whitman the Emerson of excess. Whitman inherits Emerson the priest of nature, master of digression, repetition, parataxis, and the transcendental catalogue; Dickinson inherits Emerson the Sphinx, master of the lapidary aphorism, the skeptical question, and the riddling quatrain. Both enact the power of the poet, described so lyrically by Emerson in his essay, to provoke others into seeing a familiar world anew. Putting his writings to disparate poetic uses, Whitman and Dickinson prove not only their revisionary power as readers but the richness of Emerson's writings as a mine for other writers. It is a measure of the vitality of his thought that Emerson could serve as a "vital Light" (P 883) not only for Whitman and Dickinson, whose forms and themes differ so markedly, but also for a wide range of twentieth-century American poets, from Wallace Stevens and Robert Frost to Richard Wilbur and A. R. Ammons.

NOTES

1   *Emerson in His Journals,* selected and edited by Joel Porte (Cambridge, MA: Harvard University Press, 1982), p. 484. Hereafter abbreviated *EJ.*
2   *Complete Poetry and Selected Prose,* selected by Justin Kaplan (New York: The Library of America, 1982), p. 1055. Hereafter abbreviated *CPSP.*
3   *The Complete Poems of Emily Dickinson,* 3 vols., ed. Thomas H. Johnson (Cambridge, MA, and London: Harvard University Press, 1955), from "The Spider holds a Silver Ball," Poem 605. Hereafter Dickinson poems will be cited parenthetically by P with Johnson's opus numbers. The second quotation is from Whitman's "A Noiseless Patient Spider," *CPSP* 564.
4   *Notes and Fragments,* ed. Dr. Richard Maurice Bucke (London, ON: A. Talbot, 1899), p. 56. Hereafter abbreviated *NF.*
5   *The Letters of Emily Dickinson,* 3 vols., ed. Thomas H. Johnson and Theodora Ward (Cambridge, MA: Harvard University Press, 1958), #271. Future quotations from Dickinson's letters will be cited with the abbreviation L and the opus number.
6   "Uses of Great Men," *Essays and Lectures,* selected by Joel Porte (New York: The Library of America, 1983), p. 616. Hereafter abbreviated *E and L.*
7   These manuscript notes appear in *Walt Whitman's Workshop: A Collection of Unpublished Manuscripts* (Cambridge, MA: Harvard University Press, 1928), compiled by Clifton J. Furness. Hereafter abbreviated *WWW.*
8   F. O. Matthiessen, *American Renaissance: Art and Expression in the Age of Emerson and Whitman.* (New York: Oxford University Press, 1941), p. 550.
9   Gay Wilson Allen recounts this episode in *The Solitary Singer* (New York: Macmillan, 1955), pp. 432–35. The parody was written by Bayard Taylor and published by Emory Holloway in "Whitman as His Own Press Agent," *American Mercury* 18 (December 1929): 487.
10 In his biography *Walt Whitman: The Making of the Poet,* Paul Zweig notes Whitman's talent for paraphrasing other texts: "Whitman casually pillaged the books he read, rephrasing and 'translating,' until the original has become all but invisible. . . . By means of [paraphrase], he 'digested hard iron,' while preserving the unliterary diction of his poems" (New York: Basic Books, 1984), p. 146.
11 *Whitman and Tradition: The Poet in His Century* (New Haven and London: Yale University Press, 1990), pp. 46–48.
12 In *Disseminating Whitman: Revision and Corporeality in* Leaves of Grass, Michael Moon points out that both erection and ejaculation seem to occur between the lines "And reached till you felt my beard, and reached till you held my feet" and "Swiftly arose and spread around me the peace of and joy and knowledge that pass all the art and argument of the earth" (Cambridge, MA: Harvard University Press, 1991), p. 49.
13 Joanne Feit Diehl, for example, calls Emerson's poetics "intensely exclusionary and dominated by male presence" and asserts that "what for Whitman became

a potentially saving vision becomes for a woman poet a debilitating and ultimately self-defeating vision." *Women Poets and the American Sublime* (Bloomington: Indiana University Press, 1990), pp. 5, 24.

14 Helen McNeil notes the echo of the line about Emerson in *Emily Dickinson*
(New York: Random House, 1986), pp. 98–100. McNeil argues that the poem
reflects Dickinson's response to Emerson as "a kind of travelling salesman of
optimism," a view put forth more bitterly by Melville in *The Confidence-Man*
(p. 100).

15 In *This Was a Poet* (New York: Scribners, 1938), George Frisbie Whicher
quotes this poem after marveling at Dickinson's not having met Emerson during his visit to the Evergreens (p. 198). He implies that Dickinson declined the
invitation because she was similarly "unmoved," or uninfluenced, by Emerson's ideas – a claim with which I obviously disagree, although I find his placing of the poem in this particular biographical context to be both clever and
illuminating.

16 *The Lyman Letters: New Light on Emily Dickinson and Her Family*, ed. Rich-
ard Sewall (Amherst: University of Massachusetts Press, 1965), p. 76. Cited in
Richard Sewall, *The Life of Emily Dickinson*, 2 vols. (New York: Farrar,
Strauss & Giroux, 1974), vol. 2, p. 668.

17 *Women Writers and Poetic Identity* (Princeton: Princeton University Press,
1980), pp. 189–90.

18 *Collected Poems and Translations*, ed. Harold Bloom and Paul Kane (New
York: Library of America, 1994), p. 119. Hereafter abbreviated *CPT*.

19 Joanne Feit Diehl has pointed out the problem that the Emerson imperative of
representativeness poses for the woman poet: "[T]he woman poet does not, in
the nineteenth century, or for that matter in the early twentieth century, perceive herself as speaking for commonal experience, as 'representative.' Instead,
women poets more often perceive themselves as exceptions, as isolates, depart-
ing from, rather than building upon, a tradition" (*Women Poets*, p. 2).

20 On December 10, 1878, the editor of the *Literary World* guessed that Emerson
had written the poem and quoted it entire. The story of the poem's publication
is related by Thomas Johnson in his introduction to the variorum edition of
Dickinson's poems, pp. xxix–xxxiii.

21 Barbara Packer notes that indeterminacy of tone is a hallmark of Emerson's
style: "Emerson's sentences can usually be read in more than one way, and
only the sophisticated reader will be able to supply an imagined tone or dramatic context that makes them interesting" [*Emerson's Fall* (New York: Continuum, 1982), p. 7].

22 *The Catbird's Song: Prose Pieces 1963–1995* (New York: Harcourt, 1997), p.
42.

23 *The Poetry of Robert Frost* (New York: Holt, 1979), p. 296.

10

ROBERT WEISBUCH

Post-Colonial Emerson and the Erasure of Europe

I

On a transitional November day, in the year 1872, a pair of American gentlemen could be seen roaming the rooms of the Museum of the Louvre. The elder of them was clearly in the scanning mode, moving his tall, spare frame briskly through the rooms. His younger, fleshier partner frequently would urge hesitation in the midst of one or another masterpiece, to which his companion would give friendly but only momentary assent before moving on once more, like a steer of the Western plains avoiding the rope. Again the younger man would linger with his all-absorbing gaze, then respectfully touch his friend's elbow. He would softly exclaim and modestly explicate, progressively but pleasantly puzzled by his companion's polite impatience and clear desire to gallop on, taking in everything at large yet nothing in particular with his strong, frank stare.

This is Ralph Waldo Emerson at 69 and Henry James, Jr., at 29 on a wonderful and tense day in American cultural history. This drama of different generations and opposed attitudes is played out far from home, in a French palace of power that had become a repository of the history of beauty. In March they would renew their uneasy partnership to tour the Vatican with similar results. And 15 years later, James recalls the two occasions with astonishment: "his perception of the objects contained in these collections was of the most general order. I was struck with the anomaly of a man so refined and intelligent being so little spoken to by works of art. It would be more exact to say that certain chords were wholly absent; their tune was played, the tune of life and literature, altogether on those that remained. They had every wish to be equal to their office, but one feels that the number was short – that some notes could not be given." He goes on to remark that Emerson journeyed on three occasions to Europe, where "he was introduced to a more complicated world" than his barren native New England, and yet, shockingly, Emerson's "spirit, his moral taste, as it were, abode always within the undecorated walls of his youth. There he could dwell with that ripe unconsciousness of evil which is one of the most beautiful signs by which we know him."[1]

James's condescension is complicated by the sudden turn to praise. Yet Emerson's "beautiful" failure to develop his sensibility via Europe is so crucial to James that he will not only correct it in his own experience but will also design character upon Emersonian character who will be tested by the ability to retain an American integrity while growing (as Emerson did not) into European understandings. The first of these appears just four years after James accompanied Emerson to the Louvre, in the innocent, even Adamic figure of Christopher Newman, "long, lean, and muscular" just like the "tall, lean" Emerson depicted by James in his other Emerson essay in *Partial Portraits*. We meet this allegorically named avatar of Emerson precisely at the Museum of the Louvre – which is why I have, very roughly and badly, referenced the opening of *The American* in my opening here. There, Newman finds himself "rather baffled by the aesthetic question," apparently bereft of those same "certain chords" absent from his prototype.[2]

But what if, just this once, it was James rather than Emerson who lacked the chords and missed the tune? Just possibly Emerson's opacity to art objects at the Louvre and the Vatican does not mark a limit but a determined resistance. Emerson spent real time at the Boston Athenaeum and wrote with some perception on pictorial art and sculpture. Possibly his refusal to linger in the European halls is a refusal to idolize the foreign and the past, those bullies of a culturally insecure America. Possibly too, his mode of taking it all in rather than focusing on individual works occurs because the totality of the European achievement is such a chief fact of Emerson's cultural politics. More largely, Emerson's failure to achieve via Europe a mature sensibility may not be a case of arrested if "beautiful" development but a fully sophisticated cultural strategy, an attempt to reach for a decisively different, distinctly American maturity.

I want to argue here that Emerson could not afford Europe because he believed that a post-colonial America could not, and that this issue matters so greatly that it could never be Emerson and Europe but can be only Emerson or Europe. This is a sufficiently large claim that I need to rush to four clarifications before developing it.

First, the private Emerson enjoyed Europe enormously. His three trips, in 1832–33, 1847–48, and 1872–73, each lasted for well over half a year – and no one held him hostage. His journals, especially on the middle visit, are full of commonplace appreciations of people and places. His first visit, taken less than two years after the death of his first wife and just a few months after his resignation from Boston's Second Church, dramatically restored his spirits; and much later in life he acknowledged a half wish to have lived in Rome, "a majestic city & satisfies this craving imagination," strong praise from a writer who almost always insists that the imagination never can be satisfied.[3] Even so, Emerson could praise and particularize Europe only when he took his eye from the central and tyrannical notion of the idea of Europe in relation to an imitative America that, despite some bluster, agreed by its indebtedness to its inferiority; and my claim is that his ambivalence toward Europe tends to resolve itself negatively because the crucial necessity to dignify the New World and Europe as idea or trope for Emerson overwhelms the Europe of mere fact. The typical touring American is an Anglophile well characterized by Benjamin Goluboff as "the alluder on the landscape," an insecure New World parvenu taking "a sort of examination in cultural literacy."[4] Emerson must eschew any such toadying, even if that means becoming less the alluder on the landscape than the insulter on the spot, to express a view centered on who he proudly is as a representative American.

Second, as with Europe, so too for his relations to European writers. Privately adored, powerfully formative, they must be disowned for Emerson to become himself. The writers who matter most to him are the near-contemporary British and European romantics, and at least for some real time he can never acknowledge that, again for reasons that are not selfishly individual but strategically national. To say that Emerson erases them, at least in his early essays, speaks to their prior presence; and even the nationalism that motivates him is largely owing to the valuation of folk cultures put forward by Madame de Staël and others in Germany.

But it is British writers who matter most to Emerson. In fact, it is impossible to imagine Emerson without Wordsworth's relocation of Milton's heaven of heavens within the human mind or Coleridge on imagination; and I will propose later that a sally from his friend Carlyle may have altered Emerson's writing forever. My third early clarification, though, is about England generally. For Emerson, Europe does not simply include England; Europe is largely an extension of England. The common language, America's history of colonial domination by England and its continuing cultural inheritance from England, and England's continuing standing as the most powerful nation in the Old World make England and Europe often synonymous for Emerson. Other American nationalists like Orestes Brownson might argue, "We must bring in France and Germany to combat or neutralize England, so that our national spirit may gain freedom to manifest itself."[5] Emerson won't make that differentiation even on his second trip when he is busy tallying differences between England and France: "It is doubtful whether London, whether Paris can answer the questions which now arise in the mind" because of the socialist uprisings, and "both nations promise more than they can perform"; and in Paris, "the social decorum seems to have here the same rigours as in England with a little variety in the application."[6] Thus when Emerson in *English Traits* looks for an alternative to "the tyranny and prepossession of the British element" he must go further than Brownson suggests, "by comparing with it the civilizations farthest east and west, the old Greek, the Oriental, and, much more, the Ideal standard."[7] And England is joined to the other European nations when Emerson asks in his 1860 essay "Culture," "Can we never extract this tape-worm of Europe from the brain of our countrymen?" (*W* 11: 535). Beyond real differences, the aristocracy-based nations of the Old World, French Revolution or not, lump together.

Finally, because Emerson's real alternative culture to England is an America allied with that "Ideal standard," it is worth stopping to ask whether the use of the heavily laden term post-colonial should be applied to nineteenth-century writers of the United States. Certainly there is a wide divide between the situation of settlement colonies such as the United States, Canada, New Zealand, and Australia and the situation of subjugated native populations in, say, sub-Saharan Africa and India. Race and language do not have the same kind of terrible play in settlement colonies, and the settlers themselves, however much they experience themselves as dominated by the metropolis of the empire, are an extension of that empire in the eyes of the native inhabitants – American Indians, for example, or imported slaves; reciprocally, early settlers in New England took pains to insure that they were not viewed in London as "going savage." Some, not all, post-colonial generalities nonetheless apply, most notoriously the monopolizing of prestige by imported models of high culture; the encouraging of third-rate imitations of these models; and thus a long lag between political independence and its cultural counterpart. Whatever we see as complications to the claim, Euro-Americans vehemently expressed their sense of being post-colonial in just these ways. Add to that some special features of the American situation – the pagan, then Christian notion of the westward movement of civilization and of the West as the place where the human spirit will reach its apotheosis; the claim that a democratic form of society requires cultural forms especially distinct from whatever has existed in aristocratic nations; the Puritan-derived notion of the writer as not merely an individual or even an individual carrier of his culture but a microcosmic, ideal representative of it – and one begins to understand the intensity of calls for a national literature and of protests against imported European culture.

I want first to consider Emerson in this post-colonial context to investigate more fully the motives and dimensions of Emerson's attitudes toward Europe. And while these attitudes amplify more than they change throughout his career, I want next to consider how their expression radically alters – alters in such ways in fact as to constitute in Emerson the very attempt usually ascribed first to James, to create a more mature, second stage of achieved American writing, a post-Emerson Emerson in a sense, a no-longer-post-colonial, fully freed American mind.

II

From first to last, philosophical and even spiritual conviction, personal and emotional experience, and political and social history gather around the question of Europe for Emerson. It is integral to all his thought; and had he turned from it as unknowingly as James wishes to imagine, there would be no Emerson we would wish to read.

This is not to say that Emerson's writings on Europe, especially the journal entries from his first trip in 1832–33, richly reward the reading. They largely bear out James's verdict of missing chords. For instance, Italy to a young Emerson is opera and Catholicism, both overblown pomp. "I have been to the Opera, & thought three taris, the price of a ticket, rather too much for the whistle" (*EJ* 98); or, again, upon viewing the Pope's blessings in the Sistine Chapel, "All this pomp is conventional. . . . [T]o the eye of an Indian I am afraid it would be ridiculous. There is no true majesty in all this millinery & imbecility" (*EJ* 101). But Italy is suddenly redeemed once Emerson arrives in France and requires an alternative as an attack weapon: "I have seen so much in five months that the magnificence of Paris will not take my eye today," as if the eye could be a traitor. And, for once more patriotically Bostonian than American, "I was sorry to find that in leaving Italy I had left forever that air of antiquity & history which her towns possess & in coming hither had come to a loud modern New York of a place" (*EJ* 109). Of course, when he actually was in Italy, Emerson had taken a different tone to suit his programmatic churlishness, terming Venice "a city for beavers – but to my thought a most disagreeable residence" (*EJ* 107).

I quote this silliness because it goes toward a serious purpose. Emerson's grumpings culminate in his amazing dismissal of Naples, his famous "Who cares?": "Baiae & Misenum & Vesuvius, Procida & Pausilippo & Villa Reale sound so big that we are ready to surrender at discretion & not stickle for our private opinion against what seems the human race. Who cares? Here's for the plain old Adam, the simple genuine Self against the whole world" (*EJ* 99).

This journal passage provides our key. Europe must be erased because it exists at the crossroads of Emerson's most fundamental idea and his greatest emotional fear, and they are knotted where they meet by a post-colonial set of political implications. "We come out to Europe," Emerson writes in Florence, "to learn what man can – what is the uttermost which social man has yet done" (*EJ* 106), and it is crucial that this uttermost of Europe cannot touch the lowest hem of an ideal human potential. Indeed, for the early visionary Emerson all uttermosts must be temporary and relative. The Emerson of "Circles" will proclaim that "every action admits of being outdone," that "Every ultimate fact is only the first of a new series," "that there is no end in nature but every end is a beginning." In such a view, "The only sin is limitation" and the only good is "to draw a new circle." For that, we must "forget ourselves" and become like Emerson's ideal self, "an endless seeker with no Past at my back" (W 2: 301, 304, 301, 308, 321, 318). Europe is that past, that threateningly large circle of achieved human culture, and it is the enemy to the extent that it poses as enough. Emerson knows that Europe is very great; if it is great enough, there will be no future, there will be no present. "Every man has his own voice, manner, eloquence," Emerson writes in his journal at 27. "Let him scorn to imitate any being, let him scorn to be a secondary man" (*JMN* 3: 199). And it is Europe that threatens to make us secondary. Emerson's very first sentence in *Nature* is "Our age is retrospective." He mourns that "The foregoing generations beheld God and nature face to face; we, through their eyes. Why should not we also enjoy an original relation to the universe?" Europe keeps us from experiencing ourselves as ourselves, as originary. Europe turns life into a library and creative acts into a museum.

This fear of being "secondary" leads into the more immediately psychological component of Emerson's need to erase Europe. It is succinctly expressed in the forgotten second half of his "Who cares?" passage on Naples: "Need is, that you assert yourself or you will find yourself overborne by the most paltry things. A young man is dazzled by the stately arrangements of the hotel & jostled out of his course of thought & study of men by such trumpery considerations. The immense regard paid to clean shoes & a smooth hat impedes him, & the staring of a few dozens of idlers in the street hinders him from looking about him with his own eyes." A traveler must "insist first of all upon his simple human rights of seeing & of judging here in Italy as he would in his own farm or sitting room at home" (*EJ* 99).

Emerson had an extraordinary perception of a very ordinary and awful

kind of experience, the sense of being watched, judged, and made to feel
small. He experienced the common but humiliating desire to meet an external standard horrifyingly high and mysterious, a desire which creates a
particular self-consciousness that is also a decentering of the self and a
disaster to spontaneous, original existence. At 20, dedicating himself to the
church, Emerson makes the often-quoted confession, "What is called a
warm heart, I have not" (*EJ* 47). But what he most indicts in his character
is his self-consciousness, which creates "a sore uneasiness in the company
of most men & women, a frigid fear of offending & jealousy of disrespect"
(*EJ* 46). Four years later, we hear the same refrain as Emerson contrasts
himself to his mourned brother Edward, who possessed, in a distinctive
phrase, "great power of face" whereas "I have none. I laugh; I blush; I look
ill tempered; against my will & against my interest" (*EJ* 67). His first European journey, not coincidentally, stirs these insecurities to a boil. Now
30, Emerson speaks of a desire to "hide myself in the dens of the hills, in
the thickets of an obscure country town, I am so vexed & chagrined with
myself – with my weakness, with my guilt." These feelings of self-hatred
are occasioned because "no boy makes so many blunders or says such
awkward, contrary, disagreeable speeches as I do. In the attempt to oblige
a person I wound & disgust him" (*EJ* 107). As in Venice, so in Paris. A
month later, Emerson counsels himself, "Be cheerful," decrying his "insane
habit" of "groping always into the past months & scraping together every
little pitiful instance of awkwardness & misfortune & keeping my nervous
system ever on the rack." This, he says, is the "disease" of someone "too
respectful to the opinions of others" (*EJ* 110). These entries are so richly
revealing – it is Emerson's overweening desire to please and to receive approval that somehow makes him contentious, as if a more sanguine self-
sufficiency would make him less assertive – that we may ignore their nor-
mative aspect in mourning states of awkward social behavior and
retrospective regret that afflict all of us. What is distinctive to Emerson is
his insistence that this self-diminishment must be defeated, his lack of resignation to it. Indeed, the vocation Emerson invents for himself, as public
speaker, with its extraordinary degree of literally being looked upon, challenges him to gain "power of face" and ownership of self. And the frequently pugnacious tone of his early essays may well serve to shape consciously that "contrary, disagreeable aspect" caused by his too-great respect
for the opinion of others, to oppose that desire and to achieve its goal at
the same time. In any case, for Emerson it is intolerable to be so negatively
self-aware. Years later in "Experience," he will write in his shocking way,
"It is very unhappy, but too late to be helped, the discovery we have made
that we exist" and he will define this "discovery" of self-consciousness as

"the Fall of Man," noting that "Ever afterwards we suspect our instruments" (W 3: 75). Europe brings out the worst of this self-awareness in a provincial, this disease of being "too respectful to the opinions of others" on a national scale. If we are not to be judged into that self-conscious anxiety that denotes a secondary existence, we must not let Europe make us provincial and postlapsarian at once – and so the dismissive quality of many of Emerson's notes.

The personal and philosophical thus become one in Emerson's refusal to venerate Europe. But he is not wholly original in this attitude. Emerson grows up in an America where the political wars of 1776 and 1812 have become transformed into a cultural battle with England, and this conflict is so evident to Emerson at age 19 that he self-consciously, almost dutifully, announces at the opening of his seventh journal, "I dedicate my book to the Spirit of America" (EJ 16).

He makes this dedication just two years after Sydney Smith's famous, infuriatingly accurate query, "In the four quarters of the globe, who reads an American book?" which was only the latest in a series of British taunts against the cultural vacancy of the former colony. "No work of distinguished merit in any branch has yet been produced among them," Southey wrote in 1809. An anonymous reviewer in The British Critic states bluntly in 1818, "The Americans have no national literature, and no learned men." And these discountings continue throughout Emerson's lifetime. Colburn's New Monthly Magazine, 1827: "To talk of the literature of America is to talk of that which has no existence." The Athenaeum, 1831: "This want of originality in American literature is, we think, likely long to continue." The Westminster Review, 1860: "For almost every work of note which has been produced there, the mother nation can show a better counterpart."[8] All of this sour rhetoric is reminiscent of Macaulay's famous Minute of 1835 on Indian education when he declares "a single shelf of a good European library" to be "worth the whole native literature of India and Arabia."[9] (This is why, despite differences, American literature in Emerson's time must be brought into the post-colonial discussions.) Throughout Emerson's lifetime as well, English writers would crowd their American counterparts off the shelves of the bookstalls in New York and Boston. The notoriety of the British romantics and the less controversial popularity of the English realistic novel was in stark contrast to a Euro-American literary production that only the wildest nationalists would attempt to credit.

The wiser among them looked to the future and acknowledged the present post-colonial hangover of British cultural domination as painful and even threatening to significant nationhood. As early as 1788, Philip Freneau asks,

> Can we never be thought to have learning or grace
> Unless it be brought from that damnable place
> Where tyranny reigns with her impudent face?

After another 30 years, Bryant complains that the prevailing style of poetry in America is "tinged with a sickly and affected imitation of the peculiar manner of some of the late popular poets of England" and Longfellow in 1832 similarly charges that "instead of coming forward as bold, original thinkers," American writers "have imbibed the degenerate spirit of modern English poetry." In the 1840s Nathaniel Willis and George P. Morris proclaim, "The country is tired of being *be-Britished.*" Most American books, Margaret Fuller says simply, "were English books" and Whitman editorializes in 1847 in the Brooklyn *Eagle* that all is hopeless "as long as we copy with a servile imitation, the very cast-off literary fashions of London." Still, in 1869, Lowell is taking up Emerson's notion of "this tape-worm of Europe" and ascribing the disease wholly to England: "We are worth nothing except so far as we have disinfected ourselves of Anglicism."[10]

In opposition, full-fledged literary tories were plentiful, and writers like Irving and even Longfellow and Lowell took more moderate views. But Emerson enlisted in the nationalist cause – it helps to define him – and he engages its rhetoric with real energy. England and Europe get allied to images of disease and decrepitude, to no less than innate depravity, as Emerson employs cultural time to America's benefit. But as a new nation indebted to an Old World culture, America has a contradictory status that Emerson, even as an undergraduate, would acknowledge – if only to blame England for any snakes in the American Eden: "It is the misfortune of America that her sudden maturity of national condition was accompanied with the knowledge of good and *evil* which would better belong to an older country. We have received our drama line for line and precept for precept from England and in so doing have inherited a stained and rotten web of corruptions . . . whose whole tissue is consistent in nothing but pollution" (*EJ* 10). More often, Emerson would image America as simply youthful, making European taunts of its immaturity into a virtue. He contrasts "the Genius of Britain," which treads upon "an unsound & perilous footing, burning beneath with flame to an unknown extent," to America, which "has inherited the free step & unconstrained attitude which her parent hath lost by age" (*EJ* 12). Here Emerson conjoins the images of England as aged parent and England as hell, throwing in the threat of violent social revolution for good measure.

America is ripe, Europe is rotten. "If the nations of Europe can find anything to idolize in their ruinous & enslaved institutions, we are content, though we are astonished at their satisfaction" (*EJ* 16). Internal corruptions may destroy "rotten states like Spain," a "contagion" from which America is "aloof" by the width of an ocean (*EJ* 22). In fact, it is not only America against England or America against Europe but America against the entire aged world: "Asia, Africa, Europe, old, leprous & wicked, have run round the goal of centuries till we are tired and they are ready to drop. But now a strong man has entered the race & is outstripping them all. Strong Man! youth & glory are with thee" (*EJ* 41). In all of these early statements, Europe rarely exists by itself but almost always as a negative counter to Young America, with no past at its back but the future at its feet. If the Constitution flourishes, then all the Utopianists of the past "will find their beautiful theories rivalled & outdone by the reality, which it has pleased God to bestow upon United America" (*EJ* 17). The myth of the West is invoked, "the Westward progress of the Car of Empire," to silence European influence: in this "mountain-land" "the old tales of history & the fortunes of departed nations shall be thoroughly forgotten & the name of Rome or Britain fall seldom on the ear" (*EJ* 23). If the "senates that shall meet hereafter in those wilds" are wise, "the reformation of the world would be to be expected from America." As "the despots of Europe" are now "tightening the bonds of monarchy," then "To America, therefore, monarchs look with apprehension & the people with hope" (*EJ* 29).

From this, the defensive cultural argument follows. If the redeemer nation has produced an embarrassing paucity of literature, that too can be blamed on England via "the community of language" (*EJ* 39), and in any case, "we have what is better. We have a government and a national spirit that is better than poems or histories & these have a premature ripeness that is incompatible with the rapid production of the latter" (*EJ* 49). Our reality, in other words, is what can exist for you only in visionary literature.

The youthful Emerson is an encyclopedia of the arguments made in defense of America, fighting its lack of storied history by positing instead a future, turning the tables on cultural rawness by celebrating youth and mocking the corruptions of European age, claiming a redemptive stature by which the colony is no longer a pathetically removed suburb of London but the metropolitan center for the reformation of the world. At times young Emerson's rhetoric is a performance, outracing authentic feeling, but the feeling followed over a long life; and I have quoted at length from the early, private Emerson because these ideas go powerfully toward forming the public Emerson and persist largely unchanged throughout his career. And to a degree, James is right: at times, Emerson molds his European experiences by these ideas rather than having the experiences alter them. In the midst of his first European tour he writes that, to make any good use of

what he sees, the American "needs to put a double & treble guard upon
the independency of his judgments" (*EJ* 106).

In fact, his comments on travel throughout his career illustrate his fidelity
to these early ideas even while he progressively enlarges their meanings.
Several years later, in "Self-Reliance," Emerson expands the travel anxiety
to national scope to indict "the superstition of Traveling, whose idols are
Italy, England, Egypt," as owing to "want of self-culture" (*W* 2: 80) and
that in turn is "the symptom of a deeper unsoundness" whereby "the intellect is vagabond." Even at home, "We imitate; and what is imitation but
the traveling of the mind? Our houses are built with foreign taste; our
shelves are garnished with foreign ornaments" (81–82). And finally "As
our Religion, our Education, our Art look abroad, so does our spirit of
society" (84). This is an audacious amplification of the original idea, making love of travel a form of national treason as well as self-distrust. And
two decades later, Emerson persists, noting in a sly dig that educated Americans travel to Europe "perhaps because it is their mental home, as the
invalid habits of this country might suggest." But perhaps the disease will
create its own cure in that "One use of travel is to recommend the books
and works of home, – we go to Europe to be Americanized" (*W* 11: 537).
The redeemer nation need not stray from itself to learn bad lessons of the
reprobate.

This consistency is especially striking in regard to a final characteristic of
Emerson's relation to Europe, his tendency to seek representative men. At
19 he writes, "From childhood the names of the great have ever resounded
in my ear" (*EJ* 27); and in "Culture," after proclaiming that we go to
Europe to be Americanized, he adds, "and . . . to find men." Part of this is
Emerson's strong desire to find intellectual and spiritual companionship,
but there is an extrapersonal dimension to the individuals he meets just as
there is an extrapersonal dimension to his own self as traveler. Emerson
applied the American habit of seeing the special man as a microcosm of his
culture to Europeans as well. His concluding observations in 1833 on his
first trip and in 1848 at the conclusion of his second trip both sum up the
experiences in terms of meetings with the great, and they could almost have
been written on the same day. In the first case, he begins by thanking "the
great God who has led me through this European scene, this last school-
room in which he has pleased to instruct me" – and God's primary lesson
to Emerson is not to be cowed by the great. "He has shown me the men I
wished to see – Landor, Coleridge, Carlyle, Wordsworth – he has thereby
comforted & confirmed me in my convictions." "Confirmed" here is especially interesting, as it appears that Emerson journeyed to Europe

expecting the very disappointment he will go on to describe and even cherish. In a mockery of gratitude, he now thanks the great men themselves for failing miserably to fulfill their repute:

> Many things I owe to the sight of these men. I shall judge more justly, less timidly, of wise men forevermore. To be sure not one of these is a mind of the very first class, but what the intercourse with each of these suggests is true of intercourse with better men, that they never *fill the ear* – fill the mind – no, it is an *idealized* portrait which always we draw of them. Upon an intelligent man, wholly a stranger to their names, they would make in conversation no deep impression – none of a world-filling fame – they would be remembered as sensible well read earnest men – not more. Especially are they all deficient all these four – in different degrees but all deficient – in insight into religious truth. They have no idea of that species of moral truth which I call the first philosophy.

Confessing that "Carlyle is so amiable that I love him," Emerson delightedly repeats his debunking point about all of them: "You speak to them as to children or persons of inferior capacity whom it is necessary to humor; adapting our tone & remarks to their known prejudices & not to our knowledge of the truth" (*EJ* 115).

There is much to notice here – first that the European survey has become solely British in this retrospect, second that the Anglo-American antagonism vibrates in every word. But most startling is the standard Emerson applies, the standard of what I elsewhere have termed American actualism, the demand that the writer live out in every moment of his social being, on the very surfaces of life, his deepest delvings, that the writer must become her or his most visionary ideas. Emerson's very vocation, as lecturer or priest without church, is his own attempt to fulfill this impossible demand, one which the British, keeping a sane distance between Xanadu and teatime, would find bizarre; and it surely contributes to Emerson's harsh criticisms of his own social imperfections. Yet those too are treated and transformed in this passage. Emerson eschews his usual self-lacerating worries of speaking awkwardly to note that he has knowingly fit himself to the small prejudices of these quasi-great men because the great men turn out to be so limited; thus he renovates his social anxieties into a refusal of the great that allows him the space he requires to become great himself. On the boat carrying him home to New England, facing west with his back to Liverpool, Emerson thought upon his first book. He would title it *Nature*, as if no one ever had written before him.

Fifteen years later, upon Emerson's returning once more from Europe, we get something of a ritual repetition:

> I went to England, &, after allowing myself freely to be dazzled by the various
> brilliancy of men of talent, in calm hours I found myself no way helped; my
> sequins were all yellow leaves, I said I have valued days (& must still) by the
> number of clear insights I get, and I must estimate my company so. Then I
> found I had scarcely had a good conversation, a solid dealing, man with man,
> in England. (*EJ* 391)

The emphasis is just as before, though muted perhaps (here he admits to
being momentarily dazzled at least) by the change in Emerson's own status
– he was a figure himself now, in London as well as in Boston. But he is
not so beyond it all as to forgo in the image of "yellow leaves" the usual
notion of England as past its prime, heading toward cultural winter.

Against James's notion of Emerson as Peter Pan, it is worth remembering
that the sense of cultural inferiority persists through Emerson's lifetime, for
while there is major achievement in literature and art, the full acknowledg-
ments of this will take nearly another century. It is not as if Emerson is
looking backward, incapable of change; he is looking around. But something does soften, for better or worse. During his second visit to London,
Emerson confesses, "In America we fancy that we live in a new & forming
country but that England was finished long ago. But we find London &
England in full growth, the British Museum not yet arranged, the boards
only taken down the other day from the monument & fountains of Trafal-
gar Square" (*EJ* 384). Emerson here comprehends the gap between trope
and reality as if he finally has the leisure or self-confidence to do so. And
the literary aftermath of this second journey, *English Traits, is* very different from *Nature* and from the works that follow in the '30s. The contrast
provides what thus far has been lacking in a charting of Emerson's relation
to Europe, a sense of movement through time, of that artistic and spiritual
development that James denied to Emerson. How we view the essential
differences between the handling of Europe in *Nature* and other early essays
of Emerson's first public decade and in *English Traits* (1856) or other
works of a stage initiated in 1850 by *Representative Men* determines our
view of Emerson's career, our sense of whether Emerson decidedly declines,
even submits, after an initial greatness or whether instead he exchanges one
high mode of achievement for another.

III

What is most striking about Europe in the early prose is, first, its nearly
total absence, and second, its permeating presence. It is instructive to return
to Emerson's first sentence as an author, in *Nature*, "Our age is retrospective." Emerson is writing just a few years after John Stuart Mill in 1831

defined historical perspective as the "spirit of the age," with "the idea of comparing one's own age with former ages, or with our notion of those which are yet to come" as for the first time now "the dominant idea."[11] Not only is Emerson's assertion derivative of an English writer, but clearly what "our age" honors retrospectively is most of all Europe and its achievements. And yet, in *Nature,* Emerson never quite says that. Only two decades later, in *English Traits,* will he acknowledge that our retrospective tendency is itself an importation: the English genius is "wise and rich, but it lives on its capital. It is retrospective"; or again, of the British, "Every one of them is a thousand years old and lives by his memory" (W 5: 246, 252). But in *Nature,* the culprit of this wrongheaded idolatry of the past, Britain, is never named. Likewise, Emerson's journey to Europe and his ultimate refusal to be cowed by European and, most specifically, English greatness is a final but unnamed inspiration for the work (which, apparently, he had begun before or during the trip though it would be another three years to its publication). And by its very title it celebrates the space his disparagement of the English romantic writers had cleared – even if the very word "nature" has been reinvented by those very writers. But both the influence and the rebellion against it are silent.

The work's cultural patriotism is similarly profound and similarly unremarked. At its moment *Nature* and the essays of the next several years constitute Emerson's response to the British taunts that America, lacking sufficient history and the legends that go with it, cannot produce a literature. Americans possess "neither history, nor romance, nor poetry, nor legends, on which to exercise their genius, and kindle their imagination," wrote an anonymous reviewer in an 1818 issue of *The British Critic;* and Hazlitt told Northcote that Americans "had *no natural imagination*" but that "this was likely to be the case in a new country like America, where there were no dim traces of the past – no venerable monuments – no romantic associations."[12] Cooper and James would agree in part and even a rabid nationalist like Brownson would mourn that "we have a glorious nature, no doubt, but it is barren of legends, traditions, and human associations" and, without such, "as Byron well maintained, [nature] is not poetical and cannot sustain a literature that does not soon become fatiguing and repulsive."[13] Emerson, instead, follows Tocqueville, who replied to such views with "man remains, and the poet needs no more."[14] Emerson argues that each individual "can live all history in his own person," that "all the facts of history preexist in the mind as laws," that "there is properly no history, only biography" because "we are always coming up with the emphatic facts of history in our private experience and verifying them here." If history then is merely a series of examples of those laws of existence which we know by our very nerves, then "I am ashamed to see what a shallow village tale our so called History is" (W 2: 8, 3, 10, 9–10, 40). Upon such ideas all of Emerson's thought rests, which is why he places his essay on "History" first in his book of *Essays: First Series*. Instead of following Irving, Cooper, or Hawthorne in inventing an American history to satisfy the European demand for one, Emerson refuses the rivalry and substitutes for history the vertical time of the present moment that, rightly seized, leads to overwhelming truth and a nature of transparent magnificence. "Whence then this worship of the past?" Emerson asks in "Self-Reliance," reasoning that the parent has "cast his ripened being" into the child. "The centuries are conspirators against the sanity and authority of the soul." Consequently, "He cannot be happy and strong until he too lives with nature in the present, above time" (W 2: 56, 57). If the Englishman asks how there is to be literature without history and legend, Emerson wonders how Europeans can get at the great truths when they are so buried under history's social clutter. Nature itself, and all that it portends, he will write in *English Traits,* has emigrated from the Old World to the New: "There, in that great sloven continent, in high Allegheny pastures, in the seawide sky-skirted prairie, still sleeps and murmurs and hides the great mother, long since driven away from the trim hedge-rows and over-cultivated garden of England" (W 5: 288).

Yet we find little of this nationalism identified as such in the essays and not a word of it in all of *Nature,* a book that poses the most basic metaphysical questions regarding the relation between phenomena and truth and that, tacitly at least, could be written only in an America of vast actual and meditative space, never in that Britain of actual and mental enclosures he describes in *English Traits*. This silence, I think, occurs for two reasons. One is that the nationalist quarrel with England and Europe, made explicit, would ruin the audacious scope of this amazing first book. Far better that it be a demonstration than a retort; far better that it be too busy with God and self to pick a fight. But there is a more compelling and more compelled reason for the silence. The very subject matter of *Nature,* its subject-object reconcilings, its Coleridgean lexicon and dialectics of Nature, Imagination, and Spirit, its sense of a dynamic, flowing universe, and of a commerce between nature, mind, and God all secure a New England home for a transplanted romanticism.[15] "Crossing a bare common, in snow puddles, at twilight, under a clouded sky, without having in my thoughts any occurrence of special good fortune, I have enjoyed a perfect exhilaration. I am glad to the brink of fear" (W 1: 9). Is it possible to imagine that experience in that way without having read William Wordsworth? And yet the democracy of the experience, its astonishing availability, its confessional statement, all would be undermined by the very notion of a learned idea. Emerson, simply, is covering his tracks in the New England snow, in part because any acknowledgment of influence will damage the freshness of the assertions and wreck his rhetoric. What startles in *Nature* as new is the declamatory voice, a writing strategy whereby logic is always ready to sacrifice a sequence of thought for a moment of aphoristic revelation. This is a voice against memory, which is also the personal counterpart of history. Emerson wants every moment to be a booming Now, each instant open to the farthest heaven. Writing itself is always a record of a thought, belated in that sense, and so Emerson seeks a prose that pulls itself vertically from the chronological, the voice of unfallen Adam now, the first namer confronting phenomena as if for the first time. Such a new beginning would become a ruin were Emerson to acknowledge the history of European romantic poetics and philosophy as a chief presence in his thought.

Yet he does so, in a special sense, on one of those rare occasions when Europe is allowed into *Nature* at all. Since the self experiences vividly what history and all externality can teach us only at second hand, Assyria shall be his dawn, moonrise his Paphos, "broad noon shall be [his] England of the senses and the understanding; the night shall be [his] Germany of mystic philosophy and dreams" (W 1: 17). Thus the self makes "the pomp of emperors ridiculous," announces the European parent's ripening in the child, transports the East and Europe effortlessly into the American self, and dissolves space and time. Europe appears only to disappear via a kind of transubstantiation. Its great men arise only briefly and illustratively, and they are figures from the safe distance of the Renaissance, long before American nationhood and thus in a sense available for Anglo-American sharing. Shakespeare and then Herbert are quoted, Shakespeare's rapids of metaphors to show how we can "make free with the most imposing forms and phenomena of the world, and to assert the predominance of the soul," Herbert on the self as microcosm, as "one world" that "hath / Another to attend him" to express Emerson's idea that great Nature itself is finally owned by and dissolved into spirit. Europe, then, almost never appears except when Emerson is denying the material world, the world Europe monopolizes, and its other mention is hardly surprising: "The American who has been confined, in his own country, to the sight of buildings designed after foreign models, is surprised on entering York Minster or St. Peter's at Rome, by the feeling that these structures are imitations also, – faint copies of an invisible archetype" (W 1: 67–68). So much then for the anxiety of influence, when the only original is the unbodied ideal!

In all, the silencing of Europe in *Nature* is most simply explained by a passage 20 years later in *English Traits*. Emerson notes the difficulty of observing England with a necessarily independent mind because "England has innoculated all nations with her civilization, intelligence and tastes" to the extent that "Every book we read, every biography, play, romance, in whatever form, is still English history and manners" (W 5: 36). Given such cultural imperialism, then, the sole alternative is to write instead of what America could supply in unequalled abundance and variety, nature, and make that natural resource the key to all truths, including the final one, which is "The kingdom of man over nature" (W 1: 77), with man an American consciousness and Europe as historical fact now a colony of that mind.

This same strange absence – and invisible presence, for part of my argument is that American anxieties over imitating or itself being erased by an overwhelming Europe contribute to all of Emerson's ideas – holds for the great early pieces. We would expect in an address titled "The American Scholar" much on its obvious alternative, the European scholar, but the long argument against lionizing and imitating the great says nothing of the struggle to create a distinctly American literature; indeed, as an example of unfortunate overinfluence, Emerson jokes, "The English dramatic poets have Shakespearized now for two hundred years" (W 1: 91). Otherwise, with an audacious blandness, he mentions the pleasures of reading Chaucer, Marvell, and Dryden (again, writers apparently early enough to be as much American as British); and when finally he mentions Goethe and several British romantic writers in passing, it is simply to note that they are part of an exciting trend to "embrace the common" so that "The near explains the far" (W 1: 112). Only at the last is the secret national intent of the essay disclosed, that "We have listened too long to the courtly muses of Europe" and thus "The spirit of the American freeman is already suspected to be timid, imitative, tame" (W 1: 114). But of course and silently, it is the European idolizing of the past and its importation to America that the entire essay opposes. Or again, even while its entire effort is to revolutionize the European-derived notions of Protestant religion, we find nothing directly of Europe in the Divinity School "Address" except the assertion that Puritans in England and America founded themselves away from Rome and that a new founding now is needed away from them. Likewise, aside from the indictment against real and cultural traveling, it is as if "Self-Reliance" will exemplify its own lesson by staying at home, concerned with America first and last, Europe only in passing as a barely identified danger. As for "Circles," there Emerson's insistence that whatever has been is always superseded by what will be certainly serves as an implicit response to the worry of a Europeanized America, but not one explicit word is expended upon Europe's cultural dominance. Again, in "The Poet," some brief quoting of early English poets, not a mention of a near contemporary, and finally the devastating statement, "I look in vain for the poet whom I describe" (W 3: 37). And yet the very call for a new kind of poet would not exist as it does in the absence of the post-colonial cultural situation we have considered.

This silencing is smart, perhaps necessary, wonderful in exampling a freed and huge perspective. We would not have it otherwise, but it is not quite completely satisfactory, for it is not forthright, and one of the pleasures of Emerson is his self-conscious frankness. Our common account of Emerson's career, which does see the early works as best, has never forgiven him his forsaking of the Adamic and Orphic voice, naming and proclaiming, with its acrobatic leaps that force us to recreate a logic of surprising transitions and apparent contradictions, for the more reportorial and qualificatory manner of the later works. We like Emerson best when he jumps, dances, disappears, does dialectical magic. But the later Emerson who shows some of his cards has his own audacities and provides his own pleasures.

IV

With *Representative Men,* Emerson changes, perhaps goaded by his friend Carlyle's challenge: "You tell us with piercing emphasis that man's soul is great; *shew* us a great soul of a man. . . . I long to see some concrete thing, . . . which this Emerson loves and wonders at, well Emersonized."[16] At first, Emerson proudly demurred; but finally he performed what Carlyle bid, though with typical audacity he did so by writing a book that refutes the basic ideas of Carlyle's own *On Heroes, Hero Worship, and the Heroic in History* even while employing as a title a phrase which Carlyle had invented. Carlyle sees the great man as salutary, recommends worshipful obedience to the great as a free act, and vacillates between a fear that modern society no longer will accommodate greatness and the faith that it is a permanent attribute of humanity. Emerson's democratic search for individuals who represent various human capacities at their peak will finally find each of these great men decisively incomplete, ultimately inadequate to a totality of human potential yet to be realized. Utterly without Carlyle's validation of the historical, much less his nostalgia for the past, Emerson implies that his British friend is looking for salvation in all the wrong places and will deny the value of allegiance to any but the self.[17]

But in writing of real individuals at length and in their circumstances, Emerson did become far more of an historian, and he never fully returns from that style. I don't wish wholly to argue against the general judgment that this was more loss than gain – I am not certain we still would read *Representative Men* or *English Traits* if Emerson had not written "Self-Reliance" and the other early texts – but I do believe that it is less a matter of either loss or gain than of a need to do something else: to make for himself, and perhaps for the national culture, that second act that Scott Fitzgerald later claimed was denied to American lives. The voice of the later works can afford a direct commentary, a wrestling with the problem of Europe, which was too threatening to his more prophetic strain.

While in *Representative Men* Emerson had for the first time directly engaged a contemporary English writer in (nonetheless implicit) debate, still his portraits of Shakespeare, Montaigne, and Napoleon remain shy of a full European accounting even while he briefly acknowledges each as nationally representative. With *English Traits* he is finally ready to visit the Old World in public prose. Having privately chided Carlyle in one of his journal entries as "My dear friend – standing on his mountains of fact" (*JMN* 9: 316), now Emerson recounts a national ethnic history at length, presents budgetary details from Cambridge and Oxford, provides labor statistics, quotes everyone from Aristotle to Admiral Nelson, and otherwise piles his own very tall mountain of facts. This can have its dull moments and such facticity is often accounted part of the Emersonian decline. But we might attribute this change in Emerson, this new will to deal with the cosmopolitan in cosmopolitan terms, not simply to a fatigue of nerve or a decline in energy but to his sense of a changed cultural circumstance.

Certainly it is not as if by the 1850s the British and European cultural domination of the United States is ended. But by then Emerson himself is an acknowledged author in England – his second trip is occasioned at least a bit by an invitation to speak in Manchester, and significantly that speech becomes the concluding chapter of *English Traits* – and America too is having its effect. During his second trip, he had written that while the English continue their disdain toward the New World, "Yet they are Americanizing England as fast as they can" (*JMN* 10: 434). The winds of influence may be reversing. And on that second trip as well, Emerson has been made more immediately aware of the spate of socialist revolutions affecting Europe. Socialism throws Emerson into ambivalence, as he shares its outrage over poverty but dislikes its collectivism, approves its dissatisfactions yet wishes they were less materially limited, as if to say, no, that is not what I mean. But more than anything, I think, it is unsettling to Emerson that something historically new might happen in Europe rather than America.[18] Their eventual failure, and the reassertion of privilege and tyranny that went with their defeats, finally become new proof that only America can create a future. Emerson will rail throughout the book against the huge gap between rich and poor, and he ends his concluding speech by foreseeing the dissolution of Britain "if the courage of England goes with the chances of a commercial crisis" (W 5: 314). Further, the literature of England is fully great but also greatly in recent decline. In all, it becomes safer for Emerson to write on England because he can believe that what he writes just may be an elegy. Following the very moment where he acknowledges the extraordinary influence of England upon all other nations, he spins around to assert that this is the best time to visit London as "some signs portend that it has reached its highest point. It is observed that the English interest us a little less within a few years; and hence the impression that the British power has culminated, is in solstice, or already declining" (W 5: 37). The writing of the book thus marks an American ascendancy, or at least portends such.

Even so, at times it may seem that Emerson has gone British. He twice calls Britain "the best of actual nations" (W 5: 35, 299), argues that "if there be one successful country in the universe for the last millennium, that country is England" (W 5: 35), considers America at one point "only the continuation of the English genius into new conditions, more or less propitious" (W 5: 36), and freely confesses that "they read better than we, and write better" (W 5: 211). But this is a strategy of ostentatious fairmindedness which goes finally toward a table turning in which England becomes what America is thought to be, provincial, in contrast to an American author (before James!) who is un-English precisely because he is a man of the world. His first move is to employ the tropes of cultural time to portray England as aged and his final move is to suggest the possibility of a different, energetic, and American maturity by the nature of his own person and voice.

The book begins with Emerson's account of his first visit to England in 1833 as the great British authors shock him by their personal inadequacies. These politely abusive portraits confirm that Emerson still maintains his previous allegiance to American cultural earliness, for what these English writers are, most of all, is representatively decrepit. Coleridge is still in bed at noon – not a good sign given Emerson's tropes of waking and sleeping. Met at one, he has the "bright blue eyes" that mark his own visionary characters but is otherwise a "thick old man . . . leaning on his cane." He "took snuff freely, which presently soiled his cravat and his neat black suit" (W 5: 10). Emerson provides just a touch of the senile drooler to Coleridge before allowing him to speak, which the poet much prefers to listening to Emerson or anybody. And in his speech he is first cranky and then a crank, a man of one idea in a world of ideas. Emerson finally suspects that much of the hour's one-way conversation has consisted of Coleridge's quoting paragraphs from his own writings. He is an impersonation of himself. Later, Emerson terms Coleridge "the best mind in England," thus once more insuring a sense of authorial fairness, but even this he will turn against the British by noting that Coleridge is not held in sufficiently high native esteem: "It is the surest sign of national decay, when the Brahmins can no longer read or understand the Brahminical philosophy" (W 5: 249). In the figure of Coleridge, England is decrepit; in its lack of respect for that figure, it is in decline as well.

Next Wordsworth appears, "a plain, elderly, white-haired man, not prepossessing, and disfigured by green goggles" (W 5: 19), less the drooler, more the Ninja turtle. He utters a large number of remarkably unremarkable and prudish opinions, then unexpectedly stands in his garden and recites three new poems, "the old Wordsworth, standing apart, and reciting to me like a schoolboy declaiming" so that "I at first was near to laugh" (W 5: 23). Emerson blames himself for this impulse, but the comic image of a parody of youth in senility remains. Emerson revisits Wordsworth on his second journey 15 years later and finds him, in the afternoon, "asleep on the sofa" (W 5: 294), what else? The poet laureate is once again full of cranky opinions "rashly formulized from little anecdotes" (W 5: 296), a new displaying of what Emerson earlier termed "the hard limits of his thought" (W 5: 24). As with Coleridge, to insure his evenness Emerson will insist on Wordsworth's greatness, and especially upon those aspects of Wordsworth – his sense of the godlike in the human, his capacity to extend sudden significance to the common experience – that are Emerson's as well: "alone, in his time, he treated the human mind well, and with absolute trust" and "New means were employed, and new realms added to the empire of the muse, by his courage" (W 5: 298). Yet the elderly figure of Wordsworth is what most remains with us, its "hard limits" suggestive of what Emerson elsewhere generalizes as the "limitary tone of English thought" (W 5: 251), its "cramp limitation in their habit of thought, sleepy routine" (W 5: 305) – and these great men are supposed to be the chief exceptions to that. Now these semi-senile poets stand for what Emerson will describe as "an old and exhausted island" that "must one day be contented, like other parents, to be strong only in her children" (W 5: 275–76).

Emerson is one of those American children and thus it is fitting that he relive his 1833 enabling debunking of the greatness of Europe again in 1856. He makes himself relatively young to regain a rebellious youthfulness not for himself alone but for his national culture. Though Emerson acknowledges this best of actual nations, the actual of course is never good enough. He employs his praise of England – its unduplicated emphasis on fairness, on seeing both sides, its wonderful solidity, its best of all universities, its superb common sense, its Shakespeare who is no exception though so exceptional, its sustained and total material and social success – much as he employs his paeans to nature in *Nature* or his tallyings of the virtues of each great man in *Representative Men*, ultimately to have them superseded by a superior value, whether spirit in *Nature*, the ideal whole man in *Representative Men*, or the American potential in *English Traits*. Challenged on his second visit by Carlyle's friends as to whether there exists "an American idea," Emerson responds, "Certainly yes – but those who hold it are fanatics of a dream which I should hardly care to relate to your English ears, to which it might be only ridiculous – and yet it is the only true" (*W* 5: 286–87). Admittedly "dazzled" and willing freely to admit it, Emerson nonetheless notes that "as soon as I return to Massachusetts, I shall lapse at once into the feeling, which the geography of America inevitably inspires, that we play the game with immense advantage; that there and not here is the seat and centre of the British race" (*W* 5: 275), a shocking colonial reversal announced as a done thing. And it is here that he envisions that "great sloven continent" where nature and spirit hide, fled from limitary and "over-cultivated" England, too much of a good thing to be again a great thing. "I find the Englishman to be him of all men who stands firmest in his shoes" (*W* 5: 102) and yet Emerson's final good bears allegiance to those fluid "fanatics of a dream" who seek after "the flying perfect" of "Circles."

As a personal narrative, then, *English Traits* is at once a recollection of a conversion experience by which a youthful Emerson, "much indebted to the men of Edinburgh and the Edinburgh Review" (*W* 5: 3), overthrew his venerations and became an American author, and a dramatizing of an aging Emerson capitalizing on his nation's continuing relative youth and his own to reaffirm the earlier choice. He employs England once more to reinvest America with its utopian promise at a time when the sense that the New World would be the scene for a revolution in consciousness has been threatened by the horrors of the slave trade and the hundred doubts of commercial development at home. And he can be newly, even lavishly appreciative of the Old World in the full assurance that he remains one of the "fanatics of a dream."

But that praise of England, which takes up far more of the work than our quoted passages indicate, even when it is finally gainsaid, is what makes this such a humanly attractive book. Discontent is holy, as Blake claimed, but it is the sacred quality of youth. To love the world and yet wish it to be still better or far other is the visionary courage reserved for maturity. That is what Emerson dramatizes as his gain, marrying worldliness to his

old idealism. As Julie Ellison remarks, "Emerson reverses his habitual tac-
tics – and our expectations – by depicting the British as primitives and
assuming the voice of a spokesman for cultivated society looking back in-
dulgently on its brutal past."[19] That is part of what he does while he also
characterizes England as an "over-cultivated garden." At once bestially
early and culturally fatigued, England is in what Emerson terms "a state of
arrested development," tied to "a corporeal civilization" (W 5: 304), and
this of course is a wonderful reversal of the notion that the English émigrés
to the New World were becoming primitive.

But there is a larger reversal still in the very act of making the British the
seen objects. It is the colonial subject who experiences himself as being
viewed. Emerson not only insists on his own perspective in opposition to
those Anglophile travelers against whom he long had warned, but he emphasizes the breadth of his perspective. Full of confident comparisons of
England to other societies, France occasionally but more often a host of
non-European nations from a range of times, collectedly and sanely impressed or discouraged by this or that national habit nicely and fully described, learned but not bookish, combining the genres of historical
account, scientific treatise, journalistic reporting, autobiography, and oral
address, Emerson is large, easy in his sophistication, confident, Swiftian.
The British are mostly Lilliputians, though very fleshy ones, in the palm of
a wiser Gulliver, as England is viewed often and always as one set of human
possibilities in a spectrum by an author who clearly has lived more widely
than his subjects. It is as if Emerson is saying, I will play the game not only
on your actual turf but on your literary turf as well, the observable social
realm, and by your rules of verisimilitude, particularity, and fine discrimi-
nation, and I will be very, very good at it – but I will also finally change its
rules. For if this Emerson appears to have lived more widely than his subjects, it is not only as a man of the world but also as a devotee of the
oversoul. While Emerson can surround and conquer England (and thus
Europe as well) by recourse to his knowledge of other cultures, we recall
his statement that the tyranny of English influence can be resisted best by
recourse to far civilizations "and, much more, the Ideal standard." It is that
to which he gives the most telling emphasis throughout, a standard that
takes us back to his youthful entries in those first journals which he titled,
a globalist from the start, "The Wide World."

Emerson is graduating America from its school days while, in his retain-
ing of that ideal standard and its dissatisfaction with the world as it exists,
he practices an American adulthood in which the child has been father to
the man. It is an extraordinary achievement in fact, one that probably is
not sufficiently credited because it is not sustained after *English Traits*. A

lecture Emerson gave on "France, or Urbanity" in 1848 was never revised for publication, and much of the writing after 1856 is in fact mature in a far less complex and more common manner. But in *English Traits*, even before a first generation of great American writers was widely acknowledged, Emerson indicates where a next generation might go from there; and James, without knowing that Emerson had made his own beginning journey, travels much further along that route.

Yet we might ask finally, in Emerson's devastating phrase on the glories of Naples, "Who cares?" This all took place long ago, before the United States itself became an imposing economic empire; Emerson somewhat secretly adored his times abroad anyhow; and surely there is something disappointing about a writer's devoting so much energy to a quarrel of nations, especially a visionary writer who should be clutching at universal truths. Don't serious writers play at such a quarrel with their left hands while keeping their good rights free to grasp at the cosmos? So I asked several years ago, and my answer then and now is negative. The cosmos is always culturally delivered, and Emerson could only be universal by being intensely local, given American notions of this New World soil regrounding the heavens. His early work and his late work teach two widely differing methods, by erasure and then by inclusion, for making your own world in the face of incursions. The majority of our world's population now lives in lands that are or have been colonial, and while the political fact of official empire has diminished somewhat, the cultural politics of empire in many places persist or increase. "Who cares," then, should be the slogan of all who seek cultural nationhoods and all who wish them well. For them, for us, Emerson provides possibility, even for those who must be delivered unto themselves from the dominance of an American culture he helped to invent.

NOTES

1   *The Critical Muse: Selected Literary Criticism*, ed. Roger Gard (London: Penguin, 1987), pp. 227, 213.
2   Joel Porte first points out the connection between Emerson and James's protagonist in *Representative Man: Ralph Waldo Emerson in His Time* (New York: Oxford University Press, 1979), pp. 39, 45–46. The brief quotations of *The American* are taken from the Riverside edition (Boston: Houghton Mifflin, 1962), pp. 1, 3.
3   See Porte on Emerson's more positive appreciations of Europe in *Representative Man*, pp. 37–54. For the passage quoted, see pp. 44–45.
4   Benjamin Goluboff, " 'Latent Preparedness': Allusions in American Travel Literature on Britain," *American Studies* 31.1 (1990): 66–67.
5   Orestes Brownson, "Specimens of Foreign Standard Literature," *Boston Quarterly Review* (October 1838): 436.

6   The first quoted passage is taken from the *Journals and Miscellaneous Note-books of Ralph Waldo Emerson*, ed. William H. Gilman et al. (Cambridge, MA: Harvard University Press, 1960–   ), 10: 327. Future citations to the *Journals and Miscellaneous Notebooks* will be abbreviated in the text as *JMN* and followed by volume and page number. However, most readers will find it far easier to locate passages in *Emerson in His Journals*, ed. Joel Porte (Cambridge, MA, and London: Belknap Press of Harvard University Press, 1982). Whenever possible, journal passages will be cited from this volume, abbreviated in the text as *EJ*. The second passage quoted here can be found on p. 389.

7   Emerson, *Complete Works*, Centenary Edition, 12 vols., ed. Edward Waldo Emerson (New York: Houghton Mifflin, 1903–4), V: 36–37. This edition, abbreviated *W*, is cited hereafter for all passages quoted from Emerson's essays and published books.

8   The cited articles are reprinted in full or in part in *The Native Muse: Theories of American Literature*, ed. Richard Ruland (New York: E. P. Dutton, 1972, 1976).

9   Quoted by Edward Said, *The World, the Text, and the Critic* (Cambridge, MA: Harvard University Press, 1989), p. 12.

10 Quoted in this order: "Literary Importation" in *The Poems of Philip Freneau*, ed. Fred Lewis Pattee, 3 vols. (New York: Russell and Russell, 1963), 2: 303–4; William Cullen Bryant, "Early American Verse," originally published in *The North American Review* (July 1818), rpt. from corrected copy as "An Essay on American Poetry" in *Life and Works*, ed. Parke Godwin, 6 vols. (New York: D. Appleton, 1884); Henry Wadsworth Longfellow, *Review of Defense of Poetry*, *The North American Review* 34 (January 1832): 75; Willis and Morris, quoted by Benjamin T. Spencer, *The Quest for Nationality: An American Literary Campaign* (Syracuse, NY: Syracuse University Press, 1957), p. 86; Margaret Fuller (Ossoli) *Papers on Literature and Art* (New York: Wiley and Putnam, 1846), 2: 126–27; Whitman, quoted by Perry Miller in *The Raven and the Whale: The War of Words and Wits in the Era of Poe and Melville* (New York: Harcourt, Brace, 1956), p. 187; James Russell Lowell, "On a Certain Condescension in Foreigners," *Prose Works* (New York: Riverside, 1870), 3: 272.

11 John Stuart Mill, *The Spirit of the Age* (rpt. Chicago: University of Chicago Press, 1942), p. 1.

12 From essays reprinted in part or in full in *The Native Muse*, pp. 155, 195.

13 *The Native Muse*, p. 403.

14 Alexis de Tocqueville, *Democracy in America*, the Henry Reeve Text, rev. Francis Bowen, ed. Phillips Bradley, 2 vols. (1840; rpt. New York: Alfred A. Knopf, 1945), 2: 76.

15 For one of the most extended and helpful discussions of the influence of the Romantic poets and philosophers on *Nature*, see R. A. Yoder, *Emerson and the Orphic Poet in America* (Berkeley: University of California Press, 1978), in particular pp. 29–39.

16 *The Correspondence of Emerson and Carlyle*, ed. Joseph Slater (New York and London: Columbia University Press, 1964), p. 215.

17 For an extended comparison of the two works, see my book *Atlantic Double-Cross: American Literature and British Influence in the Age of Emerson* (Chi-

cago and London: University of Chicago Press, 1986), pp. 192–203 and 232–45. For a more complete discussion of the relations between the writers, see Kenneth Marc Harris, *Carlyle and Emerson: Their Long Debate* (Cambridge, MA, and London: Harvard University Press, 1978).

18 Larry J. Reynolds provides a good account of Emerson's reactions to the spate of socialist uprisings in *European Revolutions and the American Literary Renaissance* (New Haven and London: Yale University Press, 1988), pp. 25–43.

19 Julie Ellison, "The Edge of Urbanity: Emerson's *English Traits*," *ESQ: A Journal of the American Renaissance* 32.2 (1986): 96–109.

11

SAUNDRA MORRIS

"Metre-Making" Arguments: Emerson's Poems

"I am not the man you take me for."

Consideration of Emerson's writings without significant emphasis on his verse would in some ways produce *Hamlet* without the prince, for Emerson seems to have identified himself primarily as a poet. During his New York lecture tour of March 1842, he wrote to his wife Lidian of feeling alienated from and misunderstood by his dinner companions, the social reformers Horace Greeley and Albert Brisbane:

> They are bent on popular action: I am in all my theory, ethics, & politics a poet and of no more use in their New York than a rainbow or a firefly. Meantime they fasten me in their thought to "Transcendentalism" whereof you know I am wholly guiltless, and which is spoken of as a known & fixed element like salt or meal: so that I have to begin by endless disclaimers & explanations – "I am not the man you take me for." (L 3: 18)[1]

By "poet," Emerson didn't mean exclusively a writer of verse, but instead a person whose energy was fundamentally both iconoclastic and – as he emphasizes in his lecture and essay "The Poet" – affirmative, creative, and imaginative. For Emerson, the best preachers, the best scholars, and even the best social activists are all poets. In the Divinity School "Address," he calls for the preacher to be "a newborn bard of the Holy Ghost" (*LA* 89); in "Literary Ethics," he speaks of "immortal bards of philosophy" (*LA* 98). In "The Method of Nature," whoever seeks to realize his "best insight" becomes one of the "higher poets" (*LA* 131); in "Heroism," the life of the great person is "natural and poetic" (*LA* 376); and the "Representative Man" Plato, although not literally a poet, is "clothed with the powers of a poet, stands upon the highest place of the poet" (*LA* 635). This inclusive use of its terminology shows how important Emerson felt poetry to be, and how closely he identified himself with it.

Not only was Emerson consistently referred to and thought of in his own time as a *poet*-essayist, his verse has exerted a persistent influence on other poets. It is so much like that of his admirer Emily Dickinson that readers often mistakenly attributed her anonymously published "Success is counted sweetest" to him.[2] Later, Emerson's fellow poet-essayist George Santayana chose to speak on "Emerson the Poet" during the 1903 Harvard Memorial Week celebration of the centennial of Emerson's birth. And twentieth-century poets who have admired the verse include, among many others, E. A. Robinson, Robert Frost, and A. R. Ammons.

Nonetheless, modern readers and scholars have tended to view his poetry as secondary to the "essential" Emerson. Until very recently, no current edition of the poems was available, and even now just three modern book-length studies of them exist, all dating from the 1970s.[3] This imbalance of attention, however, is beginning to be corrected. New primary material is being published, including the Library of America *Emerson: Collected Poems and Translations* and a forthcoming edition of the poems in the Harvard *Collected Works*; the poems are receiving more extensive representation in anthologies; and significant critical analyses are emerging.

Such "recovery" is fitting. Emerson wrote poetry from the time he was a boy to nearly the end of his life, penning thousands of lines (both original and translated) into his journals and notebooks – particularly into the *Poetry Notebooks,* which span half a century.[4] Using much the same method of composition as he did for his prose, Emerson would often record his initial inspiration or a preliminary draft, then later shape the material into finished pieces. He published these gleanings for over half a century, from 1829 to 1880, seeing into print more than 200 poems and translations.

Emerson collected his verse into two major volumes, both published at the urging of his admirers and after his enshrinement as an important literary figure. *Poems,* dated 1847 (it actually was printed in December 1946), contains 256 pages, with 56 poems and two translations. *May-Day and Other Pieces,* a smaller book of 205 pages, was published 20 years later, in 1867. Many of the poems in both volumes had appeared previously in gift-book anthologies or little magazines – most frequently *The Dial,* edited by Emerson and Margaret Fuller, for *Poems*; and James Russell Lowell's the *Atlantic Monthly,* for *May-Day.* A section of *May-Day* had also been published in Emerson's prose collections as individual epigraphs, for, in a virtually unprecedented gesture that I will discuss below, Emerson prefaced many of his essays with original poems.

The first of Emerson's books of poetry, the 1847 *Poems,* contains the majority of his most famous pieces – works such as "The Sphinx," "The Rhodora," "Uriel," "The Snow-Storm," "Bacchus," "Hamatreya,"

"Threnody," and the Concord "Hymn." While its earliest text is "Good-Bye," dating from 1823, the volume also includes several significant poems composed in the 1830s ("Each and All," "The Rhodora," and Concord "Hymn," for example).[5] However, most of the compositions were written in the 1840s, during Emerson's editorship of the *The Dial*, and first appeared there (they are thus in a sense "occasional" pieces – done particularly for publication in *The Dial*). The second volume, *May-Day*, is generally considered a less groundbreaking work – its poems are smoother and more conventional overall – but it nonetheless contains a substantial number of important texts, among them "Brahma," "Days," "Voluntaries," and "Terminus." Of the 30-some poems, excluding translations, that Emerson published but did not collect in these two books, eight appear in the 1876 *Selected Poems* that he prepared with his daughter Ellen and his friend James Elliot Cabot, and 15 more are printed as essay epigraphs.

This poetic canon displays considerable range. It contains quatrains and long poems; rhymed, blank, and experimental verse; patriotic tributes, social protest poems, and Romantic lyrics; elegies, free translations, love poems, and hymns. Its tones are alternately comic, meditative, narrative, and oracular. At the same time, the pieces coalesce around a set of recurrent issues and strategies central to a poem that Emerson repeatedly positioned at the thresholds of his volumes of verse, "The Sphinx." This piece opens Emerson's 1847 *Poems*, his *Selected Poems*, and the volume of poetry in the first edition of his collected works.[6] Following Emerson's lead, I, too, begin with "The Sphinx," and employ it in this essay as an interpretive paradigm for Emerson's poetry as a whole, for individual poems, and for the essay epigraphs.[7]

Originally published in the third issue of *The Dial* (January 1841), the 132-line, 17-stanza narrative is quite literally a "metre-making argument"[8] between a contemptuous Sphinx and an indomitably cheerful poet. At the beginning of the poem, the "drowsy" and brooding Sphinx calls for a " 'seer' " to answer her " 'secret,' " and thereby bring her health and animation. When she goes on to taunt humanity for its ineptitude and impotence, a mysterious "great mother" joins in to lament the condition of her juvenilized " 'boy,' " humankind. As though to refute their claims, a cheerful and confident poet appears, who praises and blesses the Sphinx. In response, the Sphinx utters an enigmatic pronouncement and soars away, evanescing into the universe.

Its notable degree of undecidability and the richness of the mythological material upon which it draws combine to make "The Sphinx" a highly suggestive choice for what I have called a "threshold poem." I use this term to identify a distinct yet previously unrecognized genre of poetry encompassing various types of introductory verse: initial sonnets, seventeenth-century emblem-book inscriptions, epic invocations to muses, the prothalamion and epithalamion, and other poems of dedication, preface, and prologue. A particular subgroup within this broad, highly self-reflexive tradition are those poems that function, like "The Sphinx," to initiate volumes of poetry.

"The Sphinx" also exemplifies another distinctive (yet overlapping) form of threshold poem. In thematizing the difficulty of poetic expression, it claims a place in the tradition of poems about the inability to write or the absence of inspiration – Milton's sonnet on his blindness, for example, or Coleridge's "Dejection: An Ode." Often these works, like "The Sphinx," function as threshold pieces for volumes of verse. We might think of Sidney's first *Astrophil and Stella* sonnet, which both begins the sequence and voices anxiety about the poet's ability to begin; or Bradstreet's poetic preface to *The Tenth Muse,* which questions her ability to write poetry even as it introduces the poetry she has written. Since the answer to their dilemma is creation, a remedy provided by the poems themselves, the category is by definition both ironic and paradoxical: these are poems about their own impossibility. Such is, of course, especially the case with *threshold* poems about lack of inspiration, for these texts "answer" blockage both through their own existence and through the verses they introduce. "The Sphinx" provides a consummate instance of this variant.

Emerson's threshold poem is also provocative because it participates in a recurrent preoccupation of its time. Nineteenth-century American writers were especially enticed by the Sphinx figure, bestowing upon it the primary regard that we, following Freud, have tended to grant Oedipus. Melville's chapter "The Sphynx" in *Moby-Dick,* for example, depicts the sperm whale's head as a Sphinx; in Poe's riddling short story "The Sphinx," the conundrum is an inscrutable and deadly disease; and Elizabeth Stuart Phelps employs the image of the Sphinx to represent women's struggle for self-expression in her novel *The Story of Avis* (originally entitled *The Story of the Sphinx*). And countless other "Sphinx"es appear in periodical literature of the time.

As befits its subject, Emerson's "The Sphinx" has always been considered especially puzzling, even for the notoriously enigmatic Emerson. Despite the abundance of critical attention the poem has received, scholars continue to debate precisely what the Sphinx is supposed to represent, what her question is, and whether the poet's reply to her is astute or absurd.[9] When he encounters her, instead of reinscribing the Sphinx's traditional association with death, the poet affirms her (" 'Say on, sweet Sphinx! thy dirges /

Are pleasant songs to me' ''). He identifies her as idealism, the " 'love of the Best' '' that paradoxically can silence with castigation, but that is also the only impetus for self-improvement.

The Sphinx responds by confirming the poet's answer and further identifying herself as part of the poet himself – " 'I am thy spirit, yoke-fellow / Of thine eye I am eyebeam.' '' Animated by poetic acceptance, the Sphinx then soars and disperses into nature. In direct contradistinction to traditional myths, which culminate in her plummeting death, "The Sphinx" ends with her ascension. Once "drowsy," "heavy," and brooding, the now "merry" creature silvers, melts, spires, flowers, and flows. And since "metaphor" is "movement," the Sphinx essentially *becomes* both metamorphosis and rhetoric. We find, then, that the answer to the riddle of existence is not so much "man" as "language" – "man" as "Sphinx" is fundamentally figuration, metaphor, poetry.

The Sphinx nonetheless leaves the readers and the poet amid uncertainty with her final enigmatic utterance, now spoken through an equally obscure "universal dame" with "a thousand voices." Emerson, in other words, closes this poem – itself a riddle about a riddle – with yet another puzzle, one that echoes the paradigmatic conundrum of the Hebrew God's self-identification, "I AM THAT I AM" (Exodus 3:14; a locution not unlike " 'Of thine eye I am eyebeam' ''):

> Thorough a thousand voices
> Spoke the universal dame:
> "Who telleth one of my meanings,
> Is master of all I am."

This "answer" leaves ambiguous the crucial issue of whether or not the poet actually has been this triumphant teller. Thus, just as she seems to assert her own supercession, the Sphinx both returns to her role as riddler and achieves vocality to a hyperbolic, even sublime, extent.

This conundrum is reflected in the poem's structure, for "The Sphinx" ends on its most significant formal deviation. Given the established metrical pattern, the poem's last lines form a half stanza – a quatrain instead of an octave. One impression the curtailment produces is that the Sphinx finally stifles Emerson and the poet – that, returning to her role of throttler, she utters a closing quatrain to which the only available response is silence. In this reading, such a thousand-voiced Sphinx, like the thousand-snaked head of Medusa, overcomes the poet with her fecundity, so that the poem breaks off to leave the poet voiceless and a blank where his corresponding quatrain should be. An opposed perspective, though, suggests that this space remains vacant precisely for poetry to fill, so that the rest of the volume represents the poet's reply – all the other poems complete the stanza. In this view, the stanzaic fragment creates an avenue to the following pages. The poem thus replicates the function of the Sphinx at Thebes: it poses a test for readers so that its difficulty will prevent some from proceeding into the subsequent poems, but will open a gateway into the verse for others (rather like Jesus' parables).

As a threshold poem, then, "The Sphinx" performs multiple tasks. It provides riddling instructions about how to approach the rest of Emerson's verse. It raises in theme and form issues crucial to the poetry. It offers an intriguing figure for Emerson's life and writings. And, finally, it suggests theories of reading, writing, and intertextuality pertinent to the poems that follow, to Emerson texts generally, and to the act of interpretation itself. By invoking the mythological *topos* of the Sphinx at the threshold, Emerson places readers in the position of the dramatized poet figure and himself in the position of Sphinx, enacting at the portal of his volume a ventriloquistic play that characterizes his poetry and his prose.[10] For "The Sphinx" activates crossings and reversals between genders, modes of discourse, forms of rhetoric, writer and reader, and subject and object that disrupt oppositional tendencies central to the cultures whose myths it employs.

In all these ways, the poem shows us how to read the rest of Emerson's verse, functioning as an initiatory riddle whose "meanings" emerge from the poems that ensue. The poem suggests that we approach Emerson's texts as the poet does the Sphinx, admiring their suggestiveness and difficulty rather than seeking to master them, all the while encouraging them to " 'say on.' " Readers are to continue through the volume, animated instead of overcome by the inexhaustibility of language and life. The subsequent poems then flow from the ongoing metamorphosis of issues raised in this threshold piece, and embody its multitude of voices and forms.

When we read Emerson's other poems through the interpretive rubric of "The Sphinx," some of their most perplexing moments, structures, and styles are illuminated. Rhetorical strategies and thematic concerns raised by that poem recur throughout *Poems* and *May-Day*. Especially in the earlier volume, the texts are characteristically multivocal, dialogic, puzzling, and elliptical. They are frequently structured according to debate or inquisition. As David Porter and R. A. Yoder have emphasized, a high percentage of Emerson's poems tell the story of a poet figure, his search for voice, and his role as an unriddler. The poems also often explore other aesthetic issues suggested in "The Sphinx." In addition, like "The Sphinx," many contain figures of blockage, flow, speech, vision, and ascension.

The most crucial connection between the individual pieces in Emerson's first volume and "The Sphinx" is their variously manifested preoccupation with riddling. *Poems* as a whole, single compositions, or sections of texts may be read as additional riddles of the Sphinx, as her oracular utterances, or as responses to her questioning. Such is the case with many of the texts literally from their beginnings, for a number of the titles function as puzzles. Many of the more enigmatic are formed from obscure, misleading, or personal allusions. "Alphonso of Castile," "Xenophanes," "Hamatreya," and "To J. W.," for example, confused many readers. Emerson's "Merlin" is not primarily the Arthurian magician, but a lesser-known Welsh bard. And several titles – "Ghaselle," "Saadi," and "Hafiz" – refer to Persian poetry, an area no more a part of his readers' usual repertoire of knowledge then than now.[11]

We get past such difficulty only to find that a surprising number of the poems are occasioned by direct or implicit questions. Sometimes these inquiries are stated at the beginnings of the poems, as in "The Rhodora," subtitled "On Being Asked, Whence Is the Flower?" Most of the pieces contain embedded questions, and many end with them: "Uriel" closes with the couplet, "And a blush tinged the upper sky, / And the gods shook, they knew not why." Other poems culminate by posing "solutions" that are themselves riddling – as "The Rhodora" 's "The self-same Power that brought me there brought you," and the assurances about "gods" and "half-gods" at the end of "Give All to Love."

At the same time, dialogue and multivocality are also pervasive, almost definitive qualities of the poems. Their tonal variety and instability may be read as further manifestations of the Sphinx, now speaking "Thorough a thousand voices." Typically, Emerson leaves these tones unreconciled, or, one might say, unappropriated, by other voices in the poems. For Emerson, the poet is one who can hear the locutions of nature and translate them (almost literally "carry" them "across") into verse. One of his most characteristic poetic strategies is to present the speech of natural objects or forces in direct quotation or paraphrase. In "Woodnotes II," we hear the "pine-tree"; in "Alphonso of Castile," the "Earth"; in "Dirge," a "pine-warbler"; in "Threnody," the "deep Heart." In other poems, the narrator quotes himself, as in "Each and All" and "Berrying." Sometimes, quoted sources quote themselves, as does Monadnoc in its poem. Or the quoted voices quote still others – the Fakirs cite Allah in "Saadi," and the Sphinx, the "great mother" in "The Sphinx." And in some of the most slippery texts, such as the "Ode, Inscribed to W. H. Channing," Emerson presents contradictory voices and disparate points of view without using quotation marks either to distinguish between speakers or to privilege a particular one.

Often, opposite interpretations of a poem arise from readers' being persuaded by one or the other contesting voice within a poem, or by readers' posing antithetical solutions to a text's fundamental riddle or conundrum. Some of the most interesting "debatable" issues involve art and sexuality, with poems seeming to posit traditional and orthodox solutions while actually suggesting more presumptuous notions. In "The Rhodora," a poem replete with the language of Romance, the "Power" that motivates the blossom and the observer, traditionally thought to be God, may partake more of sexual than of divine energy. In "The Snow-Storm," the identity of the sculptor is also more vague and threatening than readers often acknowledge. Its identification as a "fierce artificer" echoes a description of Milton's Satan as the "Artificer of fraud" in *Paradise Lost* (4:121). In a more playful note of irony, the wind in the poem might be seen as hanging "Parian wreaths" in derisive burlesque of the nineteenth-century American fad of imitating Greek architecture. And while readers often perceive the creative act of the sculptor as second-rate imitation of nature's, to "mimic" is usually to imitate "Mockingly." The term thus suggests that the artist's imitation of nature is at best ambivalent, and that the two creators agonistically mock one another.

In conjunction with riddling and argument as forms of verbal play, and with the "merry" Sphinx and cheerful poet, the volume also contains lines of even more direct humor, often missed by overly somber readers. "Fable," composed of a quarrel between a mountain and a squirrel, reveals its comic nature through a submerged closing pun. Asserting its own equal value to the mountain, the squirrel ends the poem by claiming, " 'If I cannot carry forests on my back, / Neither can you crack a nut.' " The real wit here turns subtly on the adage about a question or riddle being a "hard nut to crack," so that the reader is now expected to be the especially clever animal who can "crack" the "nut" of Emerson's poem. Accordingly, the otherwise unfortunate line in "Hamatreya" about a dog – " 'I fancy these pure waters and the flags / Know me, as does my dog: we sympathize' " – is of course *meant* to be funny, spoken as it is by a farmer who is fundamentally ridiculous in thinking that he "owns" the earth.

A review of some frequently anthologized pieces in *Poems* indicates how much of the volume develops and expands upon preoccupations initiated by "The Sphinx." "The Problem," for instance, whose title is synonymous with "Sphinx," consummately represents an "argument" with a "metre-making argument." Responding to an implicit indictment of Emerson's own decision to be an artist instead of a preacher, the poem involves debate between two points of view, dramatizes a poet confronting an obstacle to his calling, and relies upon tropes of fluidity and petrifaction. Moreover, the poem both begins with a question and contains imbedded questions – sometimes, as in "The Sphinx," in the form of catalogues.

"Uriel," another quite puzzling poem, concerns many of the same issues. A narrative of a rebellious angel who is essentially a poet figure, this text also represents a sort of indirectly autobiographical *apologia* for the poet. With rhetorical similarities both to "The Sphinx" and "The Problem," it not only contains the imbedded voice of Uriel in a riddling quatrain, but also involves argument between Uriel and the gods, speaks of Uriel as "solving," and closes with an emphasis on riddling and mystery. We never truly know Uriel's fate, and in the end the gods still "kn[o]w not why" they reacted to it as they did.

"Hamatreya" represents a literally bipartite rendition of an argument between farmers and the earth over who is more powerful – over, finally, who owns whom. This poem, like "The Sphinx," treats death as a contest between a man and a powerful mythic female figure; contains imbedded interrogation and interpolated voices, including that of a captious female figure; couches enigmas in elliptical and convoluted wordplay that centers upon pronouns ("Mine and yours / Mine not yours"); and culminates in a question that is actually a riddling paradox. In answer to the farmers' assertion of ownership and power, the earth seems to ask a question, but actually poses a conundrum that asserts the grave as the ultimate indication of mastery:

> "How am I theirs,
> If they cannot hold me,
> But I hold them?"

And the poem's title, moreover, is perhaps the most famously enigmatic among Emerson's many cryptic ones – we have yet to establish a definitive linguistic derivation of "Hamatreya," though a surprising number of scholars have tried. My guess is that Emerson coins the riddling locution by conflating "Hamadryad," or "wood-nymph," and "Maitreya," a character in Hindu scripture, perhaps to represent a bonding between two of his own seemingly opposite loves – American nature and Eastern philosophy.

The two halves of "Merlin," one of the best and most frequently read poems of Emerson's, together exemplify the recurrence of figures, structures, rhetorical forms, and concerns that I have been exploring. "Merlin I," addressed to an inadequate poet, echoes the castigating yet instructive voice of the Sphinx as it insists that the poet must "strike . . . hard" the aeolian harp strings of the imagination to create

> Artful thunder, which conveys
> Secrets of the solar track,
> Sparks of the supersolar blaze.

This section of "Merlin" receives its momentum from figures of release and ascent. The poet is allowed to " 'Pass in, pass in' " to the " 'upper doors,' " just as Oedipus was permitted to pass the slain Sphinx to enter Thebes and as readers have been allowed to pass "The Sphinx" into the rest of the poems. He is then admonished not to

> ". . . count compartments of the floors,
> But mount to paradise
> By the stairway of surprise."

Emerson often underscores the point he is making in the form of his verse. Here, the poet is told in irregular, oddly rhymed, un"count"ed lines to trust instinct rather than predetermined pattern.

The poem goes on to describe the true poet as one who, when bereft of imagination, need only "Wait his returning strength." And an especially long heptameter line follows to illustrate that the poet will soon be able to soar with his recovered muse:

> Bird, that from the nadir's floor
> To the zenith's top can soar,
> The soaring orbit of the muse exceeds that journey's length.

This tone of confidence prevails at the end of "Merlin I," answering the initial castigation. The very doors that had blocked the poet now open of their own agency to divulge their mysteries, even though no external force, however divine, could have budged them:

> Self-moved, fly-to the doors,
> Nor sword of angels could reveal
> What they conceal.

But celebration of limitlessness is only half of the equation. "Merlin," like the Channing "Ode" (and, most famously, Emerson's essay "Experience"), presents a debate without differentiating between voices or clearly endorsing a perspective. Hence, "Merlin II" complements "Merlin I," providing the counterpoise to the emphasis on freedom (and power) in "Merlin I" to stress form (and balance) instead:

> The rhyme of the poet
> Modulates the king's affairs;
> —Balance-loving Nature
> Made all things in pairs.
> To every foot its antipode;
> Each color with its counter glowed;
> To every tone beat answering tones.

With a pun on "answering," the "answer" – in politics, nature, and verse – is polarity itself. Since that polarity creates the bipartite structure of "Merlin," "Merlin II" begins with a metapoetic gesture of self-reflection.

The emphasis on doubleness then reverses to become glorification of union, but, as in "The Sphinx," the language of duality and unity wavers:

> Coeval grooms and brides;
> Eldest rite, two married sides
> In every mortal meet.

Here, Emerson has even more strongly sexualized the harmonizing work of the poet and the nature of existence itself, using figures both of androgyny and of copulation. The entire universe is paired (like the poet's couplets), so that "The animals are sick with love, / Lovesick with rhyme." Even concepts are sexualized:

> Thoughts come also hand in hand;
> In equal couples mated,
> Or else alternated.

For if they remain "Solitary," ideas are doomed to wander aimlessly, "Most like to bachelors, / Or an ungiven maid," and to remain sterile, "Not ancestors, / With no posterity."

Toward the end of "Merlin II," lines treating fate and termination "couple" into iambic pentameter:

> And Nemesis,
> Who with even matches odd,
> Who athwart space redresses
> The partial wrong,
> Fills the just period,
> And finishes the song.

This passage contains a great many puns about writing poetry that connect "Nemesis," this poem's Sphinx figure, and the poet. Nemesis "with even matches odd" – as does Emerson in these lines of alternating dimeter and trimeter. It works "athwart space" to end with a "just period" – as do these lines if they are metrically enjambed. When the poem "matches" them, the lines actually couple into classic iambic pentameter, the form of Milton, master of "period"ic syntax. Yet this closing "couplet" of pentameter rhymes, as Milton's blank verse does not, so that Emerson's prosody also alludes to the neoclassical heroic couplet of Pope, and thus in another way to formal stability.

The final lines of "Merlin II" celebrate spinning sister-poets, the fates.

These are threatening female figures like Nemesis and the Sphinx, who sing "subtle rhymes . . . / In perfect time and measure" (as the poem makes a sudden shift into irregularly but heavily rhymed tetrameter). These figures act as divine architect-artists who fashion individuals even while "two twilights," the two thresholds of birth and death, "Fold us music-drunken in." This last image of enclosure makes human life – paradoxically – a wild revelry presided over by benevolent spirits who gently tuck children into bed at night. In the "Sisters," Nemesis, the poet, and the twilights, we find figures of the Sphinx again, now (in 1846, when "Merlin" was composed) much like the "Beautiful Necessity" to whom Emerson would have us "build altars" by the time of his 1850 essay "Fate" (*LA* 967).

A similar effort to accept fate is central to "Threnody," the penultimate text in *Poems,* a work also composed in the mid-1840s. In this long elegy for his firstborn child, Waldo, Jr., who died suddenly of scarlatina at age five, Emerson confronts one of the most dread Sphinxes of all, the death of his very young son. As he does so, problems traditionally associated with Greek and Egyptian Sphinxes – inscrutability, death, time, family, guilt, and art – converge. "The Sphinx" and "Threnody" begin with humanity in similar conditions of need, both looking for someone to answer questions about offspring and fate. "The Sphinx" is concerned with "Life death overtaking," and "Threnody" with the absence of "Life, sunshine, and desire." Finally, both poems seek answers to their dilemmas, but the responses do not so much answer as reconstitute what "answering" means.

The most frequently commented upon, and criticized, feature of "Threnody" is its tonal bifurcation. The first 175 lines and seven stanzas represent a heartfelt lamentation for young Waldo – virtually an outpouring of emotion in the voice of the grieving father. The following 114 lines appear as two stanzas of direct quotation in the voice of the "deep Heart" as it responds to the grieving father. "The Sphinx" can provide readers a clue about how to read the irresolution within the latter poem, and show how its abrupt shift is actually one of its strengths. For the disparity within "Threnody" replicates the debate of poems like "The Sphinx," and the structure of those like "Merlin": Emerson allows contradictory perspectives to coexist. "Threnody"'s tones of despair and consolation are *both* real, and are fundamentally unreconcilable. The solution in "Threnody" is acceptance and love of the universe, as in "The Sphinx," but, as in the earlier poem, love and affirmation remain riddles. For the poem does not allow part two ever to neutralize the pain of part one, and it never explains how one can love a universe arranged so that one's five-year-old child would die.

We find the same philosophical and structural tension between and within two crucial Emerson essays written at the same time as "Threnody" and dealing with the same concerns, "The Poet" and "Experience." These three pieces are, in fact, best read together, with each inflecting the others' perspectives. That interrelationship illustrates how I suggest we read and teach Emerson's work generally – exploring, for example, "The Snow-Storm" with the anecdote about the snow storm in the Divinity School "Address," and poems such as "Uriel" and "The Problem," with the address itself. My point is that the moods of "Threnody," "The Poet," and "Experience," as well as their structures, share in the preoccupations and rhetorical gestures I have explored throughout the *Poems*. Although we long read "The Poet" as one of Emerson's most affirmative essays, and "Experience" as one of his most skeptical, we are increasingly coming to appreciate how fully the essays echo one another.[12] Their contiguous placement and their vacillation of tone, especially within "Experience," replicate the bipartite structure and wavering point of view of "Threnody," and, less precisely, of other Emerson poems.

Emerson's *Poems*, then, move from a narrative of overcoming threat and silence to scenes in which death itself has become the primary impulse for the poetry. In the middle, they are composed of a host of voices in a variety of personas. With "Threnody" and the poems immediately before and after it, "Dirge" and the Concord "Hymn," Emerson closes his first volume of poetry on an elegiac yet triumphant note that brings to a sort of culmination the tension between threat and affirmation that he initiated at the volume's threshold.

The second of Emerson's two primary collections of poetry, *May-Day and Other Pieces*, did not appear until 20 years later, in 1867, and thus represents one of his last significant book-length publications. The volume contains seven parts: two long poems, "May-Day" and "The Adirondacs," each of which forms its own section (together about one-fourth of the total volume); three substantial sections of midlength poems, "Occasional and Miscellaneous Pieces," "Nature and Life" (with a posthumously published poem by Emerson's brother Edward), and "Elements"; and two short sections of mostly very brief poems, "Quatrains" and "Translations." Scholars have emphasized that *May-Day*, especially in its title poem, represents the sexagenarian Emerson's answer to his own aging process.[13] The structure of the volume would seem to reinforce this connection, as though the first sections corresponded to Emerson's more productive decades and the final brief segments to the waning of his creative powers. Certainly *May-Day's* texts are preoccupied, even more than those of *Poems*, with the challenges of confronting limitation and finding rejuvenation.

In addition to reading those concerns as personally reflective ones, however, I suggest that we also view the *May-Day* volume in a way that previous scholarship has not noted.[14] Its 1867 publication, soon after the end of the American Civil War, invites us to read *May-Day* along with Melville's *Battle-Pieces* and Whitman's *Drum-Taps* as part of the literary response to the war itself. A few of the poems in Emerson's volume – "Freedom," "Ode Sung in Town Hall," "Boston Hymn," and "Voluntaries" – treat the conflict directly. Many others address it implicitly, either tropically or through such subjects as camaraderie, reconciliation, and restoration.

Some poems, including the volume's titlepiece, call upon the poetic spirit as a salve for wounds and the herald of a new age of greater freedom, with spring as a trope for national renewal. Emerson had made a similar gesture of responding to a political occasion metaphorically, and connecting politics and poetry, years earlier. Len Gougeon has pointed out that Emerson's first answer to the passage of the 1850 Missouri Compromise and its Fugitive Slave Law was in the form of poems he sent to the antislavery annual *The Liberty Bell* at the request of its editor. Ordinarily, material in *The Liberty Bell* treated abolition directly; Emerson's poems, however, translate philosophical Persian texts about poetry and rebirth. The connection of May and springtime with postwar healing (which we find in Whitman's "When Lilacs Last in the Dooryard Bloom'd") is also Emersonian. Eduardo Cadava has shown that Emerson characteristically uses nature imagery in conjunction with political events, as in "Boston Hymn," when he associates snow with the Northern forces, and in "Voluntaries" when he employs snow, and the aurora borealis, to represent the North.[15] Emerson's connection of springtime and Reconstruction extends the same strategy.

Even in its concern with the war and its aftermath, however, the volume shares affinities with the earlier *Poems* – a fact that Emerson's repeated use of "The Sphinx" as a comprehensive threshold poem implies. For with the war and again following it, America was forced to face the question of national identity – forced (as were Oedipus and the poet when they met their Sphinxes) to confront the issue of who it was. Such a challenge, the titlepiece and the volume imply, can best be met through the power of poetry, which is to bring war-torn yet now-virtuous America the vitality of spring.

Emerson does not, however, start his volume of war poetry with poems that relate to battle, then move to poems that emphasize healing and regeneration, as does Whitman in *Drum-Taps*. Rather, he inverts that more predictable structure, beginning the volume instead with a threshold poem that both describes and provides the balmic equivalent to the "rue, myrrh, and cummin" brought by the poet of "The Sphinx." Thus, his readers move immediately to the anodyne of poetry. "May-Day"'s simultaneous role as title and threshold poem, reinscribed by the book's serendipitous publication just before May Day (on April 29), attests to the importance of its sexually exuberant celebration of spring. In more than 500 lines of irregularly rhymed tetrameter (mostly in couplets and alternating rhyme),[16] the poem loosely consists of a series of odes that celebrate fertility much like classic Renaissance songs to Hymen. Its subject also makes Emerson's longest single poem a *reverdie,* a verse that welcomes the springtime regreening of the earth, in the long tradition of such poems as the Middle English "Cuckoo Song," the prologue to the *Canterbury Tales,* Shakespeare's "When Daisies Pied," Herrick's "Corinna," many of Dickinson's spring songs, and, in modern times, cummings's "in just." As such, "May-Day," like "The Sphinx," establishes the keynote of its volume.

At the same time, a number of lines in "May-Day" allude to the war through martial and emancipation imagery. The passages often employ images of blockage and fluidity to indicate the need for spring, when "the bondage-days are told [i.e., finished], / And waters free as winds shall flow." Because "The world hath overmuch of pain," Emerson writes, it is in particular need of pleasure, a time of "cheer" and "joy" when spring will "Rebuild the ruin, mend defect," just as the poet cured the Sphinx. Spring will create "liberated floods" and "new-delivered streams," bringing in summer, when – as the poem makes explicit the connection of national trauma and sexuality – the world will celebrate a "Hymen of element and race." Then, "one broad, long midsummer day / Shall to the planet overpay / The ravage of a year of war."

Thus, this threshold poem also focuses on the issue most central to the earlier poem and volume – how to respond to the sphinxes of impotence and death with cheer and potency. "May-Day" bears other resemblances to "The Sphinx" as well. It, too, represents a riddling answer to the riddle of existence, unexpectedly (especially for this aging ex-cleric) emphasizing that creativity and renewal derive from an internal "storm of heat" whose release generates life. The subsequent poems and translations illustrate that productivity even as they address it metapoetically, returning again and again to notions of regeneration and recuperation.

Immediately after "May-Day," we find a poem that is in many ways its counterpart, "The Adirondacs," a long narrative piece in a blank verse that complements its lyrical, heavily rhymed predecessor. Like "May-Day," "The Adirondacs" concerns the importance of natural renewal. Unlike "May-Day" and its glorification of heterosexual love, this poem celebrates male bonding.[17] "The Adirondacs" tells of a summer camping trip Emerson took with a group of friends, among them author and *Atlantic Monthly* editor James Russell Lowell and the naturalist Louis Aggasiz, in 1858. Despite its antebellum composition date and publication, the poem's appearance in *May-Day* would have made "The Adirondacs" 's celebration of camaraderie and renewal resonate politically for a nation just having emerged from the strife of brother fighting brother.

Though "The Adirondacs" devotes itself mostly to the tale of the explorers' energizing journey, it closes with the one direct mention of the Sphinx in Emerson's poetry other than in her own eponymous piece. As the men leave the woods to return home, Emerson writes:

> And Nature, the inscrutable and mute,
> Permitted on her infinite repose
> Almost a smile to steal to cheer her sons,
> As if one riddle of the Sphinx were guessed.

Thus, a text again culminates with a riddle about a riddle – it is very tentatively "as if" the men (like perhaps the poet in "The Sphinx") had penetrated the silence and mystery of nature.

The next section of *May-Day*, "Occasional and Miscellaneous Pieces," treats the Civil War and emancipation directly in four of its 11 poems. Emerson composed the first of these political poems, "Freedom," at the request of Julia Griffiths for the December 1853 *Autographs for Freedom*, an antislavery volume to benefit the Rochester (New York) Anti-slavery Society. At first, "Freedom," like the earlier "Ode, Inscribed to W. H. Channing," seems to be essentially an *apologia* for Emerson's lack of direct participation in the fight for freedom. However, both poems also function like classical *praeteritio*, the rhetorical device by which a speaker draws attention to something by announcing its omission ("I'll pass over the fact that the candidate stole millions"). They are thus intrinsically ironic – by virtue of their very existence, they address what they say they will not. What is more, while "Freedom" claims that Emerson is unable to "rehearse / Freedom's paean in my verse," he next proceeds even more directly to do just that. In the following poem, the "Ode Sung in the Town Hall, Concord, July 4, 1857," written to help raise money for Sleepy Hollow Cemetery, Emerson exhorts America to "bid the broad Atlantic roll, / A ferry of the free," and assure that "henceforth, there shall be no chain."

The third of these "freedom" poems, "Boston Hymn, Read in Music Hall, January 1, 1863," is even more explicit. Emerson composed it when another friend, John Sullivan Dwight, asked him to read a poem to begin the celebration for the enactment of the Emancipation Proclamation. "Boston Hymn" became famous immediately, and was sung by the African-American South Carolina regiment commanded by the white literary figure T. W. Higginson. The quatrain that alludes to the then-current debate about how emancipation was to be achieved is especially moving. A proposed solution (one that Emerson himself had supported) called for the government to recompense slaveholders for the "property" they would lose upon emancipation. Now, Emerson forcefully assumes the voice of God, whom he quotes, to command:

> Pay ransom to the owner,
> And fill the bag to the brim.
> Who is the owner? The slave is owner,
> And ever was. Pay him.

Finally, later in 1863, Emerson wrote his most frequently anthologized political poem, "Voluntaries," to honor the slain members of the Massachusetts 54th Colored Infantry and their white commander, Col. Robert Gould Shaw. This illustrious group of soldiers is also commemorated by a statue that now stands on Boston Common, and by a number of additional poems, among them the modern elegy "For the Union Dead," by Bostonian Robert Lowell. Emerson himself had earlier spoken at a fund-raising event for the group, with whom he felt a particular connection through his friendship with Col. Shaw's father, Francis Shaw. Emerson sent "Voluntaries" in September of 1863 to Mr. Shaw after the combat deaths, on July 18, of Robert Shaw and nearly half of the soldiers under his command.

"Voluntaries" begins in a mood of reverence by invoking the "Low and mournful" tones of a slave, then goes on to celebrate freedom's new cohabitation with the heroic black race. The poem asserts its faith in the ultimate triumph of the slain Northern soldiers, a victory achieved because of the probity of their cause and evidenced partly, in the Greek and Latin heroic tradition, by their immortalization in this verse. Emerson predicts that the evil Southerners finally will be "Reserved to a speechless fate," while the virtuous dead will be crowned with laurels and honored in song. And Emerson's poem, of course, participates in the commemoration it prophesies.

These war poems indicate that Emerson's concerns in *May-Day* had shifted somewhat from the time of the earlier volume. In addition, these poems are on the whole less riddling in both form and subject than their predecessors. On the other hand, many of the pieces continue a number of structural, rhetorical, and thematic preoccupations of "The Sphinx." "The Titmouse," to cite one example, begins with a question much like that in "The Sphinx" – how to overcome lethargy; it is about poet figures (narrator and bird) who cheer; it uses imagery of petrifaction; it contains interpolated voices; and its "solution" involves interaction with nature. "Days" is another riddle, and another allegorization. The speaker of this 11-line parable is as overwhelmed by the personified Days as the poet is accused of being in "The Sphinx," and as, in 1867, Emerson and the country were by the Sphinxes of age and war. The poem involves the adequacy of a respondent to mysteriously threatening and scornful female inquisitors, and requires the respondent to *ask* instead of answer – but with a question that is actually a test of her own worth. Its obscurity leads readings even now to remain, like those of "The Sphinx," divided about whether the response was successful.

Finally, two of the most famous poems in the second collection, "Brahma" and "Terminus," illustrate the evolution of Emerson's continuing concerns. Positioned at the threshold of its section, "Brahma" is the poem in Emerson's canon most often compared to "The Sphinx," in both sympathetic analyses and parodies. Fundamentally a riddle, with an implicit "What am I" as its undertone, the poem assumes the voice of what may loosely be identified as the soul or the oversoul. It begins:

> If the red slayer think he slays,
>   Or if the slain think he is slain,
> They know not well the subtle ways
>   I keep, and pass, and turn again.

Once more, then, readers receive the voice of a mysterious entity in enigmatic, oracular quatrains. The voice in "Brahma" again wants to know its own identity, and again Emerson presents his clues in opposites and paradox: Brahma asserts that "I am the doubter and the doubt," for "When me they fly, I am the wings." And the answer to this riddle is also linguistic, even poetic – Brahma's most direct statement of identity is "I [am] the hymn the Brahmin sings," and the poem itself actually *is* that hymn, in the classic long measure of Christian hymnody. Thus the god, the voice, the Sphinx, and the individual become in fundamental ways both articulation and poetry.

In addition, the readers who hear of the "slayer" and "slain" in "Brahma" are those who have just observed North and South in those roles. Although "Brahma" was written and published in the late 1850s, for its 1867 readers, the language would have been inflected with events of the war. In this context, "Brahma" also becomes a meditation on the insignificance of residual divisiveness, an affirmation of life beyond tragedy, victory, and defeat. Echoing the message of "May-Day," "Brahma" suggests that poery can provide answers to the horrors of "slayer" and "slain."

"Terminus," Emerson's meditative poem on the individual's aging process, along with the three elegiac poems that accompany it, balances "Brahma" and "May-Day" in the structure of *May-Day*'s central sections much as the closing elegies served as counterparts to "The Sphinx" in *Po-*

ems. Its title is another riddle about its allegorized subject – this time the Greek god of bounds. And "Terminus" also addresses the questions of how to deal with the Sphinxes of depletion and death: it opens, "It is time to be old, / To take in sail." Emerson's familiar concerns again cluster – the poem thematizes limitation, directly this time; contains figures of flow and blockage; portrays muses as at once helpfully provocative and potentially overwhelming; expresses anxiety about silencing; and contains interpolated voices, including that of a mysterious divinity the meaning of whose closing quatrain once more may be read in diametrically opposed ways. The poem ends by quoting a figure identified simply as "the voice . . . obeyed at prime" that tells the poet she should, even while closing in upon the shore, " 'banish fear, / Right onward drive unharmed,' " for "The port, well worth the cruise, is near, / And every wave is charmed.' " This advice, reminiscent of but different from Tennyson's in "Ulysses," seems paradoxical in a poem that ostensibly urges readers "To take in sail."

In a similar gesture of ambivalence, this time a structural one, *May-Day* indeed does not "terminate" with these elegies, as *Poems* had, but instead contains three more sections: "Elements," selected essay epigraphs; 30 "Quatrains" (or near-quatrains); and 18 "Translations," all but one, a Michelangelo sonnet, renditions of Persian poetry. The quatrains and translations, by virtue of their length, subject matter, and very existence, are quite sphingine, gnomic utterances. In addition, the translations reveal a method of composition quintessentially Emersonian, for in them Emerson blends the Persian, its German rendition, and his own revisions to create poems that disrupt boundaries between origin and elaboration.[18] That appropriative impulse is also at the heart of the final section of Emerson's verse I want to treat, his essay epigraphs, some of which are collected in the *May-Day* section "Elements." I will close by exploring the existence of these "Elements" and other epigraphs as they stood originally, at the thresholds of Emerson's prose.

For 30 essays in five separate collections Emerson chose to print his own poems as epigraphs. That decision was altogether unconventional, or, more precisely, was *anti*conventional. At the thresholds of prose pieces, as on the lintels of doorways, we expect to see "sacred" text, whether from the Bible, or from Shakespeare, Homer, Dante, or Milton. The tradition is definitively deferential. That Emerson was acutely aware of, and resistant to, this sycophantic and possibly impoverishing tendency of the epigraph convention is evident in a statement from his essay "Quotation and Originality":

Quotation confesses inferiority. In opening a new book we often discover, from the unguarded devotion with which the writer gives his motto or text, all we have to expect from him. If Lord Bacon appears already in the preface, I go and read the "Instauration" instead of the new book.   (*W* 8: 188)

He is even more adamant in his journal: "I hate quotation. Tell me what you know" (May 1849; *JMN* 11: 110).

In the epigraphs, then, Emerson boldly transposes and appropriates convention. Yet despite their peculiarity, and the fact that they are his verse that Emerson's readers most frequently encounter, the epigraph poems have received very little analytical attention. When teaching the essays and writing about them, we typically act as if the mottoes aren't there at all. It is as though readers are embarrassed by the short-lined, heavily rhymed, enigmatic pieces, and are anxious to get past them into the "important" material that follows. But not only are the epigraphs quite appealing as individual works, their presence before the essays even more insistently invites attention. As original, often lengthy, and sometimes independently printed verse "mottoes," Emerson's epigraphs are generically distinct, significant modifications of both epigraphic and poetic convention. Their peculiarity combined with their own preoccupation with enigma invites us, I think, to imagine the epigraphs themselves as riddling Sphinxes at the thresholds of Emerson's essays.

First, the epigraphs serve as problematic guardians at the gateways, representing distilled challenges that we are to grapple with before we reach the prose. At the same time, the relation of the epigraphs and the essays to their titles is frequently a puzzling, even paradoxical one. The mottoes and essay "History," for instance, are not about "History" as much as about the priority of the soul over history. And, to cite a late occurrence of the same tendency, in the companion essays "Fate" and "Power," the notion of "Fate" or "Beautiful Necessity" is paradoxical, so that the poem and motto titled "Fate" might be said really to be about "Power," and those called "Power," about "Fate." In addition, the epigraphs frequently appear in rhetorical structures and forms that are directly or indirectly based on riddling – paradox, situation *in medias res,* and fragmentary or elliptical syntax, for example. And many of the verses thematize obscurity, thus becoming poems about themselves, the essays they introduce, and what Emerson saw as the ultimate inscrutability of life. Unlike travelers near Thebes, we may choose to overlook these elusive puzzlers. But then we miss valuable hints about the essays that follow, the pleasure of playing with the runic lines, and the provocation to self-confrontation and self-examination the epigraphs provide.

As he appropriates and extends the epigraph form, Emerson writes two basic types of poems, both related to "The Sphinx": first, a sort of oracular wisdom verse that makes gnomic and riddling yet weighty pronouncements; and, second, fragmented narratives about the development of a poet-hero who can solve the enigmas that plague humankind, actually an externalization of the poetic impulse that Emerson would locate within all individuals. As a group, many of the epigraphs tell of this foundling son of Mother Nature, who in his "answers" to her produces the sort of oracular poetry that other epigraphs embody – prophetic in tone and tendency, but with an element of forbidden mystery.

Consequently, the epigraphs often double the riddle form – are frequently riddles about riddling, mysterious oracles about mystery. We find a good illustration of their terse ambiguity in the second motto to "History" (1841 and 1847):

> I am owner of the sphere,
> Of the seven stars and the solar year,
> Of Caesar's hand, and Plato's brain,
> Of Lord Christ's heart, and Shakspeare's strain.

Since the poem never identifies a subject, this quatrain is on one level the "I am" of children's riddles and a tradition extending at least back, for instance, to the Old English *Exeter Book.* The purest such construction among the epigraphs, this is the only motto in the first-person voice of its own subject, a common rhetorical strategy in riddling also employed quite frequently by Emerson's contemporary, Emily Dickinson. As in "The Sphinx," the phrase in this context also recalls the riddling "I am" of God that I mentioned in conjunction with "The Sphinx," and Coleridge's concept of the secondary imagination outlined in *Biographia Literaria,* the creating, synthesizing power of the mind that Coleridge calls "the infinite I AM." Also, especially in the context of this epigraph, the phrase imports considerable theological weight from Eastern traditions. It directly echoes a text very dear to Emerson, the *Bhagavad-Gita,* in which the speaker of the "I am" is the soul: "I am the soul which standeth in the bodies of all beings."[19]

Accordingly, that "soul" is the paradoxical topic of the first "History" epigraph, the companion to the poem I have been examining:

> There is no great and no small
> To the soul that maketh all:
> And where it cometh all things are;
> And it cometh everywhere.

This epigraph identifies the soul as the source of creation (and, by extension, poetic creation). And it makes explicit the point of the essay that follows, in which "History" is also really "soul," because "there is properly no history; only biography" (*LA* 240). In a sense, then, Emerson has provided in the first poem the answer to the second.

The lovely motto to the 1860 essay "Illusions," in *The Conduct of Life*, is my own favorite. Although Emerson did not choose to reprint "Illusions" as a separate text, the poem is increasingly anthologized. I see it as in some ways the culmination of the epigraphs, combining traits of the aphoristic and the narrative pieces finally to exist in a category of its own. An exploration of ambivalence toward perpetual change, "Illusions" finally celebrates the ongoing metamorphosis that occurs at the end of "The Sphinx." It begins in syntax that is ambiguously both imperative and declarative:

> Flow, flow the waves hated,
> Accursed, adored,
> The waves of mutation:
> No anchorage is.

These lines exemplify high Romantic apostrophe, in which the poet pretends to command what is manifestly beyond his control. In the course of the poem, these polarities of power and passivity converge: readers are reassured that the wave of progress will also restore what it subsumed. By the end of the piece, we come full circle to find that humanity, too, rides "the wild turmoil" of this threateningly perpetual wave "to power, / And to endurance."

This epigraph and others play an important role in our understanding of the relationship between Emerson's various texts and voices, and, most importantly, between his poetry and his prose. In the essay "Self-Reliance," Emerson issues an arch rejoinder to anyone who might question the value of his vocation: "I shun father and mother and wife and brother, when my genius calls me. I would write on the lintels of the door-post, *Whim*. I hope it is somewhat better than whim at last, but we cannot spend the day in explanation (*LA* 262).[20] Here, an irascible Emerson invokes Deuteronomy's rendition of the Mosaic covenant, in which God cautions Moses to keep the words he has told him that day in his heart, to teach them to his children, to talk of them, and to "write them upon the posts of thy house, and on thy gates" (Deut. 6:9). The doorway also figures prominently in connection with Passover, and with the sacrificial blood of Christ. Emerson's assertion in "Self-Reliance," then, substitutes an arrogant yet fanciful rejoinder of his own for biblical text and the words of God.

Just as in "Self-Reliance," where the word and act of *"Whim"* replace the ancient text, Emerson's own poetry does so before his essays, in the form of the essay epigraphs. They inscribe *"Whim"* upon the lintels of the prose. In this sense, the essays become elaboration, application, even "exegesis" of the initial poetic "scriptures." The epigraphs thus combine the sacred and the jovial in their existence as whimsical pre-liminary conundrums. In a larger sense, we might also imagine the epigraphs and essays as together figuring the positions of poetry and prose in Emerson's life. Emerson positions the two *together,* establishing between the genres a dialogue in which formal divisions become happily indistinct. This invitation to pause at the thresholds of his essays provides our best hint about how to read the prose that follows – poetically.

Finally, the epigraphs place Emerson himself in the position of the Sphinx and readers in the position of Oedipus. They thus initiate at the gateways to his prose the destabilization of boundaries between author and audience, reader and writer that we have come to associate with Emerson's work. For his verse as a whole asks us to challenge our intellects, imaginations, and assumptions, to *argue* with ourselves, so to speak – as does Emerson's prototypical threshold poem "The Sphinx," the crucial and complex whim upon the lintel of his first volume of verse.

NOTES

1 I use the following abbreviations to cite parenthetically from Emerson's texts: *CW, The Collected Works of Ralph Waldo Emerson,* ed. Robert E. Spiller, Alfred R. Ferguson, Joseph Slater, and Jean Ferguson Carr (Cambridge, MA: Harvard University Press, 1971–); *JMN, The Journals and Miscellaneous Notebooks of Ralph Waldo Emerson,* ed. William H. Gilman et al., 16 vols. (Cambridge, MA: Harvard University Press, 1960–82); *LA, Ralph Waldo Emerson: Essays and Lectures,* ed. Joel Porte (New York: Library of America, 1983); *W, The Complete Works of Ralph Waldo Emerson,* Centenary Edition, ed. Edward Waldo Emerson, 12 vols. (Boston and New York: Houghton Mifflin, 1903–4). Unless otherwise indicated, citations from Emerson's poetry are taken from *Emerson: Collected Poems and Translations,* ed. Harold Bloom and Paul Kane (New York: Library of America, 1994). For their help in the preparation of this essay, I am indebted to Julie Vandivere, Catherine Tufariello, Tamar Katz, Cynthia Hogue, and Joel Porte.
2 Richard Benson Sewall, *The Life of Emily Dickinson* (New York: Farrar, Straus and Giroux, 1974), pp. xxvi, 583.
3 Hyatt Waggoner, *Emerson as Poet* (Princeton: Princeton University Press, 1974); R. A. Yoder, *Emerson and the Orphic Poet in America* (Berkeley, Los Angeles, London: University of California Press, 1978); David Porter, *Emerson and Literary Change* (Cambridge, MA, and London: Harvard University Press, 1978).

4 Ralph Waldo Emerson, *The Poetry Notebooks of Ralph Waldo Emerson*, ed.
   Ralph H. Orth, Albert J. von Frank, Linda Allardt, and David W. Hill (Columbia: University of Missouri Press, 1986).
5 Carl Strauch, groundbreaking scholar of Emerson's poetry, emphasizes the importance of 1834 as "the year of Emerson's poetic maturity" in his article of
   that title (*Philological Quarterly* 34 [October 1955]: 353–77).
6 Ralph Waldo Emerson, *Selected Poems*, New and Rev. Ed. (Boston: James R.
   Osgood, 1876); and *Poems*, Vol. 9 of *Emerson's Complete Works*, Riverside
   Edition, ed. James Elliot Cabot (Boston and New York: Houghton Mifflin,
   1903–4). Emerson's son Edward explicitly chose not to begin the Centenary
   Edition *Poems* with "The Sphinx," choosing instead to start it with a much
   more accessible early poem, "Good-Bye." This sequence of events gains even
   further Oedipal inflection when we note that Emerson himself apparently very
   much disliked "Good-Bye." A letter from Ellen Emerson to Sarah Gibbons
   Emerson makes clear that Emerson allowed "Good-Bye" to be included in his
   Selected Poems at his family's insistence: "You asked me in one letter how we
   could let Father leave out 'Goodbye proud world' from the new volume [*Selected Poems*]. We were sorry, and several friends begged for it, but Father
   disliked it so much himself that all persuasion failed." [Ellen Tucker Emerson,
   The Letters of Ellen Tucker Emerson, ed. Edith E. W. Gregg (Kent, OH: Kent
   State University Press, 1982), 2: 245.] As justification for his action Edward
   argues that "The Sphinx" would deter readers at the start rather than entice
   them to read on:

   > Not without serious consideration has the editor removed the poem, which his father
   > put at the beginning of his verse, to a later place. But he has always shared the feeling of
   > regret that Dr. Holmes expressed in his book, that "Emerson saw fit to imitate the
   > Egyptians by placing the Sphinx at the entrance of his temple of song." In the mythology
   > the Sphinx let no man pass who could not solve her riddle; and Emerson's Sphinx has no
   > doubt put off, in the very portal, readers who would have found good and joyful words
   > for themselves, had not her riddle been beyond their powers.   (*W* 9: 403)

7 I discuss the importance of "The Sphinx" in my essay "The Threshold Poem,
   Emerson, and 'The Sphinx'" (*American Literature* 69.3 [September 1997]:
   547–70). Part of this chapter is adapted from that essay.
8 Emerson writes in "The Poet": "For it is not metres, but a metre-making argument which makes a poem" (*LA* 450).
9 Gayle L. Smith surveys the points of disagreement in her excellent essay, "The
   Language of Identity in Emerson's 'The Sphinx,'" *ESQ: A Journal of the
   American Renaissance* 29 (3d Quarter 1983): 136–43. While agreeing in many
   particulars, I take issue with Smith's emphasis on the "identity" of the Sphinx
   and the poet.
10 Scholars have consistently recognized the propriety of the Sphinx as a figure
   for Emerson and his work, and modern scholarship has continued this emphasis on Emerson and his writings as Sphinxes. The second chapter of Barbara
   Packer's book on Emerson's prose is "The Riddle of the Sphinx: *Nature*" [*Emerson's Fall: A New Interpretation of the Major Essays* (New York: Continuum, 1992)], and Yoder stresses the unriddling power of what he identifies as
   the recurrent Emersonian figure of the American Orphic poet. Emerson jok-
   ingly writes of himself as a Sphinx in an 1873 journal entry about his trip to

Egypt: "Mrs Helen Bell, it seems, was asked 'What do you think the Sphinx said to Mr Emerson?' 'Why,' replied Mrs Bell, 'the Sphinx probably said to him, 'You're another' " (*JMN* 16: 294).

11 Hafiz, Shams od-Dīn Muhammad Hāfiz (1326?–?1390), of Shiraz; and Sa'di (whose name Emerson spells Saadi, Said, Seyd, and Seid), Mosharref od-Dīn ibn Mosleh od-Dīn Sa'dī, of Shiraz (ca. 1213–92), are two of the most famous Persian poets.

12 See, for example, B. L. Packer, *Emerson's Fall: A New Interpretation of the Major Essays* (New York: Continuum, 1982); Richard Lee Francis, "The Poet and Experience: *Essays: Second Series*," in *Emerson Centenary Essays*, ed. Joel Myerson (Carbondale: Southern Illinois University Press, 1982, pp. 93–106); David Hill, "Emerson's Eumenides: Textual Evidence and the Interpretation of 'Experience,' " in Myerson, *Emerson Centenary Essays*, pp. 107–21; Joel Porte, "Experiments in Creation," in The *New Pelican Guide to English Literature*, vol. 9: *American Literature*, ed. Boris Ford (London: Penguin, 1988).

13 See, e.g., Porter, pp. 130–33. Porter also emphasizes the title poem's thematization of the poetic process in relation to what he calls Emerson's "crisis of the imagination."

14 Len Gougeon has treated the importance of issues associated with abolition and the Civil War as a part of his emphasis on Emerson as, in the title of Gougeon's book, *Virtue's Hero: Emerson, Antislavery, and Reform* (Athens: University of Georgia Press, 1990); see also Gougeon, "Emerson, Poetry, and Reform," *Modern Language Studies* 19.2 (Spring 1989): 38–49.

15 Eduardo Cadava, *Emerson and the Climates of History* (Stanford: Stanford University Press, 1997), especially pp. 171ff.

16 "May-Day" exists in several versions. The first-edition text, that in the 1876 *Selected Poems,* a third in the Riverside Edition, and a fourth in the Centenary.

17 For a discussion of Emerson and the gendered construction of selves, see Julie Ellison, "The Gender of Transparency: Masculinity and *The Conduct of Life*," *American Literary History* 4.4 (Winter 1992): 584–606.

18 On Emerson's translations, see *The Topical Notebooks of Ralph Waldo Emerson,* vol. 3, ed. Ronald A. Bosco (Columbia and London: University of Missouri Press, 1993); Richard Tuerk, "Emerson as Translator – 'The Phoenix,' " *Emerson Society Quarterly* 63 (1971): 24–26; and J. D. Yohannan, "Emerson's Translations of Persian Poetry from German Sources," *American Literature* 14 (1943): 407–20.

19 Charles Wilkins, trans., *The Bhagavat-Geeta* (London: C. Nourse, 1785), p. 85.

20 Stanley Cavell has devoted a good deal of attention to this same passage. See especially his two essays on Emerson in *The Senses of Walden: An Expanded Edition* (San Francisco: North Point Press, 1981).

12

MICHAEL LOPEZ

The Conduct of Life: Emerson's Anatomy of Power

I THE WHICHERIAN PARADIGM

Is there a "late" Emerson? Certainly there was an *elder* one. Emerson lived a long and extraordinarily prolific 79 years. It seems only natural and reasonable to assume that his *thought* – like his life, like the metamorphic history of his times – can be divided into chronological periods. Emerson seems, in fact, to invite us to read him in terms of early and late phases. In the opening pages of *The Conduct of Life,* generally considered his last important book, he speaks of a former naiveté (the optimistic assurance that the world is all "positive power") and a new realism (the chastened acknowledgment that "negative power" is really something to be reckoned with): "Once we thought, positive power was all. Now we learn, that negative power, or circumstance, is half."[1]

Stanley Cavell has questioned the simplistic way in which these often-cited lines have persistently been reduced to "sheer autobiography." "It would be more like Emerson," Cavell writes, "to be speaking of the human race, or human maturation, generally."[2] Yet it is precisely the interpretation that takes these lines as Emerson's confession of his own intellectual coming-of-age that a long scholarly tradition has set firmly, perhaps irremovably, in place.

I speak here of the approach to Emerson's life *and* thought that has now become the dominant paradigm in Emerson scholarship. That approach, still taken as self-evident in most of what is published on Emerson, was set most securely in place in the thesis Stephen Whicher expounded in his groundbreaking *Freedom and Fate: An Inner Life of Ralph Waldo Emerson* (1953) – considered by many the single most important study of Emerson ever published – as well as in its companion piece, Whicher's widely used textbook, *Selections from Ralph Waldo Emerson: An Organic Anthology* (1957).

At the root of Whicher's thesis lies a large assumption which has seemed so eminently unobjectionable that it has, at least in the history of Emerson's reception, rarely even been remarked. That is the assumption that the thought of a writer like Emerson will accurately mirror the personal evolution of the man, and that just as a long life may be divided into natural periods of maturity and immaturity, growth and rupture, so too may the outlines of his philosophy be best understood through a similarly developmental approach that looks for phases, periods, and transitional moments of crisis and change.

Building on this assumption, Whicher postulated a fundamental division in Emerson's thought. Emerson's career as essayist and lecturer began, according to Whicher, with a decade-long burst of egocentric, anthropocentric, revolutionary Transcendentalism. (This decade falls, roughly, between Emerson's resignation from the ministry of Boston's Second Church in 1832 and the publication of *Essays: Second Series* in 1844.) This early period constituted, for Whicher, the essential and most important Emerson. But this initial attitude of idealistic protest, this early affirmation of human "sovereignty" and "mastery" was, Whicher argued, followed by a nearly tragic descent into a newfound skepticism, a new "acquiescence" (one of Whicher's key words) to "negative power" and "circumstance." "In youth," as Emerson puts it in "Fate," "we clothe ourselves in rainbows, and go as brave as the zodiac. In age, we put out another sort of perspiration, – gout, fever, rheumatism, caprice, doubt, fretting, and avarice" (963).

That description pretty well sums up the way we now routinely differentiate between an early and late Emerson. The first is purported to be ambitious (for both himself and humankind), courageous, nonconformist, risk taking – though his idealistic head is in the clouds – while the later is deemed conservative and skeptical about his former radicalism. The Emerson of *Nature* is a "naive rhapsodist";[3] the Emerson of *The Conduct of Life* has learned that "No picture of life can have any veracity that does not admit the odious facts" (952). The late Emerson, it is alleged, has finally grown to respect the immovable forces of nature; he has even become fatalistic about man's helplessness before them. The rise-and-fall pattern to this interpretation, which gives Emerson's career the symmetry of classical tragedy, is as perfectly balanced as the two acts ("Parts I and II") that make up Whicher's *Freedom and Fate*. Emerson's youthful proclamations of limitless freedom meet their inevitable comeuppance, giving way, at last, to his mature recognition of the constrictions of fate.

We have reached, however, one of the main limitations of Whicher's paradigm: the bias inherent in the very tags "mature" and "immature." It is not just that categorizing Emerson's ideas as either youthful or mature is too simple – though it is – but that schematizing his thought in this way also accords all too easily with two long-standing sets of prejudices. The first of these prejudices, the Modernist/New Critical reaction against Romanticism generally, is well known. The Romantic poets, as T. S. Eliot famously put it, citing Matthew Arnold, "did not know enough." A similar impatience with Romantic literature as inherently immature accounts, at least in part, for the widespread rejection of Emerson, in the first half of the twentieth century, by writers like Eliot, Yvor Winters, Allen Tate, and Ernest Hemingway. But the particular position that Eliot took toward Emerson – acknowledging that he had obtained a certain historical "dignity," but insisting that he was not intrinsically "very important" and "ought to be made to look very foolish" – is also typical of a secondary and subtler prejudice that any consideration of Emerson must sooner or later address. That "anti-Emerson tradition," as I have elsewhere called it, has been far less noticed, though it has become an ingrained, largely unconscious part of Emerson scholarship.[4]

I refer to that long line of critics who have elevated Emerson to unquestioned canonical status, all the while dismissing his work as unworthy of serious attention as either philosophy (even as morally complex thinking) or coherent prose. There were, in the first decades of the twentieth century, a few, like John Dewey or O. W. Firkins, who decried the double-edged tradition that has both honored and forsaken Emerson, or routinely written him off as a philosopher. More recently, Stanley Cavell has returned our attention to that ambivalent, "fixated critical gesture toward Emerson both on the part of his friends and of his enemies." The hugely influential way in which F. O. Matthiessen canonized Emerson as the central writer of the American Renaissance – though one who had failed to create "a form great enough to insure that his books will continue to be read" – is perhaps the key instance of that conflicted gesture which has concurrently celebrated and buried him. But it is merely one of countless examples. Perry Miller's belief that Emerson's ideas were "too utterly fantastic to be any longer taken seriously" or Leslie Fiedler's description of his writing as "a notable monument to an insufficient view of life" – such judgments are typical of a critical tradition which has identified Emerson's work as worthy only of what D. H. Lawrence called "museum-interest." Whicher's own approach, it is important to note, led him to a similar conclusion: both phases of Emerson's career were, as far as the modern reader was concerned, "obsolete stages in an evolution of thought that seems unlikely ever to make them tenable again." It is this prevailing "condescension" toward Emerson which has, Cavell concludes, helped "to keep [American] culture, unlike any other in the West, from possessing any founding thinker as a common basis for its considerations."[5]

The Whicherian approach has further undermined Emerson's reputation by lending its scholarly weight to that view of him which has, more effectively than anything else, embalmed him in six feet of amber: the perception that he had – at least in his early, major phase – no appreciation of the tragic aspects of real life. From Henry James's allegation that Emerson's eyes were "thickly bandaged" to all "sense of the dark, the foul, the base," to George Woodberry's belief that he could "find no room for evil in the universe," to John Updike's recent charge that "a world of suffering" has been "scandalously excluded" from his work – the impression that Emerson was, morally and philosophically, Pollyanna has been repeated for so long now, by so many, that it has hardened into the axiomatic cornerstone of his Transcendentalist image, both within and without academe. There are, increasingly, dissenters from that opinion. "As for that 'ripe unconsciousness of evil' that James found in Emerson," Harold Bloom writes, "I have not been able to find it myself, after reading Emerson almost daily for the last twenty years." But the received, scholarly wisdom continues to maintain, with R. Jackson Wilson, that "denying the reality of evil" was "an important part of Emerson's philosophical program." Popular opinion hardly differs. A recent reviewer for the *New Yorker* identifies a movie that is "reluctant to handle the unpleasant grit of life" as an "Emersonian work."[6]

The Conduct of Life can, in fact, read – particularly if one comes to it expecting Whicher's chastened, late Emerson – like a self-conscious attempt to exorcise an earlier innocence. From the book's opening imagery of slaughterhouses and massacres, its recurrent meditations on death and disease, its reverence for the real over the spiritual, the present world over the promise of another, its obsession with power in all its forms and contempt for weakness in all its forms – ("The worst of charity," Emerson sniffs, "is that the lives you are asked to preserve are not worth preserving" [1081]) – to its abiding, celebratory vision of the pain that begets strength, the poison that brings health, or the brutality that gives birth to civilization – there is much that seems calculated to provoke, if not repel. No wonder Harold Bloom has dubbed it "that great, grim, and most American of books." Or that Bartlett Giamatti, rereading the essay "Power" in 1981, was shocked to find not "the Lover of Nature, [the] sweet, sentimental, Yankee Kahlil Gibran" who has come to inhabit the popular imagination, but a quite other Emerson – one "as sweet as barbed wire . . . his sentimentality as accommodating as a brick." In Emerson's own time, reviewers complained of *The Conduct of Life*'s "want of heart," its appeal to "the lowest depths of man's nature," its rejection of Christian morality and the Christian "law of love." More than one contemporary reader wondered if Emerson had not "lost the power to sympathize" with common human suffering.[7]

II THE GOOD OF EVIL

That Emerson's thought, or anyone's thought, may be seen as the record of a lifetime of development seems, as I have suggested, so reasonable a presumption as to be self-evident. The contrary presumption is, however, no less reasonable. Is it not equally possible that a writer's "philosophical biography," as Thomas McFarland calls it, may exist not as a record of progressive periods, a history of renunciations and epiphanies, but as "a continuing process of elucidation of primary orientations"? "Nothing can be taught us," Leibniz said, "the idea of which is not already in our minds."⁸ It is a principle Emerson himself restated many times: "What can we see, read, acquire, but ourselves?"⁹ The attempt to achieve an organic awareness of an author's *Weltanschauung* through chronological tagging has inherent limits. "Chronology," McFarland writes, "can often have a specific value; but its reverence by the scholarly tradition is largely a convention of that tradition, complementing the scholarly prejudices that require 'development' in the sense of progressive steps. The textbooks exult in the proliferation of developmental stages; but such stages do not allow us to see clearly the unfolding of a single, constant orientation to life."¹⁰

That caveat regarding the scholarly predilection for finding development may stand, in fact, as a fair description of what has happened in Emerson studies. The "chronological rubric," as McFarland calls it, has had, and always will have, enormous "specific value." It has helped us recover Emerson's wavering opinion on a multitude of discrete issues (individual figures, like Webster or Thoreau, for instance, or specific topics, like social reform or abolitionism). It has helped us perceive the human drama of changes in mood and temperament chronicled in Emerson's journals. But it has also made it hard to see "the unfolding of a single, constant orientation to life." "Single, constant orientation to life" is another way of saying consistent philosophy, and it is precisely a coherent philosophy that scholarship has concluded, for a century and a half now, that Emerson lacks. Thus John McDermott, surveying the criticism in 1980, noted one of the most curious but telling characteristics of Emerson studies: "In the vast secondary literature on Emerson, distinctively philosophical considerations are virtually absent."¹¹ So much scholarly energy has been expended in dutifully detailing the crises that propelled Emerson into "maturity" – or in determining the precise boundary that is supposed to exist between the naive and the disillusioned Emerson – that there has been little time or inclination left for allowing the possibility that Emerson's thought might exist as a more complex, philosophical whole. To suggest – as I wish to do here – that there exists, from his first book to his last, a fundamental, unchanging Emersonian psychology/philosophy (the two are one for Emerson, as they were for Nietzsche) – is still, as far as Emerson criticism is concerned, to indulge in something akin to heresy.[12]

But let us move directly to *The Conduct of Life,* to a paragraph that is, in its pan-historical scope, one of the most remarkable in Emerson's canon, yet, in its psychology, one of the most characteristic:

> In front of these sinister facts, the first lesson of history is the good of evil. Good is a good doctor, but Bad is sometimes a better. 'Tis the oppressions of William the Norman, savage forest-laws, and crushing despotism, that made possible the inspirations of *Magna Charta* under John. Edward I. wanted money, armies, castles, and as much as he could get. It was necessary to call the people together by shorter, swifter ways, – and the House of Commons arose. To obtain subsidies, he paid in privileges. In the twenty-fourth year of his reign he decreed, "that no tax should be levied without consent of Lords and Commons;" – which is the basis of the English Constitution. Plutarch affirms that the cruel wars which followed the march of Alexander, introduced the civility, language, and arts of Greece into the savage East; introduced marriage; built seventy cities; and united hostile nations under one government. The barbarians who broke up the Roman empire did not arrive a day too soon. Schiller says, the Thirty Years' War made Germany a nation. Rough, selfish despots serve men immensely, as Henry VIII. in the contest with the Pope; as the infatuations no less than the wisdom of Cromwell; as the ferocity of the Russian czars; as the fanaticism of the French regicides of 1789. The frost which kills the harvest of a year, saves the harvests of a century, by destroying the weevil or the locust. Wars, fires, plagues, break up immovable routine, clear the ground of rotten races and dens of distemper, and open a fair field to new men. There is a tendency in things to right themselves, and the war or revolution or bankruptcy that shatters a rotten system, allows things to take a new and natural order. The sharpest evils are bent into that periodicity which makes the errors of planets, and the fevers and distempers of men, self-limiting. Nature is upheld by antagonism. Passions, resistance, danger, are educators. We acquire the strength we have overcome. Without war, no soldier; without enemies, no hero. The sun were insipid, if the universe were not opaque. And the glory of character is in affronting the horrors of depravity, to draw thence new nobilities of power: as Art lives and thrills in new use and combining of contrasts, and mining into the dark evermore for blacker pits of night. What would painter do, or what would poet or saint, but for crucifixions and hells? And evermore in the world is this marvellous balance of beauty and disgust, magnificence and rats. Not Antoninus, but a poor washer-woman said, "The more trouble, the more lion; that's my principle." (1083–84)

Is this paragraph an example of "idealism"? Of "acquiescence" to fate? Those are the two poles which have traditionally been used to define the

THE CONDUCT OF LIFE

boundaries of Emerson's intellectual life. Yet passages like the above – and *The Conduct of Life* may be considered a series of like-minded passages – make it clear how useless the customary tags are in explaining the kind of thinking that actually goes on in an Emerson essay. It may be possible to take Emerson's faith that "there is a tendency in things to right themselves" as support for the usual criticism of his purported idealism: that he espoused a prim meliorism indifferent to evil. But Emerson's belief that things will "right themselves" is so vividly grounded in his acknowledgment – his celebration – of antagonism, of "negative power" in all its forms, that the usual rubrics of idealism or optimism hardly seem adequate. There is a crucial difference, as Josiah Royce once remarked, speaking of Nietzsche, between the denial of evil and the insistence that it be transfigured or incorporated so as to enrich, in some way, one's own life and philosophy. As Christopher Lasch notes, "The statement that 'evil is good in the making' [as Emerson puts it in "Fate" (960)] does not deny the existence of evil; what it denies is the possibility that we can abolish it."[13]

Understanding of the post-Christian, proto-existential philosophy Emerson propounded in each of his essays, from *Nature* to the concluding essay on "Old Age" in *Society and Solitude,* must begin in the recognition of this central tenet of his thought: that he taught, like his admirer Nietzsche, not the avoidance of evil and pain, not "an excision of ills from life," but "the conquering of defects by their inclusion in a richer life."[14] If we accept this as a root premise of his thought, and jettison the Transcendentalist image that has perenially made it impossible to take him seriously as a philosopher, we can begin to appreciate the philosophy that *is* so apparent in the above passage.

That philosophy/psychology is not a matter of those categories habitually trotted out, in textbook anthologies and introductory lectures, as the foundation stones of his thought: his monism, his pantheism, his philosophical absolutism, his unyielding belief in the moral law, his idealist naiveté, his yearning for unity, his desire for transcendence of this world rather than struggle within it. It is not that his syncretic yearnings, his belief in an Over-Soul, in a Platonic or Neoplatonic "all-dissolving Unity," as he calls it in "Beauty" (1112), or "Blessed Unity" as he addresses it in "Fate" (967), are not prominent features of his thought. But his idealist and organicist sympathies constitute only one strain of his thought – a strain that is consistently balanced and frequently undermined by a quite opposite kind of thinking.[15]

That kind of thinking may be encapsulated in six key words from the paragraph above: "power," "antagonism," "resistance," "overcoming," "use," "education." These words represent a way of thinking that Emerson returns to, with unflagging emphasis, restating and extending it on every page of the nine essays that comprise *The Conduct of Life*. To make this list of key Emersonian words complete, we need add only three; the concepts each represents are implicit in the paragraph above and each is a recurrent, pivotal word in *The Conduct of Life*. Those words are "reality," "necessity," and "work." "Reality" is invoked repeatedly in the above paragraph: in the insistence that "the glory of character" lies in "affronting," not evading, "the horrors of depravity" – advice we see Emerson himself acting upon in his diligent catalogue of "sinister facts," his zealousness in allotting so much space to war, disease, and all manner of disaster, and in his concluding deference to the realistic common sense of "a poor washerwoman." "Necessity" is no less conspicuous: the catalogue of history's "sinister facts" is, in fact, the record of the way in which individuals or whole peoples have learned that necessity, or unavoidable misfortune, can be turned to good. Thus despots like Henry VIII ultimately "serve men immensely" by curtailing the power of the Pope. Thus Edward's desperate need for money and armies leads to the founding of the House of Commons and the English constitution. Thus "blacker pits of night" make possible new and more powerful forms of art. Thus even the horrors of "crucifixions and hells" give birth to painters, poets, and saints.

Each of these examples is, of course, also an instance of use, education, overcoming – even antagonism or resistance. This is one reason writing about Emerson can be so difficult: the particular Emersonian philosophy exemplified in the above paragraph exists as a taut, complex web of infinitely crisscrossing threads; unraveling it in a systematic way, strand by strand, category by category, can be all but impossible. (This is not at all to suggest that Emerson's thought itself has no underlying system or unity. I am suggesting, in fact, that it does. But it is characteristic of Emerson, both as a prose stylist and as a thinker, to practice the kind of compression and ellipsis that demands active or, as Emerson puts it, "creative reading" [59]. Emerson "does not," as Morse Peckham observes, "build us bridges; he makes us leap.")[16] Emerson's paragraphs and sentences usually illustrate not one key word, not one philosophical or psychological principle, but several simultaneously. His characteristic insistence on "work," for instance, is certainly implicit, in the passage above, in all the examples of destructive force transformed into civilization, or darkness "mined" and worked up by the artist or saint. Yet work is, in this instance, subsumed in the concepts of use or overcoming. All of the key words I have listed may, in fact, be subsumed, to some degree at least, in another large category that was always an Emersonian imperative: "action." (And action is itself, in *The Conduct of Life,* at times replaced by the synonym "performance," which is in turn used synonymously with "work," as in Emerson's command in "Worship": "The only path of escape known in all the worlds of God is performance. You must do your work, before you shall be released" [1075].)

There is, however, one idea, one image, which is so overriding in *The Conduct of Life* that we may take it as Emerson's fundamental conceit: power. Joel Porte, noting the book's obsession with power, particularly physical or sexual energy, suggests that "[t]ime and again, Emerson's thoughts on a wide variety of subjects tend to become a 'physiology of' whatever is under consideration."[17] This reductive technique – the redefinition of things in terms of their primary or "lowest" constituents, particularly their most primary source of power – is, indeed, so routine a feature of *The Conduct of Life* that it is worth examining in some detail.

Emerson, for example, begins *The Conduct of Life* by alluding to the momentous, contemporary debate over "the theory of the Age" and the viability of social reform ("the hope to reform men"). But by the third paragraph he has begun what will turn out to be a relentless reduction of those lofty issues to their sheer physical components. First, political reform is reduced to the necessity for individual reform ("The riddle of the age has for each a private solution" [943]); then the possibility of even individual change is reduced to a question of temperament, sex ("vital power"), and genetic inheritance ("Men are what their mothers made them. . . . When each comes forth from his mother's womb, the gate of gifts closes behind him" [947]). Emerson's language, inspired by medical books and phrenological pseudoscience, is, as he says, "gross" and satirical. Squints, potbellies, and pug noses are signs of ineluctable fate. A man's future is "already predetermined . . . in that little fatty face, pig-eye, and squat form" (947). Within a few pages of the book's beginning, politics (was there any issue of greater significance to Americans in 1860?) has been reduced to simple physiology ("A good deal of our politics is physiological" [948]), and that logic has been taken even a step further, to its *reductio ad absurdum*, in Emerson's recommendation that elections be decided by body weight – by, in other words, whichever party has the fattest candidates: "On the whole, it would be rather the speediest way of deciding the vote, to put the selectmen or the mayor and alderman at the hayscales" (949). No wonder Emerson feels compelled to acknowledge, in the book's second half, that he may have been keeping discussion "on too low a platform" (1055).

Directing our attention to life's lowest level is, however, one of *The Conduct of Life*'s major goals. "Let us learn to live coarsely, dress plainly, and lie hard," Emerson declares in "Culture" (1027): it is one of his recurrent appeals to *low* reality, one of his many pledges to keep his discussion of a conventionally "high" topic like culture focused on the bedrock level of its coarse and hard origins.[18] *The Conduct of Life* maintains that coarse, reductionist perspective not only in its grotesque or satiric imagery ("New York is a sucked orange" [1017], "The German and Irish millions, like the Negro, have a great deal of guano in their destiny" [950], " 'Tis odd that our people should have – not water on the brain, – but a little gas there" [1026]), but in its persistent attempt to strip off the veneer of high civilization in order to reveal the "aboriginal might" or "aboriginal source" (981, 979) from which it springs. The examination of the way in which a universe of primordial, amoral, self-regenerating power *expresses* itself, either to overwhelm us or to be channeled and transformed into health, art, and culture, is Emerson's main theme.

"The whole economy of nature," as he says in "Behavior," "is bent on expression" (1041). "Life expresses" (1037). (Or, to rephrase Emerson's title slightly, and clarify a pun he undoubtedly intended, "life *conducts*.") "[T]he core," as Emerson says, "will come to the surface" (1047). Life's primal power "vents" (1048) itself in a universe of forms, from the mundane to the extraterrestrial. It expresses itself in the "tell-tale" look and gait of the body (1041), in fashion (in "the power of form" [1101] or the "power of a woman of fashion" [1038]), in manners ("the power of manners is incessant" [1037]), in the "force of beauty" (1112), in the power we can derive from other people (friends and enemies are both "channels of power" [1032]), in athletic competition (which provides "lessons in the art of power" [1021]), in "the power of happiness" that "puts us in a working mood . . . and untunes the active powers" (1089), and in that unrelenting "love of power" (994) that compels man to "take such advantage of Nature that all her powers serve him" (1110). That innate love of power drives man to the capitalistic "use of his planet" and, as Emerson predicts, to the use "of more planets than his own" (991).

The Conduct of Life is, finally, an anatomy of power – or, to use a description made current by Michel Foucault, an "archaeology of power" – in all its protean forms. "There is," as Emerson announces at the beginning of "Power," "not yet any inventory of a man's faculties" (971). (We lack, as he phrased it in his lecture "Aristocracy," an "anthropometer" – a machine capable of measuring the degree of power a man could be entrusted to "carry and use.")[19] *The Conduct of Life* is clearly intended to fill that void. It is an attempt to excavate and catalogue all the ways in which the *life force conducts* itself unrestrained by man, usually with destructive results – as well as all the ways in which it can *be conducted* or, as Emerson says repeatedly, "concentrated" into life-affirming results (results that are empowering to human beings) through the human acts of education, use, work, resistance, overcoming, and antagonism. All human activity is a manifestation of life's primal will to power; man has an instinctive drive to use and to become master. Man's "instincts," Emerson writes, "must be met, and he has predisposing power that bends and fits what is near him to his use. . . . As soon as there is life, there is self-direction, and absorbing and using of material" (961–62).

The image of "absorbing" things or, as Emerson calls it in "Culture," "the assimilating power" (1020), is – like the image of "taking up" or "converting" things – a long-standing Emersonian synonym for use or over-coming. And, here again, use is often a synonym for "working things up": "In our life and culture, everything is worked up, and comes in use" (1088). "We acquire," as Emerson promises in the paragraph cited above, "the strength we have overcome." "Man's culture can spare nothing, wants all the material. He is to convert all impediments into instruments, all enemies into power. . . . He will convert the Furies into Muses, and the hells into benefit" (1033–34). The world is man's "tool-chest, and he is successful . . . [to] the degree in which he takes up things into himself" (991). Those readers who wish to consider the full extent of Emerson's psychology of use/assimilation/overcoming might begin with the passage in "Power" de-tailing the way in which a "man of force" will "absorb" or "use" those around him (973–74). "He is the rich man," as Emerson puts it in "Wealth," "who can avail himself of all men's faculties" (991). And it is not, despite *The Conduct of Life*'s heavily androcentric imagery, only men who use and shape "everything in our life and culture." There is, as Emer-son makes clear, "in both men and women, a deeper and more important *sex of mind,* namely the inventive or creative class of both men and women" who are able to use "the uninventive or accepting class" (973).

John McAleer calls this Emersonian principle of "creative assimilation" a form of "psychic vampirism."[20] But life simply is, as Emerson says, "a search after power" (971). "Men of sense," he declares, seek the "convert-ing," "the assimilation of nature to themselves": "Power is what they want, – not candy; – power to execute their design, power to give legs and feet, form and actuality to their thought" (993). And the will to power does not end with such "men of force." As soon as the rare "good man" (or "mas-ter") comes along he is in turn put to use: he becomes a source of power, a "centre of use," for all those around him. (Thus civilization can be traced back to "the thoughts of a few good heads" [1082].) It is no coincidence that every essay in *The Conduct of Life,* with the possible exception of "Illusions," quickly turns, whatever its ostensible topic, into Emerson's own search for power, as he gets down to his real subject: the investigation of the ways in which fate, wealth, culture, beauty, even worship, are further manifestations of the will to power omnipresent in nature and man.

"Fate" introduces, in its third paragraph, the imagery of human power ("the power of character," man's ability to "learn at last [the] power" of every obstacle he confronts) which Emerson will posit as the counterforce in the universal battle between man and fate. "Wealth" similarly defines its topic in terms of the way man practices "the useful arts" – or learns to put "to better use" – nature's "forces and resistances" (989). "Culture" begins with the acknowledgment "that all the world is in pursuit of power" and Emerson's hypothesis of a natural "rank of powers" (1015). "Behavior" is another inventory of power, this time as it expresses itself in the world of manners and fashion. "Manners impress as they indicate real power" or a "[s]trong will" (1047); they provide that "rough-plastic, abstergent force" that rouses human beings out of their "quadruped state" (1038). "Considerations By the Way" reasserts the book's main theme: "Yet vigor is contagious, and whatever makes us either think or feel strongly, adds to our power and enlarges our field of action" (1079). "Beauty" opens with the complaint that "Our botany is all names, not powers" (1099). Our science, our culture, fail us, Emerson claims, if we "do not come out men of more force" (1101). The lost art of alchemy, which sought "to prolong life, to arm with power" is offered as an example of a science "that was in the right direction" (1099).

"Worship," an essay whose very title suggests an act of submission, a stance of humility, would appear to be the book's single exception to its preoccuption with the aboriginal roots of power, its emphasis on what we can will in *this* world, what we can use and "work up" in the often coarse reality of the present day.[21] ("Come out of the azure. Love the day" [1051] is one of *The Conduct of Life*'s central mandates and a further example of the premium it places on reality.) Indeed, Emerson begins by implying that his essay on faith will be on a "higher platform" than the previous entries. And he proceeds to speak of his unshakable confidence in "the moral sentiment" (1065), his certainty that "Religion, or Worship" is "the flowering and completion" of culture (1057), and his desire to reaffirm "the doctrine of Faith" (1055) in an age when "the old faiths . . . have spent their force" (1058). But if faith or spirituality, in any conventional sense, is Emerson's goal, then he chooses to take a curious path to it, for his path leads him to conclusions that go beyond Christianity, beyond a loose, general theism – beyond even the limits of a religion-neutral, Judeo-Christian ethics. "Worship" turns out to be neither a reaffirmation of faith nor even about its apparent subject. It is, rather, an example of the way in which Emerson's idealist/transcendentalist leanings are undercut by his pragmatic, antitranscendental psychology.

Emerson remains, in "Worship," the same psychologist of power who anatomized wealth, culture, and behavior by scratching through their surface significance to get at the essential power-reality at their core. The language of "Worship" is still the language of power, its method still the analysis and exaltation of power that Emerson has always practiced. Its emphasis is still on the existential realities and necessities of *this world* (Emerson insists on our "necessitated freedom" [1076]), its focus still the human acts of use, work, and overcoming. Its very idiom and mode are, in other words, hardly conducive to a defense of a theistic *other world*. (Emerson's ideas, as John Dewey once remarked, "are not fixed upon any Reality that is beyond or behind or in any way apart. . . . They are versions of the Here and the Now.")²² A traditional theism is, in fact, one of the many illusions Emerson attempts to dispel in his closing essay. "We are coming," he writes, "on the secret of a magic which sweeps out of men's minds all vestige of theism and beliefs which they and their fathers held and were framed upon" (1120).

"Worship" 's true subject is the act of *work* itself, the act of resistance, learning to work *against* "adversity . . . against failure, pain, and ill-will" until one's task is complete. (Work, as Emerson defines it, is another form of use, of education, another example of turning evil to good. Working against failure means learning "to welcome misfortune," learning that "adversity is the prosperity of the great" [1072].) "Work," Emerson proclaims, "is victory. Wherever work is done, victory is obtained" (1068). Work, as Emerson presents it, is nothing less than redemption. It is "the only path of escape known in all the worlds of God" (1075). "Every man's task," as he alternately phrases it, "is his life-preserver" [1071]. "Of immortality," Emerson writes, "the soul, when well employed, is incurious" (1075). That is an astonishing epigram to find in an essay on worship: it devalues worship, devalues, in fact, any attention to an "other world," and urges us, instead, to work. Emerson's heroes are not believers in another world, but the resolute "finishers" of tasks in this one (1068). The true subject of "Worship" is, in short, the subject of every essay in *The Conduct of Life*: strong will, practical power, the concentration of force toward some productive end – the ability, as Emerson says throughout the book, to "stick" to one thing. ("Concentration," as he states it in "Power," "is the secret of strength in politics, in war, in trade, in short, in all management of human affairs" [982].)

Emerson has traditionally been honored (and dismissed) as the patron saint of "those who would live in the spirit." But the philosophy of power and use manifest in all his essays places no value on an inner or spiritual life unless it issues in some form of work. "Every man is a consumer," Emerson writes in "Wealth," "and ought to be a producer" (989). (This devaluing of "subjectivity" unless it leads to some act of production, transforming man, in the process, from a consumer into a producer or creator, is a major theme of two other nineteenth-century philosophers of power: Marx and Nietzsche.) The "pitiers of themselves," the "cravers of sympathy," as Emerson calls them – and they are the object of his derision throughout *The Conduct of Life* – are most contemptible because they belong to "the unproductive classes" (1090). "To make our word or act sublime," as he declares in "Worship," "we must make it real" (1068). Men, ideas, truth: their worth for Emerson depends not on some presocial, ideal, absolute value, but on their "total powers and effects" (1069), on the work they do in the world. Societies, saviors, religions: all are the consequence of the force of "will" (957). "All the great ages," Emerson writes in "Worship," "have been ages of belief. I mean, when there was any extraordinary power of performance" (1063). Belief, like truth, has no value in and of itself: its value lies in its translation into "performance." Emerson's famous "moral law" is, similarly, so persistently described in *experiential* terms – in terms of the power it grants – that we move beyond a traditional conception of morality and close to Nietzsche's existential belief that truth is "proved" not by its correspondence to an objective reality, but "by the feeling of enhanced power" it gives to those capable of *using* it as a "tool of power."[23]

There are other Emersonian principles in "Worship" that are equally contrary to morality in its traditional Christian form. Two in particular are worth noting. The first of these we might call his "contempt for sympathy." Though it has been largely ignored by scholars, it is a fundamental principle of Emerson's psychology, one that was repeated by Thoreau (in his attack on the selfishness of philanthropists in *Walden*) and by Nietzsche (in his scorn for the Christian "religion of pity").[24] It surfaces, in "Worship," in Emerson's vow that "the multitude of the sick shall not make us deny the existence of health" (1061) or in his remark that "The Spirit does not love cripples and malformations" (1074).

One can hear Emerson wince in disgust, not when he speaks of suffering itself – disease, poison, and poverty are all extolled as potential sources of power throughout *The Conduct of Life* – but whenever he considers the loss of power that results, for both parties involved, in the act of bestowing "charity" or "sympathy." At the root of the "craving for sympathy" (1016), as Emerson diagnoses it, lie all the self-delusions of self-pity. And pity, for himself or from another, takes from the sufferer his only opportunity for true health: the opportunity to resist pain and overcome it. Power for Emerson is never the simple absence of negative force. It is the overcoming of powerlessness. Health is never the mere absence of disease, but the overcoming of weakness. Health – and the command to "get health" (1088) is another of *The Conduct of Life*'s central mandates – is thus defined as "*recuperative* force," as "power, life, that resists disease, poison and all enemies" (974–75; my emphasis).[25] "No labor, pains, temperance, poverty, nor exercise, that can gain [health], must be grudged" (1088).

"Every man is a rascal," Emerson contends, citing Dr. Johnson, "as soon as he is sick" (1088). "The pitiers of themselves," the "leaky" complainers, the self-"coddlers" are "a perilous class" (1039, 1051, 1027). We must therefore treat the sick with the same firmness we show to drunkards, "giving them, of course, every aid, – but withholding ourselves" (1088). Mental suffering, because it requires the same process of self-overcoming, requires the same withholding of pity. As Emerson states it at the beginning of "Worship": "I have no sympathy with a poor man I knew, who, when suicides abounded, told me he dared not look at his razor" (1055). "*Loss of sympathy*" is what we need: only the act of overcoming "humiliations" or "defeats" will move us toward a greater "humanity" (1087; my emphasis).

Emerson appeals to another equally unorthodox principle at the end of "Worship," when he promises "honor and fortune . . . to him who always recognizes the neighborhood of the great, always feels himself in the presence of high causes" (1076). Such enthusiasm for great souls has usually been classified as an example of Emerson's Victorian hero worship. But his hero worship is actually one subcategory of a much larger, less recognized, Emersonian principle: his guiding belief that "Nature is upheld by antagonism." It was not heroes themselves Emerson loved, so much as the competition and conflict that creates them.

Emerson's championing, in the long paragraph above, of war, revolution, barbarian invasions, or any violence that "shatters a rotten system" and gives birth to new strength and "new men" is not an aberration or a momentary lapse in his thought. The Heraclitean notion that "War is the father of all things" is, on the contrary, the cornerstone of his philosophy of power.[26] "More are made good," Emerson insists, citing Democritus, "by exercitation than by nature." We should welcome the "friction in nature" because it leads to the "overcoming" of "resistances" and, consequently, to new power (984–85).

The Conduct of Life, like all of his collections of essays, upholds repeatedly Emerson's vision of life as a theater of conflict. The whole world, as he put it in his journals, "is a series of balanced . . . antagonisms";[27] man himself is "a stupendous antagonism, a dragging together of the poles of the Universe" (953). (Capitalism, as Emerson describes it in "Wealth," exists according to the same principle: each speculator is "met and antagonized by other speculators as hot as he. The equilibrium is preserved by these counteractions" [993].) True friendship, or a true culture, is not a matter of sympathy and Christian charity, but of mutual resistance and competition. We should "engage our companions not to spare us" (1089), find "somebody who shall make us do what we can" (1093). "But it is certain," Emerson writes, "that there is a great deal of good in us that does not know itself, and that a habit of union and competition brings people up and keeps them up to their highest point" (1094). "You cannot have one well-bred man without a whole society of such. They keep each other up to any high point" (1024).

Emerson's endorsement of great men and "high causes" at the conclusion of "Worship" may seem, at first glance, as pious as a Sunday hymn. But it takes on a curious resonance coming in the midst of his persistent celebration of "trial[s] of strength" (59), "tests of manhood" (261), or the natural "rank of powers" (132) that obtains when any two people meet. (Whenever two people meet, "one instantly perceives that he has the key of the situation, that his will comprehends the other's will, as the cat does the mouse" [184]. Men have an instinctive knowledge "of each other's power and disposition"; they "take each other's measure, when they meet for the first time, – and every time they meet" [190]. Every man, Emerson concludes, has a precise "rank in the immense scale of men, and we are always learning to read it" [181].) It is difficult to take Emerson's appeal to the human potential for greatness as a conventional call for spiritual renewal. For he seems to be returning – like Nietzsche, in his analogous descriptions of an antagonistic universe – to a pagan morality based on a realistic acceptance of a natural hierarchy of power, not on the Christian ideals of charity and "meekness."

It is, in fact, Emerson's theory of power that makes *The Conduct of Life* a fundamentally anti-Christian book. The will to power, the "spawning productivity" (1082), that sets the universe in motion exists, for Emerson, outside the boundaries of any Christian definition of good and evil, moral and immoral. This is Emerson's central philosophical lesson: the always tangled coexistence of positive and negative force. While Christian morality defines good and evil as opposites, Emerson portrays them as simply different points on the same continuum of power. Vice is not the opposite of virtue, but "the excess or acridity of a virtue" (1082). There is, consequently, an inherent paradox or hypocrisy underlying Western tradition: what civilization glorifies as "good" may merely be a different degree of the same power it condemns as "evil." Civilization may in fact, Emerson suggests, depend precisely on the same, natural "love of power" it attempts to banish as immoral. "The pulpit and the press," Emerson writes, "have many commonplaces denouncing the thirst for wealth; but if men should take these moralists at their word and leave off aiming to be rich, the moralists would rush to rekindle at all hazards this love of power in the people, lest civilization should be undone" (994).

Egotism is, similarly, one "excess of power" – Emerson calls it a disease – that becomes all too evident, and noxious, whenever the egotist enters society. Yet "the goitre of egotism," metaphysical malady that it may be, has its roots in "individuality" – and individuality is one prerequisite of culture. "This individuality is not only not inconsistent with culture, but is the basis of it" (1016). The remedy is not to censure and attempt to eradicate what is a natural, and potentially creative and benign, expression of power. The "cure" for negative force lies, rather, in those acts which constitute the core of Emerson's psychology: its use, assimilation, incorporation, its "overcoming." "And the end of culture is not to destroy this [egotism], God forbid! but to train away all impediment and mixture, and leave nothing but pure power" (1016–17).

"Good energy and bad" are not antitheses, but the kindred offspring of nature's "spawning productivity" ("all kinds of power usually emerge at the same time . . . the ecstasies of devotion, with the exasperations of debauchery" [976]). Civilization depends not on the extinction of "bad energy" – the natural overflow of aboriginal force is in itself a good – but on the use we make of it. "All *plus* is good," Emerson says, speaking of power in whatever form it may take, "only put it in the right place" (979). Civilization cannot, in other words, simply be defined as virtue, morality, and "good energy"; it exists, rather, as the complex end product of what we now call, in the wake of Nietzsche and Freud, the "sublimation" of destructive or immoral impulses. "This aboriginal might," Emerson writes, "gives a surprising pleasure when it appears under conditions of supreme refinement, as in the proficients of high art" (981). Culture cannot exist without those "wicked" energies that give it "muscle"; even our "representations of the Deity" depend on those forces we associate with hell (978).

If there is an essential harshness, even a cruelty, in Emerson's thought, it is not the Whicherian brand of midlife disillusionment scholars usually talk about. There was always, as Christopher Lasch suggests, an underlying "fatalism" in Emerson's essays, though it has been carefully downplayed by his putative defenders from his day to ours.[28] Emerson's "fatalism" may be most accurately situated, however, not, as Lasch suggests, in the tradition of Edwardsean Calvinism, but in the context of that largely contemporaneous tradition with which it has so many intellectual affinities – that modern tradition of continental thought that runs from Fichte and Hegel, through Marx and Nietzsche, to Freud. It is a tradition that, in the course of its development, placed ever-increasing emphasis on "power" and "will," posited the search for some universal motive force as the aim of science and philosophy, and defined history and identity in terms of the way a world spirit, or mankind, or an individual, sublimates, uses, or incorporates a universe of antagonistic energies. The fatalism inherent in this tradition is not a matter of Calvinist predestination; it is fatalistic, rather, in its steadfast vision of existential struggle between mind and nature, freedom and fate. (That existential tension – the "marvellous balance," as Emerson calls it in the paragraph cited at the beginning of this section, of "beauty and disgust, magnificence and rats" – is most intensely explored in the extraordinary, prolonged attempt Emerson makes, in "Fate," to suggest the endless, "intricate, overlapped, interweaved" way in which our notions of freedom and fate are forever knit together in one "web of relation" [961].) Nietzsche was not the first to base his philosophy on the "antithesis character of existence";[29] that point of view was already a dominant feature of Emerson's essays. Before Nietzsche, it was Emerson who devoted his career to anatomizing the will to power as it variously expressed itself in all aspects of an antagonistic universe. Emerson was, as George Stack concludes, the modern era's first philosopher of power: "Although others had spoken of the power-motive in human nature . . . it is not too much to say that Emerson was the first thinker to examine not only the human desire for power, but . . . the first to disclose its multiple forms and its presence in *all* existence."[30]

III "FATE": THE DOCTRINE OF USE

The Conduct of Life's philosophy of power does not represent a new stage in Emerson's development. The emphasis on humanity's search for "elemental power" (46), the vision of life as a stupendous antagonism in which man and nature vie for dominion, the insistence that "the relation of man to the globe" is "a relation of use":[31] these precepts were firmly in place in Emerson's thought as early as the publication of his first book, in 1836, or the series of lectures (1833–36) that preceded it.

The psychology of overcoming and sublimation that underlies Emerson's belief in "the good of evil" is introduced, in *Nature,* as "the doctrine of Use" (29). "Nothing in nature is exhausted in its first use," Emerson explains: "Nature's dice are always loaded. . . . [I]n her heaps and rubbish are concealed sure and useful results" (27–28). Emerson's point here – that our fate or our natural condition, however unlucky it may seem, can be put to use (and thereby overcome) – is exemplified, in even more memorable terms, in his account of the ultimately "good office" performed by poverty. That same "grinding debt" whose "iron face the widow, the orphan, and the sons of genius fear and hate" is also "a preceptor whose lessons cannot be foregone": it is, Emerson insists, "needed most by those who suffer from it most" (26–27). This is the guiding psychological principle that will inform the rest of his career, reappearing in his descriptions of "the good of evil," the medicinal effects of poison, or the power to be found in "poverty." (Nietzsche's dissection of the inherent contradictions underlying Western morality would make him master of such paradoxes; he, too, would define "everything good" as "the evil of former days made serviceable," and exhort us to "reinterpret" our "poverty into a necessity so that . . . we no longer sulk at fate on its account." For Nietzsche, power and creativity begin in "authentic distress." "Neediness," as he puts it in *The Gay Science,* "is needed!")[32] "So use all that is called Fortune," Emerson urges us in "Self-Reliance" (282). "Disasters of all kinds, sickness, offence, poverty" will, he writes in "Compensation," "prove benefactors" (297). "We must," he reminds us in "Experience," "hold hard to this poverty, however scandalous, and by more vigorous self-recoveries, after the sallies of action, possess our axis more firmly" (490). "The calamities are our friends," he contends, once again, in *The Conduct of Life,* citing Ben Jonson's lines on "blessed Poverty": poverty is one of the necessary conditions of "truth-speaking" (1031). Or, as he restates this central doctrine in "Considerations By the Way": "The wise workman will not regret the poverty or the solitude which brought out his working talents" (1086). "[S]uccess, reality, joy, and power" all reside in the "rich poverty" of "the deep today."[33]

The frequent homage *The Conduct of Life* pays to "Necessity" is not evidence of Emerson's "acquiescence" to fate. It represents, rather, an essential tenet of that philosophy of power Emerson had been articulating and refining, in essay after essay, from the beginning of his career. Necessity, like all forms of negative power, was never, for Emerson, something one *acquiesced* to – it was, on the contrary, something one put to use as a potential source of power. "Beauty," as Emerson says, "rests on necessities" (1106). Necessity is the true source of culture, knowledge, mastery, and freedom. "The material of freedom consists of necessities."[34] "Power is never far from Necessity."[35]

Emerson may seem, in the closing paragraphs of "Fate," to be bowing down, at last, to the destructive force of fate, to that impersonal, "savage element" that so easily "dissolves persons." His refrain – "Let us build altars to the Beautiful Necessity" – may seem to tip the rhetorical balance away from human power, toward all those nonhuman forces that can nei- ther be countered nor controlled. But the essay's final words – Emerson's injunction that we "draw on all [the] omnipotence" of that same fatal power – tip the balance back to his constant theme: the doctrine of use. The famous catalogue of disasters offered early in the essay (945–46) ends with a description that similarly suggests our ultimate use of evil. Fate's endless array of negative powers may "respect no persons," but they are also, as Emerson describes them, "mixed instrumentalities": fate is a "ter- rific benefactor" (945–46).[36]

"Every spirit makes its house," Emerson writes early in "Fate," "but afterwards the house confines the spirit" (946). This remark has, as Ger- trude Hughes notes, "persistently been seen in terms of decline."[37] But by the essay's close, that image of defeat has been revised to fit a conception of ultimate human mastery. The idea of fatal "limitation" has been rede- fined as the foundation for further growth – an unending process not unlike that unstoppable expansive force Emerson envisioned, nineteen years ear- lier, in "Circles." In 1844, Emerson had defined nature as man's "differen- tial thermometer" (546), the tool for measuring human power. In "Fate," the limits of our natural existence are once again redefined as limits no longer, but as human tools – "the meter of the growing man." Nature's contingencies are the dragonlike, yet necessary, "retarding forces" we learn to "ride and rule." Such lordship, Emerson promises, is inevitable:

> We can afford to allow the limitation, if we know it is the meter of the growing man. We stand against Fate, as children stand up against the wall in their father's house, and notch their height from year to year. But when the boy grows to man, and is master of the house, he pulls down that wall, and builds a new and bigger. 'Tis only a question of time. Every brave youth is in training to ride and rule this dragon. His science is to make weapons and wings of these passions and retarding forces. (957–58)

The point is made repeatedly: we must learn life's "odious facts," learn to turn them to our benefit. Our "sound relation to these facts," Emerson says, "is to use and command, not to cringe to them" (953–54). "A man's power is hooped in by a necessity, which, by many experiments, he touches on every side, until he learns its arc" (952). All facts, all apparent constric- tions, however immovable they may seem, can be saddled and made to serve. All power, however threatening to man, can be converted to his good use. The violent torrent is at last "taught to drudge for man." The wild beasts man "makes useful." Chemical explosions he learns to control "like his watch." Man masters all modes of energy: legs, horses, wind, steam, gas, electricity. "There's nothing he will not make his carrier" (959). The once diabolic force of steam becomes the perfect "workman." The anarchic force of the mob becomes, through the transformations of democracy, "the most harmless and energetic form of a State." The Watts and Fultons, the great statesmen of the world, have all grasped the same principle: "where was power was not devil, but was God" – if only properly put to use (959–60).[38]

NOTES

1 *Essays and Lectures,* ed. Joel Porte (New York: Library of America, 1983), p. 949. All subsequent citations from Emerson, unless otherwise indicated, will be from this edition. Page references will appear parenthetically in the text.
2 Cavell, *In Quest of the Ordinary: Lines of Skepticism and Romanticism* (Chicago: University of Chicago Press, 1988), p. 35.
3 *Selections from Ralph Waldo Emerson: An Organic Anthology,* ed. Stephen Whicher (Boston: Houghton Mifflin, 1957), p. 253.
4 Eliot's judgments are in *The Sacred Wood* (1920; rpt. London: Methuen, 1960), p. xii, and his essay on Henry James, reprinted in *The Shock of Recognition,* ed. Edmund Wilson (1943; rpt. New York: Octagon Books, 1975), 2: 859; see my *Emerson and Power: Creative Antagonism in the Nineteenth Century* (DeKalb: Northern Illinois University Press, 1996), pp. 19–52.
5 Dewey, "Ralph Waldo Emerson" (1903), in *Emerson: A Collection of Critical Essays,* ed. Milton Konvitz and Stephen Whicher (Englewood Cliffs, NJ; Prentice-Hall, 1962), pp. 24–30; Firkins, "Has Emerson a Future?" in *Selected Essays* (Minneapolis: University of Minnesota Press, 1933), pp. 79–93; Cavell, *This New Yet Unapproachable America: Lectures after Emerson after Wittgenstein* (Albuquerque: Living Batch Press, 1989), p. 78; Matthiessen, *American Renaissance: Art and Expression in the Age of Emerson and Whitman* (New York: Oxford University Press, 1941), p. 75; Miller, *Errand into the Wilderness* (Cambridge, MA: Harvard University Press, 1956), p. 186; Fiedler, "American Literature," in *Contemporary Literary Scholarship: A Critical Review,* ed. Lewis Leary (New York: Appleton-Century-Crofts, 1958), p. 174; Lawrence, in *The Recognition of Ralph Waldo Emerson,* ed. Milton Konvitz (Ann Arbor: University of Michigan Press, 1972), p. 169; Whicher, *Freedom and Fate: An Inner Life of Ralph Waldo Emerson,* 2d ed. (Philadelphia: University of Pennsylvania Press, 1971), p. 172; Cavell, *Conditions Handsome and Unhandsome: The Constitution of Emersonian Perfectionism* (Chicago: University of Chicago Press, 1990), p. 133.
6 James, *Partial Portraits* (1888; rpt. Ann Arbor: University of Michigan Press, 1968), p. 31; Woodberry, *Ralph Waldo Emerson* (1907; rpt. New York: Haskell House, 1968), p. 152; Updike, *Odd Jobs: Essays and Criticism* (New York: Knopf, 1991), p. 154; Bloom, *Modern Critical Interpretations: Henry James's "The Portrait of a Lady,"* ed. Harold Bloom (New York: Chelsea House, 1987), p. 6; Wilson, *Figures of Speech: American Writers and the Literary Marketplace, from Benjamin Franklin to Emily Dickinson* (Baltimore: Johns

Hopkins University Press, 1990), p. 183; Anthony Lane, "Against the Law," *New Yorker*, 27 Dec. 1993/3 Jan. 1994: 149.

7 Bloom, *Modern Critical Views: Nathaniel Hawthorne*, ed. Harold Bloom (New York: Chelsea House, 1986), p. 4; Giamatti, *The University and the Public Interest* (New York: Atheneum, 1981), p. 174; I cite contemporary reviews in *Critic, Westminster Review, New Englander*, and the *Athenaeum*, reprinted in *Emerson and Thoreau: The Contemporary Reviews*, ed. Joel Myerson (New York: Cambridge University Press, 1992), pp. 294, 306, 303, 284.

8 McFarland, *Coleridge and the Pantheist Tradition* (Oxford: Clarendon Press, 1969), pp. 175–76; Leibniz quoted in Thomas McFarland, *Shapes of Culture* (Iowa City: University of Iowa Press, 1987), p. 170.

9 Emerson, *The Journals and Miscellaneous Notebooks of Ralph Waldo Emerson, Volume III, 1826–1832*, ed. William H. Gilman and Alfred R. Ferguson (Cambridge, MA: Harvard University Press, 1963), p. 327. As Emerson puts it in "Worship": "We can only see what we are"; "That only which we have within, can we see without" (1067, 1070). In "Fate," Emerson introduces Schelling's idea that "there is in every man a certain feeling, that he has been what he is from all eternity, and by no means became such in time" (948).

10 McFarland, *Shapes of Culture*, p. 172.

11 McDermott, *Streams of Experience: Reflections on the History and Philosophy of American Culture* (Amherst: University of Massachusetts Press, 1986), p. 244, n. 35.

12 There have been important dissenters from the Whicherian orthodoxy. James Cox, for example, finds Emerson "an alarmingly repetitive writer": "I do not see Emerson as 'developing' or 'progressing' or 'declining'. . . . [V]isions of Emerson's career in terms of crises and turning points, in ups and downs, in directions from revolution to compromise or from idealism to realism have their own distortion." ("R. W. Emerson: The Circles of the Eye," in *Emerson: Prophecy, Metamorphosis, and Influence*, ed. David Levin [New York: Columbia University Press, 1975], pp. 71, 75–76.) Other studies that define Emerson's career in terms of repetition, not evolution, are Julie Ellison, *Emerson's Romantic Style* (Princeton: Princeton University Press, 1984) and Gertrude Reif Hughes, *Emerson's Demanding Optimism* (Baton Rouge: Louisiana State University Press, 1984).

13 Royce, "Nietzsche," *Atlantic Monthly*, Mar. 1917: 327–29; Lasch, *The True and Only Heaven: Progress and Its Critics* (New York: Norton, 1991), p. 264.

14 Royce, "Nietzsche," p. 329; George J. Stack is not the first to have called Emerson's essays "post-Christian" and "proto-existential," but his pioneering work, *Nietzsche and Emerson: An Elective Affinity* (Athens: Ohio University Press, 1992), is one of the few studies in which an existentialist interpretation of Emerson has served as the basis for a sustained, philosophical analysis. I am indebted to Stack's extensive discussion of many of the Emersonian/Nietzschean concepts – overcoming and sublimation, the necessity of radical honesty, the universal will to power, "the paradox of good and evil," the necessary tension between freedom and fate – I examine here.

15 The conflict in Emerson's work between transcendental and antitranscendental ways of thinking is not, as his critics often conclude, the result of his reputed

incoherence or his personal failure to achieve a consistent philosophy. It is a tension profoundly characteristic of nineteenth-century, Western thought.

16 Peckham, introduction to R. W. Emerson, *Essays: Second Series* (Columbus, OH: Charles E. Merrill, 1969), p. viii.

17 Porte, *Representative Man: Ralph Waldo Emerson in His Time* (New York: Oxford University Press, 1979), p. 229.

18 "Nature forever puts a premium on reality," Emerson says in "Behavior" (1047). We must, as he later states it, risk everything in our quest to "know the realities of human life" (1087). "Divine Providence," he writes in "Worship," has "hid from men neither disease, nor deformity, nor corrupt society, but has stated itself out in passions, in war, in trade, in the love of power and pleasure, in hunger and need" – and we must "not be so nice that we cannot write these facts down coarsely as they stand" (1055). The premium placed on getting *down* to reality is reflected, as well, in the emphasis Emerson gives, throughout *The Conduct of Life*, to "honesty" or what he calls speaking (or "doing") "truth" at "the zero of indifference" (1092). The honesty he advocates is, most particularly, a severe, private honesty about ourselves. This theme reaches its crescendo in the concluding essay, "Illusions": "Whatever games are played with us, we must play no games with ourselves, but deal in our privacy with the last honesty and truth. . . . Speak as you think, be what you are, pay your debts of all kinds" (1122).

19 *The Complete Works of Ralph Waldo Emerson,* ed. Edward Waldo Emerson (Boston: Houghton Mifflin, 1903–4), 10: 49.

20 McAleer, *Ralph Waldo Emerson: Days of Encounter* (Boston: Little, Brown, 1984), pp. xiv, 8.

21 In his 1861 review, Noah Porter, Jr., correctly noted *The Conduct of Life*'s commitment to "the present" as "enough . . . to think and care for" – though Porter could only condemn such "Epicureanism" (*Emerson and Thoreau: The Contemporary Reviews*, pp. 303–4); David Robinson examines the conflict in Emerson's essays between aggressiveness and "a stance of humility" in "Grace and Works: Emerson's Essays in Theological Perspective," in *American Unitarianism, 1805–1865*, ed. Conrad Edick Wright (Boston: Massachusetts Historical Society and Northeastern University Press, 1989), pp. 129–31.

22 Dewey, "Ralph Waldo Emerson," p. 28.

23 The "moral sense," Emerson writes in "Worship," is "the fountain of beauty and strength"; "To this [moral] sentiment belong vast and sudden enlargements of power" (1061). The "moral," as he says later in the essay, "enriches, empowers all" (1072). The "experience of the moral sentiment" is, in "Fate," similarly associated with "unlimited power" (956–57). The citations from Nietzsche are from *The Will to Power*, trans. Walter Kaufmann and R. J. Hollingdale (New York: Random House, 1968), pp. 149, 266 (sections 455, 480).

24 Nietzsche seems, Stack notes, "to have completely assimilated [Emerson's] belief that in order to retain spiritual or psychological strength, it is important to overcome the weakening feeling of pity or sympathy" (*Nietzsche and Emerson*, p. 281; for Nietzsche's objections to a "morality of pity" see, also, pp. 282, 333). For the long philosophical tradition of "anti-pity thinkers" – a tradition that goes back to the Greek and Roman Stoics, to Descartes, Spinoza, and Kant

– see Martha C. Nussbaum, "Pity and Mercy: Nietzsche's Stoicism," in *Nietzsche, Genealogy, Morality: Essays on Nietzsche's "On the Genealogy of Morals,"* ed. Richard Schacht (Berkeley: University of California Press, 1994), pp. 139–67. Nussbaum comments briefly on this pivotal, though neglected aspect of Emerson's thought (p. 166, n. 49); Gustaaf Van Cromphout examines it thoroughly in "Areteic Ethics: Emerson and Nietzsche on Pity, Friendship, and Love," *ESQ: A Journal of the American Renaissance* 43 (1997): 95–112.

25 *The Conduct of Life* alludes often to the "use in medicine for poisons" (978). Such descriptions are, like his recurrent testimony to the benefits of poverty, one of Emerson's many, diverse reassertions of "the good of evil." "If we will make bread," he writes, "we must have contagion" (975). "The poisons," as he puts it in "Considerations By the Way," "are our principal medicines, which kill the disease, and save the life" (1086). "The huge animals nourish huge parasites, and the rancor of the disease attests the strength of the constitution" (975). The science of botany, Emerson observes, is doomed to remain "all names, not powers" so long as the botanist idealizes the "herbs of grace and healing" and neglects the "virtues of his weeds" (1099).

26 Like Nietzsche after him, Emerson cited Heraclitus's doctrine approvingly. See his 1865 "Harvard Commemoration Speech," in *The Complete Works of Ralph Waldo Emerson*, 11: 341.

27 *The Journals and Miscellaneous Notebooks of Ralph Waldo Emerson, Volume XI, 1848–1851*, ed. A. W. Plumstead et al. (Cambridge, MA: Harvard University Press, 1975), p. 371.

28 Lasch, *The True and Only Heaven*, pp. 243, 262, 547.

29 Nietzsche cited in Stack, *Nietzsche and Emerson*, p. 186.

30 Stack, p. 156.

31 From Emerson's 1834 lecture "On the Relation of Man to the Globe," *The Early Lectures of Ralph Waldo Emerson, Volume I, 1833–1836*, ed. Stephen E. Whicher and Robert E. Spiller (Cambridge, MA: Harvard University Press, 1966), p. 48.

32 Nietzsche, *The Will to Power*, p. 530 (section 1025) and *The Gay Science*, trans. Walter Kaufmann (New York: Random House, 1974), pp. 90, 117–18 (sections 17 and 56). Cf. Stack, *Nietzsche and Emerson*, p. 235.

33 *The Complete Works of Ralph Waldo Emerson*, 7: 175.

34 *The Topical Notebooks of Ralph Waldo Emerson, Volume I*, ed. Ralph H. Orth and Susan Sutton Smith (Columbia: University of Missouri Press, 1990), p. 80.

35 A saying of Pythagoras noted by Emerson; see Edward Emerson's notes to *The Conduct of Life* in *The Complete Works of Ralph Waldo Emerson*, 7: 358.

36 As Emerson states it in his late essay "Perpetual Forces": "We see the causes of evils, and learn to parry them and use them as instruments." (*The Complete Works of Ralph Waldo Emerson*, 10: 73.) Even death – the death, at least, of others – is described by Emerson, in *Nature* ("Discipline"), "Nominalist and Realist," and "Experience," in terms of the use we can make of it.

37 Hughes, *Emerson's Demanding Optimism*, p. x.

38 The concluding two paragraphs of this essay are taken, in slightly altered form, from my *Emerson and Power*, pp. 95–96.

SELECTED BIBLIOGRAPHY

TEXTS

The Complete Works of Ralph Waldo Emerson. Centenary Edition. Ed. Edward Waldo Emerson. 12 vols. Boston and New York: Houghton Mifflin, 1903–4.

The Early Lectures of Ralph Waldo Emerson. Ed. Stephen E. Whicher, Robert E. Spiller, and Wallace E. Williams. 3 vols. Cambridge, MA: The Belknap Press of Harvard University Press, 1959–72.

The Letters of Ralph Waldo Emerson. Ed. Ralph L. Rusk and Eleanor M. Tilton. 9 vols. New York: Columbia University Press, 1939–94.

The Journals and Miscellaneous Notebooks of Ralph Waldo Emerson. Ed. William H. Gilman et al. 16 vols. Cambridge, MA: Harvard University Press, 1960–82.

The Correspondence of Emerson and Carlyle. Ed. Joseph Slater. New York: Columbia University Press, 1964.

The Collected Works of Ralph Waldo Emerson. Ed. Robert E. Spiller et al. 5 vols. to date. Cambridge, MA: Harvard University Press, 1971– .

Ralph Waldo Emerson: Essays and Lectures. Ed. Joel Porte. New York: Library of America, 1983.

The Poetry Notebooks of Ralph Waldo Emerson. Ed. Ralph H. Orth et al. Columbia: University of Missouri Press, 1986.

Complete Sermons of Ralph Waldo Emerson. Ed. Albert J. von Frank et al. 4 vols. Columbia: University of Missouri Press, 1989–92.

Emerson: Collected Poems and Translations. Ed. Harold Bloom and Paul Kane. New York: Library of America, 1994.

Emerson's Antislavery Writings. Ed. Len Gougeon and Joel Meyerson. New Haven: Yale University Press, 1995.

SELECTIONS AND ANTHOLOGIES

The Heart of Emerson's Journals. Ed. Bliss Perry. Boston: Houghton Mifflin, 1926.

Selections from Ralph Waldo Emerson: An Organic Anthology. Ed. Stephen E. Whicher. Boston: Houghton Mifflin, 1957.

Selected Writings of Ralph Waldo Emerson. Ed. William H. Gilman. New York: New American Library, 1965.

Emerson in His Journals. Ed. Joel Porte. Cambridge, MA: The Belknap Press of Harvard University Press, 1982.
Ralph Waldo Emerson. Ed. Richard Poirier. New York: Oxford University Press, 1990.

RESOURCES FOR RESEARCH

Burkholder, Robert E., and Joel Myerson. *Ralph Waldo Emerson: An Annotated Secondary Bibliography,* Pittsburgh: University of Pittsburgh Press, 1985 [spans 1816–1979].
———. *Ralph Waldo Emerson: An Annotated Bibliography of Criticism, 1980–1991.* Westport, CT: Greenwood Press, 1994.
Carpenter, F. I. *Emerson Handbook.* New York: Hendricks House, 1953.
Harding, Walter. *Emerson's Library.* Charlottesville: University Press of Virginia, 1967.
Hubbell, George S. *Concordance to the Poems of Ralph Waldo Emerson.* New York: H. W. Wilson, 1932.
Ihrig, Mary Alice. *Emerson's Transcendental Vocabulary: A Concordance.* New York: Garland Publishers, 1981.
Irey, Eugene F. *A Concordance to Five Essays of Ralph Waldo Emerson.* New York: Garland Publishers, 1981.
Myerson, Joel. *Ralph Waldo Emerson: A Descriptive Bibliography.* Pittsburgh, PA: University of Pittsburgh Press, 1982.
von Frank, Albert J. *An Emerson Chronology.* New York: G. K. Hall, 1994.

BIOGRAPHIES

Allen, Gay Wilson. *Waldo Emerson: A Biography.* New York: Viking Press, 1981.
Baker, Carlos. *Emerson Among the Eccentrics.* New York: Viking Press, 1996.
Brooks, Van Wyck. *The Life of Emerson.* New York: The Literary Guild, 1932.
Cabot, James Elliot. *A Memoir of Ralph Waldo Emerson.* Boston: Houghton Mifflin, 1887.
Emerson, Ellen Tucker. *The Life of Lidian Jackson Emerson.* Ed. Dolores Bird Carpenter. Boston: Twayne, 1980.
Firkins, O. W. *Ralph Waldo Emerson.* Boston and New York: Houghton Mifflin, 1915.
Holmes, Oliver Wendell. *Ralph Waldo Emerson.* Boston: Houghton Mifflin, 1884; rpt. with an introduction by Joel Porte: New York: Chelsea House, 1980.
McAleer, John. *Ralph Waldo Emerson: Days of Encounter.* Boston: Little, Brown, 1984.
Pommer, Henry F. *Emerson's First Marriage.* Carbondale: Southern Illinois University Press, 1967.
Richardson, Robert D. *Emerson: The Mind on Fire.* Berkeley: University of California Press, 1995.
Rusk, Ralph L. *The Life of Ralph Waldo Emerson.* New York: Columbia University Press, 1949.

Wagenknecht, Edward. *Ralph Waldo Emerson: Portrait of a Balanced Soul.* New York: Oxford University Press, 1974.

Whicher, Stephen. *Freedom and Fate: An Inner Life of Ralph Waldo Emerson.* Philadelphia: University of Pennsylvania Press, 1953.

CRITICISM

Anderson, John Q. *The Liberating Gods.* Coral Gables, FL: University of Miami Press, 1971.

Anderson, Quentin. *The Imperial Self: An Essay in American Literary and Cultural History.* New York: Alfred Knopf, 1971.

Arnold, Matthew. *Discourses in America.* London: Macmillan, 1885.

Barish, Evelyn. *Emerson: The Roots of Prophecy.* Princeton, NJ: Princeton University Press, 1989.

Bercovitch, Sacvan. *The Rites of Assent.* New York: Routledge, 1993.

Berthoff, Warner. *Fictions and Events.* New York: Dutton, 1971.

Bishop, Jonathan. *Emerson on the Soul.* Cambridge, MA: Harvard University Press, 1964.

Bloom, Harold. *Figures of Capable Imagination.* New York: Seabury, 1976.

———. *A Map of Misreading.* New York: Oxford University Press, 1975.

———. *The Ringers in the Tower.* Chicago: University of Chicago Press, 1971.

Bruccoli, Matthew J. *The Chief Glory of Every People.* Carbondale: Southern Illinois University Press, 1973.

Buell, Lawrence. *Literary Transcendentalism: Style and Vision in the American Renaissance.* Ithaca, NY, and London: Cornell University Press, 1973.

Cadava, Eduardo. *Emerson and the Climates of History.* Stanford: Stanford University Press, 1997.

Cameron, Sharon. "Representing Grief: Emerson's 'Experience.' " *Representations* 15 (Summer 1986): 15–41.

Cavell, Stanley. *Conditions Handsome and Unhandsome: The Constitution of Emersonian Perfectionism.* Chicago: University of Chicago Press, 1990.

———. *In Quest of the Ordinary.* Chicago: University of Chicago Press, 1988.

———. *The Senses of Walden.* San Francisco: North Point Press, 1981.

———. *This New Yet Unapproachable America.* Albuquerque: Living Batch Press, 1989.

Cayton, Mary Kupiec. *Emerson's Emergence: Self and Society in the Transformation of New England, 1800–1845.* Chapel Hill: University of North Carolina Press, 1989.

Chapman, John Jay. *Emerson and Other Essays.* New York: Scribner's, 1898.

Cheyfitz, Eric. *The Trans-Parent: Sexual Politics in the Language of Emerson.* Baltimore, MD: Johns Hopkins University Press, 1981.

Colacurcio, Michael. *Doctrine and Difference.* New York: Routledge, 1997.

Cowan, Michael. *City of the West.* New Haven: Yale University Press, 1967.

Duncan, Jeffrey. *Power and Form in Emerson's Thought.* Charlottesville: University of Virgina Press, 1973.

Ellison, Julie. *Emerson's Romantic Style.* Princeton, NJ: Princeton University Press, 1984.

Engel, Monroe. *The Uses of Literature*. Harvard English Studies 4. Cambridge, MA: Harvard University Press, 1973.

Gass, William H. *Habitations of the Word*. New York: Simon and Schuster, 1985.

Gelpi, Albert. *The Tenth Muse: The Psyche of the American Poet*. Cambridge, MA: Harvard University Press, 1975.

Gelpi, Donald. *Endless Seeker: The Religious Quest of Ralph Waldo Emerson*. Lanham, MD: University Press of America, 1991.

Gilmore, Michael. *American Romanticism and the Marketplace*. Chicago: University of Chicago Press, 1985.

Gonnaud, Maurice. *Individu et société dans l'oeuvre de Ralph Waldo Emerson: Essai de biographie spirituelle*. Paris: Didier, 1964; English version: *An Uneasy Solitude*. Trans. Lawrence Rosenwald. Princeton, NJ: Princeton University Press, 1987.

Goodman, Russell B. *American Philosophy and the Romantic Tradition*. New York: Cambridge University Press, 1985.

Gougeon, Len. *Virtue's Hero: Emerson, Antislavery and Reform*. Athens: University of Georgia Press, 1990.

Greenberg, Robert M. *Splintered Worlds: Fragmentation and the Ideal of Diversity in the Work of Emerson, Melville, Whitman, and Dickinson*. Boston: Northeastern University Press, 1993.

Grusin, Richard A. *Transcendental Hermeneutics*. Durham, NC: Duke University Press, 1991.

Gura, Philip F. *The Wisdom of Words: Language, Theology, and Literature in the New England Renaissance*. Middletown, CT: Wesleyan University Press, 1981.

Hansen, Olaf. *Aesthetic Individualism and Practical Intellect*. Princeton, NJ: Princeton University Press, 1990.

Harris, Kenneth Marc. *Carlyle and Emerson: Their Long Debate*. Cambridge, MA: Harvard University Press, 1978.

Hodder, Alan D. *Emerson's Rhetoric of Revelation:* University Park: Pennsylvania State University Press, 1989.

Hopkins, Vivian. *Spires of Form: A Study of Emerson's Aesthetic Theory*. Cambridge, MA: Harvard University Press, 1951.

Howe, Irving. *The American Newness: Culture and Politics in the Age of Emerson*. Cambridge, MA: Harvard University Press, 1986.

Hughes, Gertrude Reif. *Emerson's Demanding Optimism*. Baton Rouge: Louisiana State University Press, 1984.

James, Henry. *Partial Portraits*. London: Macmillan, 1888.

Kazin, Alfred. *An American Procession*. New York: Knopf, 1984.

Lange, Lou Ann. *The Riddle of Liberty: Emerson on Alienation, Freedom, and Liberty*. Atlanta, GA: Scholars Press, 1986.

Lee, A. Robert. *Nineteenth-Century American Poetry*. New York: Barnes & Noble, 1985.

Leverenz, David. *Manhood and the American Renaissance*. Ithaca, NY: Cornell University Press, 1989.

Loewenberg, Robert J. *An American Idol: Emerson and the Jewish Ideal*. Lanham, MD: University Press of America, 1984.

Lopez, Michael. *Emerson and Power: Creative Antagonism in the Nineteenth Century*. DeKalb, IL: Northern Illinois University Press, 1996.

Loving, Jerome. *Emerson, Whitman, and the American Muse.* Chapel Hill: The University of North Carolina Press, 1982.

Matthiessen, F. O. *American Renaissance: Art and Expression in the Age of Emerson and Whitman.* New York: Oxford University Press, 1941.

Michael, John. *Emerson and Skepticism: The Cipher of the World.* Baltimore, MD: Johns Hopkins University Press, 1988.

Miller, Perry. *Errand into the Wilderness.* Cambridge, MA: The Belknap Press of Harvard University Press, 1956.

———. *Nature's Nation.* Cambridge, MA: The Belknap Press of Harvard University Press, 1967.

Morris, Saundra. "The Threshold Poem, Emerson, and 'The Sphinx.' " *American Literature* 69.3 (September 1997): 547–70.

Mott, Wesley T. *"The Strains of Eloquence": Emerson and His Sermons.* University Park: Pennsylvania State University Press, 1988.

Neufeldt, Leonard. *The House of Emerson.* Lincoln: University of Nebraska Press, 1982.

Newfield, Christopher. *The Emerson Effect: Individualism and Submission in America.* Chicago: University of Chicago Press, 1996.

Packer, B. L. *Emerson's Fall: A New Interpretation of the Major Essays.* New York: Continuum, 1982.

Paul, Sherman. *Emerson's Angle of Vision: Man and Nature in the American Experience.* Cambridge, MA: Harvard University Press, 1952.

Pease, Donald. *Visionary Compacts: American Renaissance Writings in Cultural Context.* Madison: University of Wisconsin Press, 1987.

Poirier, Richard. *Poetry and Pragmatism.* Cambridge, MA: Harvard University Press, 1992.

———. *The Renewal of Literature: Emersonian Reflections.* New York: Random House, 1987.

———. *A World Elsewhere: The Place of Style in American Literature.* New York: Oxford University Press, 1966.

Porte, Joel. *Emerson and Thoreau: Transcendentalists in Conflict.* Middletown, CT: Weseleyan University Press, 1966.

———. *Representative Man: Ralph Waldo Emerson in His Time.* New York: Oxford University Press, 1979; rev. ed.: New York: Columbia University Press, 1988.

———. *In Respect to Egotism: Studies in American Romantic Writing.* New York: Cambridge University Press, 1991.

Porter, Carolyn. *Seeing and Being: The Plight of the Participant Observer in Emerson, James, Adams, and Faulkner.* Middletown, CT: Wesleyan University Press, 1981.

Porter, David. *Emerson and Literary Change.* Cambridge, MA: Harvard University Press, 1978.

Roberson, Susan L. *Emerson in His Sermons: A Man-Made Self.* Columbia: University of Missouri Press, 1995.

Robinson, David. *Apostle of Culture: Emerson as Lecturer.* Philadelphia: University of Pennsylvania Press, 1982.

———. *Emerson and The Conduct of Life.* New York: Cambridge University Press, 1993.

Rosenwald, Lawrence. *Emerson and the Art of the Diary*. New York: Oxford University Press, 1988.
Santayana, George. *Interpretations of Poetry and Religion*. New York: Scribner's, 1900.
Sealts, Merton M. *Emerson on the Scholar*. Columbia: University of Missouri Press, 1992.
Steele, Jeffrey. *The Representation of the Self in the American Renaissance*. Chapel Hill: University of North Carolina Press, 1987.
Stoehr, Taylor. *Nay-Saying in Concord*. Hamden, CT: Archon, 1979.
Strauch, F. Carl. "Hatred's Swift Repulsions." *Studies in Romanticism* 7 (Winter 1968): 65–103.
———. "The Mind's Voice: Emerson's Poetic Styles." *ESQ* 60 (Summer 1970): 43–59.
———. "The Year of Emerson's Poetic Maturity: 1834." *Philological Quarterly* 34 (October 1955): 353–77.
Teichgraeber, Richard F. *Sublime Thoughts/Penny Wisdom: Situating Emerson and Thoreau in the American Market*. Baltimore, MD: Johns Hopkins University Press, 1995.
Thurin, Erik Ingvar. *Emerson as a Priest of Pan: A Study in the Metaphysics of Sex*. Lawrence: University of Kansas Press, 1981.
Toulouse, Teresa. *The Art of Prophesying: New England Sermons and the Shaping of Belief*. Athens: University of Georgia Press, 1987.
Van Leer, David. *Emerson's Epistemology: The Argument of the Essays*. New York: Cambridge University Press, 1986.
Waggoner, Hyatt H. *Emerson as Poet*. Princeton, NJ: Princeton University Press, 1974.
Weisbuch, Robert. *Atlantic Double-Cross: American Literature and British Influence in the Age of Emerson*. Chicago: University of Chicago Press, 1987.
West, Cornel. *The American Evasion of Philosophy*. Madison: University of Wisconsin Press, 1989.
Wilson, R. Jackson. *Figures of Speech*. New York: Knopf, 1989.
Wolfe, Cary. *The Limits of American Literary Ideology in Pound and Emerson*. New York: Cambridge University Press, 1993.
Yoder, R. A. *Emerson and the Orphic Poet in America*. Berkeley: University of California Press, 1978.
Zwarg, Christina. *Feminist Conversations: Fuller, Emerson, and the Play of Reading*. Ithaca, NY: Cornell University Press, 1995.

CRITICISM – COLLECTIONS

Bloom, Harold, ed. *Ralph Waldo Emerson*. Modern Critical Views Series. New York: Chelsea House, 1985.
Bode, Carl, ed. *Ralph Waldo Emerson: A Profile*. New York: Hill and Wang, 1969.
Buell, Laurence, ed. *Ralph Waldo Emerson: A Collection of Critical Essays*. Englewood Cliffs, NJ: Prentice-Hall, 1993.
Burkholder, Robert E., and Joel Meyerson, eds. *Critical Essays on Ralph Waldo Emerson*. Boston: G. K. Hall, 1983.

Cady, Edwin, and Louis J. Budd, eds. *On Emerson*. Durham, NC: Duke University Press, 1988.

Donadio, Stephen, Stephen Railton, and Ormond Seavey, eds. *Emerson and His Legacy: Essays in Honor of Quentin Anderson*. Carbondale: Southern Illinois University Press, 1986.

Konvitz, Milton R., ed. *The Recognition of Ralph Waldo Emerson: Selected Criticism Since 1837*. Ann Arbor: University of Michigan Press, 1972.

Konvitz, Milton R., and Stephen E. Whicher, eds. *Emerson: A Collection of Critical Essays*. Englewood Cliffs, NJ: Prentice-Hall, 1962.

Levin, David, ed. *Emerson: Prophecy, Metamorphosis, Influence*. New York: Columbia University Press, 1975.

Myerson, Joel, ed. *Emerson Centenary Essays*. Carbondale: Southern Illinois University Press, 1982.

———. *Emerson and Thoreau: The Contemporary Reviews*. New York: Cambridge University Press, 1992.

Neufeldt, Leonard Nick, ed. *Ralph Waldo Emerson: New Appraisals: A Symposium*. Hartford, CT: Transcendental Books, 1973.

Porte, Joel, ed. *Emerson: Prospect and Retrospect*. Harvard English Studies 10. Cambridge, MA: Harvard University Press, 1982.

Sealts, Merton M., Jr., and Alfred R. Ferguson, eds. *Emerson's Nature – Origin, Growth, Meaning*. New York: Dodd, Mead, 1969; rev. ed.: Carbondale: Southern Illinois University Press, 1979.

Simon, Myron, and Thornton H. Parsons, eds. *Transcendentalism and Its Legacy*. Ann Arbor: University of Michigan Press, 1966.

INDEX

Adams, Henry, 2, 30, 68
Adams, John Quincy, 53
Agassiz, Louis, 99, 232
Ahab, Captain, 113, 114, 115
Akenside, Mark, 42
Alcott, Bronson, 20, 21, 22, 63, 97; "Orphic Sayings," 20
Alcott, Louisa May, *Little Women,* 142
Allen, Gay Wilson, *Waldo Emerson,* 140
American Revolution, 37
Ammons, A. R., 190, 219
Anderson, Quentin, 3, 5, 8; *The Imperial Self,* 3
Aristophanes, 4
Aristotle, 210
Arnold, Matthew, 1, 174, 245
Athenaeum, The, 199
Atlantic Monthly, 219, 233
Augustine, Saint, 103
Aurelius, Marcus, 42, 104

Barker, Anna, 121, 126–28
Bellamy, Edward, 70
Bercovitch, Sacvan, 50, 53, 65; *The American Jeremiad,* 53
Berkeley, George, 43
Berkson, Dorothy, 137
Bhagavad-Gita, 238
Biglow, Hosea, 10
Blake, William, 213
Bliss, Daniel, 32, 33, 34, 36, 47
Bliss, Phebe, 32, 33
Bloom, Harold, 40, 164, 246
Bradstreet, Anne, *The Tenth Muse,* 221
Brentano, Bettine, 132
Brisbane, Albert, 218
British Critic, The, 199, 205
Brook Farm, 22–24, 61, 62, 63, 64, 153, 155
Brooklyn Eagle, The, 200
Brooks, Van Wyck, 70
Brown, Gillian, 143, 144, 150, 153
Brown, John, 155

Browning, Elizabeth Barrett, 163
Brownson, Orestes, 23, 64, 65, 71, 194, 195; "The Laboring Classes," 23, 64
Bryant, William Cullen, 200
Bulkeley, Peter, 5, 32
Burke, Kenneth, 51
Burkholder, Robert E., 50
Butler, Joseph, 41
Byron, George Gordon, Lord, 205

Cabot, James Elliot, 30
Cadava, Eduardo, 231
Cage, John, 100
Calvinism, 14–15, 44, 65, 259, 260
Cameron, Sharon, 148–49, 156
Carlyle, Thomas, 11, 18, 165, 194, 202, 203, 205, 210; *On Heroes, Hero Worship, and the Heroic in History,* 205
Carpenter, Dolores Bird, 140
Cavell, Stanley, 158, 242, 243, 245
Cayton, Mary Kupiec, 71
Channing, William Ellery, 15–16, 43
Channing, William Henry, 23, 132
Chaucer, Geoffrey, 91, 94, 208; *Canterbury Tales,* 232
Chauncy, Charles, 14
Chopin, Kate, *The Awakening,* 1
Church, Frederick, 100
Cicero, 37
Civil War, 24, 231
Clarke, James Freeman, 16, 21
Clarke, Samuel, 41
Colburn's New Monthly Magazine, 199
Coleridge, Samuel Taylor, 6, 7, 45, 101, 146, 151, 182, 194, 202, 206, 210, 212, 238; *Biographia Literaria,* 151, 238; "Dejection: An Ode," 221
Columbus, Christopher, 107
Conway, Moncure, 1, 160
Cooper, James Fenimore, 205, 206
Cox, James, 264
Cranch, Christopher Pearse, 20, 172
Croly, Herbert, 70

Whitman, Walt (*cont.*)
166; "Song of Myself," 106, 163, 164,
169–70, 171, 176; "When Lilacs Last in
the Dooryard Bloom'd," 231
Wilbur, Richard, 190; "The Persistence of
Riddles," 188
Williams, Raymond, 59, 60
Willis, Nathaniel, 200
Wilson, Edmund, 56, 58
Wilson, R. Jackson, 246
Winters, Yvor, 245
Wolfe, Cary, 50
Woodberry, George, 246

Woolf, Virginia, 151
Wordsworth, Dorothy, 151
Wordsworth, William, 6, 11, 18, 42, 151,
152, 174, 194, 202, 206, 212
Wright, Frank Lloyd, 100

Yaeger, Patsy, 143, 144
Yarbrough, Stephen, 125
Yoder, R. A., 216, 223
Young, Edward, "Night Thoughts," 41

Ziff, Larzer, 3
Zwarg, Christina, 147
Zweig, Paul, 190

Cambridge Companions to Literature

The Cambridge Companion to Brecht
edited by Peter Thomson and Glendyr Sacks

The Cambridge Companion to the Eighteenth-Century Novel
edited by John Richetti

The Cambridge Companion to British Romanticism
edited by Stuart Curran

The Cambridge Companion to English Poetry, Donne to Marvell
edited by Thomas N. Corns

The Cambridge Companion to Shakespeare Studies
edited by Stanley Wells

The Cambridge Companion to Milton
edited by Dennis Danielson

The Cambridge Companion to English Medieval Theatre
edited by Richard Beadle

The Cambridge Companion to English Renaissance Drama
edited by A. R. Braunmuller and Michael Hattaway

The Cambridge Companion to Old English Literature
edited by Malcolm Godden and Michael Lapidge

The Cambridge Chaucer Companion
edited by Piero Boitani and Jill Mann

The Cambridge Companion to Dante
edited by Rachel Jacoff